LOS_
WEXFORD

LOST
WEXFORD

THE FORGOTTEN
HERITAGE

NICKY ROSSITER

The
History
Press
Ireland

*Dedicated once more to my family especially Ellie, Finn, Lola,
Ziggy, Jude, Jack & Noah*

Special thanks to Sean Tyghe for his information

First published 2017

The History Press Ireland
50 City Quay
Dublin 2
Ireland
www.thehistorypress.ie

The History Press Ireland is a member of Publishing Ireland,
the Irish book publishers' association.

© Nicky Rossiter, 2017

The right of Nicky Rossiter to be identified as the Author
of this work has been asserted in accordance with the
Copyright, Designs and Patents Act 1988.

British Library Cataloguing in Publication Data.
A catalogue record for this book is available from the British Library.

ISBN 978 1 84588 588 5

Typesetting and origination by The History Press
Printed and bound by CPI Group (UK) Ltd, Croydon, CR0 4YY

CONTENTS

INTRODUCTION

MOST OF the material used in this book has come to light as I researched other volumes on the history of Wexford. The criteria for 'lost' is fairly wide. Most of the people, places, expressions and other categories used here have gone completely from our lives; others still exist but in different forms. Also included are a number of items of history from many decades ago that were previously lost to us and, where possible, the method of reportage of the time – another lost art – has been reproduced.

Like all towns, Wexford has been evolving for centuries but it is relatively unusual in the cosmopolitan air that it has – a hangover from the days of sea travel when our residents could visit foreign ports more easily than they could some Irish towns and cities. This gave Wexford a history quite different from other Irish locations but it has also made it more difficult for a writer to claim any expressions, words or activities as being unique to

the town. This was brought home to me recently when I found the word 'get', referring to a person – usually young – who was a nuisance, quoted as in common use in Glasgow in the 1800s. So please bear with us if you find some of our Wexfordisms in distant lands or cultures.

The book will range over a number of areas of loss using relatively recent items as well as those from a few centuries ago. Like all books, it is finite in size and schedule so inevitably material has had to be left out.

To try to make the research as inclusive as possible, I invite readers to give feedback on the ubiquitous Facebook where the group 'WISH – Wexford Industrial & Social History' will relish your personal recollections and strive to preserve and share them.

1

WEXFORD'S INDUSTRIAL HERITAGE

FROM THE earliest times, a shipping industry of sorts brought the first settlers to the shores of the mud flats and small industries were the lifeblood of Wexford in days when road travel beyond the county was expensive and dangerous and when we could travel more easily by sea than land.

The first mention we have of Wexford industry is quoted in Hore's *History*. It tells us that in 1540 The Faythe was called 'Ffayghtt Strete' and its cabins were 'snug', with their 'dwellers most industrious on earth, employed in weaving nets and spinning hemp'.

Some of the next earliest verifiable records to be found go back to 1820, such as the following list of small industries with people and addresses. I am fascinated not just by the variety of goods imported but by some of the surnames that seem to have disappeared in the last two centuries (all names are spelt as they appeared originally):

1820

Boot and Shoe Makers
Henry Box, Corn Market
James Colfer, Corn Market
Lawrence Colfer, Main Street
Patrick Edwards, Main Street
John Jones, Main Street
Nicholas Kelly, Main Street
Thomas Lett, Main Street
Andrew M'Hugh, Castle Street
Nicholas Murphy, Faith

Braziers (made brass objects)
John Byrne, Main Street
Daniel Cullen (brass founder, etc.), Main Street

Brewers
Matthew Pettit, Mount-Folly
Lawrence Scallan, Spa-Well
Michael Wickham, Main Street

Brush Manufacturers
Anthony Hughes, Main Street
William Trigg, Main Street

Cabinet Makers
Hercules Atkin, Georges Street
Loftus Codd, Monk Street
Nicholas Cullen, Corn Market

Gun Makers

William Anglim (who was also weigh master), Monk Street
Benjamin Green, Corn Market

Hat Manufacturers

James Corish, Main Street
Thomás Jefferies, Main Street

Maltsters

Robert Kane, Faith
James Murphy, Faith
James O'Connor, Main Street
Philip Walsh, Main Street

Rope Makers

James Barry, Faith
William Carroll, Faith
John Cody, Main Street
Gregory Scallan, Faith
Stephen Wall (and flax dealer), Faith

Soap Boilers and Tallow Chandlers

Rebecca Jeffares, Main Street
Shepherd Jeffares, Main Street
Frederick Jones, Corn Market
Patrick Ryan, Main Street
John Valentine, Main Street
Enoch West, Main Street

Tanners
John Cooney, John Street
Patrick Donnelly, Main Street
John Doyle, John Street
Ann Frayne, John Street
William Redmond, Mary Street

Watch and Clock Makers
Nicholas Hatchells, Main Street
Joseph Higginbotham, Main Street

Miscellaneous
Walter Connor, whitesmith, Slaney Street
Stott Howard, wire machine maker, Main Street
William Landers, coach maker, John Street
Timothy Timson, silversmith, Main Street
Robert Wyke, artist, Slaney Street

In 1831, thirty-eight Wexford malt houses produced almost 80,000 barrels of malt, mostly for export to Dublin. The town had three breweries, four tan-yards, three ropewalks, three soap and candle manufacturers, one tobacco factory and one foundry.

1885

Cabinet Makers
Brien & Keating, 9 and 14 Main Street and Anne Street
Patrick Howlin, 24 High Street
Patrick Shaw, 87 Main Street
Patrick Sinnott & Sons, Main Street

Cart And Car Makers
R. & R. Allen, Custom House

Coach Builders
Mary A. Boardman, Main Street
Thomas Cullothan, Selskar Street
J. Dempsey, John Street
John Dodd, Westgate
H. Higgins, Allen Street
Henry Leary, Henrietta Street

Cork Cutters
Thomas Lacy, Allen Street
William Lawler, Main Street
Frank Whitty, Slippery Green

Rope Walk
John Wall, Faythe

Census 1911

The urban population of Wexford in 1911 was 11,531, of whom almost 5,000 were aged under 20 years. Among the occupations recorded were: forty-nine printers, eight watchmakers, twelve maltsters or distillers and fifty-five bakers. Twenty-one men were involved in coach building and fifteen shore-based ship's carpenters were recorded. Two ladies were engaged in upholstery or cabinet making and one was a brewer, while there was also a lady forge keeper or blacksmith. Another three ladies were employed as quill or feather dressers.

Bishopswater Distillery

The distillery covered 6 acres and was built of fine Wexford stone, erected in the year 1827 by a small company of gentlemen in the locality. It afterwards passed into the hands of the Messrs Devereux, who were the original and principal shareholders and directors of the company. The works are enclosed by a stonewall and, at the top of the hill, at the entrance in Talbot Street, there is a handsome gateway; whilst at the bottom, in King Street, where the Wexford Corn Market is held, there is another entrance. The frontage in King Street is 582ft, and the depth of the buildings therefrom nearly 200ft, whilst the height is about 60ft. A spring known as Bishops Well, blessed by a Bishop of Ferns, was said to be the source of the water. This stream issues from the heart of the Forth Mountain and is supposed to possess rare qualities for brewing and distilling purposes. The annual output was 110,000 gallons per annum at its height.

The company had its own cooperage and cart-making shops. The partnership ended on 1 February 1836. In 1912 the lands for auction on 14 February comprised of:

1. Boiler house, engine room, brewer's office, elevator room, spirit store, waterwheel, still room, corn loft, nine distiller's warehouses, grain house, gauging house, excise office (4 acres 30 perches).
2. Forge, grain shed, distiller's house and garden, dwelling house, managers' and clerks' offices, boiler house, stables, coach house, harness room (8 acres 18 perches, under tenancy from CWA Harvey).
3. Cow house (2 roods 4 perches, Harvey).
4. Cooper's shop; racking store (15 perches, Harvey) all within half a mile of town centre.
5. Bonded store at Paul Quay, frontage 49ft depth 245ft.

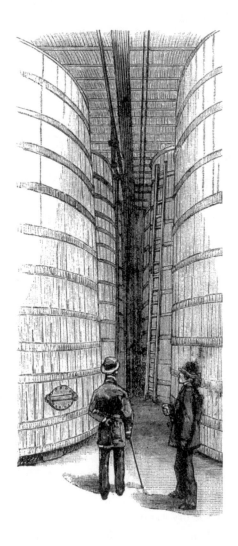

It was wound up in May 1914 after which there were rumours it was to be a POW camp.

Breweries

In July 1808 there was a to let advertisement in the *Wexford Herald*: 'Brewery concerns and dwelling house in Back Street now occupied by Laurence and John Murphy. The copper, capacity 30 barrels, is good as new. Perfect command of excellent water.'

In 1824 brewers were listed at St Magdalene's, Mount Folly (Matthew Pettit), Redmond Park (Lar Scallan), The Old Pound (Philip Walsh) and South Main Street (Michael Wickham)stretching to the quay. This later became part of The Long Rooms public house.

There was also a brewery at Heffernan's corner in 1840.

Bricks

Belvedere Road was the road to a sand pit and brick kiln in 1880. In 1891 there was an advertisement in the newspapers: 'Best bricks for sale, Mr Malone of Belvidere'.

Clay Pipes

The Clay Pipe Factory was on Main Street, almost opposite Bride Street. Mr William Murphy owned it. The factory was set up in opposition to the Waterford Pipe Factory. The clay was stored in the old corn store in the Folly, just above Pierce's Foundry. He later bought Miss Browne's factory at the King Street end of Barrack

Street around 1889. The pipes were popular until wooden pipes became cheaper.

Clogs

James Billington was born in Preston, Lancashire, where he learned the traditional craft of clog making. A County Wexford girl called Mary Maher fetched up in Preston and married Billington. On a holiday in Ireland James saw great potential for his footwear and they eventually moved first to Avoca in Wicklow, then to Arklow, but the lure of Wexford must have proved too strong. In the fateful year of 1911 the family moved to 85 South Main Street. They had a shop front with a clog-making enterprise at the rear. Within a few years clogs were the favoured footwear of Wexford farmers. They also proved the ideal footwear for foundry workers such as those in Pierce's.

Coaches

Morris' shop in Upper John Street was formerly the coach-building factory of J. Dempsey, while opposite the top of Slaney Street was Mr Dodd's coach-building factory. Molloy's coach-building factory was in Selskar and Mr Landers had a coach-building firm on the quay. In 1902 William Higgins, coach builders, were in Gibson Street.

Cousins Mineral Factory
In 1917 Cousins Mineral Factory advertised a genuine secret improvement in drinks made 'with the same palate heat as the

summer so you could drink them on the coldest day with the same satisfaction', presumably meaning that they tasted good in summer or winter. Their soda water was 'suitable for mixing in either milk or whiskey'.

Creamery

In the year that Mandrake the Magician appeared on stage at the Dun Mhuire and a plaque to Jem Roche, the boxer, was unveiled in the Bullring, Edelweiss Dairy Products set up a factory on the outskirts of Wexford. The base was Rockland's House and, in true Wexford tradition, we seldom if ever used the official name. To us it was The Cheese Factory. From those beginnings in October 1961 the factory grew and grew, with a few name changes along the way (but we still used the original nickname). As Wexford Creamery it produced quality cheeses such as Wexford Cheddar. Then a whey products section was added. It later produced baby foods in the world-famous 'Cow & Gate' stable and continues to offer steady employment decades on, now as Danone.

Dockyard

In 1832 the Redmond family opened a dockyard in Wexford on reclaimed land to the south of the quays, causing Lewis, in his *Topography of Ireland*, to remark:

Shipping interests have been materially promoted by the construction of a patent slip and shipbuilding yard at the southern end of his embankment (Redmond was responsible for the reclamation of the land where Trinity Street now stands), from which a vessel of 70 tons has already been launched. Vessels belonging to the port had previously been built at Milford and Liverpool.

The first vessel built here was *The Vulcan*, for a local ship owner, Nathaniel Hughes. It was launched in 1833. However, on 18 January 1837, a letter to Archer & Leared, Slip Dockyard, was sent requiring payment of £28 4*s* 0*d*, 'for hire of boat from Mathew Doyle for use as a pilot boat due to company's failure to build boat as agreed'.

The dockyard employed 100 men at its peak and was responsible for building schooners and barques of up to 360 tons. Kohl, writing in 1842, reported that:

> At Wexford I saw, for the first time, an interesting piece of machinery called Parkin's patent slip, by means of which ships when building can be raised or lowered in the dock, as may be required by the state of the tide. A machine of this description, which in this country is found in so small a place as Wexford, is not to be met with even in the largest seaport towns of Germany.

By 1875 its workforce had dropped to ninety people and it closed in 1920.

Drinagh Cement

Limestone quarries had operated at Drinagh for many years before Harry Cooper established the cement works in 1871. Drinagh Cement Factory was the first success at manufacturing Portland cement in Ireland. In 1883 Wexford cement secured first prize in the international industrial exhibitions held in Dublin and Cork in competition with the leading manufacturers of England, America and many continental countries.

In the 1890s there were about 100 men employed in the cement works, mostly quarry men and indoor labourers. Two shifts were worked each day. The day shift started at 6 o'clock in the morning and finished at 6 in the evening with an hour and three-quarters for meals. The night shift started at 6 o'clock in the evening and continued until 7 in the morning without a break. The men worked seventy-two hours for a six-day week. The majority lived about 3 miles from the cement works and probably walked to Drinagh. They were paid at the rate of 1*s* 8*d* a day or about 10*s* a week.

In 1936 it was announced by the government that it had been decided to establish two new cement factories – one at Drogheda and the other at Limerick. The Department of Industry and Commerce informed Wexford. Sadly the cement industry in Wexford was over and only a few abandoned kilns and a smoke-stack survived into the late 1900s.

Fine Wool Fabrics

Stafford's owned the Mouldex factory making plastic and rubber goods in 1947. They later opened Fine Wool Fabrics on the site. It subsequently became Senator Windows and is now Enterprise Centre.

Wexford Gas Consumers Company

James Furniss of Anne Street founded the first Wexford Gas Works in 1830. It went bankrupt in 1865 but a new company, the Wexford Gas Consumers Company, started in Trinity Street in 1869. Considering the extent of the network of piping that they had to install to supply their product to factories, homes and street lighting, one must stand in awe of the undertaking. In addition there were the logistics of streetlights to be lit and extinguished every day of the year as well as maintained.

In 1918 a strike at the gas works put the town in darkness and factories were closed.

As the town expanded, the gas network also grew with new housing estates being gas powered for cooking long after electricity took over in lighting. I still recall gas lighting in a Wexford house as late as the 1960s. The gasman was a familiar sight in all areas in the 1960s. He travelled by bicycle and had a leather satchel to carry the money. Today he would probably have a van with security guards. The reason for this collection was that gas was prepaid by meter. When the gasman came he emptied the meter, totted up the usage and sometimes there was a surplus to be handed back – due to variations in the tariff. You also got a receipt for the money collected.

In the 1970s there was consternation in Wexford as the Gas Company suddenly closed. Gas cookers had to be replaced and government funding was needed to ease the burden. Trinity Street lost the towering gasometers and new developments grew on the sites.

Gainfort's Boot Factory

Gainfort's Boot Factory was at 73 (North) Main Street in 1902. They had been in business since 1852, making hand-sewn boots. Orders came from as far afield as Gibraltar, Capetown and Transvaal. Apprentices worked on small boots in the first few years.

Hardob's

This factory opened on the Quay in 1967, giving training and employment for Wexford workers in the clothing industry. When the roof was erected a fir tree with streamers was used to check the alignment as per an old German custom. During this a worker with a bottle of spirits walked on the roof, drinking. Aidan Roche, mason, of Bishopswater had the honour. All the other workers celebrated inside.

Hat Manufacture

There were four hat manufacturers recorded in 1824, including Lett of Church Street. The first Tuskar hats, a type of straw hat, made in Wexford went on display at Hadden's in January 1903.

Howards

In 1832, S. Howard had a factory making machines for dressing flour and brushing corn. For the more domestic market they produced wire riddles (an implement for sifting sand or clay) and

wire safes (these were the forerunner of the refrigerator when meat was kept cool in an outside cupboard of wire). They also repaired umbrellas.

Letts

In 1887 there was mention of a Wexford man called Lett exporting mussels to North Wales. A century later the same name was on the boxes of mussels but the market was worldwide.

23

The family operated seven boats out of Wexford in the 1950s and were said to be the largest exporter of live eels in the United Kingdom at the time. It was while in Billingsgate Market selling eels that Laurence Lett was made aware of a shortage of mussels and fielded enquiries about the possibility of any being available in Wexford. By 1963 the company was harvesting wild mussels in the Wexford area. Later, due to growing demand, they moved into cultivating their own stock. To cover the off-season for mussels they also harvested and supplied prawns and scampi.

Malthouses

In 1785 Wexford had 195 small malthouses. In 1808 an advert in the *Wexford Herald* read:

> To be let, Dwelling, Brewery, Malthouse and Stores in town of Wexford, occupied by the late W. Kearney. 300' in depth, has advantage of the only fresh water river in town, running front to rear. Value will increase when new line of quay is completed.

There were thirty-eight larger enterprises in 1831.

The shipping trade facilitated a major malting trade in Wexford. One maltster, named John Barrington, 'turned out 60,000 barrels in a season'. Others involved in the trade in the mid-nineteenth century included Patrick Breen of a Castlebridge family, Richard Walsh, Robert Stafford and William Whitty.

There was severe distress reported in 1887 as malthouses were closed with hundreds out of work. Work was never so scarce and outdoor relief doubled within a year.

Umbrellas

In 1914 F. Carty of Selskar ran an umbrella factory.

Wexford Paint and Varnish Company

In the 1930s Wexford Paint and Varnish Company at King Street, who manufactured Capitol Paint, were located behind the Capitol Cinema.

Printing

A printing industry once thrived in Wexford, with newspapers printed here since the 1700s. The *Wexford Journal* dated from 1776 and the *Wexford Chronicle* from 1777. The *Journal* became *Wexford Independent* and was still going in 1877.

Fred Wood's Liberty Press was also located here, at Commercial Quay.

As late as the 1960s and into the 1970s we had two weekly newspapers. In addition to the newspapers the printers provided the invoices, receipts, posters and all the other paperwork that is now computer generated or purchased from multinational companies. English's in Anne Street had a vibrant book-printing and binding business, producing publications such as the *Capuchin Annual*. In addition, The Free Press had contracts to print leaflets and forms for the Government Publications Office. A few older members of the audience may recall the days when stamping a card was a very real part of employment. Those countless thousands of insurance and wet-time cards were printed in The Free Press.

Farms throughout Ireland had leaflets on Colorado beetle, scabies in sheep and dry cow mastitis that were printed by Wexford men at 59 South Main Street and parcelled by Wexford women before being collected by the dray horse of CIÉ to be transported by train to Beggar's Bush in Dublin.

The People Office, built partly over Archer's Lane, produced a magazine that would rival the original British tabloid magazines like *Titbits* and *Weekend*. Back in 1902 County Wexford was part of the British Empire. British law prevailed and British magazines predominated. It was against this background that the Walsh family, originally from New Ross, decided to start a magazine. But this was to be no ordinary publication. The idea was to produce a magazine that combined the best of world information with all that was good in Ireland. From the very beginning it subtitled itself as 'A Journal of Fiction Literature and General Information', a description that would last for ninety years. Over the years, the rivals grew, shrivelled and died, but *Ireland's Own* continued.

From the narrow back street in Wexford it moved to Dublin for a few years, but it was to return to its roots in the southeast from where copies were sent around the world. As early as 1911, the Readers Page had correspondents with addresses ranging from Portugal to Bombay to Ohio and Buenos Aires – helped, no doubt, by its rather unique request to its readers to 'Pass on your copy to a friend'. It is still going strong today.

Sawmills

There was a court case in 1902 of Patrick and Teresa Cullen *v.* Edmond Moody t/a R&R Allen, arising out of the death of John Cullen, aged 15, at a sawmill. The boy was collecting waste oil from a gas engine in the factory. He was found on 25 February 1902 in a store called The Forge, lying near a flywheel with an oilcan nearby. He was probably struck on the head. John Sills, carpenter, saw the body, as did Mr Tobin who was in charge of the forge and engine. Cullen was a spoke polisher as was a boy named Gaul. He had to take oil from machines for blowers and shafts three times a day. A spoke polisher finished spokes on an emery- or leather-covered shaft in the wheel department. It was decided that Cullen was responsible for his own death because he was doing something other than his own job.

Foundries

Blacksmiths' forges and later foundries were once a common sight in
Wexford. Joe Murphy is recorded
as having a forge in Abbey Street
by the round tower of the town
wall in the 1800s. In 1809 the
Wexford Herald reported on a
fire in Back Street – now Mallin
Street – saying that 'sparks fell
on a smith's forge some distance
away and burned so quickly
that even the bellows was lost'.

In 1829 Nathaniel Hughes
was looking for an apprentice
for his whitesmith and bell-
hanging business.

Behind 80 and 82 John
Street, in what is now the garden
shed of no. 80 and the kitchen of 82, was a
factory that manufactured shovels for the malt stores, while Dan
the Nailor's was at 56 South Main Street.

We even had a Foundry Lane – now called Patrick's Lane.
Donnelly's in Foundry Lane made bowls. They also erected the
ironwork in Stafford's stores at Paul Quay and made sewer grates.
It later became Lees.

Malone's on Newtown Road employed many Pierce's workers
during the Lockout.

How many of you recall a company with a product called Waico
Springs of Brockhouse Industries? The company was established

in Maudlintown in the 1930s and operated very successfully for about forty years. It later moved to part of the Pierce's complex.

Wexford's Three Main Foundries

Like in so many towns throughout the world the industrial revolution would prove a blessing that turned to a curse. It increased production, employment, wages (to some extent) but it also led to specialisation and to towns becoming almost solely dependent on single industries. In Wexford it was the foundries producing top-quality farm machinery that generated the ancillary jobs in allied trades, in commerce and in construction.

Today when most people think of them they think of the Lockout of 1911. In fact, that was but six months out of over a century of production.

We seldom realise how the three main foundries of Wexford were connected and might very well have come to pass as one major entity. Matthew and Bridget Doyle moved to Wexford town in the 1800s and their first home was in Abbey Street, in what is now a doctor's surgery.

Another young blacksmith, James Pierce, had also moved to Wexford from Kilmore, around this period. He started a forge opposite Mount Folly and lived in front of it, in a small, white-washed house. He had four sons – Philip, Martin, James and John – and four daughters – Kate, Johanna, Annie and Alice. James Pierce, blacksmith, joined with Matthew Doyle, fitter. Matthew made ploughs and James helped him in the forge. They prospered and in time were joined by their sons, four Pierces and William and Andrew Doyle. William, like his father, was a fitter and Andrew became a moulder.

The Doyles decided it would be better if they started their own foundry and in 1880 the Selskar Iron Works was founded.

Doyle's Selskar Iron Works

In 1880 the Selskar Iron Works was founded. It flourished and in 1902 converted to a limited company, sparking a newspaper to report:

> William Doyle started the great works on a very modest scale about twenty years ago and went in for making machinery, rather than engaging in the national industry of making 'glorious eloquence'. His Iron Works now stand on a site of nearly three acres. We hope the new company will go on progressing and making Irish industrial history.

Doyle's were fortunate in not being involved in the strike of 1890, as their men did not join the National Union of Dock Labourers. They were not so fortunate in 1911, though relations were good and neither brother wanted involvement, especially Andrew, who worked with the men in the foundry.

Because of his patriotism, Doyle refused orders for British war production in 1914. Pierce's took up the offer, mainly as it meant young Philip Pierce, who was in the British Army, would be released for essential war work. When the 1916 Rising took place, Doyle's gave work and refuge to many men on the run. Doyle's made guns, bullets and hand-grenade casings in the foundry. These were moved out by night.

In its prime, Doyle's was famous all over the country, regularly appearing at agricultural shows. The firm had its own stand and displayed a full range of products. The firm's interest in promoting the improvement of agricultural standards is demonstrated in the Enniscorthy Museum, where a Doyle Cup, donated to the

Enniscorthy Show for a competition among farmers, is among the exhibits.

Wexford Engineering Ltd or The Star

This company originated in Cappoquin, in approximately 1880 as R. & E. Keane, but in 1899 work was already well advanced on the development of the Wexford site. A meeting had been held to which William Doyle (of Selskar Iron Works) was invited. It was proposed that he should join with the new company, which would then be the largest in Wexford, but William Doyle turned down the invitation. It was to the south of the South Station and became the second largest foundry in the town.

One of the incentives to increase their Romanian market was the fact that cargoes of timber were being imported into Wexford from the Black Sea port of Odessa at that time. Rather than have ships go out 'in ballast', very competitive rates were available for the shipment of cargo to Odessa, e.g. machinery in lieu of ballast. This may also have been a factor in deciding to locate in Wexford. Considerable doubts were raised in Wexford and elsewhere as to the feasibility of reclaiming a minimum of 5 acres, much less 8½ acres, from the sea but a lease was granted by the Wexford Harbour Board on 2 March 1897. An access way-leave lease was agreed with an adjacent property owner, John Knox Hughes, on 4 November 1899. A similar lease was also agreed with Mary Josephine Devereux on 24 April 1900.

The work of dredging and reclaiming the site commenced. Initially, an agreement was made with the Wexford Harbour Board to hire their dredger but this method was too slow and laborious. It was decided, therefore, to hire another larger dredger from Wales with capacity to suck up material, much of it being sand, and pump it on to the site.

Various roof designs were considered before deciding to accept Thompson's quotation of 14 August 1899. Despite the difficulties of the site, virtually no problems were experienced with settlement of foundations.

Much thought was given to the design of a siding to enable wagons to be manually moved towards the east end of the siding, as they were unloaded or loaded by the company crane. Remnants of this can still be seen.

However, the company was not making enough profit to pay the agreed 6 per cent to its debenture holders, which included the Bank of Ireland, who wanted to put the company into liquidation, so the debenture holders voted to appoint John S. Hearn as receiver. An order to wind up was issued on 24 March 1908 and a 'new' Wexford Engineering Company Limited was incorporated on 29 November 1909.

John S. Hearn attended all the exhibitions in which the company participated, including the RDS and Balmoral Spring Shows and the Smithfield Show, then held at Islington in London. He was present on the stand when royalty purchased a Star sprayer from the stand for their Sandringham estate, visited it.

In 1964 the company had an approach from Smith Holdings, for whom it had been manufacturing a range of budget ploughs under a different brand name. The proposal was to market all Star farm machinery through their organisation or alternatively to sell the company to them, as they were buying Pierce's and wanted to assemble Renault cars in the Star Iron Works. The first Wexford-assembled Renault 8 drove through the factory gates on Tuesday, 23 November 1965. Sadly both foundries are now gone.

Pierce's

James Pierce founded his business in 1839, manufacturing fire fans called 'Fire Machines', which can still be found in older farmhouses. The first premises were in Allen Street.

Around 1835 an English warship was wrecked on the south coast. Pierce negotiated a contract with the government to salvage a number of heavy artillery pieces on board and transport them to Wexford. The success of this contract probably provided the capital he needed to set up a business.

We often do these men a great disservice in thinking only of the setting up of businesses. Many like the legendary Henry Ford were inventors, adapters and engineers. James Pierce worked on threshing machines. These had been previously made largely of timber and were worked by hand. He successfully made them in cast iron. He made a further technical breakthrough by perfecting a gear-and-drive-shaft system whereby horses could replace people in working the machines.

In addition they could be artists. For example, regarding an elaborate cast-iron conservatory for Sir John Power of Edermine House it was commented that the building of it was 'the work of an ingenious Wexfordman, Mr. James Pierce'. The circular glasshouse at Castlebridge House is the work of Pierce's from this time, too.

The company moved to the Mill Road Works in 1847. They built a quarter-mile-long bridge over the Slaney at Carcur in 1856. They later built a printing press for a local printer and the railings, made by hand at Pierce's, for the new twin churches still pay testament to the skills of the workers. By the 1880s, Pierce's had a staff of 130. By the turn of the century staff numbers had grown to around 400 and the company was the principal industrial employer in the county.

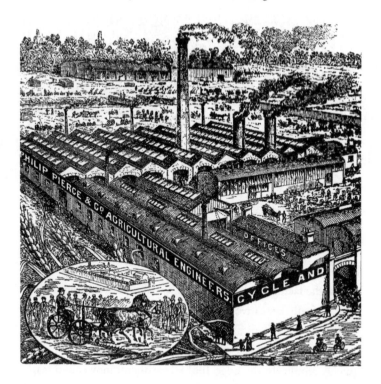

Gold medals for excellence were awarded to Pierce's at Dublin and Paris exhibitions in 1882. This saw business increasing, with exports to England, Asia, the colonies and South and Central America. The company slogan was, 'The World our Market'. In 1889 the firm of 'Philip Pierce et Cie' were carrying on business at 59 Rue de Flandre in Paris with depots in Rouen, Bordeaux, Marseilles and Nantes while the Pierce Tumbler Rake was especially popular in Australia.

From start-up in 1897, Pierce's were soon offering eleven different models of bicycle, including a double-barred heavy-duty model suitable for RIC men. In 1902 Lloyds Mexican Circus visited Wexford and the Brothers St Clair performed 'cycling teacup'

(wall of death) on a 75-degree sloping track. One of troupe was Tom Smith, formerly of Barrack Street, whose father was band-master of 3rd Battalion. Pierce's decided to present them with a bike so that it would be used worldwide. When Michael Collins visited the factory in April 1922 he was also presented with a new bicycle. Sadly later investigation shows that the famous photo of Collins does not feature a Pierce's bike.

A major fire in 1910 destroyed most of the factory but it was quickly rebuilt. In the Edge Tool Department, mower and reaper sections were tempered by passing along endless belts and through a series of gas flames before being dropped into a tank of whale oil.

There was some correspondence in the newspapers in January of 1914 about meals being supplied at a cheap rate in the factory. This was seen as a good idea as it would avoid those living some distance from work eating meals in the nearby church grounds or rushing home in the 50-minute dinner break.

Pierce's Social Club was opened at Paul Quay in March 1914. Over 400 attended the ceremony, performed by Miss Pierce of Rocklands and Miss Pierce of Park House who presented the keys to Patrick Murphy representing the men of the factory.

The factory was used to manufacture shell cases during the First World War, with a large female workforce operating shift systems.

About fifty young girls were employed in connection with munitions work at Mill Road Iron Works. Prior to the introduction of female labour in this establishment, a number of young women had emigrated to similar work in Herefordshire.

By 1930 Pierce's phased out bicycle manufacture in favour of ploughs and mowers. They also dropped the manufacture of bedsteads. This was a business they had started around the turn of the century to cash in on the move away from timber beds to metal ones. Growing public health concerns about personal hygiene and official attempts to tackle widespread tuberculosis led to a big clear-out of old timber beds. Pierce's were offering both children's cots and beds for private and institutional use.

The great durability of the farm machinery made by Pierce's was such that a purchaser might get a lifetime of use from a machine. Farmers expected Pierce's to be able to supply spare parts for machines that were often 60 to 80 years old. Pierce's met this demand and also supplied parts for machines made by English competitors.

In the late 1940s Harry Ferguson contacted Philip Pierce about the possibility of the company manufacturing implements, especially ploughs, for his revolutionary new tractor. Pierce's would have had the necessary skills and technology to do so but Philip Pierce was said to have been convinced 'that the tractor would never catch on'. By the 1950s he was converted and produced such implements.

In 1964 the Smith Group bought both Pierce's and their main rival, the Wexford Engineering Company. The Star Iron Works by the latter company was closed and a major rationalisation of the product range of the two companies was undertaken.

On 16 July 1965 124 men were laid off permanently as follows: forge 23; machine shop 18; paint shop 3; foundry 43; wood shop 4; fitting shop 13; edge tool 19 & stores 1.

The company was sold to the TMG Group in 1978. More staff were laid off, despite some diversification, and with liquidation in 1980 the remaining 240 jobs were lost. The factory was bought and reopened in 1981 with a much smaller workforce. It would eventually close and remain derelict for some years before becoming the site of today's Tesco.

Legacy

What of the legacy of our industrial past? If not for the prosperity of those times, when Wexford sort of ruled the seas and the agriculture, we would not have the twin churches, the buildings on the quays or the paved surface of the Horse River used as a millrace for the distillery, because the money would not have been there.

The most tangible legacy of our industrial past happens to be dwelling houses. Few people may know that the houses of Casa Rio, Alvina Brook and Avenue De Flandres, along with the little hut-like spout near The Gaelic Bar, are the remnants of the industrial might that was Pierce's and, by extension, of Wexford's industrial past.

Pierce's is commemorated in a piece of sculpture and a clock; Selskar Iron Works by a mural on a supermarket wall; and The Star lives on in a few sheds built with Renault boxes.

2

THREE DECISIVE
DECADES

THIS BOOK is written while I am in my sixties and, as such, it allows me look back on three decades in my early life that proved so decisive in the story of Wexford.

It is difficult for anyone who did not live through it to understand what Wexford in the 1940s and '50s of the twentieth century must have been like and even as I write this I admit that my knowledge comes from research rather than memory.

As in all history, the decades were only words – not numerically accurate times. The 1950s probably started in 1945 and lasted to about 1962. Our '60s were a short decade from about 1963 until 1971 with the 1970s running from then into the 1980s.

In what we call the 1950s Wexford was suffering the effects of the so-called Economic War with Britain and the Second World War, which had a deep impact on us even if we only called it the Emergency. Work was hard to come by and when obtained it was badly paid and all too often very insecure. This led to widespread emigration, quite often of just the father of the family. The foundries were booming but very often this meant night work or shift work in busy times and 'laid off on the dole' in slack times. Shops were local and small. Electricity was still being rolled out and inside plumbing was only starting to be part of newly built houses. On the plus side, housing was improving, suburbs were being populated and things were starting to turn.

By the 1960s education was becoming a more equal franchise, especially as free second-level education came to Ireland. Few people realise that prior to 1966 parents had to pay for secondary school and many left school at Primary Certificate Level with only that certificate for reading, writing and arithmetic. In this short decade the teenagers of the USA and UK began to influence those of a similar age in Wexford. The transistor radio and the television brought a democracy of sound and with it of ideas and thought to the booming population of teens.

Those teens grew to maturity in the 1970s and, with their education, outward-looking ideas and outside influences, began to change the town and its institutions on a scale and speed never seen before as they married, raised families with different outlooks and became involved in growing numbers of cultural organisations. Let us look at key events in those decades.

Sadness of Summer in Wexford

Little did many children of the 1950s realise that quite often in the summer months foundries such as Pierce's laid off their workers for a few weeks when orders were slack. This was not paid annual holidays but rather a time to 'sign on' for social welfare. The men made the most of things, putting a brave face and bringing the swimming togs with them to go for a dip at Ferrybank, Kaats Strand or Browne's Bank after the visit to the Labour Exchange.

A few weeks of summer also saw the return of the emigrant. These were people who had had to leave Wexford to find work and often lived in London, Liverpool or Birmingham. They usually got their annual holidays from the factories or building sites in the same two weeks.

During those weeks the town came alive. Morning saw the men strolling down the streets leading to the town and quays. They were often decked out in new suits, new shirts and ties. They sported tiepins and maybe cufflinks. In the many pubs of the town and quays they met old friends and relations for a few jars and maybe a singsong as the day wore on.

The wives would emerge to saunter the town in the afternoon. Earlier in the day they might have been glimpsed with hair in curlers and covered with scarves. Now they were in their element as they visited the shops with the aroma of perfume wafting on the air and the best of Crimplene C&A dresses and coat/dresses on display.

For those forced to seek employment abroad those summer visits meant cramming those other fifty weeks into this two and storing memories to sustain them in the long winter months looming ahead.

Week one of that fortnight was a round of catching up, meeting for chats and cheerful pub nights. Then after the Sunday the air would turn. They were now on the downward spiral. The songs got more maudlin and the handshakes tighter and longer.

By the Saturday the summer was over for them and their loved ones in Wexford. That evening the hackney cars were busy taking couples with the brown cardboard cases to the North Station. The platforms were packed with those leaving and those wishing them

Godspeed. The train approached from the Ferrycarrig direction. The whistle never sounded more mournful as the steam hissed and the train stopped.

Hugs and handshakes were exchanged. Tearful farewells were said. They boarded the carriages like condemned prisoners and waved through tiny slots in the top of the windows or at the doors where windows were lowered on the leather straps.

The guard raised the green flag and blew the whistle. The driver gave that farewell toot and the train chugged off down the quays. Still they stood paralysed at the windows seeing old friends and strangers on the quay and younger relatives running beside the train, waving and shouting. The adults had left the station for a foot-dragging trip back to the houses that now felt so empty.

The emigrants eventually sat down after passing the South Station, heading for the pierhead, the boat, the jobs and to begin saving for another summer fortnight in Wexford.

Another Side of Emigration

For those not so directly touched by emigration as in losing a parent, partner, son or daughter to 'the boat', having relatives in England could have its benefits.

Those who had emigrated as singletons often found themselves better off financially than the people left behind and they showed this good fortune in the regular 'parcel home'. These brown-paper parcels, tied with string and sealing wax, were eagerly awaited in the homes of Wexford. They would usually consist mainly of clothes for the woman of the house and the children. These would have been purchased cheaply in the chain stores that had not yet sprung up on our shores. The 'coat dress', a sort of matching dress and light 'coat' of similar material, was one of the fashion items to grace many a Wexford wedding at the time. They were easy-care fabrics usually bought in places like C&A. The children got jumpers and shirts in colours and designs seldom on offer in the local stores so that it was very easy to spot families who had 'someone living in England'.

But the clothes were of the least interest to the youngsters. Packed in between all that fabric would be the comics. We had a number of the more popular titles on sale in shops like Bucklands, but there were others that were not imported, like *Radio Fun*, and these provided an extra 'hard currency' in the hugely popular area of swapping comics, which helped us read a lot more titles than parents could afford.

There was a summer bonus for such families as well as time went on and the people living abroad were prospering to the extent of either owning a car or being in a position to rent one for the two weeks of the summer holiday. If they owned a car and went to the expense of bringing it home the children were in for a wildly exciting treat. Coming home on the 'mail boat from Fishguard' meant that the family might travel to Rosslare Harbour by train to greet them. In those days of infrequent use of cars there was no roll-on, roll-off option and the cars were lifted from the hold by crane. To achieve this the car was held in a huge net that was attached to the crane and hauled up like a catch of herring to be deposited on the pier.

Having a car parked outside the door was a huge bit of prestige for those two weeks and children often just sat in them and savoured the envy of their pals. The car also opened up new horizons. Rosslare Strand was a great attraction for summer beach visits but the car meant that Ballyhealy, Curracloe and Ballinesker were now possible options and the whole family vied for their day at one of those less accessible beaches.

The car also allowed visits to family members who lived in country areas where bicycle, small motorbike or even, in the 1950s, pony and trap were the only ways to facilitate a visit. It also meant trips to country graveyards where ancestors were buried, because most residents of Wexford had roots of some sort 'in the country'.

The visitors also brought the 'more exotic' sweets on sale in the UK and more up-to-date cameras than the ubiquitous box brownie that most homes had and this meant more family photographs and memories to be cherished.

The 1960s

To see what we have lost in a little over fifty years let's go back in time to visit a house of the 1960s in one of the new suburban streets of Wexford.

One of the first things we notice is children at play. There are about ten of them, boys and girls together, aged from maybe 8 years to 12 years. They are playing games like 'Queenie I Oh', 'Scotch' and 'Statues'. They are not in a playground or big garden but on the open public road. In fact, this is one of the main thoroughfares into Wexford but traffic is so sparse they are only interrupted very occasionally.

The house is what is commonly called 'a corporation house', meaning that it is rented from the local authority, as were the majority of houses in Wexford of the 1960s. There is no driveway; instead there is a small garden with grass on the right and a single bush in the centre, while on our left is a much narrower garden of flowers.

Net curtains are on all windows with heavier curtains pulled back on the larger ones upstairs and down. There is most likely a

bicycle parked under the parlour window or maybe even a Honda 50 or its predecessor.

Initially all doors would have been painted 'corporation green' but over time the tenants stamped their individuality with different colours and later replaced some of the panels with glass to let more light into the hall. Empty milk bottles would be placed on the sill of a small window beside the door for collection by the milkman. A piece of paper wedged into one of them would give the next order – in pints, not litres.

It was common practice to leave the key in the door, unless the house directly fronted a street – in that case the key would most likely be attached by a string to the doorknocker and dangle inside the letterbox. A stranger would knock on the knocker – doorbells were not common yet. A friend would knock then turn the key and enter, often calling out their name.

Inside the door a stairs led to the bathroom and bedrooms while a hall led straight to the 'back kitchen'. A common feature in the hall was for the lower portion of the wall adjoining the stairs to be covered with wallpaper – often 'embossed' covering the section above the dado rail. This was a practical idea because quite often a bicycle was stored in the hall at night. In older homes that painted portion might have been timbered and painted. This was called wainscoting, but in the middle 1900s we used that term only for the 6-inch timber around the base of the interior walls. It was later called skirting board.

In the Wexford of the 1960s the 'back kitchen' was what we might now call the kitchen. The 'kitchen' was our dining room and 'the parlour' was our sitting room.

The back kitchen was where the cooker, powered by 'town gas', was located as well as the sink. It was a relatively small room for cooking but more often than not it was also used as the 'everyday dining room'. There would probably not be a washing machine or fridge. In the 'back kitchen' there was a door closing off the under-stairs area. This was used for storage and it was the location of the red gas meter.

Town or mains gas was paid for before being used. Putting money in the meter regulated it. In the 1960s the usual denominations were shillings or sixpences. The money was placed in a slot on a dial and a handle turned to put it through the meter, releasing a supply of gas. It was common to see small towers of the coins stacked ready in case 'the gas went out', otherwise the children were sent off 'looking for change for the meter'. In later years, after the demise of mains gas, many people removed the door and placed cookers or fridges in the 'under-stairs cupboard'.

Beside the 'back kitchen' was the kitchen. This was used for dining 'on state days and special occasions' such as Christmas or visits by important people such as boyfriends or girlfriends. By the 1960s it was also the location of the television and therefore had become the heart of the house. Its open fire with marble surround added to the importance of this room. It also accommodated the hot press where the copper tank stored water heated by the back boiler. It was in this cupboard that clothes needing airing after being washed were kept. The kitchen in most houses was where the red 'Sacred Heart lamp' burned perpetually before the Sacred Heart picture. This red bulb – usually with a crucifix-shaped filament – was wired especially into the house. The lamps were a fixture in houses from the time of electrification, replacing candles or 'night lights' (as tea lights were called) that were usually housed in red-tinted glass containers.

From the early 1960s the other feature of the room was 'the telly'. Like the houses, these were usually rented at the time with RTV being one of the biggest companies offering the service. The television sets of the era were massive, produced black-and-white pictures and were forever breaking down. A 'snowy picture' was probably atmospheric and especially affected the foreign ITV channels such as HTV Cymru and later Harlech. A 'rolling picture' or one that suddenly flipped sideways to just 'lines' sent the householder to the twiddly knobs at the rear of the set marked 'horizontal hold' and 'vertical hold'. Many a pre-teen became expert at manipulating these settings. The aerial wire usually entered the house through a hole bored in the wooden window frame. There it was connected to a little off-white box. From that another cable was connected to the socket at the back of the set. If there was more than one channel this latter cable needed to be changed to different windowsill boxes. Over time this caused the connections to become loose and the usual remedy was tearing a piece off a newspaper and wrapping it around the connector to steady it.

The household could not deal with the calamity of loss of picture or sound so Fergie had to be called to book a visit from David. To ring for service meant a dash to the phone box on the green or down to the local shop to report the fault. This was the upside of renting but the wait could be hard to bear.

The kitchen furniture usually comprised of a table with a few chairs and the 'three-piece suite' of sofa and two armchairs.

The widows often had a wooden pelmet at the top, covering the runners for the 'heavy' curtains and the wire holding the net curtains.

The other room on the ground floor was the parlour. If the family was big this was converted to a bedroom, otherwise it was seldom used. It usually had the 'best suite' and maybe a coffee table – although coffee was seldom, if ever, drunk. There might be a radiogram or a china cabinet. The latter was a glass-fronted cabinet wherein the knickknacks of holidays, best china and other items would be displayed. It was in the parlour that the Christmas tree was installed and extra-special visitors such as the priest on his rounds for the dues would be entertained. As children grew up it was often the unofficial 'courting room' for those evenings they did not 'go to the pictures'. At such times the Dansette record player was plugged in to play the 'Music for Pleasure' special offer LP records from Woolworths or later the K-Tel compilations.

Upstairs there would have been two bedrooms and a bathroom. The bathroom had toilet, sink and bath. If the man of the house was handy the latter two were often enclosed with a cupboard built under the sink and a sort of wooden laundry box at the end of the bath. There were no immersion heaters so baths were planned for times when the back boiler had provided a 'tank' of hot water.

The back bedroom had an open fire mirroring the kitchen but with a less elaborate surround. The front bedroom had a nook where it jutted out over the stairwell. Once again from the annals of *Practical Handyman*, the periodical that many bought, this might have been enclosed with hardboard, giving a 'walk in wardrobe'. The beds comprised a headboard and footboard connected with bolts via two iron bars along each side. On top of this went the 'base' and then the mattress. They were furnished with feather pillows and sheets covered by blankets with a candlewick bedspread over them.

Back down the stairs and out through the back kitchen was the yard and garden. Depending on the position on the street the outdoor elements might vary. In general the yard was lower than the garden and enclosed by a retaining wall with a few steps up to the garden.

Just outside the back door would have been a meat safe attached to the wall about 5ft from the ground. This was the fridge of the era. It was used to store meat and other perishables and was sometimes where the jelly was left out to set after the ritual of stirring it into boiling water on the Saturday night in preparation for Sunday dinner.

At the top of the steps in many council houses was a massive semi-detached shed joined to the neighbour's. This was the coal shed but was big enough for storage of all sorts of items such as the last for shoe repair, the vice attached to the workbench for carpentry and a makeshift loft for things to be kept out of young hands, such as the bayonet left over from the LDF service years. Many people built extra sheds on to the rear of the coal shed to pursue hobbies like breeding canaries or raising pigeons or as sheds for the family dog.

Most families cultivated the gardens, with cabbage and rhubarb being the more common crops. The latter was 'forced' under galvanised buckets or basins and the former kept kids busy at times removing caterpillars. The more adventurous might grow straw-berries or even gooseberries.

The washing line was also a feature of the garden with a high pole and the line attached by a pulley to the back wall of the house.

Such was the typical corporation house of the 1960s in Wexford.

The 1970s

They say that if you remember the Sixties you weren't there and in many ways the Eighties are best forgotten so I decided to look at some of the local happenings on the Seventies to help to jog a few memories.

Down in Kilmore the local newspapers reported that Johnny Sinnott had a lucky escape when his car went over the quay. Luckily it caught on a rope securing a trawler and was pulled out with the help of a tractor.

In Rosslare Harbour, CIÉ was seeking planning permission for an open-air swimming pool, squash and tennis courts at the Great Southern Hotel.

Miss Mary Dunphy, who was on holiday from her home in California, found a message in a bottle at Rostoonstown. Sadly it was not from an exotic desert island but rather from someone in Bishopstown in Cork.

In Enniscorthy Michael Smith of Drumgoold Villas retired after serving fourteen years with Sisk & Co. He got a presentation of a wallet of notes, which appears to have been the approved retirement present – more useful than a travel or carriage clock or gold watch, which seemed to feature in many fictional retirements.

Patrick Power and Dick Hayes Junior travelled to Hull to study echo sounders, indicating the arrival of new technology in the fishing industry.

John Murphy's 166-acre farm at Ballingale Taghmon was sold for £60,000. Meanwhile a bungalow at Mulgannon in Wexford fetched £12,000.

Pat Quinn – famous for his bald head and white polo-neck sweaters (a fashion item of the era) – was the new owner of the Castle Motor Hotel back in 1973. This is now Hotel Ferrycarrig. He paid a visit to the hotel by helicopter at a time when such occurrences were reported in the papers. He landed in the GAA park.

The Regal Lodge Roadhouse out the Newline or Duncannon Road was a very popular entertainment venue at the time. The acts on offer ranged from the local band Kinsella Country to Brendan Grace. You got both on a single bill with the Kinsella billing bigger than the comedian.

The Castlebridge Hotrod Club organised racing at Kilrane. Admission was 20p. There was also a children's sports programme on offer. It was noted that Fintan Murphy gave use of the field.

Wexford Rifle Club presented a film show at the Dun Mhuire. The double bill included *The Art of Small Bore Shooting* and a nature film called *Oisin*. Admission was free.

In Broadway there was a charity walk led by St Patrick's Fife & Drum Band and there was a dance the same night with Bob Ormsby and his band. Both were in aid of the Old Folks Party.

Tommy Carroll was popular in those days with two gigs in one week although his cordovox appears to have been billed only once. The Menapia Folk remind us that the ballad boom had not died in rural Wexford.

Taking the car, bus or bike into town opened up a world of variety in the Dun Mhuire. Top of the bill were The Pattersons – another folk outfit. Joe Lynch was billed in advertising as coming directly from a TV station but not Glenroe. At the time he was starring with David Kossoff in *Never Mind the Quality – Feel the Width* on ITV.

George Boyle was popular on what we then knew as Telefís Éireann with a show called *Seorsa agus Beartlai*.

For the younger dancers disco had arrived with go-go dancers, light shows and 'films – with sound'. Admission was only 10 bob and you got chicken and chips thrown in. For a more sedate and probably romantic night out how could you pass up Castlebridge Ballroom for 8s with dancing from 9 to 1? You also had the chance to see the three Kinsella brothers as part of The Blue Mountain Boys.

MARITIME TALES

WEXFORD'S MARITIME past was integral to its development. Here are a few nautical tales and snippets. They are reproduced verbatim where possible, to give the reader a better understanding of how the people of Wexford in that period were informed of the incidents and to make long-lost reports feel more resonant.

Murder at Sea

Captain Glass was originally a surgeon but after making several voyages to the Guinea Coast he became a captain. He became captain of a privateer and was only three days at sea when his crew mutinied, but a French Prize coming into sight saved the situation. They captured the vessel and it proved to be of great value. Shortly afterwards an enemy frigate appeared and although the privateer put up a hard fight, they had to strike their colours, but not until they had lost half the crew and the captain had been shot through the shoulder. Capt. Glass was taken prisoner and was landed at the West Indies, where he was treated with great severity as a prisoner of war, but he was at last exchanged.

He again started privateering and was again taken prisoner. During his career he was taken prisoner no fewer than seven times. Finally he obtained exclusive right to trade with a port he had discovered on the Guinea coast. He interested a number of merchants and made a venture there but the natives would have nothing to do with him. They murdered the men he sent on shore and attacked the ship but were repulsed.

The ship began to run short of food and the captain started off in an open boat for the Canary Islands to obtain a supply. On arrival there he was arrested as a spy and thrown into prison. After being some months in confinement he managed to communicate with the captain of a British man-of-war, who secured his release. In the meantime, as he failed to return to the ship, the mate abandoned the voyage and returned to England. When the captain's wife heard the news she started off for the Canaries accompanied by her young daughter, and there they found Captain Glass. They all embarked on the *Earl of Sandwich* to return to England. The ship left the Canaries under the command of Captain Cochran in late 1765.

Four of the crew murdered the captain and passengers and several of their fellow crewmembers under terrible circumstances. After loading a boat with money valuables, they scuttled the ship off the coast of Wexford. They landed at Ross and went into a public house and took a room. They gave the landlady jewellery worth about £20 and they gave the maid $36 dollars and a necklace and earrings set in gold. They also changed $1,250 dollars into gold with a local merchant and would have changed more if there had been any more gold obtainable. It afterwards came out that their boat was so loaded that they had to throw a quantity of treasure overboard to keep the boat from sinking and they buried a large part of the treasure between high and low water at their landing place.

In January 1766 eleven casks containing 250 bags of dollars, part of the treasure that was on board the *Earl of Sandwich* and 'which had been secreted by the four inhuman villains now in confinement for the murder of Captains Cochran & Glass, Mrs. Glass, Miss Glass etc.' were brought to town from Ross, escorted by two troops of General Severin's dragoons, and lodged in the Treasury.

The four men were arrested and tried for murder in Dublin.

On the 3rd Mar 1766 George Gidley, Richard St. Quinton, Peter McKinlie, and a Dutchman Andres Lukerman, late mariners on board the brig Earl of Sandwich, belonging to London, whereof John Cochran was master, were executed near St. Stephen's Green pursuant to their sentence for having murdered their captain, Captain Glass, his wife and daughter, also Charles and James Pinchert. Their bodies were brought from the place of execution to Kilmainham Gaol and they were afterwards hung in chains in the most conspicuous places at Poolbeg.

The treasure from the ship was found in Booley Bay, County Wexford.

Loss of an Emigrant Ship

The following story was reported from the *Wexford Independent* in 1852:

Lost Wexford: The Forgotten Heritage

Wexford, Sept.18, 10.a.m. –

The Oyster-boat *Teetotaller* has just arrived at our quay, having in tow two boats containing about 60 male and female passengers and part of the crew of the ship Bhurtpore, of Liverpool, Bambridge master, bound to New Orleans, about four miles eastward of the Forth, at three o'clock this morning. As well as I can ascertain from the passengers, the following is an account of the disaster: This vessel was about 1,500 tons burden, having a crew of 35 hands and 485 souls (men, women and children) as passengers, the latter, with the exception of 56, being all Irish, and generally young people of the peasant class of life. She left Liverpool on Thursday morning in tow of a steamer, which left her off Ormsby Point. During Thursday night she rather lost ground than gained, but on Friday morning she had fair wind. The coast of Wales was seen by the passengers before nightfall last evening. All the passengers were, at the time she struck, in their berths, and whether any blame is to be attached to the captain or officers is yet to be ascertained. The description given by some of the sufferers of the scene that followed is horrifying. When the two boats here alluded to left the wreck there were still two other boats left, and Captain Devereux, the master pilot, was using all exertion to get to the assistance of those on board.

On the calamity being known in town, the merchants, together with Mr Devereux, MP, and his worship the Mayor, Mr John Walsh, assembled in the Chamber of Commerce to devise the best means to send to the assistance of the sufferers, and several oyster-boats have been despatched, properly manned, to the scene of disaster. A spirited and humane townsman, Captain Crosbie, has accompanied them, to afford the benefit of his assistance.

Half past 3 p.m.

A pilot boat has just reached our quay, bringing about 100 more off the wreck. Others have been landed at the Forth. When the last boat left about 100 still remained on the wreck, but it was expected, with the assistance of the *Oyster* and other boats, most of the people would be saved. The Mayor was in attendance on the arrival of the pilot boat, and had the unfortunate sufferers conveyed to the poorhouse for shelter, where no doubt every attention will be given them. Later accounts since received state that the ill-fated ship had gone to pieces, and that the remainder of the passengers and crew, with the exception of five persons, who were unfortunately drowned, had been got ashore and landed at Wexford. The Bhurtpore was a fine ship, of about the register before stated, and was only on her second voyage.

Further Particulars

The *Wexford Independent* of Wednesday gave the following particulars of the wreck:

At day-break, when the perilous situation of the ill-fated vessel we discerned from the pilot station at the Fort of Rosslare, Captain Mark Devereux (pilot master), with a chosen crew, promptly put off in the cutter *Rapid*, and reached the Bhurtpore in about an hour afterwards. The long-boat, life-boat, and pinnace, had just left the ship, filled with passengers, and were picked up, the two latter by the fishing smack *Teetotaler*, and the long-boat by Captain Devereux, who, with much difficulty, persuaded the crew to return again to the ship; however, he made a second and third trip, and succeeded in taking the full complement the boat was capable of containing each time. That portion of the crew picked up by the *Rapid* was so exhausted that they remained on board the pilot boat, being unable to assist the brave fellows who manned the latter in rescuing any more lives from the wreck. Captain Devereux had then no other alternative but to proceed to town with the number he had already saved, which amounted to one hundred and ninety. The revenue cutter *Gypsy* was prevented from rendering any service, her bowsprit having been carried away at 4 A.M., by the fishing smack *Adventure*, of Liverpool. The tide surveyor (Mr Costelloe), however, promptly proceeded to Wexford where, from the imperfect account that reached town, nothing had as yet been done. The Rosslare and Kilmore lifeboats were immediately in requisition – the ship's boats that had now reached town taken in tow and despatched to the scene of the disaster. Mr. C. [Costelloe?] returned to his station, and with one-half his men, and an excellently picked crew of English and Jersey fishermen, at once proceeded to the wreck in the Jersey fishing smack *Frisk*, taking his own splendid four-oared boat in tow. All the boats made the ship about 3 P.M. It was now blowing strong, a heavy sea breaking alongside; and the masts and spars that had been cut away still hanging by the wreck rendered it extremely dangerous to approach the vessel. Mr. C.'s boat, however, taking the initiative, after repeated attempts, succeeded in getting alongside, but such was the excitement or fear of the poor unfortunates on board the wreck, that they could not be persuaded to leave the vessel for some time. The revenue boat at length brought seven off the wreck the first, and eight the second trip. The ship's pinnace and Kilmore lifeboat followed, and made one trip each. Night was now closing in; it became the duty of those in charge of the boats to make the land; the gale increased as night fell; the rain pourerd down in torrents, and it was pitch dark. It would be in vain to describe the feeling with which those brave fellows abandoned for the night the unfortunates that yet remained on board; but they did all that was possible for men to do under the circumstances. After landing in Wexford those he had already saved, Captain Devereux returned to the good work, leaving the fort station at half-past twelve the same night, in order to be ready at day break, on Sunday morning, at the wreck, when he resumed his "labour of love" in the cause of humanity, rescuing one hundred more human beings making in all two hundred and ninety lives saved by that intrepid and truly philanthropic man – a fact that entitles him to the imperishable and affectionate gratitude of friends of humanity throughout the universe. The crew of *Frisk*, including the tide-surveyor, the tide-waiters and Jerseymen, deserve much credit also for staying by the ship to the last moment on Saturday evening, and risking life and limb in the cause of humanity. On Sunday

morning, we regret to say, that her brave master lost his own life in endeavouring to save the lifes [*sic*] of others; for, about seven o'clock, A.M., in trying to board the wreck, the life-boat was driven by a sea in contact with the bower anchor of ship, which perforated the bottom of the boat, and the captain getting foul of the gear that hung from the vessel, was unfortunately drowned. Although one of his men was seriously wounded in the head, by striking against the vessel, he still made an effort, in conjunction with his fellow shipmate, to keep the boat afloat by lashing the airtight tanks to the beams, when she drifted to the perch of Carrigs, and the two poor fellows were picked up much exhausted by a boat from shore. We understand that all the passengers and crew of the ill-fated ship, whose disaster we have been detailing, were saved, with the exception of five or six of the former, including three children, that died from cold and exhaustion on Saturday night; and now we come to the part which the inhabitants of Wexford acted on this trying occasion. As soon as the unfortunate creatures, brought first by Captain Devereux, reached our quays, the mayor sent round the bell-man to request that clothing should be supplied forthwith to the half-denuded and wretched beings thrown on our bounty by the inscrutable decree of Almighty Providence within one hour the appeal was responded to in the most generous spirit; and we know ladies that nearly cleared their wardrobes to perform this exalted work of charity. Mr. Richard Devereux opened his house at Paul-quay for them as a temporary asylum; and other accommodation was obtained at private lodgings and the auxiliary workhouse.

The *Liverpool Mercury* says: 'The agents of the Bhurtpoor, have despatched a steamer to bring over the passengers, and have arranged for another ship to convey them hence to their destined port, New Orleans.'

Dreadful Shipwreck – Sixty-One Lives Lost

In 1852 the *Wexford Independent* featured the following account:

Liverpool, Sunday, Eleven p.m.

We have received intelligence this evening of the total loss of the American ship *Mobile*, Captain Furber, which sailed from this port on Monday last for New Orleans. The particulars of this melancholy occurrence, so far as we have been able to learn, are as follows: The Mobile sailed from the Mersey, as above stated on Monday last with upwards of forty passengers, and a crew numbering about thirty men, and proceeded safely until half-past 2 o'clock on Wednesday morning, at which time she struck on Blackwater Bank; and shortly afterwards began to break up.

At the time she struck the wind was blowing a perfect hurricane from ENE [East North-East], with a very heavy sea running, the only sails she carried at the time being the fore and main topsails, close reefed. Shortly after she struck, efforts were made to launch the boats, but, in consequence of the heavy sea running at the time, they were fruitless. The scene on board the ill-fated ship a few minutes after striking baffles all description. The poor passengers were running about in all directions, crying out piteously for help, but, alas! there was none at hand, and at every succeeding wave one or more of their number was washed off the wreck, until, in a very short time, all had disappeared, with the exception of eight seamen and one passenger, who had fortunately lashed themselves to the channels. A few hours after the vessel had struck, the weather moderated considerably, and about eleven o'clock on Thursday morning two schooners hove in sight, and immediately bore down to the wreck. One of the schooners, which was bound for Glasgow, took four of the sailors and the passenger on board, and the other took the remaining four off, and landed them at Wexford.

When rescued they were in a very exhausted state from cold and exposure. They were forwarded to this port in the Wexford steamer, and arrived this evening, destitute of everything but what they stood in. Captain Furber, the commander of the ill-fated ship, together with all his officers, perished. There is no doubt that the ship went to pieces on Friday, as great quantities of wreck, crates, several water-casks, and portions of a vessel, were passed on Friday night and Saturday. The *Mobile* was a fine ship of upwards of 1,000 tons burthen, and nearly new.

Emigration

Between 1814 and 1815 11,000 Irish emigrants came to St John's, Newfoundland. They endured terrible conditions of passage. One such voyage quoted is that of the schooner *Fanny*, from Wexford, which sailed in April 1811. Due to shortage of food and water, five passengers died during the forty-one-day voyage. There was an enquiry and John Lannon, the master, was fined £500 for 'putting to sea with insufficient food and water'.

4

RELIGION

RELIGION WAS a much stronger component of Wexford life in the decades and centuries before now. When the Angelus bell rang out from the churches at noon and 6 each evening all work and even walking stopped as people young and old doffed hats and blessed themselves before silently praying. On meeting a priest or nun all people stepped from the footpath and saluted. The 'dead bell' rang throughout the town as a funeral Mass ended and people stopped to bless themselves. The polar opposite, 'joy bells', pealed over the town on all sorts of occasions, accompanied by the flocks of birds disturbed by the sound taking flight around the church spires. To give a flavour of this here are a few instances of regulations and happenings that illustrate it.

Banns

They are now a thing of the past in the Roman Catholic Church, but not so many decades ago, if a couple wished to marry, the 'wedding banns' had to be read on three consecutive Sundays at Mass. These were very specific and while announcing the intention asked the congregation to report any 'impediment' of affinity or consanguinity that would prevent the marriage.

Charity Sermons

Imagine paying to go to church to hear a sermon. That is exactly what used to happen in times past, when church sermons were used to raise funds for various charities.

In December 1830 it was advertised that the 17th Annual Charity sermon was to be preached in the Catholic church of Wexford by Revd Dr Donovan. This sermon, to which the faithful paid admission, was in aid of 'educating, clothing and apprenticing to useful trades, the Poor Children, 340 male and 250 female, of the Lancastrian and Nunnery Schools'. If you did not wish to give away your afternoon, donations from non-attenders could be paid to the preacher or to Very Revd Corrin PP, any of the Catholic clergy or Richard Devereux, who was the treasurer. It was pointed out that children were received at the schools without religious distinction. Subscribers included: Mrs Redmond, Bettyville; Thomas Walker, Belmont; Ryan, Main Street; Kellett, Clonard; Wiliam Hughes, Mulgannon; Williamm White, hotel; Mrs Talbot, Rocklands.

As similar sermon was advertised in 1832 to take place in St Iberius' church on 16 December to provide clothing for 120 children of Wexford Free School.

Christmas

A report for Christmas 1939 states that 'the weather was fine, few candles were seen in windows as the custom was dying out'. The Confraternity Band paraded to Midnight Mass at the Immaculate Conception and the Loch Garman Band to the Friary. Each played carols in the grounds. On Christmas Eve a large crowd sang traditional carols in the friary. Solos included 'Nazareth' by James Browne; 'Adeste' by Miss Chrissie Hayes; and 'Holy Night' by Statia Keyes. Fr Angelus, guardian, was the celebrant. Violins and cellos were used. The crib was opened at the Gloria for the first time in Wexford. Two low Masses followed. About 300 children got free toys and fruit at the Social Club. Parcels of tea, sugar and 'other necessities' were distributed to 450 poor from Mayoralty Relief Fund. Even into the 1960s the Christmas Mass in the Friary was so popular that people vied for tickets to attend.

High Mass

High Mass is a thing we seldom hear of anymore. These were high theatre in many ways with large numbers of priests and deacons as well as altar servers in attendance. In the Friary during the Mass the friars would raise their cowls on every mention of the holy name. At the Gloria of the Mass, choirs and bells would compete for attention. Incense played a large role in the service with priests incensing each other, incensing the deacons who incensed the altar boys who then incensed the congregation. In fact, Dermot Walsh tells a story that so great was the impact of the Mass that young boys often 'played Mass' on the steps of the Bank of Ireland building on The Crescent with genuflecting, imaginary thuribles and prayers.

Mourning

Like for religion, the outward signs of mourning were once huge in Wexford. Upon the death of a family member clocks were stopped, mirrors (and some pictures) were covered and all curtains of the house were drawn. A crepe of black material with a card giving funeral details was attached to the 'street door'. Close family members dressed as completely as possible in black. Others wore a black 'mourning band' on the outer sleeve of clothing. With the shortage of material during the Emergency the band was replaced by a 'black diamond' of material sewn on to the sleeve of the overcoat or suit. Funerals were attended by hundreds of people and while women never walked after a hearse the funeral procession with hundreds of men would weave its way through the streets of the town. The direction and streets used varied depending on the church chosen. As the funeral passed, shops closed their doors and dimmed their lights and people on the street stopped and blessed themselves. On the quay the train stopped as the hearse passed. The widow seldom attended the funeral. Instead she and others travelled to the cemetery – by hackney car – on the 'ninth day'. The family usually refrained from all sources of entertainment until after that day, including radio in many families. Sundays were important days for visiting cemeteries and hordes of people, often still in black, could be witnessed crossing the 'old bridge' at Carcur throughout such days with bunches of flowers freshly cut from their gardens.

Older Days

In 1634 it was reported that there were 'many Papists in the town, unashamed of their religion and Mass is tolerated and publicly resorted to in 3 or 4 houses'.

The Auxiliary Hibernian Bible Society was meeting in the courthouse in 1823 and '300 children were confirmed at Wexford church'.

Prior to 1840 there were set charges throughout Ireland for various religious duties: charge for a house of family 2*s* 6*d*; collection of corn per house 1*s* 3*d*; Christmas and Easter Sunday 6*d* per house; confessions 6*d* per family; marriage £1 8*s* 2*d*; baptism 3*s* 4*d* each; Mass to remove a soul from Purgatory 10*s*; anointing 1*s* 1*d*. The bishop received half a guinea from each marriage and two guineas each for holy oils, dinners and oats for the horse. The usual garb of clergymen consisted of a full suit of black cloth, a coat 'long and broad in the skirts and a waistcoat deep in body and close up to the neck', with knee breeches with silver buckles, black cloth gaiters and boots to the knee. A good horse was a prerequisite.

5

CHARACTERS

WHEN WE think of characters from our past we seem to look for the 'off the wall' or more disreputable but such is not the case here. Looking back at what we have lost or are in danger of losing, I find that it is the people who stood out from the crowd because of their jobs – now gone – or their larger-than-life appearance. Because such characters were local they never made headlines so much of this chapter depends on my recollections and I apologise in advance for anything incorrectly recalled or omitted.

Black Lead

Black Lead 'appeared' in South Wexford in the months following the First World War. He was a rather sinister-looking character with long hair and beard. His hat was always bent like a sou'wester.

He carried a bag like a sporran held around his neck by a string. To add to the mystery he covered himself, his clothes and bag in the substance that gave him his name — black lead. During his time in Wexford he is said never to have named himself or professed any religion. It seems that he spoke several languages and showed great manners and gently begged for alms. He always said, 'God bless you' and gently looked at you as if it was a combined responsibility and privilege to support him in frugal comfort.

He lived for some time in one of the houses owned by the late Mrs Katherine Scallan of Drinagh. Occasionally, he resided in the grandly titled Shelbourne Hotel at Cornmarket or, as it was occasionally known, 'The Flying Flea', where many men of the road lodged. There is a tradition that he went for a swim every day of the year in the canal of the South Slob.

He was a harmless character who attracted affection as he roamed the roads, but maintained a perpetual cloud of secrecy. No one, even Mrs Scallan, ever knew his name, and looking at a picture of him one would seem to need great courage to ask him directly.

It is said that he called for the priest in his final hours and was attended by Fr Michael O'Neill and local lore states that he left between £300 and £600 in cash for charitable purposes in Wexford. He carried his origins, his profession and the secret of his life previous to his arrival in Wexford with him to the grave. He may well have been one of the millions of victims of the terrible First World War, at a time when shell-shocked wanderers abounded. We will never know what brought him to our town. Because he stayed in County Wexford we must assume he was contented and at peace here.

Colman Doyle

Colman Doyle was the epitome of the old-style shopkeeper well into the digital age. He was to be observed most mornings, strolling the Main Street with a hearty 'good morning' for all and sundry. In his earlier hardware shop it was common to hear his refrain 'if we haven't got it we will get it for you'. Another time I recall hearing a customer ask the price of an item and be quoted £5. The customer declared, 'but Pierce's have them for £4'. Colman asked why they had not bought it there and was told they were out of stock. Quick as a flash he replied, 'When we are out of stock we only charge £3 for them'.

Cruelty Man

Cruelty Man was the awful title we gave to the officer who represented the Society for Prevention of Cruelty to Children. A lot of youngsters were kept in line with the warning that 'the Cruelty Man will get you'. This inspector was paid a salary and was provided with a house that doubled as a local office. They were nearly all recruited from the ranks of retired army personnel and police.

Dr Hadden

Doctor Hadden was a man of outstanding stature not only physically but also in the contribution he made to Wexford. He was born in Wexford but spent his early years studying abroad. Later, with his wife Helen, he worked as a missionary doctor in both China and Siberia. Returning to Wexford in the 1930s he entered fully into the political and social life of his native town. As well as being involved in the Boat Club and the Cage Bird Society, Dr Hadden was founder member of two organisations that have become Wexford institutions. These are the Wexford Male Voice Choir and Wexford Historical Society which was originally called The Old Wexford Society. The good doctor, who can still be recalled striding along our streets with white hair, beard and staff, was also a member of Wexford Corporation and was made a freeman of the borough in 1972. He wrote and lectured widely on our heritage up until his death in 1973 at the age of 91 years.

Frank Sinnott

Frank is not just a Wexford character: he is probably a character of Wexford in that he has achieved so much. Few people realise how good a guitar player he is and that he has tutored hundreds of young people in the art. He was one of the moving forces behind the Wexford Festival of Living Music that brought top-class international acts to Wexford and, as few people recall, had the Bishop of Ferns as patron. He still excels at promotion of live entertainment from time to time.

He pioneered the free sheet newspaper in Wexford with *The Boker*, originally from his 'office' (the telephone box in Peter's Square). You might need to blame him for this book too because for some reason he took me on to write for *The Boker* in those early days and by offering 'a penny a word' probably incited much more descriptive prose than was necessary. His 'View from the Bridge' column in The Boker and later various local 'freesheet' newspapers showed his philosophical side and with the right breaks, who knows, he could have given Kevin Meyers or Fintan O'Toole a run for their money.

John Wilson

Mention the word 'character' anywhere in Wexford and one of the names that instantly springs to mind is that of coalman John 'Buller' Wilson. The old world of John Wilson's Wexford was one where coal delivery involved an intimacy with the customers, 'If people were stuck for coal on a Sunday, he'd help them out'. John's horse 'Blackie' used to haul 40-45 bushels (32 bushels = one tonne of coal). On a slippery, frosty morning it would drag a load like that all the way up the hill to Wolfe Tone Villas. It was probably the last full-time working horse in Wexford town.

Margaret Hurley

Margaret 'Maggie' Hurley has been an entertainer on Wexford streets for many years. For most of that time, her signature song has been 'Nobody's Child' along with the good old Wexford greeting of 'Howaya Hun?' At Christmas she changed her repertoire for a seasonal 'Rudolph the Red Nose Reindeer'.

Mercy Laundry Girl

In the days before washing machines became common in our homes most families used 'the laundry' for large items and for special items. Wexford was well served by commercial laundries such as The Celtic – pronounced with a 'hard C'. But the Mercy Convent also operated a commercial laundry at its premises in Summerhill, which was also the orphanage. Many will recall their collection and delivery service with a jolly young lady knocking on doors, returning the freshly laundered items wrapped as a parcel in brown paper.

Paddy Brady

Paddy Brady was a formidable presence in Wexford. Although physically disabled, he traversed the town and surroundings in a magnificent vehicle that was a sort of cross between a large mobility wheelchair of today and a small car. Paddy was a common sight on almost every street as he 'sold the pools'. These sheets were used to bet on the soccer games in the UK every Saturday and caused the wireless to be commandeered at about 5.30 on such days as men and women 'sweated on the results'.

Paddy Roche

Paddy Roche had a forge at Crescent Quay in the middle of the twentieth century. Surprising as it may seem, only a few decades ago there was enough horse-drawn transport to allow him to have a thriving business in the whitewashed building in the middle of

Wexford. Dermot Walsh recalled visits to the forge with Paddy incanting 'hup hup hoo' as he lifted the hoof to attach the red-hot horseshoe and then snipped off the nails to the smell of burning keratin. Manning the bellows that kept the fire burning was Bertie Murphy, described as a smartly dressed smiling gentleman reminiscent of the movie star Stan Laurel.

Public Health Nurses

Nurse Gaul and Nurse Dunbar were probably the best known Public Health Nurses in Wexford back in the 1950s. Anyone watching the television series *Call the Midwife* will understand their vocation. This was a time when most children were born at home, assisted by these nurses or their colleagues and the family doctor such as Dr Toddy. They would also have undertaken the general health chores now conducted in outpatients or health centres.

Sanitary Man

The Sanitary Man was the person who would now be called an Environmental Protection Officer. In 1889, when a person reported that his father was buried in the wrong grave, permission from sanitary man was needed before the body could be exhumed and re-inter six months later.

Sign Writers

Sign writers once abounded in Wexford before the advent of the plastic shop fronts. These men were true artists who devised and designed the name over a shop along with a few words denoting the goods on offer. They were as well versed in fonts as any printer or today's graphic designers. But theirs was not a cosy office. They produced their masterpieces atop rickety ladders in all sorts of weather. They probably had to put up with the usual Wexford smart remarks such as the latchico shouting up that they had left out a letter.

Much Further Back

An old Barony Forth alliterative rhyme conveys the hereditary characteristics of some of those who once lived in Wexford:

Stiff Staffort, Stiff Stafford.
Dugged Lamport, Dogged Lambert.
Gay Rochfort, Gay Rochfort.
Proud Deweros, Proud Devereux.
Lacheny Cheevers, Laughing Cheevers.
Currachy Hore, Obstinate Hore.
Criss Colfer, Cross Colfer.
Valse Vurlong, False Furlong.
Shimereen Synnott, Showy Synnott.
Gentleman Brune, Gentle Browne.

The Story of a Life

The *Wexford Guardian* once contained the following interesting biography:

Some four or five years ago, there was in Wexford a poor, illiterate, thoughtless, improvident man, with a wife and three children, named Myles Martin. He knew no trade or handicraft to earn subsistence by, only hard common labour; and in obtaining that he often found much difficulty, and too frequently did not succeed in retaining it when found. The Wexford poorhouse finally received him and his family within its walls; but the spirit of Martin was restless; he could not brook this restraint; and he escaped on board a vessel to Newport, and soon after got employment at the Merthyr Tydfil Iron Works. On it becoming known that the husband had employment, the family could no longer be retained in the poorhouse, and ultimately were helped over the channel to join him; but what he earned, though sufficient to keep himself, was not equal to the support of a family that could not render him any assistance, and they had to leave Merthyr. After many hardships, he again separated from his family, and the wife and children became inmates of the Wexford poorhouse. Nothing was heard of Martin for nearly a year, until a rumour rose that he had made his way to Liverpool, and being employed there on some job in an American vessel, he stowed himself away in the hold, and was not discovered until the voyage to Savannah was extended to ten or twelve days. On discovery, his abject condition, his simple but melancholy story, operated favourably on the heart of the humane captain, and he was well treated during the remainder of the passage, he promising to work hard to pay a just compensation. On landing, he faithfully kept his word; he worked hard and successfully, and not only paid his passage, but, continuing in the merchant's employment, saved, moreover, some money and, through the merchant, forwarded to Messrs. Allen, of Wexford, 6 pounds towards conveyance of his family to him. Mr. Allen made the fact known to the board of guardians, but no aid from that quarter was extended, and Miles Martin was forgotten, when lo! a short time ago, another letter from the same merchant arrived, covering a money order to Mr. Allen sufficient to free the money outwards, and moreover, informing him that Martin was not only saving and industrious, but that he was the present proprietor of a farm of sixty broad acres, and that what he most needed was the presence of his wife and family to cheer him on and assist him in its management. On Thursday, Mrs Martin and her three children took passage from this port (Wexford) to Savannah, on board Mr. Allen's barque Brothers, heartily thanking God for her altered position and changed prospects. The poor, heedless, despised, ne'er-do-good runaway in Ireland is now a farmer of promise and patient industry in the neighbourhood of Savannah.

6

NICKNAMES

NICKNAMES SEEM to be a dying art. Just as the Christian names are following media trends, many modern nicknames tend to follow suit. In compiling this section there is a slight dilemma. Were the older names accepted, were they even known by all the recipients or were they found to be insulting? In case of giving offence we will avoid identifying the person if at all possible. Those who recall the actual person will no doubt add the missing name. This of course may ignite debate and recollections in many a pub in the coming months.

The nicknames were often amusing but then again some might have had deeper meanings; however, they did give a certain flavour to the period. I suppose they all knew they had nicknames in some way and one can have little sympathy because some of them were adept at christening others, like one teacher who referred to a pupil who walked with a stoop as 'here's me head me arse is coming'.

In this section we thank Sean Tyghe (Sheener) for providing most of the entries. Many of the nicknames defy explanation of their origins but we will try to deduce wherever we can. Some nicknames went with a number of people or surnames. Others required the prefix 'The' and are placed alphabetically with 'T'.

Babóg – a name sometimes given to a young apprentice.

Back the Horse – not as one would expect from betting on horses but rather from reversing a horse.

Bagga – possibly a mispronunciation of a Christian name at some stage.

Bardog Roche – This is an interesting one coming from young Roche being called a 'roacheen', which is a small fish that was also called a bardog.

Basket Arse – sounds somewhat descriptive.

Biffo Fowler – might be from something to do with a character in *The Beano* comic.

Big Tiny – a sarcastic reference to size.

Bonner O'Connor – very common rhyming nickname for almost every O'Connor.

Briar – probably someone a bit moody.

Buggy Wuggy – was used for a man who had a shop called Bugsy Malone.

Bullet Rossiter – a very good athlete in his day.

Canary – possibly a good singer.

Cha – not an abbreviation of Charles.

Clock in the Basket – the story goes that a lady did not use a wrist watch but carried a clock around in her basket.

Crow Newport – he had a pet crow that used to stand on his shoulder.

Dabber – usually applied to painters, recalling the profession.

Dooshie – possibly a small person based on the adjective.

Flash – was used for a photographer.

Forty Coats – a common nickname for 'knights of the road' because they usually wore all their clothes at once. Asked why he wore so many coats, even in summer, one knight of the road replied, 'If they keep out the cold in winter they will keep out the heat in summer.'

Ga – might derive from involvement in GAA.

Gabby Jack – a talker.

Goering – someone who had obtained a second-hand military style coat.

Gunner – said to be because his father had been a gunner in the army.

Hornick – nickname taken from a well-known murder attached to some people held in less than the highest regard.

Hoss – many believe this referred to his bulky resemblance to Hoss Cartwright in the TV show *Bonanza*.

Leg in the Hollow – was sometimes used to refer to a person with an odd gait.

Lourdes Water – sold water that he said came from Lourdes.

Lu Lu – derived from the Christian name Luke.

Mensa – from his profession as a teacher of Latin.

Mug o' Tar – someone who likes really strong tea.

N'yuck N'yuck – for a fan of Curley in The Three Stooges.

Sailor Murphy – based on his occupation.

Shilling a Stitch – for a dressmaker.

Slap the Rasher – a grocer. The name came about because when a person went to his shop for a pound of rashers he would slam the meat on to the scales, causing the dial to go up and whip the rashers off again before the needle settled. He would say, 'There's a good pound there now for ye Mam.'

Snowball – white haired.

The Bear – because he was a rather grizzly old character.

The Boss – for the school principal.

The Crab – a contrary person from the sideways gait of a crab.

The King – for person who saw the place as his domain.

Third Order – a pious person.

Trapper – he was renowned for trapping the football like modern soccer players.

Vistavision – a cinema projectionist.

Winkie with Gig – was used in Pierce's for the man pushing the gig to carry items around.

The Man – for the boss or foreman.

Here are some nicknames that defy explanation:

Ba Swift

Bisto

Bucket

Burn the House

Curse a God Jack

Diddler

Dinger Bell

Do Do

Duck Egg

Flogger

Gadget

Gawney

Hairy Paw

Hop the Cod

Jazzer

Jingle of coin

Nicknames

Kitser

Krypton Factor

Lamb of God

Moll Trot

Mutton Cutlet

Nanny Honey

Nettle

No Stocking

Pancake

Peter Wa Wa

Rocket

Scootchie

Six Eggs

Slippy Fippence

Sputnik

Sugar Al

Teapot

The Compo King

The Demon Barber

The Hooded Crow

The Ice Man

The Midnight Milkman

The Quavering Tenor

The Silver Dollar

Old-Style Entertainment

ENTERTAINMENT IS ONE AREA that reflects most on our changing lifestyles. Not all of the following are lost but most have changed utterly.

Bird Shows

One very popular pastime in the mid-twentieth century was the rearing and showing of birds. These ranged from canaries to budgies and linnets to more exotic imported varieties. Almost every street had a bird fancier – identifiable by the shed built in their back garden.

These were a very different species to the pigeon fanciers who also dotted the urban landscape and could be identified by either the flocks of pigeons circling the area or by being spotted in the early morning heading off with a large wicker basket on the carrier of their bicycle.

Bird shows were held all over the country and Wexford enthusiasts were to be seen heading for the railway station with big black crates. Inside these were show cages all neatly designed to fit snugly into the space available.

Show cages were works of art in themselves. I cannot recall if different styles were used for different species but I do remember the ones for canaries. They were painted black on the outside and sky blue on the interior. Many of the birdmen constructed these cages themselves.

Wexford was also a venue for these bird shows and two of the buildings that I recall were the Loch Garman Bandroom in High Street and the St Iberius' Hall in Common Quay Street – now the ESB shop. In later years shows have been held in the Vocational School. The shows were major logistical undertakings. Crates of birds had to be collected from the station and night watchmen had to be appointed from the committee to look after these precious charges. The cages were sorted and arranged, category stickers attached and a catalogue produced.

The judges were usually from outside the area and, after long deliberations, rosettes, plaques and cups were awarded with the presentation taking place usually on the Sunday afternoon.

Rearing these show birds was almost a full-time task and required a rudimentary knowledge of biology, nutrition and husbandry. Many of the fanciers bred their own birds and even crossbred to produce winners. I remember some canaries had a special food to bring out a redder hue to the generally accepted yellow plumage. Breeding the birds was like a lottery. There was the anticipation of the egg laying. Then there was the worry about incubation. Thunder was a major problem with many birds being lost if a thunderstorm erupted at a crucial stage. Many a father and son or daughter could be seen walking head down on areas like the Rocks Road – now Mulgannon – after Sunday Mass. They were not looking for lost coins but picking dandelions to feed to the birds.

Hardware stores and many small shops also stocked birdseed, millet and other requirements. As a spin-off to the shows many other people had canaries and budgies as pets. These powered an industry for little ladders, mirrors, bells, cuttlefish and a rake of other treats for the Joeys and Pollys.

Bird shows still take place and there are still fanciers and enthusiasts but these do not seem to have the community-wide appeal of that golden age.

Carnivals and Circuses

In July 1914 Heckenberg's Circus visited Wexford, featuring 'Chloe Cinvere and her Marvellous Cake Walk Horse; The Weldon's, Continental Eccentrics from Berlin; Togo, a real

Japanese who has appeared in every hall of note in the world to walk on a slant rope; Cecelia, sweet singer and her cello.' The advertisement stated: 'This is a class concern and not a penny show masquerading as a circus and £100 will be given to charity if any of the acts have not appeared at Hengler's Dublin; Barnum and Bailey's Pantomime, Hippodrome London and every building of note in the world.' It boasted the largest marquee ever erected, holding 4,000 people. Prices ranged from 6*d* to 3*s* with children 2*d* for midday performance.

Duffy's Circus arrived in town in May 1917. It promised a noble stud of horses and coloured ponies along with a troupe of male and female acrobats. Also to be looked forward to was 'Mademoiselle

Petresque', the female human serpent, advertised as 'a mystery to all the medical experts of America'; Texas Jack, the famous rough rider; a merry gathering of men in motley; ten clowns and several rare attractions. To add to the excitement Duffy's promised a gorgeous street procession.

Such a circus tradition continues to the present but was probably in its heyday in the 1960s with huge circuses like Fossett's and Chipperfield's playing to packed tents over many days on end and announcing their arrival with a parade of animals through the streets. The more popular circus venue was the racecourse.

Carnivals usually took place at Harvey's Field in Talbot Street or Kirwan's Field at Carrigeen. These were our travelling funfairs with swing boats, chair-o'-planes, roll a penny, rifle range and the like. They drew huge crowds on every evening of their stay, being especially popular as a meeting place for the teenagers of the town. Many of the attractions of carnivals were adapted in the 1960s by local clubs in their 'field days', raising funds with somewhat more rudimentary but just as effective slides and stalls.

Cinema

So great was the interest in film in its first fifty or sixty years that towns like Wexford supported as many as three cinemas. Such cinemas or picture houses also offered four separate programmes of two films each week with two showings per night and matinées on Saturday and Sunday.

The programme changed on Mondays, Wednesdays, Fridays and Sundays. The evening began at about 6.30 p.m. with the main or 'big' film. At around 8 p.m. the support was screened and the feature film was repeated at 9.30 p.m. approximately. This had early goers seeing the programme in reverse. In addition there were advertisements, *Pathé News* and trailers for forthcoming attractions. The local advertising consisted of single-frame slides proclaiming field days, fetes and sales of work.

Every so often, a major film came to town and was expected to draw such crowds that it was screened for a full week. These were usually biblical epics such as *The Ten Commandments* or *Ben Hur* and came complete with an interval. Being instructive films, these attracted school attention and many a pupil will recall bringing the ticket price into class, lining up in the schoolyard and marching en masse during school hours to the local 'flea pit' for a bit of religion, Hollywood style.

The popularity of such films also witnessed postal booking forms being printed in local newspapers so that people would not miss out on seeing them.

At evening performances, courting couples were the main clientele. While the male queued for the tickets, the female queued at the shop. Her task was to buy the food. Orange Crush, Double Centres and Scots Clan were the 1950s equivalent of Cola, popcorn and crisps.

Once inside there was another ritual to comply with. The tickets were handed over to a lady in the booth, who interrupted her knitting for the occasion. She tore the tickets in half and impaled her section on a needle and thread. This was also the 'lady of the lamp', who rooted out troublemakers who interrupted the films on occasion.

After-film rituals were also popular. Usually these centred on chips. Most picture-houses had one or two chippers in their vicinity where crowds grew after the shows. Fish and chips, chips and rissoles, chips and peas were the more popular orders. Wrapped in newsprint with lashings of salt and vinegar, they kept hands warm and stomachs filled on many a frosty night as people walked home. There were also the 'eat on the premises' chippers where pigs' feet were most popular. Such establishments used enamel plates and myth has it that some even had such plates nailed to the table to prevent pilfering. While consuming chips and mushy peas, patrons could read about the coming cinema attractions on long narrow playbills that only ever seemed to be used by cinemas to advertise their films.

Clubs

In an era when most houses were designed purely for sleeping and eating people flocked to a wide variety of clubs in Wexford.

These included Brunswick Club (exclusively for Protestants) at The Assembly Rooms (established in 1828); Wexford Independent Club at The Commercial News Rooms (1828); The Catholic Young Men's Society at Common Quay Street (1855) along with The Young Men's Christian Association (1858). The Wexford Harbour Boat Club was established in 1873, joined by The Union Club on The Quay; The County Club on Spawell Road as well as The Home Rule Club meeting in The Tholsel and The Temperance Club at Temperance Row.

These were later joined by St Patrick's Social Club, The Thomas Moore Social Club at Cornmarket and St John's Tontine Society as well as The James Connolly Social Club and The Crescent Boat Club.

In 1939 the following were listed: Blues & Whites (GAA); St Patrick's Social Club; Thomas Moore Social Club (Cornmarket); James Connolly Social Club; Crescent Boat Club; Cathal Brugha Football Club; Bishopswater Mummers; Whitemill Social Club.

In 1954 we could join the CYMS, YMCA, Fr Gaul's (Selskar), Harriers (Faythe), Catholic Girls (South Main Street), Liam Mellowes FF (Grogans Road), Mechanics, Foresters, Gaelic League, An Realt, St Christopher (cycling), Wexford Fishing, Harbour Boat, and Crescent Boat. The GAA clubs included The Volunteers (John Street), Sarsfields (Carrigeen), Davitt's (Davitt Road), Young Ireland (Selskar) and The Parnell's (Parnell/William Street).

There were also St Aidan's Social Club at Frank Murphy's, Whitemill Social Club (established in 1946); Whiterock Social Club (1939); St Mary's, Bride Street (1939); Mulgannon Harriers Club, Faythe (1939). There were billiards clubs at CYMS, St Patrick's, Harriers, Irish National Foresters and Pierce's on Paul Quay as well as Drinagh Hall; Gaelic Hall Paul Quay, Redmond Hall, Town Hall, Iberius Hall.

The story is told that as far as The Crescent Boat Club in Gibson's Lane was concerned the closest any of them got to a deck was the deck of cards.

Folk Music

There has always been a cohort of people playing traditional Irish music in Wexford as in any other town being used as the music for a ceilidh.

With the international resurgence of folk music in the 1960s an appetite for what we often called ballad music blossomed. A regular Saturday night crowd puller at the Talbot Hotel were McMurrough or, as they were earlier known as, Shades of McMurrough. For years they drew full houses to the bar and released some excellent albums.

In the Wexford Ballad Festival of 1966 the £10 first prize was won by The Johnstons and the Wexford group The Kinsellas were placed fourth. Meanwhile any public house worth its name featured regular ballad sessions of varying quality and in many ways ushered in the 'lounge bar' where couples felt more at ease in the atmosphere of comfortable seating and oh so sophisticated drinks such as Babycham or Baileys with ice.

International Artistes

Today seeing their favourite stars or singers on TV or Youtube enthrals people but a few decades ago we in Wexford saw our idols live and up close in person at local venues. Just to give a sample, here are some of those who appeared in Wexford.

In 1961 Mandrake the Magician was advertised as playing at the Dun Mhuire. This may have been a sort of touring version of a

popular cartoon character who appeared in the newspapers under
that name. It may even have been our first unknowing view of a
franchise.

Pop fans could see Edison Lighthouse live at the Dun Mhuire.
The Dun Mhuire also hosted Love Affair, The American Drifters,
The Tremeloes (after their Brian Poole days) and Slim Whitman.
Meatloaf played White's Barn. In 1973 Herman's Hermits topped
the bill at The Dun Mhuire while Mungo Jerry was at Whites Hotel
and Christie at Whites Barn. In 1975 Joseph Locke appeared at the
Dun Mhuire while folk diva Julie Felix was at Whites Barn. Helen
Shapiro also starred there, costing 75p admission. Later in the
year Sandie Shaw was at Whites while Val Doonican was in The
Dun Mhuire, costing £1.50 a ticket. Marianne Faithful was in The
Talbot Hotel in 1976 and The Boomtown Rats were advertised
at The Dolphin Bar in Maudlintown while Billy J. Kramer was
billed for Butlers of Broadway. The following year saw Marmalade
at Whites Barn and Makem & Clancy in The Dun Mhuire. Later
in the year Dick Emery appeared at the Dun Mhuire and Kenneth
McKeller at Whites Hotel.

The first Wexford Festival of Living Music occurred in
1970 and the international artistes appearing included: Tara
Telephone, Danny Doyle, Gay & Terry Woods, Fairport
Convention, BP Fallon, St Sepulchres Consort, Thin Lizzy, The
Hennesseys.

Lectures

In the early part of the twentieth century lectures were a popular part of entertainment. In 1902 Dr Usher gave a lecture titled
'Bird Life', with the Venerable Archdeacon Latham DD presiding.

There was a temperance lecture by Revd D. Henry of New York YMCA while 'Rooms in the Vatican' was the subject of a lecture by Count Plunkett and Arthur Conway MA FR VI revealed the science behind 'Wireless Telegraphy'. 'Land of Song', by Revd J.W. O'Byrne, which was illustrated vocally and instrumentally in aid of Boys Confraternity, provided a true blend of wisdom and entertainment. Mrs Benjamin Lamb, a representative of World Women's Christian Temperance Union, spoke to a large crowd at the lecture hall in the Methodist church, Wexford in 1914. Many people took the pledge and a local branch was formed.

The following year's lectures included, 'Origin of the Irish Fairy', 'How Ireland became an Island'; 'The Holy City'; 'The Wily Germ' and 'Life in the Far East'. In 1914, 'The Romance of London Streets' lecture cost 1*s* 3*d*.

Marching Bands

Today when we hear of bands we think of the performers on *Top of the Pops* or its modern equivalent, 'Somewhere's Got Talent'. In times past marching bands were extremely popular in Wexford as in many other towns. St Bridgid's Fife & Drum Band was founded in Mr Sinnott's house on Roche's Terrace in 1893. They bought their instruments at Furlongs Music Depot on South Main Street. Their first public appearance was at the anniversary of the Manchester Martyrs in 1894. They played at the funeral of Philip Pierce 1895 and at the unveiling of the Pikeman statue in 1904. They played at the Jem Roche fight in Theatre Royal Dublin 1908. The band was reorganised in 1922 as St Patrick's Fife and Drum Band and were the first band to play the Irish national anthem in Wexford Park in 1925. They are often locally known as the 'Boys Band'.

The Wexford Militia Band played at the regatta of the Wexford Boat Club on 18 August 1902.

In May of 1917 the local branch of the Irish National Foresters were making arrangements for the establishment of a pipe band while the Infirmary Brass & Reed Band was started in 1914 as was a pipe band established at the Mechanics Institute in 1914.

Through the middle part of the twentieth century Wexford town boasted a number of marching bands, including The Loch Garman Silver Band, The Holy Family Confraternity Band, The CBS Band and later the Clonard Band, complete with majorettes.

Thankfully not all our marching bands are gone – Saint Patrick's, augmented by The Castlebridge Fife & Drum Band, still turns out on major occasions.

Pantomime

Some of the biggest fundraising events of the early twentieth century were the annual pantomimes and one of the biggest of these took place in the Theatre Royal, in aid of the Friary. The pantomime was a night or afternoon out for all with the 'principal boy' entrancing the daddies, the tenors mesmerising the mammies and the dame entertaining the children. The most noteworthy and creative element of pantomime was the topical song that usually recalled the news or main events of the past year. In the performance of 1959 the eight-year-old Festival Opera was recalled in this ditty:

Oh, come all you people now
And I will tell you how
This old town of ours has gained high renown.
When they come from far and wide
To this place called Slaneyside
And the Pikeman from his pedestal looks down.
Oh, it happens once a year,
When there is plenty of good cheer
And everyone is opera minded then.
Oh, the dockers know the score
Of La Plaisir D'Amour
And the messenger boys all whistle La Boheme.
Oh, the town is such a sight
When it comes to Gala Night
To High Street we all wend our way to stare.
Cos there's velvet and there's fur
And 'sure what would you with her',
For only for her bouquet she'd be bare.

Opera

The year 1951 witnessed the beginning of a major cultural event in Wexford, the Wexford Opera Festival. The brainchild of Dr Tom Walsh, Dr Des Ffrench, Eugene McCarthy and Seamus Dwyer, it began at the Theatre Royal in that year. The first production was *The Rose of Castile* by Balfe, who by coincidence lived for a time in Wexford. Lord Longford, whose touring theatre group had often played at the Theatre Royal, opened the first festival. The opera festival was to grow into a top-class international event, with many fringe events embracing all forms of art. The policy of staging top-quality but often neglected operas proved a winner. One of the benefits of this festival has been the blossoming of latent artistic talents in Wexford people.

Radio

Raidió Éireann was on the air from around midday to 11 p.m. – long before the twenty-four-hours-a-day sounds of today. The Sunday fare offered a mixture of excerpts from Shakespeare through to sports reports and a symphony concert from the Gaiety Theatre.

During weekdays they had schools broadcasts with poetry, nature study and essay competitions. There was also a programme on school choirs with hints and instructions for plain chant. Weeknight offerings included *Tales from the Tailor's Shop*, *Talks for Farmers*, *The Gentle Art*, which was a talk for fishermen, *Music from the Counties*, *Great Singers of the Past*, plays, foreign reports and talks for foresters.

They seemed to have talks for everyone. In these days of controversy about diets, how about the offering in July 1937 in a talk – *The Liver Diet for Anaemia*?

Each night ended with the national anthem.

The Kennedys of Castleross was the biggest soap in Ireland in the 1950s and surprisingly it was broadcast at 'dinnertime', when the children were home from school on the lunch break and the mothers were busy dishing up food. Nevertheless it held the country spellbound. It aired on Tuesdays and Thursdays, sponsored by Fry Cadburys, and mainly let us eavesdrop on the goings on in Mrs Kennedy's shop. It was on this show the renowned playwright Hugh Leonard cut his teeth. The show was true family fare to the extent that even pregnancy had to be dealt with obliquely. It is said that when John F. Kennedy visited Ireland in 1963 he was asked if he was related to the Kennedys from Castleross.

A foreign soap usually heard by accident daily was the BBC's *Mrs Dale's Diary*. No, the Irish people had not developed an interest in this middle-class lady and her life. It just happened that the programme preceded the daily horse racing results.

That 1 o'clock slot was very popular probably because most people were eating at the time and radios and dining tables sat side by side. Fruitfield Jams brought us *Tom & Peggy* to answer cooking, gardening and household queries and Jacobs was letting the nation have its agony queries answered by Frankie Byrne with the catchphrase 'the problem I answer today may not be yours but it could be some day'. Her theme tune was Frank Sinatra singing 'Come Fly with Me'. On Friday at lunchtime Urney Chocolates sponsored *The Planet Man*. Many of us missed this because we went to the chipper on Friday.

Other sponsored programmes, each of 15 minutes' duration, included: *The Walton's Programme* ('if you feel like singing do sing an Irish song') *Urney's* ('anytime is Urney time'), and *The Glen Abbey Show*.

Many of these brought us the emerging pop music of the era but we do not know how lucky we are that it got aired. Just after the Second World War Raidió Éireann placed an unofficial ban on dance music. Wexford TD Dick Corish welcomed it, saying that if Irish people had been subjected to crooning and jazzing much longer we would have little music in the country within the next generation.

But that next generation were already fighting a guerrilla war of music. Every Saturday morning the younger generation were tuning in to Children's Favourites on the *Light Programme* from the BBC where they heard 'Running Bear'; 'Battle of New Orleans' and many more international hits. The teenagers were discovering crystal radio sets and then transistor radios, which allowed them freedom to tune in to American Forces Network or Radio Luxembourg without being castigated for listening to 'jungle music'.

Showbands

In the 1950s and '60s with the 'invention' of the teenager and the economy on the rise Ireland saw a major growth in the live entertainment scene.

While there had always been a great musical tradition nurtured by the marching bands of the town people now saw an opportunity to play different music and maybe earn a few bob into the bargain. If they played trumpet or other wind instrument the advent of Eddie Calvert and Acer Bilk showed them another area of performance. The availability of television encouraged hundreds of young people – mostly male – to take up the guitar, with varying degrees of success. This explosion of musical talent led to the formation of showbands and ballad groups. Many only played within a narrow geographical area – often because the members needed to be home to 'turn into work' early the following morning. Others took a more professional approach, maybe going on tour during the holidays from work or even making music the main occupation. Among the locally based bands that entertained Wexford audiences in the past were The New Eire Orchestra (leader Johnny Reck), Tommy and the Collegians, Joe Lowney's Band, John Lowney's Band, The Supreme and The Travellers.

Showbands were also a national phenomenon and we were never short of visiting bands at The Dun Mhuire, White's Barn or The Slaney Ballroom in the Talbot Hotel. The catch phrase of the bands was 'send them home sweatin'' and, with non-stop performances of two or three hours of triple song sets, they achieved their aim.

In Wexford in 1962 dancing to The Majestic Showband cost you 5s. Among other popular showbands performing in Wexford were The Cadets (with Eileen Reid singing about her wedding dress), The Clipper Carlton, The Black Aces and The Footappers. The Dixies from Cork added comedy routines and others developed particular performance routines that foreshadowed the tribute bands of today such as The Freshmen, who were a sort of Irish Beach Boys. The latter showband broke new ground in the 1960s with the concept album featuring a specific theme and even spoke word tracks for 'Peace on Earth'.

Theatre and Drama

Theatre and drama had a long tradition in Wexford. In the *Wexford Herald* of 1809 we find the following: 'A few gentlemen whose ambition is to alleviate the distress of the poor will present "Othello, Moor of Venice" and a variety of entertainments. Boxes will cost 3/3, pit 2/2, gallery 1/1. Tickets from Mr Lord, printer and Mrs Duffy's, Cornmarket.'

By 1830 they were well into their stride with 'Rules for establishing an amateur theatre in Wexford. Committee of 3/5 appointed by manager to control money. Run December to April with 2 plays per month. Profits to go to charity at end of each season. Pit and boxes only used, actors apply to the company, accounts public. Committee Capt. Cullen; Capt. Harvey; Mr Martin, Manager Capt Bolton, orchestra manager Mr Hickey'.

January 1832 was the opening date for the Theatre Royal in High Street. It was built for newspaper owner Mr Taylor. The new theatre, lit by candles and oil lamps, attracted huge crowds, with carriages clogging the surrounding streets on a regular basis. It was leased to Mr McGowan of Belfast and opened his management in December. Mr Daly and Miss Graham performed but newspapers reported, 'It was not packed out'. On 31 December *Romeo and Juliet* was performed by permission of the mayor. In November 1906 it had international performers for the Wexford audiences with the new comedy, *To Marry or Not To Marry*, coupled with *My Grandmother* with Mr and Mrs Lacy of Theatre Royal Covent Garden and Mr and Mrs Neyler of Theatre Royal Crowe Street.

In April 1914 the renowned Irish songwriter Percy Ffrench was in the Town Hall to give a 'humorous song and art recital'. He was the superstar of his day, having written songs and poems that were performed widely and some of which are still heard on record. His songs like 'Delaney's Donkey' were popularised again in the 1960s by stars such as Val Doonican. Tickets and a plan of the hall were available at Miss Malone's, North Main Street.

Drama came into its own during Lent when dancing was forbidden and the locals flocked to various drama festivals as local groups battled for honours. This has since evolved into national festivals attracting entries from around Ireland to various venues – still in Lent.

Tops of the Town

Religion played a huge role in Wexford in the middle of the twentieth century and, through its dancing ban during Lent, it would inadvertently provide the impetus for an important piece of live entertainment. Tops of the Town was staged for the first time in Wexford in 1962. This knockout competition gave employees from local businesses a chance to perform and led to competition between the different industries as each supported their own employees. The shows were a great mixture of variety acts – all performed in those early days by actual employees of the firms or relatives or friends. It is amazing to reflect on the dedication and ingenuity that went into this form of entertainment. Over the weeks of Lent the contests raged with great intensity. But before that the amateur members of staff in shops and industries had to decide on content, write scripts, devise dances and rehearse to the highest degree. A flavour of the interest in Tops of the Town may be gained in recalling that among the contesting groups could be County Council, Woolworth's, People Newspapers, the Free Press and even the Gardaí. As time went on, the national finals of Tops of the Town became huge ratings shows when broadcast live on national television. The local contests gave rise to a number of entertainment icons for Wexford such as Toddy Rossiter, John Hayes and Slim Redmond as ballet stars in *The People Show*.

Weddings

Weddings might not be seen as entertainment today but in times past it was at weddings or wakes that most of our forefathers gathered and were entertained or more than likely entertained one another.

Until about the 1960s wedding ceremonies were much more

family-only affairs with the ritual often taking place on a side altar before or after rather than during the Mass. The 'reception' was a wedding breakfast, usually in a family home. I recall my Aunt Marie's wedding breakfast in her parents' house in Alvina Brook. Records on the radiogram provided the music. The next generation moved the reception to small hotels. It was still an early-day affair and there might be a musician or two after the food. My abiding memory of such early weddings was the singing of my aunts and uncles. The standards were 'Carrig River', 'The Old Bog Road' and 'Noreen Bawn'.

8

SWEETS AND TREATS

TODAY MANY young people appear to be almost of independent means. Back in the 1950s we had to earn the few pennies for our treats. One of the most common was 'doing the messages'. This might range from going to the local shop to get the bread or other necessities and could earn a penny or two. Longer ranging were the messages required 'down town'. This was usually a Saturday-morning task involving going to a few shops where payments were made 'on the book' for more expensive clothing or household items. This could earn the 'price of the pictures' that afternoon.

When it came to spending the few pennies, we were spoilt for choice. Some treats are still with us, some are probably banned on health and safety grounds and others are just sweet memories.

Aniseed Balls were, to the best of my memory, brown in colour and quite small so you got a lot for your penny. They were also long lasting as they were sucked rather than eaten although that biting temptation was permitted close to the end when you chomped and that little seed of aniseed was released.

Aztec Bars were a combination of chocolate nougat and caramel and first appeared in 1967. One memory of these was not of taste but rather of advertising where life-size cutouts of Aztec warriors appeared outside the sweet shops.

Barley Sugar was one of those sweets that remind us that there were always manufacturers trying to sell us health through treats. This orange-coloured 'stick' was said to be good for you so we probably got a few more bits of this than we did of chocolate. I suppose we all thought barley being a cereal was beneficial and sugar was still an innocent ingredient.

Black Magic chocolates were never really a children's treat. Few of us liked that dark chocolate but if a few were on offer – possibly after the mother getting a box for Christmas or birthday – we reluctantly took them and probably grew to enjoy them. Interestingly research has shown that different countries like different chocolate tastes, perhaps because of the original formulas that developed separately. Maybe this is why we love milk chocolate but find the American Hersey Bars less appetising.

Broken Biscuits – back in the days before all our biscuits came pre-packaged the retailer got them in tin boxes about 12 inches high with one variety per tin. Naturally there would have been some rough handling in transport and some of the merchandise would have been broken. Breakages also occurred in the rudimentary self-service era when the tins were displayed with glass tops that allowed the customer to pick their own biscuits into a paper bag to be purchased by weight. Back in those days biscuits were a bit more than a treat – they could also be a status symbol, dished up on a plate to distinguished visitors. Naturally no host wanted to present anything but the most pristine fare and therefore would not accept the broken biscuits. These biscuits were gathered into separate tins in most shops and sold at a discount. Sometimes they pre-empted the packet biscuit by being sold in pre-packed paper bags at a fixed price. This gave us the added magic of surprise when we opened the bag to find maybe a chocolate one in among the Nice and Marietta.

Brunch was something different to us when we grew up. It had nothing to do with a fry-up. The Brunch Bar was ice cream covered in multicoloured biscuit pieces. I suppose we saw it as a sort of meal on a stick.

Choc Ices started out without the now-familiar stick. Basically they were a bit like the ice-cream wafer sandwich without the wafer but covered in chocolate. Eating them without losing too much or getting too messy was a skill requiring that we keep the foil wrapper – I can still feel that rough paper – around it until we got to the final mouthful. Miscalculating that meant too big a bit and 'brain freeze' or too small a bit and ending up licking it off the paper.

Clarnico Murray is a name I always associate only with Iced Caramels. These tooth-decay time bombs combined toffee centres with pink or white icing shells.

Cleeve's Toffee came in bars that you probably needed a small hammer to break into the mouth-sized squares we got. I think this was manufactured in Limerick and despite the danger to teeth and gums it was popular as a school treat.

Conversation Lozenges were the forerunner of our current Love Hearts. Young lads had little interest in sweets touting those romantic phrases so the manufacturers had Conversation Lozenges. They were not heart shaped but came in a variety of shapes and used every-day phrases rather than the later lovey-dovey guff.

Crisps – we had Smiths, Perri and Tayto Crisps back in those days. Of the three Tayto were the ones that came to be used as a synonym for crisps and are still popular today. Few of us ever knew or cared that Joe 'Spud' Murphy was the man behind this phenomenon although the crisp originated in 1908. In 1920 Smiths Crisps appeared in London with the little twist of paper containing salt included to flavour the crisps. The crisps were popular and spread worldwide but Joe thought them bland, even with the salt. With some experimenting he developed the cheese and onion crisp and the rest with its many variations is history.

Double Centres were the favourite treat for the courting couples heading for the pictures. As the name suggests, some marketing head had decided that people wanted extra and hated choosing between the centre flavours in sweets like Roses or Quality Street so they put two tastes under each chocolate coating.

Flash Bars were a wonderful combination of toffee and chocolate. The toffee made them a longer-lasting treat but we often preferred to get ones where the machine made a mistake and the bar had more chocolate than toffee.

Golly Bar was a sort of 'nude choc ice' in that it was just a block of ice cream with no chocolate covering. This made it cheaper but also increased the hazards encountered with eating the choc ice. It later attained a stick that made the process easier.

Ice Cream – today we get our ice cream in all sorts of shapes and forms but in the 1950s we really only had ice-cream wafers. These were sort of sandwiches of ice cream between two thin wafers. The ice cream came in blocks and the shopkeepers cut the slices according to price. Earlier this was at the discretion of the vendor but later stainless-steel measuring instruments came into use. These marked the block into equal segments (at one time the standard measure was a threepenny slice with double that being cut for sixpence). The vanilla flavour was joined by a ripple (a strawberry or raspberry swirl in the middle), then flavours like banana and even tricolour slabs. In the 1960s the ice cream on a stick finally reached Ireland and was touted for its convenience and avoidance of sticky fingers.

Imps – these were not the creatures of legend but sweets. They were small and black and came in boxes smaller than matchboxes. They were called sweets but although they looked like liquorice they were hot, hot, hot. They were not little devils but they probably singed the tastebuds of a generation.

Jelly Babies were originally called Unclaimed Babies when they were devised as far back as 1864. Then Bassett's took them over in 1918 when they marketed them as Peace Babies at the end of the First World War. They were rebranded as Jelly Babies in 1953. We all had favourite flavours in Jelly Babies and when offered one from a bag we had a good rummage to get our favourite. A common

109

joke regarding Jelly Babies was that we preferred male babies because there was more jelly.

Lemons Pure Sweets was the slogan and it must have been taken to heart because boxes of these hard sweets were the treat in school. After the religious inspector gave us a clean bill of health the teacher might pass around a box of these for the class as a treat. Similarly this might happen on the last day of term, before the school holidays. The choice was probably influenced by their Irish manufacture.

Liquorice Allsorts started out as various separate liquorice sweets in about 1899. The story goes that the Allsorts came about when a salesman dropped a tray of loose sweets, thereby mixed them. Again the problem with the package is favourites. I bet everyone who ever had a packet of these was left with the plain black tube ones at the bottom as the last resort.

Love Hearts developed from Conversation Lozenges as we all became so much more romantic.

Lucky Balls were lumps of almost pure sugar with a red coating and inside one might find a threepenny bit if one was lucky. One can just imagine the insurance claims on these today for broken teeth, tooth decay and choking on money.

Macaroon Bars were wonderful chocolate bars with coconut flakes mixed in. The problem was that they disappeared so quickly.

Packet Biscuits – most people will recall their arrival. What they may have forgotten was the first packets. These were small waxed or greaseproof paper packages of about four to six biscuits and were usually relatively plain varieties like Marietta (later Marie) or Nice or more exotic Bourbon Creams. The packages grew bigger with time and evolved into the staple of the Sunday teatime or special visit as USA Assorted or Afternoon Tea. These had a variety of biscuits and everyone wanted first pick because there were always the pink wafer or a plain biscuit that few wanted on that special occasion.

Peggy's Leg is an oddly named sweet in that it was just a stick that in no way resembled a leg, regardless of who Peggy was. It was a relatively cheap sweet that was as long lasting as it was bad for teeth.

Polo Mints were an amazing item in that they were sort of advertised for the bit that was missing. We heard of them as 'the mint with the hole', as if it was better to buy something with less substance. Sticking the tip of the tongue through the hole as it expanded was essential to the process of consuming them.

Rock was colloquially 'Dublin Rock' because in the 1950s that was just about the only place people went on a visit, and a bar of rock was the traditional treat brought back to the children by parents, relatives or siblings lucky enough to travel. Again it was almost pure tooth killer with the added attraction of 'the name going right through it'. In these days of international air travel Toblerone Bars are the equivalent last thought-of treat.

Sherbet Fountains date from around 1925 and are thought to have been a new way to market the sherbet powder originally sold to be dissolved in water. They were paper rolls with sherbet inside and this was sucked out through a liquorice 'straw'. Many of us ate the 'straw' and either ate the sherbert with a spoon or dissolved it as originally intended.

Silvermints were an Irish creation in the 1920s. They were bigger in size and a lot rougher in texture than the Polo. Steve Silvermint was invented as the symbol in the era of private eyes.

Sundaes – these were another ice-cream treat but were much more sophisticated as they meant dining out. The primary location that I recall was Ally White's, a little shop on South Main Street. As well as the takeaway service for ice cream and sweets there was a sitting area where we might be treated – by adults – to the Ice Cream Sundae. It was served in a bowl with a spoon and varied from a scoop or two of ice cream to a 'bundle of scoops' of different flavours sprinkled with 'hundreds and thousands' or doused with a spray of raspberry syrup. Jelly might also be added or even chopped bananas.

Turkish Delight was marketed under the name Hadji Bey by a family who fled Armenia to Cork around 1903. This was the unadulterated product. It was later refined and covered in chocolate to become more commonly sold as Fry's Turkish Delight.

9

STORIES OF
LOST WEXFORD

LIKE MOST TOWNS, Wexford had numerous stories related to inhabitants over the years. I am indebted to Sean Tyghe, among others, for recounting the following selection to me before they are lost forever. To spare blushes some names have been changed.

In the days before Eircode and electronic sorting were introduced there was a sort of 'knowledge' like that of the London cabbie required if you were a postman with mail being sorted in the local office.

There were various aids to this but little could improve on the local knowledge of the Wexford-born postmen. During sorting, rather than consult the lists on the wall, it was common practice to shout out any item that was not 100 per cent clear. On one such occasion a sorter shouted 'Claremorris', to which the geographic answer would be County Mayo, but Tom Healy with a superior

knowledge replied 129 Bishopswater. This was because he knew that Claire Morris lived at that address.

On another occasion a letter was received in the post office addressed simply to Annie Murphy, Bishopswater. Tom brought the letter out and popped it into the letterbox of the first Murphy in that street. The lady of the house rushed out after him to say it was not for her. 'Sure' he said, 'it's addressed to any Murphy in Bishopswater!'

At one time a new postman took over a route in the town and set out on his deliveries. A few hours later there was a telephone call to the post office. It was the local military barracks, wondering why they had no delivery that morning. The postmaster agreed to check this and asked the postman on his return. He was told that yes he had delivered some letters to the barracks on the first post and he had some more for the second post. Later that day there was another call from the barracks. The postman was called in and told there was nothing delivered. He took the call and explained that he had left the letters in the letterbox at the end of the avenue. But that is the litter box, the soldier said. 'Ah sure, I thought that was the Irish for letter.'

One day a friend called for Sykie Savage. He wasn't ready to go out so he showed him in to the parlour to sit at the electric fire. When he was ready to leave the friend said that the electric bill would be huge with those three bars going all the time. 'Not my problem,' said Sykie, 'I only have a loan of the fire from a neighbour.'

One evening a hardy man called Santy Byrne went for a stroll. A few 'hard chaws' or 'teddy boys' started to harass and call him names. He put up with this for a while but then drew out and flattened two of them and the other ran away. What they had not realised was that Santy was a top-class boxer in his day.

Ba Swift lived in Kaysers Lane in a very small house where he was 'snug as a bug in a rug'. He decided it would be humorous to paint a staircase on the back wall to give the impression that there was an upstairs. He was a great GAA fan and would often pretend to jump in the air to catch a football if he met some friends on the street. One Sunday afternoon he tuned in to the radio to listen to a commentary on a match. Unfortunately the broadcast was in Irish and Ba had no Irish. He listened as best he could to the match. As was the custom of the time he met up with some friends later that evening on the corner of King Street. Discussion centred on the match with some who had attended giving the usual expert view. Ba asked if they were at the match at all because none of them mentioned Agus and he said 'he was all over the pitch in that match'.

'Lamb of God' was the nickname of a man who was very religious and attended all Third Order and Confraternity events. He went to every procession and during Lent attended the Mission. The Mission was a series of religious events given by visiting priests whose forte was preaching. There would be the Children's Mission followed by the Women's Mission, to be topped off with the Men's Mission. When the ceremonies were going on the local clergy would be out 'patrolling the streets' and confronting anyone who should be at the Mission and enquiring why they were missing it. So if you didn't fancy attending the best strategy was not to 'stick your nose outside the street door'. There was little point in venturing out because the cinemas, clubs, shops and snooker halls were closed.

On the final night of the Mission everyone brought a candle. During the ceremony each person held the lighted candle aloft as the missioners asked, 'Do you renounce the Devil?' He bellowed this from the pulpit without amplification and would shout at the crowd to make it more convincing and asked them again, 'Do you renounce the Devil?' The congregation replied, 'We do'. He said he was still not satisfied and asked again and the crowd shouted back, nearly raising the roof. The missioner tried again and 'Lamb of God' was getting a bit carried away by then. When the missioner asked again he shouted, 'We do, we do, we do, we hates him, we hates him, we hates him.'

Marty Hayden was a very popular barman in Wexford in his day, to the extent that he was known to bring his own crowd of customers with him if he changed employment. He was a very witty man and on one occasion after he pulled a pint of Smithwicks the customer held it up to the light and said, 'that's very cloudy'. Marty retorted, 'What do you expect for ten and sixpence, thunder and lightning?'

Swanker Malone was a cooper by trade but also ran a fish shop where his cat would sit in the window beside the platter of fish. He was a very religious man and to attend ceremonies he would dress in his best suit, white shirt and shiny shoes. The story goes that when answering prayers or singing hymns Swanker always stood out because he was always a few seconds behind everybody else. People would comment on him 'standing out' and he would be delighted.

At a meeting of the local soccer referees one of them reported on an incident at a match the previous day. He said he asked the offender's name and was told Roy Rogers, so he told him 'get up on Trigger and ride out of here'. In a similar vein a player told a referee that his name was Humpty Dumpty. He was told, 'The best you can do is go over there and sit on that wall.'

At one time in Wexford a man was looking for a transfer from one of the older houses in the town. He went to the Municipal Buildings to see the town clerk but the girl at reception said he was at a meeting. He tried again the following day with the same result.

On the third attempt he was given the same answer. 'Tell me this,' he said, 'is it Leopardstown or the Curragh he's at?' The next day he was going up Hill Street and met the town clerk and introduced himself. He explained the problem saying that the walls in the old house 'are so thin that if the person in number 1 asked his mother what time it is the person in number 2 would answer half-two.' So they agreed to go to his house and he left the town clerk in his house and went next door. After a few minutes the town clerk called, 'Can you hear me, mister?' The reply came, 'Hear you? I can see you!'

One winter a local farmer had run out of hay and asked a neighbour to help him collect a load from another farm. They completed the deed and on the way home the neighbour asked if it had been expensive. 'No,' the farmer said, 'we robbed it.' The neighbour was upset about this and they parted in silence. A few days later they met and the farmer asked if he felt any better. The neighbour said he did because he had told the priest in confession. 'Next time you go there tell the priest your sins, not your business,' replied the farmer.

One wet and windy 14 February some years ago a local postman got a bit upset to find his bench was piled high with cards and boxes of all sorts for delivery. This was in the day of huge cards and those quilted ones that were posted in cardboard boxes. He turned to a colleague and said, 'That feckin' Rudolph Valentino has a lot to answer for.'

The story goes of a local man who wanted a new van for his work so he got on to the clerk of works to ask for a replacement. When asked what the problem was he said, 'It's only an ould banger. Every time I put her in reverse she goes backways.'

Sean tells of his younger days when he and his friends plucked chickens and also picked blackberries for O'Leary's of John Street with a target to earn nine pence. This allowed them to spend four pence on admission to 'the hard seats' in the Abbey Cinema, a penny for an ice lolly, another for a penny toffee and three pence for a 'bag of chips in Maggie Stamps'. In Stamps chipper he recalled a sign in the 'sit down' area – 'Knives & Forks are not medicine and are not to be taken after meals'.

Sean also recalled a time when his friend had been asked to tidy up the attic of an old house. Sean went down that evening to swap comics with him and was brought inside to see what he had found in the attic. It was an old gun dating from the 1800s. The lads decided to clean it up and oil it and, of course, to try it out. So they went to George Bridges and bought a few rolls of caps as used in toy guns. They scraped these off to make a pile of 'gunpowder'. Then they needed a 'bullet'. This being the era of marble or taw playing they fixed on the metal 'steeler' as the projectile. Next day they headed for Redmond Road and pointed the gun at a tree about 15ft away. There was an enormous bang and the lads 'took to their heels' up Tom the Cock's Lane. The next day they returned and found the steeler embedded in the tree. Sean later sold the gun into the collection of weapons then displayed in the Crown Bar.

Another of Sean's stories related to his career as postman. It involved a letter addressed to P. Pierce, Mill Road, Wexford, PA. He took it out on his rounds to deliver to Pierce's Foundry but the girl in the office did not think it was for them. A similarly addressed letter arrived a week later and Sean realised that PA was the abbreviation for Pennsylvania in the USA. It was quite a coincidence that there were such similar addresses and people worlds apart. As a postscript to this I checked and there is a Pearse Mill Road in Wexford, Pennsylvania.

One Valentine's Day Sean was on deliveries and had a card addressed to Wendy Doyle, George's Street but with no house number. This was made more difficult because there are many flats in the street. He asked a few people – as postmen often did then to ensure delivery – but no one knew her. He brought it back to the post office and thought he would try again the next day. Going up the street the following day he came upon a couple having an argument. He introduced himself, asking if they knew a Wendy Doyle. It turned out that she was Wendy and the row was about him not sending her a Valentine Card. So he went off delighted to have saved a romance. The following year he noticed her wedding photo in the local paper – but she had married a different fellow.

One day at Mass one of the friars was reading the notices. He came to one announcing a coffee morning in aid of the Friary Heating Fund – 'hmpph,' he said, 'you are going to have to drink an awful lot of coffee.'

Singers and singing came in for a lot of 'stick' in Wexford in the past and gave way to lots of amusing tales. The town of the Festival Opera has been famous for the singing in its pubs and rightly so. In times past most of these singers had never seen the lyrics written down and learned the songs from the radio. This of course left words open to interpretation. A very popular song of the 1950s was 'Saint Theresa of the Roses' but when rendered in many a Wexford pub of the era the words emanating were 'Saint Theresar of da Roses'. Another singer would give a wonderful rendition of

'Mona Lisa' but with a lisp. 'The Holy City' was another favourite but with the immortal line 'Rosanna in the highest'.

There is story told that back in the early part of the twentieth century a local band won a national prize and were to be photographed for the newspaper. Photography was not too common at the time and this caused major excitement. One band member was said to have a 'swarthy complexion' and a local wag remarked, 'Should we black up the rest of the band or give him a good wash?'

WEXFORD WORDS
AND EXPRESSIONS

IRISH WRITERS like Joyce and Wilde have given the English language more than a fair share of words and expressions over the centuries. On Wexford streets, many similarly important sayings were coined, adapted and most often stolen from other lands. Our mariners brought home foreign words and phrases and Wexfordmen serving in distant lands also imported new words.

Very few of these words can be claimed as exclusive to our area but all are or have been used in conversation in Wexford over a long period, yet sadly they are now losing their currency.

After in Wexford means later as in 'I'll do it after'. This is a contraction of 'I'll do it after I do this'.

Angish means sickly, as in the phrase 'She's very angish looking'. It comes from the Yola language of Forth and Bargy that is a form of Middle English dating back to the time of Chaucer.

Any joy is our way of asking if there is any news. It probably derives from US Forces slang for 'good news'.

Back means to bet on as in 'he went to back a horse'. It probably comes from the idea of betting on something in the context of giving backing as in investing.

Bags is used to denote a mess as in 'He made a bags of it'.

Bamped is used to denote blowing a car horn. The phrase, 'He bamped at her' is common.

Bardog is a type of small fish. It is often used as a nickname for people called Roche. This may come about through confusion with another small fish called a roacheen, which could be translated as a small roach, hence bardog for a young Roche.

Baw ways denotes crooked as in 'he hammered the nail on baw ways'.

Blow in is any non-native of an area. Although common in Wexford it is descriptive slang from Australia from around 1942.

Bockety is another term for crooked, as in 'it's a bockety table'.

Bow is the common Wexford term for the banshee. The word comes from Bugh, a fairy queen of the Tuatha De Danann, the mythical Irish tribe.

Bowsie is a guttersnipe or disreputable person, usually male. It probably derives from 'boozey', as in drunk.

Box means a blow, for example one might say, 'He got a box in the forehead'. It comes from the Danish *baske*, meaning slap.

Brudge is a common mispronunciation of bridge.

Caibosh is used in reference to having a detrimental effect on something, usually an event or action. The usage might be that 'he put the caibosh on it'.

Canat is a young trickster or troublemaker. Common usage would include, 'He was just a little canat'.

Chaney alley was our reference to a type of child's marble.

It probably comes from a corruption of china as in the glazed pottery that they resemble.

Child sometimes meant specifically a girl as in the phrase 'Is it a boy or a child?'

Chrissnen is an odd corruption of crescent. It is most common when referring to Crescent Quay in Wexford.

Clock was the name for black beetle. A superstition was that it caused rain if you killed one.

Cod is to fool or deceive. It may be related to the codpiece of earlier times that was used to deceive or exaggerate.

Codology is foolishness. The slang dates from 1910 and comes about from putting 'ology' at the end in mocking imitation of psychology etc.

Comeallye is used to denote a ballad or other popular song. It comes from the most common first line of many such songs as in 'Come all ye …'. It is also used as a derogatory term for some songs.

Cop on means to get some common sense, as in 'cop onto yourself'. It comes from 'cope with'.

Court can be a friendly person of the opposite sex or the act of being extra-friendly with such a person. In the former the phrase might be 'she was a great court' and in the latter, 'he was determined to court her'. It comes from to court meaning to find favour with.

Cowslick was a very common reference a piece of hair that stuck up and was difficult to tame, even with hair oil or cream. It was used in the *Book of the Dun Cow* about Cúchulainn.

Crab was a contrary person. It could come from the sour juice of crab apples or the sideways gait of the crab.

Cranky meant bad tempered. It comes from the Anglo Saxon *crank*, meaning sick.

Crator is a corruption 'poor creature' and usually refers to an unfortunate person.

Craw meant the chest and was most commonly used as in 'He was a right crawthumper', usually meaning a hypocrite, especially in a religious sense. The word comes from the name of the first stomach of a fowl.

Crepe was used most commonly for a crumpled tissue paper, rather than today's common parlance for pancakes. The paper, in various colours, usually made its most common appearance at Christmas to cover the bucket holding the Christmas tree, to wrap presents or to make decorations. A characteristic of crepe paper was that it was sort of elastic and this gave rise to another expression that can seem a bit rude today but it was very common in the late 1900s. If an item shrunk in the wash, one might say 'it crapped', meaning it went like crepe paper. The word also had a more sombre meaning in that it referred to the bow, often of black net-type material, that was fixed to the front door of deceased people with a card attached, giving funeral arrangements.

Cut was our name for a lovely cake usually made up of leftovers. The proper name is a Chester Cake. The expression probably came about because the original cakes were large slabs from which customers bought 'cuts' or portions. Cut was also used by people when drinking things like lemonade or Orange Crush to remark on the strength or 'tartness' as in 'There is right cut to that'.

Deadly meant great, as in 'she looked deadly'. The origin is from 'dead on', as in dead on target.

Deish meant lovely – 'She looked deish in her new coat'. It comes from the Gaelic *deas* for nice.

Dekko meant a look or glance, 'Give us a dekko at the picture'. It is derived from the Romany *dekho*, meaning to see.

Ditch is a built-up boundary. Curiously it has the directly opposite meaning in England, where it means a hole or trench.

Doubt was once used to mean the opposite of what we now mean by it. It is immortalised this way in the song 'The Fair Do' with the line, 'I doubt they had steam in the clipper fair do' meaning 'I believe'.

Dressed to the nines was a very common expression in Wexford to denote someone who had dressed up, especially for a date or the like. They might also say he or she was 'quare swankey'.

Dull meant stupid, mad or insane.

Dying alive was used to tell us that a person was in love as in 'He was dying alive about her'.

Feck – any adult could, and did, use this word with its various adaptations without 'fear or favour' when everyone knew they really meant a similar word with an alternative vowel. Mind you, the word was also used as an alternative to steal as in, 'Did you feck that book?' It was also useful as 'leave' in the sense that 'He fecked off home'. It is said to have also been used as a substitute for 'throw' but I have not experienced this in Wexford.

Fecker was a blackguard, again it was used as an alternative to a similar, ruder, word.

Feckin' was often used as an affirmative adjective as in 'You're feckin' right'.

Fetch meant a double or an apparition such as a ghost. It may derive from 'to recall' or 'fetch back'.

Figary meant a notion, for example, 'He took a sudden figary to go down the field'. It comes from *vagary*, meaning to wander, from whence we also get 'vagrant'.

Fillums was a common pronunciation for films.

Fired – this was used as we use the word 'throw', as in 'He fired a stone at me'.

Furt meant a blow, as in, 'he got a furt in the back'.

Get was a trickster. It might also be pronounced as git, a word more common elsewhere. I recently found this to be common in Scotland.

God bless the mark was usually used as a sort of blessing or show of sympathy for children or those who might have been chronically ill.

Grand meant fine e.g. 'I'm grand', as in splendid.

Great meant friendly – 'He's great with the Murphys'.

Heel ball was a block of colouring that may have been wax. It gave the colouring for the edge of the leather used for soling and heeling the shoes to blend with the shoe colour. Heel ball also occurred in an expression relating to appearance or attitude in the phrase 'He was all heel ball', meaning a person looking well spruced up for a date.

Heft was weight. You might be invited to 'get a heft of that'. It probably comes from the word 'heave'.

Ho boy was similar to a canat or latchyco in being a bit a chancer.

Hop (on the) meant playing truant. It may derive from 'hop' as an alternative to 'skip'.

Hoult could refer to a fine body, for example, 'She was a fine hoult'. It may be a corruption of 'hold'.

Jujus were almost any fruit jelly sweets. Some were said to resemble the fruit of the jujube tree.

Kayli was a sherbert that came sometimes in a bag with a lollypop and at other times it was in a sort of tube, like a stick of dynamite, with a liquorice straw.

Lard might mean good in the sense of, 'I'll beat the lard out of you'.

Lip meant to pout, as in, 'He had a lip on him'.

Ma – I have noticed over the years the way people from different countries refer to mothers. In America she is usually Mom or Mommy, in Britain this changes to Mum or Mummy and in Ireland in general it is Mammy or less often Mam. In Wexford the most common cry is 'Me Ma'.

Made in Pierce's – this Wexford phrase is unique to the town but probably has counterparts using alternative factory names in every other town in the world. To say, 'He must have been made in Pierce's' was to comment that a person showed little or no emotion, indicating a non-human origin.

Maiden names – it was very common in Wexford, especially in the days before the population swelled so much with 'blow-ins', for married women to be still referred to by their maiden names by way of identification. This was not like the current norm of double-barrelled names or not changing a name on marriage. It was especially true when women talked of other women. Expressions like: 'That's Mary Kelly's son. You know, her married to Tom Murphy'.

Manse – although it generally means a big house, this word has often been associated with the house of a Protestant clergyman with Presbytery used for the Roman Catholic equivalent. In Wexford most people would have called the priest's residence in School Street 'the Manse'.

Minerals – as in a 'bottle of minerals' or as others might say, a 'bottle of pop' or 'a soda', indicating a soft drink. 'Give us a bag of crisps and a bottle of minerals for the young fella.'

Mitch was another name for playing truant.

Nap cards were a sort of early national lotto. They were used as fundraisers for clubs and pub social clubs.

Parching with the droot – this was parching with the drought and, as you will agree, it was a very descriptive way of saying you were thirsty by bringing visions of parched lands and an actual drought.

Peg was a reference to throwing – 'He went to peg stones at the dog'. It is Australian slang dating from around 1930.

Perish in both its meanings was quite commonly into recent times although it has fallen out of general usage. One phrase, of course, was 'perishing with the cold'. This was a quite eloquent use of the word and is actually very descriptive if a little fatalistic. But another great phrase was when you vexed someone they would say, 'That will be the rock you will perish on'.

Pictures was our reference to cinema – 'We went to the pictures'.

Pierhead was the usual name Wexford town people called Rosslare Harbour, as in 'He went to the pierhead to catch the boat'.

Pismires – ants were often referred to as pismires, which was a specific name for a species of ant with the first part coming from Middle English for 'urine', based on the smell of the acid they secrete and *myre* from Danish for 'ant'. Here we see an example of those non-local Wexford words.

Rack was a large-toothed comb and probably came from 'rake'.

Rantan meant having a spree – 'He was out on the rantan'. It originated from the German *ranten*, meaning to move noisily.

Right few – this was a compound expression. We seldom said a specific number and instead used phrases like, 'He had a few drinks'. Likewise we used 'right' as an adjective as in 'He's a right fella' or 'She was a right ould'. Used together the expression would be 'We went for a right few'. It was also the adjective for words like 'crowd', 'cur' etc.

Roacheens were small fish, probably originally referring to ones that looked like young roach.

Rounds, as in 'rounds of bread', was very common in Wexford. It referred to the whole slice.

Scoops – this was used when people talked of having some alcoholic drinks – 'he went for a few scoops'.

Scootch meant either a ride or to shuffle along. You could say, 'He got a scotch on the bike' or 'She scotched along the seat'. It may originate from boat-like boots used to move on sloblands or wetlands.

Scratch was the cheapest seats in an auditorium – possibly implying flea ridden.

Shagged could mean tired, as in 'I was shagged after running down the road'. It could mean threw, as in 'He shagged him into the car'.

Signify was an expression often heard in Wexford, meaning that something does not make any difference, as in 'That does not signify'.

Silent collection – collections were always important at Mass as a way of amassing funds. When there was a special occasion or a special need the priest would suggest a silent collection as in only put in paper money – higher denominations that the usual coin.

Silver circle – these were fundraising processes whereby one signed up to pay a fixed sum every week, rather than the other system where you 'bought a line' on a card. The silver circle could run for five or ten weeks with either a small draw each week or one major prize at the end.

Sniving meant full of, as in 'the place was sniving with blackberries'. In an original context referring to a lake or river full of fish it might derive from the Gaelic *snamh*, meaning 'to swim'.

Soft referring to a child or baby meant young or immature.

Spar blasted is closely related to perishing and is a lovely expression for being very cold. My mother often said, 'We were spar blasted waiting for the bus'. The expression probably has nautical origins as in relating to the spar on a ship.

Sparbles was the name for the little nails used for tacking on the leather sole or heel.

Sprong – if you use the Internet to look up the word sprong, be prepared for a surprise. However, for years Wexford people used this word for a garden fork. Could it have arisen from a corruption of the word 'prongs'?

Stave – was used to describe a session in a pub or house where music and song had featured, as in 'There was a right stave in Browne's last night'.

Swing swong was a swing, for instance, 'the children played on the swing swong'.

Taped meant sized up, as in, 'She had him taped'. It possibly comes from measuring tape.

Taws meant marbles – 'We played taws after school'.

Terrible was very, as in, 'He was terrible nice'.

Three sheets in the wind is another nautical expression used to denote someone who is drunk. It is not native to Wexford; indeed, one explanation that has been given is from a Nantucket sailor referring to sailing ships where 'Four sheets to the wind are okay because they are balanced, so are two sheets now and then but three would be very unbalanced'.

Turk could mean angry or annoyed as part of the phrase – 'she turned Turk'. It may have maritime origins if Wexford sailors did not get on with Turkish people on voyages to places such as the Black Sea.

Twigged meant to figure out – 'I soon twigged to him'. It comes from the Gaelic *tuig*, meaning to understand.

Vexed was our way of saying we were annoyed.

Wainscoting is said to refer to the wood panelling used to cover the lower half of the walls of a room, most commonly an entrance hall. In Wexford the name was often applied to what we commonly call the skirting board.

Ward was a division in the municipal area and well into the twentieth century local elections had people elected to represent each ward rather than as at present where it is for the whole town area. The equivalent would be DED or district electoral divisions. The old wards of Wexford generally followed the old parishes.

Wash was the name for leftover food that was collected for feeding to pigs.

Yez was the plural of you, as in, 'Where are yez going?' 'Youse' might also be used.

WEXFORD STREETS

I N AUGUST 1847 the Corporation appointed a committee to label the streets. But change is always with us and in Wexford, like in any other area, the names of our streets were often subject to change. Sometimes this was through colloquial usage and at other times it came about through over-zealous politicians trying to tell us what we should prefer. The latter was tried a few times since Irish independence with varying degrees of success.

In 1764, according to Griffith's Valuation, Wexford boasted Flesh Market, Cornmarket, Back Street, Shambles, Keizars (*sic*) Lane, Ferryboat Quay, Medows (*sic*) Quay, Bennett's Quay, Common Quay, Gibson's Lane and Custom House Quay (principal quay).

In 1820, according to Pigot's Directory, the streets listed included Back Street, Main Street, Selskar Street, John Street, Cornmarket, Slaney Street, Westgate, Old Pound, Common Quay Street, The Faith (*sic*), Custom House Quay, Bullring, Castle

Street, Monck Street, Anne Street, Mary Street, Ram Street, Paul Quay, Stonebridge and George Street.

On various dates after 1920 the Borough Council agreed to adopt new names for nineteen streets. The changes were:

Charlotte to Colbert – this did not catch on

Gibson to Peter – the names are both used but Gibson as Lane rather than street

George to Oliver Plunkett – the old name is still most common

King to Partridge – very few would even recognise Partridge Street

William to James Connolly – the old royal name remains

Wellington Place to O'Rahilly Place – this is also still using the old name but many locals would not even know its location

Ram to Skeffington – both names are used with Ram Street often preferred by older people

Monck to McDonagh – another retaining the old name

Barrack to Macken – this is still Barrack Street

Talbot to Pearse – this is more often Talbot Green now

Henrietta to O'Hanrahan – the old one still used

Hill to Sean McDermott – the more descriptive is the common name

Back to Mallin – both names are used today

Duke to Thomas Clarke Place – the new name is used but mainly because Duke Street or Lane is gone

Waterloo Road to McCurtain Road – the name recalling the battle is still used

Anne to Thomas Ashe – even though the GPO is located there Anne Street is the common designation

Common Quay to O'Hanlon Walsh – again the old name is still used

Castle Hill to Kevin Barry – this street can be found using both names

High to McSweeney – this street has never been anything but
High Street

In a plebiscite in 1932 to legalise the changes only four could be
changed – Castle Hill, Back, Ram and Gibson. Others were officially changed later.

In true Wexford fashion regardless of changes the general public
retained the use of the old names.

Other Name Changes Over Time

Trimmer West was Meylor's (*sic*) Lane
Well Lane was Bolan's Lane
Abbey Street was Lower Back Street
High Street was Upper Back Street
John's Gate Street was John's Lane
Allen Street was Broad Street
Salthouse Lane was listed as Slaughterhouse Lane in 1649
Abbey Street was Selskar Street
Charlotte Street was Custom House Lane
Anne Street was marked as Flesh Market on Fannin's Map of 1800
Green Street was Black Cow in 1856
Roche's Road was The Deddery
Cinema Lane was Moran's or Harpurs
Anne Street was The Shambles and Waterloo was Methodist Row
(according to the book *Centenary of Twin Churches*)

Let us take a walk through the Wexford that once was. On our tour we
will imagine the town in past decades or centuries, and this will give us
a picture of what has been lost to present and future generations.

The Quays

We begin our tour at O'Hanrahan Station or, as we in Wexford say, the North Station, recalling a time when two railway stations served the town. This station welcomed celebrities such as Michael Collins and Countess Markievicz, in the days of the struggle for independence. It was the point of departure for Simon Bloom after the murder of Miss Wildes and it resounded to the music of bands and the crying of families as men emigrated to seek work in England. So big were the crowds bidding farewell to those men initially and on their returning to work after a short holiday that the authorities charged 1*d* for tickets to go on to the platform.

Heading south, we pass on our left a structure that is less than a shadow of its former self and so qualifies as lost. The goods depot of

what was CIÉ until the 1970s was the lifeblood of Wexford trade. The vast majority of the goods for shops and industry arrived by rail, although this had diminished since its heyday. A very large staff was employed in the goods yard, including my grandfather Joe Walsh. It was to the yard that wagons arrived daily, carrying all sorts of goods. Open wagons brought coal or fertilisers, while covered wagons transported the merchandise now arriving by container or courier. The yard was the distribution centre for all this with many shop owners arriving throughout the day to collect items. There was also a delivery system using flat carts pulled by dray horses that conveyed the merchandise to the shops and businesses of the town and surrounding areas.

Next along, on the left, was 'The Dead House'. This was a mortuary for those bodies pulled out of the river or harbour or washed up on the nearby coastal regions, as well as sailors who died on the thousands of annual voyages from Wexford Quays.

In the early nineteenth century a magnificent Oak Bridge would have stood here on our left. The man employed to erect this stunning oak bridge was Lemuel Cox, an American. The oak bridge was 1,554ft long and 34ft wide. To build it, seventy-five piers of oak, each with six timbers, had to be driven into the harbour bed. In addition it needed a portcullis so that shipping would be able to proceed upriver. At low tide there was a depth of water, known as a draught, of 16ft. The Oak Bridge had Chinese railings and two orchestra points in the centre with recesses and seats offering shelter. The bridge was a fashionable promenade where the gentry took their strolls and the bands attached to the military units stationed in Wexford frequently played on it.

It was a working bridge with tolls and these repaid the shareholders handsomely over the years. The shareholders were canny business people and while the bands were not charged the promenaders had to pay. In 1807 the toll company, which changed in a sort of franchise every three years, decided to charge the Tyrone Militia Band. Their commander moved them off the bridge.

Disaster struck in October 1827 when the central portion of the bridge collapsed. There is no report of injury but traffic ceased and there was no income. Mr Robert Hughes of Ely House was instrumental in getting the bridge repaired on that occasion, perhaps because without it he had to travel around via Castlebridge and Ferrycarrig to get to town. As part of the repair job stone causeways were erected at either end, thus reducing the wooden structure, thought to be dangerous. You may still see the abutment at Ferrybank a few feet from the current bridge.

There were calls for the end of the tolls and eventually the Grand Jury – a forerunner of the County Council – purchased the rights of the bridge from the shareholders for £10,000. Taking into account the income from the tolls over fifty years this had certainly proved to be a good investment. Opening the bridge in this way increased traffic but the bridge's popularity ultimately led to its downfall. Traffic became too much for it and in the 1850s a plan was unveiled for a new bridge. As a tragic footnote, many of those who were the original shareholders on the Oak Bridge at Wexford were executed there in the insurrection of 1798.

From 1805 we could have admired a magnificent courthouse on what is now our right-hand side. It was built on what is called Wellington Quay, reminding us of our colonial past, and was located beside the White Horse Inn, which would have been the first hostelry reached on entering Wexford via the bridge. Bombing in the early hours of 18 June 1921 heralded the end of that illustrious building.

Continuing south, we walk along the magnificent old stones running parallel to the railway line. This marked the limit of a linear quay front and dated only from around the early 1800s in Wexford. Prior to that, quays or wharves were at right angles to the waterfront and were usually private edifices allowing merchants to land goods at the rear of their premises. Until about 1880, walking here we had the waters of the harbour below on the left.

From the 1880s we might have walked a wooden-pile wharf extending the full length of the quays and this would have allowed one to stroll about a further 2 yards from the stone edge. You would have walked on only about 5 inches of heavy timber 'sleepers' holding you above the harbour waters. You would have heard the sloshing of the waves against the quay wall and, looking down through the gaps between the sleepers, seen the water and seaweed undulating only a few feet away. Walking the route in stormy weather you could experience the water splashing up through the openings. Beautiful wooden stairways gave the possibility of getting 'down close and personal' with the harbour waters.

There was a story that when the railway arrived at Wexford there were discussions as to whether it should skirt the town to the west but the story went that it would prove too expensive and it was decided to build the pile wharf instead. There is little truth in that tale because why would the railway be built away from the major import point of the ships on the quay? Furthermore, the main railway line actually runs on the land rather than on the pile wharf. The purpose of the pile wharf, or Woodenworks as we knew them, was as a shunting area where wagons were placed for loading and unloading to the boats. This wooden structure was another feat of engineering with huge wooden piles driven into the harbour bed strong enough to support sleepers and rails and fully laden wagons. There were lovely cast-iron cranes installed on the Woodenworks to assist in the loading and unloading. It is important to note that where we now walk was not generally open

to the public a century ago. It was a working port with all the restrictions, dangers and policing required for what was in essence a factory or industrial site.

In the middle of the twentieth century the quay front became a public road and from there you would have experienced a regatta on almost every Sunday of the summer season. There would have been dinghies, gabbards, cotts and other boats, all individually owned by men whose families probably had ancient mariner blood – even Viking – as they raced in spirited competition. This was a great sport but also a dangerous one as capsising and sinking often resulted from the racing. Another aspect of regatta to be viewed rather than experienced was 'the greasy pole'. This pole – like a mast – covered in grease jutted out over the water and the lads tried to outdo one another walking out as far as possible without slipping. On a more sedate note at regattas and often just any Sunday morning you might find ranks of 'young lads' sitting on the edge of the quay with their backs to the town dangling pieces of twine or 'lashing' into the water with a mussel tied on. These were the crab fishers of Wexford.

Further out one would have seen a broad harbour dotted with islands and shallows and mudflats including Beg Érin or Little Ireland. The fields surrounding that coast were known as 'The Dairy Fields' and were a popular courting location into the middle of the twentieth century.

Ferrybank itself was a lovely little beach area for the inhabitants of Wexford and would be thronged on a sunny Sunday afternoon or a summer evening, even at a time when it had to be accessed via the bridge that stood at Carcur. In the 1960s men would have been out in the mud at Ferrybank, each with a sprong and bucket. Their quest would have been the cockles that were abundant there. These were a local favourite cooked in milk.

On the right as you stroll Commercial Quay, named for the original use of this section of the new quays of the 1800s, you would have seen Kinsella's Coalyard a century ago among many others taking their coal directly from the boats docked at the quay. That coal was hand shovelled into huge metal bins to be hoisted from the hold and tipped either into coal lorries or open railway wagons.

On the corner of Charlotte Street there is an interesting historical point to note: it is the recessed or 'cut off' lower corner of the building. This was common in the days of coach travel when control of the horses was not always possible and the wheels often clipped buildings. The interestingly named Entiknapp's sold sweets, ices and tobacco in the adjoining shop in the early 1900s.

Across Charlotte Street the wonderful little building surrounded by the Centenary Stores reminds us that it was a post office in the 1800s and was the premises of Doyle's Plumbers in the 1900s.

Where the lane emerges under a building Kevin Morris, many times mayor of Wexford, had his auctioneering business. Prior to that it was the first premises of McCormack Brothers, hardware, and earlier still it was Breen's Ironmongers.

The tall building beside Mooney's was the original site of the Provincial Bank before it moved in the early 1880s to Anne Street corner. Hugh McGuire then acquired the premises and used it as a ship's chandler's.

Beside that you might have seen one of our oldest and most mysterious lanes. It is known as Roman Lane, although we never had any record of a Roman settlement. In some English towns Roman Lane denoted a lane or street where Roman Catholics had places of worship during the early centuries of the Reformation. The lane was less than 3ft wide and extended to the Main Street.

In the 1930s one of the shops here you could have visited was Roger's shop, selling bicycles and wirelesses. Later it became a furniture store run by Billy Rackard, one of the three legendary Rackard brothers of the mid-twentieth-century Wexford hurling team. The rear entrance to O'Connor's Steam Bakery stood here with a date of establishment of 1860.

Harry Wilson operated his shipping and coal importing business on the quay here. He was also a Lloyd's agent. The shipping connection of the site went back to Gafney's, who earlier had a coal and iron yard there. Yes, it was spelt with a single 'f'.

The wonderful façades on the buildings near the junction recall that these were originally one building and part of the St Iberius Club that ran up most of Common Quay Street.

Common Quay was something similar to common land. In times past all quays were privately owned and operated. The Common Quay may have been an access point for the ordinary sailor or small boat to dock and load or unload.

On the opposite corner stood the coal and wool yard of Ffrenche's and an old malt store. Next door the beautifully kept old building was built as the Union Club around 1830 and later became the Commercial Club.

Cooper's Solicitors also had offices in the area. Boggan's Garage fronted the quay here and the workshop stretched up from the quay, parallel to Church Lane.

On Custom House Quay, the dominant building was formerly the National Bank. The carved head over the door, thought to represent Slaighne from whom our river Slaney takes its name, reminds us of the artistic architecture of such buildings in the past. To the right of the door there was the entrance to a garden at the rear of the bank. It was built over in the 1900s.

To the south of the bank were Thompson's sawmills and hardware shops. These later became McCormack & Hegarty's and then McCormack's, housing the same type of business. In more recent history, it was the original home of Hardob's Textile Factory when it set up in Wexford in the 1960s before moving to the industrial estate at Whitemill.

At the northern corner of Anne Street was English's Printing Works. This was one of a number of printers in Wexford in the twentieth century. It produced mainly jobbing printing but also excelled at book production and was the printer of the *Capuchin Annual*, among others, for many years.

The redbrick building on the opposite side was the Provincial Bank from around 1880. Observe the rounded roof on the adjoining building. Walsh and Corish of Taghmon moved here in 1918 with an auctioneering business. Contrary to perceived knowledge, the roof is not part of the old United States airbase on 1918.

Next door was George Murphy's garage with petrol pumps at the kerb and an enamel plate with a map of Ireland attached to the wall. To the rear was Allen's timber yard in the 1800s.

The lane here is Cullimore's Lane and probably takes its name from the original landowner.

The old Bank of Ireland building, dating from 1835, leads us round on to Crescent Quay. This quay, referred to in a document of the early 1800s as 'Elliptical Quay', is situated on the old Deep Pool of Wexford.

The next building along was one of the hundreds of malt stores that dotted Wexford in the eighteenth and nineteenth centuries. Sleggs Lane opens off the car park to the rear.

Into the late 1900s numerous small buildings filled the Crescent Quay. One was Underwood's, who appear to have been very varied in their trade, offering everything from tinsmith through bicycles to undertaking.

Beside this was a timber yard that was owned by Staffords and earlier by Ennis.

One of my favourite buildings here was formerly Browne's Forge. It was an establishment for shoeing horses and ponies. It later housed Bookends, one of our first second-hand bookshops, and was run by Jimmy Lacey.

A magnificent archway once spanned the goods entrance for Penney's.

The Ballast Office was built as headquarters of the Harbour Commissioners in the 1800s. An interesting feature is the apparent carvings of the window ledges. It is said that the shapes were made by sailors using the sills to sharpen their knives.

Crescent Mall is built on the old Stafford's Sawmill and timber yard. Beside that was the Talbot Garage, also a Stafford enterprise. The entry to the car park here once was a lane leading to Wickham's Brewery on South Main Street.

The two lovely old houses, still residences, sport slate fronts to protect against rain much in the way plastering does now. It is said that such Welsh slate arrived in Wexford as ballast in sailing ships and was recycled in the building trade.

On the corner here is one of the many custom houses that operated in Wexford as the port thrived. It once had a 'belvedere' or small glass area in the roof where the officers could observe ships using the port.

Paul Quay's title is often attributed to Paul Turner, a landowner in earlier times, but this is unlikely as the name would probably have been Turner Quay. An alternative is that the original title was 'the Quay of the Pale' or Pale Quay. This latter name is shown in a document dated 1610. Pale is another name for a fort or fortress and seems fitting when one considers the proximity of both Wexford Castle and Stafford's Castle. It may also derive from Pole Quay – such is the joy of trying to trace our past.

Another grain store dating from around 1900 called Old Mill House stood beside the customhouse. It was demolished overnight in the late 1900s.

Oyster Lane was a lane with a number of hotels and inns back in the 1800s. Carr's was the more prominent, offering oysters, brown bread and porter as a speciality. Oysters were a common commodity in those times and were regular fare for the common people.

Stafford's were ship owners, importers, exporters and much else besides. The buildings along here dating from 1936 into the late 1900s housed the coal import and sales. It was here that we went to order coal for household delivery. The yards were huge and they had their own weighbridge. It was in this vicinity that the company's ships had their cargoes of coal, timber and goods of all description unloaded for its many enterprises. Staffords were the last major sailing-ship owners in Wexford and had sail-making lofts on this quay. The Stafford family bought their first steamships in 1919, named *Elsie Annie* after their daughter, and *JFV* (James,

Francis, Victor) after their sons. By the outbreak of war in 1939, they operated the most modern fleet in Ireland under the title of the Wexford Steamship Co.

The stonewall beside the railway tracks here recalls the original outfall of the Bishopswater River into the harbour, but whether there was ever a bridge there is open to question.

Pierce's Foundry had a social club for its employees in this area. It was on these premises that the Tontine Society was introduced to Wexford from France, where the company had offices. The system entailed members paying a fixed sum each week and withdrawing the savings at times such as Christmas. In addition, when a member died, each subscriber gave a small sum called a 'death' and the money collected was put towards the burial costs. It sounds like a very simple matter today but at a time before credit cards, credit unions and easy loans when fear of a pauper's grave haunted many, it was a great and very popular idea.

An adjoining building was used to store finished implements from the foundry awaiting shipment and also the coke and pig iron imported for the industry.

Howard Rowe had a flourmill here too and at one time the Sisters of Mercy provided 'penny dinners' to the poor of the town from premises on Paul Quay.

Looking seaward again and slightly to the north, we see a rather curious man-made island in the harbour opposite Paul Quay. This is the Ballast Bank. It was erected in 1831 to provide a place for loading and unloading the ballast essential to stabilise ships sailing without cargo. Prior to its construction the ballast was stored on ballast wharfs on the quay.

Before 1974 facing south at this point your eye would have wavered between the twin tanks of Wexford Gas Consumers Company in Trinity Street and Clover Meats (later Smiths and then Wexford Electronix) occupying the land jutting seaward. Between these two the railway lines would have led your eye to the South Station with a platform situated between two lines of rails. Earlier still you might have boarded ship for Tenby in Wales or Liverpool or Dublin at a wharf just a few yards ahead.

The Main Street

We head away from the sea and up King Street. The Corporation tried to call it Partridge Street in 1920 but, despite a name plaque, it never caught on. In times past walking up here would have taken you between stone-built malt stores that lined both sides of this street.

At the top we turn right and what we are entering is called Stonebridge. The actual bridge was about 100 yards from the corner and was, until recently, delineated by a tarmacadam strip. In the past it has been called Wexford Bridge and in 1764 it was known as Jew's Bridge. The bridge was built over the Bishopswater River and may have marked the northern gate of the earliest Norse or Viking settlement. The first recorded story of murder or manslaughter in Wexford town happened at Stonebridge. At about mid-afternoon on 25 February 1560, a quarrel took place between Thomas Walsh, a shoemaker, and Geoffrey Brian, a mariner. The insults led to blows being exchanged and finally Brian stabbed Walsh below the heart. Walsh died from the wounds received.

On our left once stood the old Capitol Cinema and, at the beginning of the twentieth century, Staffords Furniture Store was here. The Capitol Cinema opened on Sunday, 15 February 1931, with a film called *The Big Trail*. The Capitol was the second purpose-built cinema to open in the town but was also used as a concert venue. Among those who appeared at the Capitol were Jack Doyle and Movita (she later married Marlon Brando) in January 1944, and, in 1945, the Wexford Theatre Players with *Variety Spotlight* starring Martin Crosby, a big star on the Irish circuit whose family came from Wexford, and Cecil Sheridan. Imagine for a moment the cinema queues stretched around the corner into Upper King Street being kept in order by the cries of 'Two deep now, two deep' coming from a cinema attendant.

A notable character of the time was Tommy Swift; he was a man of low stature, who sold newspapers from a little pram-cum-hand-cart to people who queued at the Capitol Cinema. The Capitol closed in the early 1990s. The adjoining premises was the Granada Grill, more popularly known as Joe Dillon's, a venue for popular entertainment including bingo sessions.

O'Toole's in the mid- to late 1900s it was a very popular gathering place for young people. There they sat for hours over 'bottles of minerals', ice-cream sundaes or cups of coffee. The front of the shop was an Aladdin's cave of exotic tobacco products, Swiss army knives and toys. The Capitol Bar was a popular venue for a pint before or after a visit to the cinema.

To the right at Stonebridge is Larkin's Lane, also known as Sinnott's Place. In the early 1900s the right-hand side of this lane accommodated Stafford's offices, and provision cellars. On the other side there was a forge. The Larkin name derived from an extensive bakery, which came later. The bakery is long gone and the premises became home to Wexford's Theatre Workshop in the 1980s. A generator was housed in the lane, which provided electrical power for Stafford's Enterprises between 1921 and 1928. It was Wexford's first major electrical plant.

To the left of Stonebridge is Stonebridge Lane. It was called 'The Hole of the Wreck' in the past. There is no historical record of

why but this area of Wexford would have been marshland into the Middle Ages and may have witnessed wrecks. In 1800s there were twenty-seven houses listed there; James Prendergast, who lived in the lane, owned the majority.

Moving north along South Main Street would have shown us Stafford's Castle on our right. It became a gaol in 1665 and was used to house prisoners during the 1798 Rebellion. In 1812 a new gaol was built at Spawell Road and the castle became a lunatic asylum and house of industry. By 1831 it was called the House of Industry and Insane Asylum to provide shelter for beggars, prostitutes and the insane. Poor people housed there were allowed keep half of any earnings; vagrants were allowed none. It was financed by subscriptions from the local gentry with members paying £3 per year. Inmates were also used to raise revenue. Until 1847, the inmates were street cleaners with the house being paid £10 per annum. Remember this was the era of animal-drawn transport with street cleaning being quite a messy occupation. Annual subscription from Thomas and Charles Walker (of Belmont) was recorded as £3 in 1831. The *Wexford Chronicle* reported in 1832:

> A special meeting of the governors decided that due to the increase of cases of Asiatic Cholera in the past few days better treatment of mendicants was needed. In future a good breakfast was to be provided with meat for dinner on 3 days each week and boiled bread and milk for supper.

Among the reported deaths that week were William Westnot (aged 87), Israel Daly (84), Catherine Scott (68), Mary Cloak (68), Robert Rowe (80) all from cholera. The castle was eventually demolished in 1866 to provide land for development.

Where Bride Street joins Main Street on our left was known as Coffin Corner in 1812. This may stem from a time when military personnel from Wexford Castle were buried in St Mary's graveyard and passed along this way. Funerals from Bride Street church usually went this way too, on to Main Street and the quays – until excess traffic resulted in the roads being rerouted. An older red-brick house on this corner was home to one of the many Tontine societies in the town in the 1900s.

Archaeological evidence of our Viking past, including post and wattle walls and some footwear and pottery, was uncovered in this area. Similar remnants were found at Oyster Lane almost opposite.

Opposite Bride Street was the site of Murphy's Clay Pipe Factory. I also recall Barry's fish shop on the site.

At the top of Oyster Lane Malone's fish shop once stood, with a cat sunning itself in the window beside a large Wedgewood plate where the fish was displayed. On the opposite corner of Oyster Lane the Pettit supermarket empire started in about 1947. The original house was the birthplace of Father James Roche, driving force in the construction of Wexford's twin churches.

There was once an old-style manned public convenience on the corner of the appropriately called Mann's Lane.

The site of the Dun Mhuire entertainment complex, which opened in 1960, was the Devereux townhouse over a hundred years ago. It was later the residence of the clergy of the church of the Assumption until 1889, when it became a barracks for the Royal Irish Constabulary. With the advent of Irish independence it housed the Civic Guards, who later moved to Roche's Road. The local branch of the Legion of Mary started here in 1934 and acquired the building in 1938. The Legion operated a Catholic Girls Club there.

Opposite Dun Mhuire Jem Roche, a favourite for the title of World Heavyweight Boxing Champion in 1908, operated a public house. The advertising motto was 'Only champion drinks served'.

Heffernan's pub is on the site of Hay's Castle. Walter Hay was recorded as living in Wexford in 1641. The street next to it is Peter Street, known locally as Gibson's Lane. The name came from William Gibson who had the malt store at the corner. It is one of the named streets as Gibson's Lane in 1764.

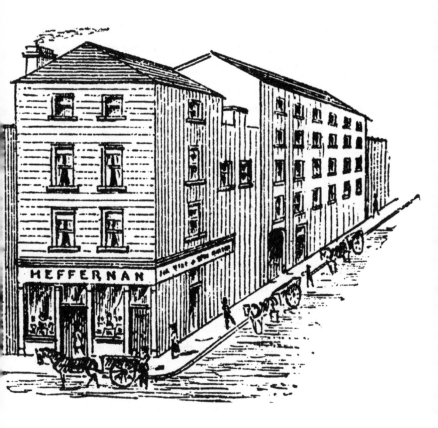

Never an official name, Cinema Lane has officially been Moran's Lane, Harpur's Lane and Hay's Lane. The more commonly used name comes from the Palace Cinema (locally always referred to as the Cinema Palace probably because of the design of the playbills) that was opened in the lane on 7 December 1914. The first concert performance was in aid of Belgian refugees of the Great War. It has the name Moran's Lane in a map of around 1812. The cinema was opened in a former bonded warehouse where The Receiver of Wrecks stored goods salvaged from shipwrecks before they were auctioned. The title of Harpur's Lane comes from Francis Harpur,

155

businessman, ship owner and Lloyd's agent, who lived here in 1827. He was also a town councillor and three times mayor of Wexford. In 1853 Francis Harpur had a ship store here.

The slight incline here on South Main Street is known as Coffey's Hill and actually gives the title to a piece of popular music played by St Patrick's Fife and Drum Band which was founded in Wexford in 1893. Coffey's was a family store that traded for over a century on this site selling clothes, footwear and nursery products in the latter years. The premises were the Hat and Cap Warehouse in 1877. Coffey's also owned the pawn shop, managed by and colloquially referred to as Davy Tobin's, in Abbey Street into the 1960s.

On your right going up Coffey's Hill was the Temperance Hotel. These were common throughout the British Isles in the late 1800s and early 1900s. Miss Maggie Dempsey operated a wonderful second-hand book and comic store in this area in the mid-1900s. It was there that many people made the acquaintance of Dan Dare, Flash Gordon, Batman and Superman, among others. With emigration came a few benefits. Aunts and uncles in Britain and the USA often included these comics in the parcels home. The comics then began a circular journey through the hands and minds of countless Wexford children thanks to Maggie's emporium.

Allen Street branches west from Main Street. It is named after the Revd Joseph Allen but was known as Broad Street in 1649 and was first paved in 1793. In 1824 Corbett and Rochford's Ladies Boarding School was located in this street. John Hickey was master of a post office in Allen Street in 1824. In Pigot's Directory of that year it is noted that mail from Dublin arrived at 10.15 a.m. and was dispatched at 3.30 p.m. and letters were to be posted by 3 o'clock. Mail from Broadway (south of the town) arrived every Sunday, Wednesday and Friday at 10 a.m.

Nolan's sweet shop and café was a popular meeting place for the youth of the town over the years. Here they listened to the latest hit records played on the jukebox.

An old lane called Kenny's was incorporated into Hore's Stores beside Penney's. It exited in the lower section of Henrietta Street. At 31 South Main Street, now part of Hore's drapery business, Edward Walsh established *The People* newspaper in 1853. It incorporated the *Wexford Guardian* of the previous year. *The People* went from strength to strength and is still published in Wexford, albeit at another location. Hore's was famous in the mid-1900s for its rhyming advertisements in the local newspapers.

Penney's department store is on the site of Kenny's Hall, where Oliver Cromwell is said to have stayed for a short time in October 1649 after the fall of Wexford. The current store replaced Woolworth's in the 1980s. Kenny's Hall is believed to have been a castellated mansion, perhaps of medieval origin. During the Confederate War David Sinnott, the military governor of Wexford, lived there. The name Kenny's Hall dates from the 1700s, when the Kenny family lived there. An alderman of the town, Mr Sinnott, took a lease on the building in the 1840s and operated a very successful hardware, undertaking and cabinet-making business on the premises. In 1870 Richard Devereux purchased the head rent on the building and bequeathed it to the Society of St Vincent De Paul. The hardware business continued under Frank Gaul until just before the arrival of Woolworth's, when major renovation and re-modelling was carried out.

Barkers Shop incorporates two interesting old Wexford shops. One was the giftware store that gives it its name, Barkers. As well as buying giftware you could book sea passages there in the early 1900s. The shop was established in 1843 as Marine Stores, again reminding us of our maritime past. The other shop was Paddy Lyons shoe shop. This is reputed to be the first Wexford shop giving plastic bags with the shop name printed on them.

Fitzgerald's store was the hardware, seed and ammunition shop of S&R Pierce until the 1980s. This was a huge old style hardware shop full of nooks and crannies, big counters and brushes and shovels hung outside throughout the day.

Sleggs Lane on the seaward side is one of my favourite lanes in Wexford. It is entered via a low arch opposite Fitzgerald's shop. One then descends a short flight of steps under the shops giving a real feeling of going back in time – especially before it had public lighting – to emerge into a car park. In earlier timers one would continue down the narrow thoroughfare to the Deep Pool or Crescent Quay. In October 1866 this lane was one of three mentioned as being in a filthy state and a danger to public health with cholera in the town. This lane still gives the best feel of old Wexford.

Keysar's Lane, beside Fitzgerald's, is one of our oldest lanes and it is often confused with Slegg's Lane. Keysar's Lane joins South Main Street to High Street. It was called Keizar's in Griffith's Chronicles in 1764. Tradition tells the lovely story that the name derives from 'kiss arse lane' because the steepness caused people to fall on their rears or be in a position to kiss the posterior of those in front when climbing the lane. Today, we have a car park where many houses once stood in this lane. In 1853 there were twenty-five premises recorded here, primarily houses with yards. Among the inhabitants were Ba Swift and Nicholas Murphy, a 'baker's oven keeper'.

Charlie Pierce's shop is on the site of one of our first chippers, where the appropriately named Mr Fisher sold fish and chips and ice cream. We also had the L&N here. That was the London & Newcastle Tea Company reminding us of our colonial past.

Moving along, Matty Furlongs was on our left. This is where Wexfordians, including the fledgling St Bridget's Fife & Drum Band, bought musical instruments, sheet music, religious items and wallpaper among other items into the mid-1900s.

We had Allie Whites where, if we behaved well, we were treated to an ice-cream sundae. I also remember lovely spearmint bars without a maker's name but they had a sort of cobweb design on the wrapper.

Healy and Collins Department Store were renowned among the youngsters at least for the innovative cash system. Little boxes flew back and forth on wires throughout the shop. Cash was put into the container and whizzed off to the office, where a receipt and change were inserted and returned to the counter and the customer.

The Book Centre was previously Stones, a grocery and provisions store. Opposite stood Roche's greengrocers, which was previously owned by Doyles. In old photographs one can see the bottom of a sign on this building. It shows the 'AL' of Theatre Royal and the reason for this is that an exit or entry from that theatre in High Street passed through the shop at one time. Mr Charles Vize had a photographer's studio once. He also operated at another time from High Street. He was the projectionist at the Palace Cinema and also played in the orchestra in the days of silent movies.

Our very own gas company closed in the 1970s. Their showroom was at 3 South Main Street. On the first floor was a lovely bay window jutting out over the Main Street.

At the top of Anne Street was the wonderfully named Lamb House – some steps leading to a side entrance can still be seen. This area of Wexford had numerous basements in the shops and may have given rise to the fabled tunnels said to connect The Friary with the quays.

Anne Street, to our right, housed numerous clubs such as Masonic and Orange halls. The lower south side in 1828 had the Harbour Commissioners and Ballast Office, which later became an Inland Revenue office. A sandy beach was excavated in 1950s at the base of the hill, near the General Post Office. The GPO was built in 1894 and the Methodist church in 1836. Number 8 Anne Street housed Anglim's, the printers of the *Wexford Illustrated Almanac*. The Shamrock Hotel of 1885 became the Shamrock Bar, proprietor P. Meyler by 1945; it was later owned by Pierce Roche and features fictitiously in his son Billy's novel *Tumbling Down*.

Clancy's Hotel was originally a house owned by Clancy, a victualler. A room in Clancy's Hotel was let to the Temperance Club 1850. This was the first popular reading room and charged a subscription of 1*d* per week. Clancy's became the County Hotel when it was sold to the Sinnott family in June 1947. In 1853 number 3a was classed as a slaughterhouse. Thomas and Mathew Boggan opened a garage in Anne Street in 1920s and ran a bus fleet from Anne Street. 'Banshee' and 'Bluebird' were the names of two of the buses. They also operated a parcel-delivery service along the routes. Anne Street has changed beyond recognition in recent years with government offices replacing the Shamrock and the County.

The Mechanics Institute was opened on 13 July 1849. The rules included: no papers to be read at the fire and no paper to be held more than 15 minutes. It offered classes, a museum and a library. The membership cost per annum was: apprentices 4*s*, operatives 6*s* and others 10*s*. Life membership could be gained for £5 or in exchange for suitable books to the value of £10. The three-storey house was purchased for £800. The original meeting to establish the institute was held in the Temperance Hall.

Present were: James Johnson, first editor of *The People* newspaper, who later became a priest; Revd William Moran; Michael Hughes; George Codd; Thomas McGee, who became lieutenant colonel of the 69th New York Regiment, and Benjamin Hughes of the *Wexford Independent*. Opinions on the project were sought from Charles A. Walker, deputy lieutenant of County Wexford and Sir Francis Le Hunte RN. Both were in favour. Le Hunte, who was leaving home at the time, gave £100 and 1,000 volumes. Books were donated by Mrs C.S. Hall, noted for the travel book 'Hall's Ireland'. Thomas Hutchinson, British consul at Fernando Po, gave forty books plus African curiosities including a bamboo crown used by the King of Bassapo in 1857; Queen Victoria gave an autographed volume and Ambrose Fortune of Wexford gave a portrait valued £50.

Archers Lane, which connected Main Street to High Street, was marked on maps in the mid-1800s. It was covered in and reclaimed over a century ago when it became part of *The People* newspaper offices and works. Some of the steps could still be seen when People Newspapers were on the site. It exited on to High Street through an arch just along from the Theatre Royal. Archer's Lane was the location of the Friar's chapel in the seventeenth century. There was a meat market with approximately thirty stalls off Archer's Lane. Clement Archer lived at Anne Street in 1834 and may have given his name to the lane.

Dick Whelan had a barbershop along on the right-hand side. It was an apothecary shop for Mrs Pierce and before her for Mr Richards. There was a grill set into the footpath here to allow light into a basement. Many people refused to stand on it for fear of it collapsing.

Hasset's chemists held the distinction of having a telephone number of 'Wexford 1' in the 1920s.

Fettett's Lane, on the right, was shown on the sketch map of the town of 1812. Access to the working port was via the lanes and these were locked at night and patrolled by the harbour constables.

Corish Memorial Hall was two doors from Church Lane. It was named to honour Richard (Dick) Corish, Mayor of Wexford for twenty-five consecutive years and member of Dail Éireann until his death in 1945. In this building a school was started under the Agricultural and Technical Scheme. This school developed into the Vocational School and was transferred to West Gate in 1908. The building belonged to the Irish National Foresters.

Church Lane leading seaward takes its name from St Iberius' church, which it adjoins. It was originally narrow all the way from here to Custom House Quay. Here the Duke of Ely had his townhouse. It later became a Workingmen's Free Reading Rooms. It was behind St Iberius' church and can be seen in some old photographs. In September 1827 an application was made to Councillor Richards for the opening of Church Lane. In 1832, S. Howard had a factory there where they made machines for dressing flour and brushing corn. For the domestic market they produced wire riddles for sifting sand or clay and wire safes.

In Rowe Street the Wesleyan church is now converted to other use but retains its façade. It was opened on 9 March 1863 with a congregation of 500. The minister of the Bethesda church at Cornmarket reduced his Sunday services to allow people to attend, to help pay for the building. The Excise Office was located in Rowe Street in 1846 and the Inland Revenue office was at number 7 in 1875. The National League regularly met in rooms at 2 Rowe Street in 1884 and the Wexford County Board of the Gaelic Athletic Association was founded there on 21 November 1885 – a plaque on the wall reminds us of this.

Iberius' church on Main Street is said to be on the site of an older church, originally built outside Norse Market Gate. The date of the present church is not clear. We have records that St Iberius' was repaired in 1693. Money was requested to build a gallery in 1728. In 1831 Revd Storey proposed Major Wilson of Roseville as churchwarden with Mr Dance and Mr Trigg as sidemen. The parish clerk was to get £20 for three services each Sunday and four in the week. Revd Storey supplied wax candles for the reading desk and tallow candles for the congregation at a cost of £3 10s 0d. The vestry paid £5 11s 3d for coffins for the poor in 1831. This church has many interesting monuments and is worth a visit. In February 1868 the Corporation paid £5 to St Iberius' church for special pews for visiting judges of assizes. The mayor could also use them.

The Bullring is one of the focal points of Wexford. It was called the Common Plain before bull baiting took place under a charter granted to the butchers of the town in 1609. Baiting was later transferred to John Street near the George Street junction. This spectacle of a huge beast tethered and then attacked by dogs took place at the Bullring and the hide of the animal was presented to the mayor, with the flesh being distributed to the poor of the town. In 1764 there was a courthouse with clock. It was also called Fountain Square around 1790 to 1800 when it housed a fountain; unlike the extravagant structures of European cities this was a more modest, wall-mounted item. In 1833 the Bullring was stated to be 'unlit and unpaved'.

The Cape of Good Hope or The Cape Bar that attracts so many photographers to snap its legend of 'bar and undertaker' was once the home of the '13 club', where members were required to consume thirteen glasses of punch in quick succession. In 1831 Ambrose Fortune, in premises stated to be near the Bullring, 'manufactured razors, penknives etc. to highest standard'; there was also a clock and watch business. Where the bank now stands the Court of Conscience for debts under 40s and the Corporation offices were at the Tholsel in 1837 with a butter market underneath. Sixty feet of the former Shambles was purchased from Mr Sparrow for building this Tholsel with five arches. At turn of the nineteenth century, 'onion women' sat on Tholsel steps twining onions and selling second-hand clothes. The Fish Market was said to be called the 'Piaze' by sailors more familiar with the Mediterranean than with Dublin The Tholsel was demolished 1898.

The New Market was built in 1871. The north-side buildings replaced six thatched houses. On 6 May 1872 it was noted in the local newspapers that the Corporation had been allowed borrow £1,000 to erect this new market. Tolls charged at the New Market included fowl 1d per basket and turkeys 1d each at Christmas.

In 1881 Laurence Murphy sold stationery next to Daly's Bakery on the northern corner of the Bullring. The premises later became the Ritz Café. In the corner of the Bullring the old rectory was the home of the Elgee family and Speranza, mother of Oscar Wilde. The house later became Pitts Coaching Inn and Morris' Hotel before being bought by Lamberts.

Sheppard's statue, the Pikeman, recalls the Rebellion of 1798 when the first Irish Republic was declared here. The Pikeman was unveiled on Sunday, 6 August 1905 by Fr Kavanagh OFM. Eleven special trains brought visitors to the event and over twenty bands attended.

A fire engine house was located in the Bullring in 1880.

Rallies such as P.T. Daly addressing a crowd on 3 August 1911 to say that 'dockers had won their claim and now factory workers urged to unionise', a Suffragette meeting in April 1914 and an anti-vaccination protest in 1919 were regular occurrences in the Bullring. In later years victorious sporting teams were feted here.

There were two air-raid shelters in 1941 and an old milestone was defaced as a wartime precaution although its 64 was in Irish miles to Dublin.

The plaque to Jem Roche was unveiled on 1 October 1961. Roche is probably best known for his unsuccessful challenge for the World Heavyweight Boxing Championship against T. Burns in Dublin on St Patrick's Day, 1908, but in a career of thirty-eight fights he won twenty-two by knockouts and seven on points. One of those he knocked out was John L. Sullivan.

Leaving the Bullring and continuing north, we enter what was once called Foreshore Street. The name tells it all: here we would have been walking along the seaside a few centuries ago.

Frank O'Connor's Bakery was established in 1860 and boasted some of the most modern machinery in the world. In 1889 their bread cost 5*d* per four pound loaf. The fine mosaic tile floor inside the door is worthy of examination. The façade still sports the legend recalling its bakery days – 'Bread is Still the Stuff of Life'.

Further along Hadden's was the first store in Wexford with fixed prices although not from the year it opened, 1848.

Oaks' Lane, on our right, runs parallel to Charlotte Street. It was once worth the effort to follow the lane from North Main Street to the Quay just to view the house stretching across the arch on the quayside exit. This lane was referred to as the Old Shambles on a map of the 1840s.

Charlotte Street on the right, past Oak's Lane, was originally known as Custom House Lane. The name changed in the early 1800s as recorded by a harbour commissioner note of 1830, 'Widened the street at Old Custom House now called Charlotte Street'. In 1828 there was a request that the 'street be powder paved, new street at custom house'.

At the time, it was the coach terminal, 'Shamrock Coach Co. leaves Thomas Kehoe's, Charlotte Street at 6.00 a.m. and arrives College Green, Dublin (White Horse Cellar) at 6.00 p.m. Fare 8/='.

In 1917 Walter Carter of Charlotte Street was fined 6*d* for playing football on the street. He said that on returning from the chapel some children had kicked the ball to him and he kicked it back. The constable stated that Carter had picked up the ball, a football case filled with hay, and kicked it from Charlotte Street into Main Street. This caused inconvenience to people using the street for business or pleasure.

Across Charlotte Street was Walkers, an institution in Wexford of the first half of the twentieth century. For most native Wexfordians Walkers meant the smell of coffee, freshly ground. That was the aroma that permeated the store. Inside the large premises there were all the provisions one could find in the most modern supermarket. They blended their own teas. They had cellars full of wine, whiskey, stout and beer. There was a dispatch department and stabling for their horse and vans, stretching down to the quays.

On the narrowest point on Wexford's Main Street in the mid-twentieth century was the entrance to the coffee shop of Whites Hotel. The hotel was founded as a coaching inn in 1779 and provided refreshment and accommodation for visitors to Wexford ever since. The building incorporated Mr Wheelock's house, where Sir Robert McClure, who discovered the North-West Passage, was born. The composer William Balfe lived for a time in a house opposite the hotel. His opera, *The Rose of Castile*, was one of the first featured in the Wexford Festival Opera.

The beautiful redbrick building was the YMCA or Young Men's Christian Association club, established in 1858. The wonderful old wooden staircase still winds its way to the second floor, dividing in two on its first landing.

The *Wexford Independent* was published at No. 96 North Main Street in 1875. It incorporated the *Wexford Journal*, established in 1769.

Monck Street, on the right, takes its name from General Monck, Duke of Albemarle, who was granted the lands in 1658 by Cromwell. The grant also included the rights to the ferry, which ran from the area of the Rock of Wexford to Ferrybank prior to the erection of the bridge in 1794. At that time Monck Street was called Ferryboat Lane. The Crown Hotel in Monck Street was established in 1885. On 7 July 1922, the first Wexford casualty of the Civil War died from a shotgun blast in Monck Street.

Strictly speaking, we are now leaving North Main Street and entering Selskar Street. This area is probably the longest inhabited section of Wexford, predating the arrival of the Norsemen. Skeffington Street leads to the sea; it used to be named Ram Street after Bishop Ram.

George's Street stretches landward with its many old townhouses, such as the Colcoughs and Harveys, on the left. Some of the old boot scrapers of an earlier period are still evident here outside the front doors reached by several steps. The official name is Oliver Plunkett Street. Colcoughs of Tintern had their townhouse beside the entrance to the hotel. They had a theatre in the attic where visiting actors and singers performed. In 1821 a letter to Cesar Colclough on 3 November referred to a plan to open a passage or street between John Street and George Street. A cabin, occupied by Colcough's tenant, was in the line of the proposed road and he was asked to have the tenant removed, as the Wexford Harbour Commissioners could not afford to relocate him. The letter pointed out that the new road would greatly improve the land value.

The Christian Brothers School opened on Upper George's Street on 1 October 1853 and closed in 1971. The Constabulary

Barracks was at number 5 in 1853 and was still there in 1914. It later became Miss O'Brien's Girls School. The Loreto Convent started in Wexford at 14 Lower George's Street on Assumption Day 1866. They moved to Richmond House, then a vacant hotel, within three months. The first interment in Crosstown cemetery in 1892 was a Carroll of 14 George's Street.

John Duffy & Son Circus set up in Red Pat's field on 28 May 1923. Livestock auctions were held there in 1918 and Pioneer Rallies in the 1950s. The Abbey Cinema, originally to be called the Ritz, was later built on the site.

Trimmers Lane cut east to west through Selskar or Main Street, following the route of an ancient causeway linking Selskar Abbey to the ferry rock. The eastern lane still exists. A walk down here gives a good impression of the old town, although most buildings are bricked up.

Selskar Avenue on the left incorporates Trimmers Lane west. A number of houses were demolished to create the wider street.

Well Lane was previously called Bolan's Lane. In the 1800s there were fourteen houses there. The name Well Lane comes from a well in the area. It was later equipped with a pump. Towards the turn of the nineteenth century Blind Mary lived in Well Lane. She earned a living as a water carrier and was one of the gentlest and best-known characters in the town. She walked inside a barrel hoop, outside which she carried two buckets of water. She wore a short petticoat, a man's frieze coat and a deep poke bonnet. She delivered water to 'half the quality in town' until 'the newfangled water works and pipes put the pumps out of fashion'.

Redmond Square and the monument remind us of the Redmond family. We would be standing on water or marsh here but for their reclamation work. This family was involved in politics, business and banking as well as land reclamation. Redmonds and their contemporaries reclaimed most of the land from Redmond Place to Carcur.

The North Railway Station, or as it is officially known O'Hanrahan Station, was opened on 12 August 1874. The railway originally terminated at Carcur. The station still boasts the Victorian ironwork in the platform canopy. Many people will recall the station for the machine on the platform where you paid a penny and stamped out a number of letters on a band of metal to make name tags.

Back Streets and Lost Delights

We start our next walk from Redmond Square. This time we will dart back and forth, looking for the little gems of history and heritage.

Heading west, Slaney Street was home to the families of lighthouse keepers at Tuskar Rock. They were given the house after complaints had been made by Sir Randolph Churchill about conditions for such people when they lived on the rock in winters of the 1880s. This street once formed part of the shoreline of the River Slaney.

To our right, at the top of Slaney Street, is Westgate. Sir Stephen Devereux built the original Westgate (also called Cowgate) in 1300 as part of the extended town wall. It was the entry point for goods and travellers using the ancient Coolcotts Trail. The tower had an area for collecting tolls on the ground floor with cells for the detention of offenders beside it. The guards' quarters were situated above this. The town gate of Westgate was removed in 1759, along with the other four gates of the town. They were hastily re-erected at the time of the 1798 Rebellion but finally removed in 1835. The town gates were demolished to allow free access for the increasing traffic of the nineteenth-century town.

Turning left at the top of Slaney Street, we enter Temperance Row. A Temperance Hall was built here in the 1800s at the time of Father Matthew's Crusade.

Selskar Abbey is probably the best-known building of old Wexford but the tower is the only remnant of the abbey; the other edifice is the old Selskar church. The original abbey was dedicated to St Peter and St Paul and by tradition was founded near the causeway used by St Ibar to reach the ferry point of departure for his monastery on Begerin, in the fifth century. The local legend states that the abbey was founded by Alexander Roche, a knight returning from the Crusade to the Holy Land, in the time of Richard the Lionheart. On reaching Wexford he was informed that his true love, believing him slain, had entered a convent. He then decided to dedicate his life to God. To that end, he had an abbey erected and became its first abbot.

The abbey was used for a synod in 1240 and a parliament in 1463. It suffered with the dissolution of the monasteries in 1540 and was sacked by Cromwell in 1649. The abbey was called St Peter's of Selskar in 1240, Holy Cross in 1439 and St Sepulchre at another time. The roofless building adjoining the ancient tower today was built in 1818 at a cost of £1,400. The roof was removed in the middle of the twentieth century to avoid the cost of rates. In the 1970s the play *Murder in the Cathedral* was performed within the walls. This tied in well with the other story that King Henry II did penance there at Easter 1172 for the murder of Archbishop Thomas Beckett by his knights. The churchyard contains many interesting graves, including some 1798 loyalist soldiers and one belonging to the family of Thomas D'Arcy Magee, poet, scholar and politician, who left Wexford and became a founding father of the Confederation of Canada. He was assassinated in 1867.

With the historic abbey tower at our back, we proceed along the street named after it, Abbey Street. The modern infill housing has replaced numerous small homes, forges and shops.

Left, across George's Street, is Pembroke House, which was the site of the Central Constabulary Barracks. It later became a girls' school and then a sweet shop known as 'The Gem'. On the right-hand corner was Coffey's Pawn Shop, best known in later years as 'Davy Tobin's', and many good suits spent their weekdays there in pre-Social Welfare days, being redeemed only for Mass on Sunday.

On the bandstand, incorporated into the town wall, a plaque commemorates the twinning of Wexford and the French town of Coueron. It was unveiled in 1982 by Mayor of Wexford Padge Reck and Mayor of Coueron M. Morandeau. The town wall and one of its towers are nicely visible here. A forge owned by Joe Murphy was sited beneath the tower over 100 years ago.

Cornmarket survives from Norman times when specific areas of the town were designated for the sale of different commodities such as meat, fish and corn. The Cornmarket of a century ago was very different from today. It had at least twenty busy shops of all descriptions. In the area now occupied by Kelly's were five separate businesses. There was a Bethesda church but this became a theatre around 1830 with actors from London appearing on its stage. Among the other businesses of Cornmarket over the years were: the Shelbourne Hotel, Michael Hanrahan's Private School, Paddy Healy's shoe repairs and Molly Mythen's pub. The latter establishment is now the Thomas Moore Tavern and celebrates the name of the composer whose grandfather lived there and whose mother was born on the premises. On being honoured by the Slaney Amateur Society, Moore referred to his grandfather as 'honest Tom Codd of Cornmarket'. The premises was then called 'The Ark' and in 1835 was the headquarters of a club catering for the small shopkeepers and tradesmen of Wexford. It was a favourite haunt of nocturnal oyster-eaters, who could buy 100 for 10*d*.

Wexford Arts Centre has provided art and entertainment for native and visitor alike since opening in 1974 but even a century before it was a place of enlightenment, amusement and leisure. It was built in 1775 as a market house. The lower windows of today were arched recesses for the traders. Inside was a magnificent ballroom and supper room. The Protestants of Wexford formed the Brunswick Club here in 1828. In 1836 the viceroy, the Earl of Mulgrave attended a banquet here. The founder of the Methodists, John Wesley, is said to have preached here and recorded in his journal that it was one of the best public rooms he had ever spoken in. A breakfast of tea, coffee, eggs and cold meats was served here on the occasion of the reopening of the Wesleyan church at Rowe Street, on 10 March 1863, following renovation. The Assembly Rooms, as they were also known, were popular venues for lectures such as the Gilchrist and musical evenings with entertainers such as Percy French, composer of 'The Mountains of Mourne', among other popular songs, appearing on a number of occasions. They became the headquarters of Wexford Corporation in the early part of the 1900s and were known as the Town Hall. Meetings of the town's elected representatives were sometimes interrupted by the latest dance music in their new home, as the Town Hall was for many years a popular dance hall. Indeed, the members of the Corporation even had to adjudicate on complaints, such as the dance the 'Jitterbug', which caused alarm to more serious dancers in the Town Hall in the middle of the 1900s.

Moving along this 'shelf of Wexford', we enter Back Street, officially Mallin Street, where we can trace the old town wall. The Square Tower on this portion of the wall identifies it as one of the older sections. A lesson learned on the Crusades to the Holy Land was the effectiveness of circular towers for defensive purposes, and such structures were incorporated into the walls built at a later period. The *Wexford Chronicle* was printed in Back Street, by Mr George Lyneall, in 1782.

Crossing Rowe Street, we enter High Street. This street, perhaps, more so than the Main Street, gives a feeling of the almost claustrophobic atmosphere of the narrow streets, with high buildings so common in the towns of an earlier age. On the eastern side of High Street (once called Upper Back Street), through a narrow arch, was part of the production area of People Newspapers Group until the 1990s. This group of newspaper titles grew from *The People*, established in 1853 at 31 South Main Street by Mr Edward Walsh. The premises was built over Archers Lane, where the Shambles or meat market was located in the 1880s. High Street is the home of the internationally famous Wexford Festival Opera, established in 1951. In January 1832, the Theatre Royal in High Street opened to the public. It was built for a Mr Taylor, owner of the *Wexford Herald* newspaper, and took the place of another playhouse, which had stood in Cornmarket, where Kelly's shop now trades. The magnificent Theatre Royal, lit by candles and oil lamps, attracted patrons from near and far. The vicinity of High Street was regularly filled with the carriages of the 'gentry', flocking to one of the finest theatres in any town of Wexford's size. It was common practice, after the show, to adjourn to Carr's Hotel in Oyster Lane for a supper of oysters from Wexford Harbour, accompanied by brown bread and porter.

Mary's Street, on our right, was called Chapel Lane and a glance up the hill quickly explains why. Filling the view of the upper part of the street is the Bell Tower of the Franciscan chapel or Friary. At approximately the midpoint of Mary Street, the thoroughfare widens abruptly. This was the location of Mary's Gate, called Raby's Gate, one of our town entry points.

Clarence House on High Street was built in 1830 'on the site of Bishop Caulfield's palace'. In the same year the building was listed as a prize in a lottery. Seven houses and one garden were raffled on tickets costing 3 guineas each. The target figure for ticket sales was £45. When this target was not reached the draw was postponed indefinitely. Clarence Buildings were later disposed of by the more traditional methods. For a time they were owned by the Redmond family and the Sisters of Mercy lived here prior to taking over the Talbot Orphanage at Summerhill.

The premises, with a small grassed garden fronting it, is the Loch Garman Silver Bandroom. The Quakers or Society of Friends established the house in 1842, as a meeting house.

Leaving High Street we move into St Patrick's Square. Behind the high stonewalls is St Patrick's graveyard and the ruins of St Patrick's church. The graveyard is the final resting place of many of the people who fought in the rebellions in 1641 and 1798. The head of Colcough of Ballytigue, who was executed on Wexford Bridge in 1798, is buried here. A portion of the old town wall and its defensive ditch is visible near the church. Adjacent to this property was the Parochial Protestant School, which in 1824 catered for seventy-seven boys and sixty-two girls. The school was relocated in Davitt Road in the 1970s.

With St Patrick's graveyard on our right, we enter Patrick's Lane. Patrick's Lane was also called Foundry Lane from Donnelley's Foundry that was located there. One claim to fame was that they made the bowls used in 'road bowling', a sport now more associated with County Cork. For many years St Patrick's Fife and Drum Band had a bandroom in the lane. The band was commonly known as 'The Boys Band'. There was a slaughterhouse beside the lane. On a warm day you would get a very lifelike feel of the streets of a medieval town. They would not be the scrubbed cobbles and airy plains of Hollywood movies but bustling, crowded places without running water or drains, with animals kept close to the houses and the entire related aroma.

Keeping to the lanes, we cross Gibson's Lane and enter Mary's Lane. Mary's Lane is one of our finest examples of the old lanes. It stretches by a meandering route that takes us past some old malt stores, a churchyard and an old oratory. The initial section is a typically utilitarian lane with stores and walls. We pass Mann's Lane on our left, leading to South Main Street and then round the corner into the loveliest section of Mary's Lane.

Up the steps to our right is St Mary's church and graveyard. If the gate is open it is worth exploring. This cemetery is the last resting place of many people of military background, perhaps because of its proximity to the military barracks, formerly Wexford Castle, situated in Barrack Street. According to the chronicles in Hore's *History*, St Mary's was a particularly beautiful building, 'similar to but smaller and more ornamental than, Selskar Abbey and St Patrick's Church'. There was a rector of St Mary's referred to by Hore in the year 1365. This church was the parish church devastated by Cromwell. This left a period of approximately 200 years, until the opening of the town's twin churches in the mid-nineteen century, when Wexford had no official parish church. The last parish priest of St Mary's was Dr Ffrench, who held the position from 1638 to 1651. He lived in Peter's Street and used to enter the church through his garden. After the Cromwellian occupation, the bell from this church was given to a Protestant church in Castlebridge. It was later sold as scrap, but rescued for use in Wexford dockyard. After some years of sounding shift changes at the dockyard, it was purchased and presented to the Christian Brothers for use in their monastery in Joseph Street. The annual patron day at St Mary's was on the feast of the Assumption.

The houses in this lane are excellent examples of an old town; there are dormer windows and steps leading to the door; and some retain the whitewash finish. The house with the dormer windows, midway up this lane, is traditionally held to have been a Mass House. From 1672 to 1691 it was forbidden by law to celebrate the Eucharist publicly. Therefore houses such as this were used. When the penal laws were relaxed the house continued as a prayer centre. In 1853 it is referred to as a chapel and schoolroom. In the 1850s the Wexford Catholic Young Men's Society was founded in this house. The society moved to larger premises at Common Quay Street in 1856 and the house returned to domestic use.

Turning right, we are on Lower Bride Street. This street is mentioned in chronicles of 1650, when reference is made to a gaol belonging to a Mr Reade situated there. It measured 30ft by 21ft and was used to house prisoners prior to Stafford's Castle being opened as a county gaol. In the present car park on the left was Wetherald Court. The property may have belonged to Catherine Wetherald who had a wine a spirits business at North Main Street. No trace remains.

From this car park we take the steps down into another car park. This incorporates Stonebridge Lane and the Ropewalk Yard. A ropewalk was a common sight in most port towns. As you might imagine, they were places where ropes were manufactured. They were usually long and narrow to allow for the twining of strands in the manufacturing process. The yard here stretched up behind the houses of King Street Upper. The yard became a livery stable owned by Stafford's, where people travelling to town tethered their animals and carts, and also parked their bicycles.

We exit the car park on to King Street and turn right. This area was prone to very serious flood into the latter years of the twentieth century. The water often reached the second-floor windows.

The imposing stone buildings visible in the upper part of the street were malt stores and are a reminder of a time when Wexford had around thirty such stores providing malting barley to small local breweries and to major breweries such as Guinness in Dublin – transported by sea. The stores have been converted to apartments called The Pillar. This name is taken from the colloquial name of the malt stores. Legend relates that it was derived from a tavern called the Golden Pillar that stood in the vicinity some centuries ago.

We take the first left from King Street and walk into Lambert Place or, as the locals call it, Bunkers Hill. Standing at the junction at the top of this hill we can see Barrack Street on our left, leading back to South Main Street. This street takes its title from the military barracks standing on a hill where Wexford Castle and possibly the original Viking settlement stood.

Opposite is Parnell Street. It was called New Street for a number of years. On the top right-hand corner of Parnell Street stood Peter Dempsey's chipper where people from the south end of Wexford enjoyed chips, peas and pigs' feet after a visit to the cinema or pub.

Behind it was Taylor's Castle, one of the fine old houses built on what was once the outskirts of the town. It had gardens sweeping down towards the shore of the harbour.

To our right is Michael's Street where the seminary that preceded St Peter's College was founded in the early 1800s.

Taking the road between Michael's and Parnell Streets, we are in what is officially called Kevin Barry Street, but most people still refer to it as Castle Hill Street from the time when it was literally the hill leading from the castle. Behind the high wall on our right is St Michael's graveyard, which served the town until St Ibar's cemetery at Crosstown opened in 1892. Traditionally, the graveyard is on the site of the Norse church of St Michael the Archangel. It is believed that they built their church here, on high ground above the harbour, and that a beacon fire was lit nightly beside the house of God. This meant that the Norse sailors' first and last sight of land, by day or night, was that of their church.

Our vista opens as we enter the Faythe at Swan View. In 1540 this was called 'Ffayghtt Strete'. The name Faythe is traced to '*faiche*', an Irish word translated as 'a green' or 'fair green'. A fair was held here on 24 August each year. In the 1700s it was referred to as a poor area with no schools and was where the Huguenot refugees settled.

Like all parts of Wexford, the Faythe has a share of lanes. One leads to Cody's Well. By tradition this well is associated with the

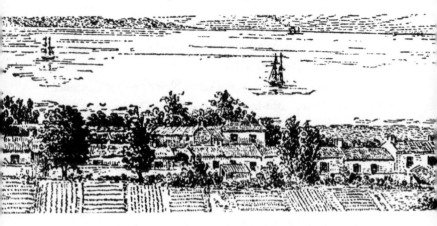

family of 'Buffalo Bill Cody', whose parents were reputed to have lived in King Street. There is no evidence of this but it is a good story. Directly opposite this lane was another, called Ovenhouse Lane, now identifiable by a house set back from its neighbours. At Ovenhouse Lane was one of four public bakeries of the Faythe in the early 1900s. There the locals could have their dinners, especially at Christmas, cooked at a small charge. That was in an era of houses without the gas and electric cookers of today.

Swan View was probably the site of the fairs. The swan, which gives the area its title, is one of metal. Robert Stafford, a merchant who was also Mayor of Wexford, erected the fountain in 1851. The trees here are relatively new. Previously there was just a wide, open square. This open area was a popular place for meetings and rallies. Most of the public meetings of the 1911 Lockout were held here, including that addressed by James Connolly. In 1941 Éamon De Valera reviewed a large gathering of military volunteers, nurses and Local Defence Forces at Swan View.

We leave Swan View via a short road to the left and come to the junction of Michael's Street, the Folly or Mill Road and Mulgannon or the Rocks Road – we have no shortage of alternative titles here.

At the corner of Mill Road and Mulgannon Road stood Pierce's foundry on a huge site. Its official title was Mill Road Works.

Mulgannon Road was called Duncormick Road, in 1837.

Proceeding up Mulgannon Road, Nunn's premises, at Harris's Lane, was part of the vast malting industry of Wexford and the Nunn family were a major force in the business. It was in the country home of Mr Nunn, at Castlebridge, that the seeds of the *Guinness Book of Records* were sown, during a discussion on the speed of the plover after a day's shooting.

The major housing developments on the left along Mulgannon Road are on the former lands of the Stafford family. Their house was Cromwell's Fort but there is no evidence that it had any connection with Oliver Cromwell. It was built in 1783 and was the Hawkes Cornock residence in 1902.

Turning right, we would have entered a road that did not exist in the 1930s. It was opened on land once belonging to Pierce's to connect Mulgannon to Distillery Road. That is Avenue De Flandres. It is a Pierce's development of houses, mainly for senior management. The name is French and recalls the location of Pierce's Paris office on Rue De Flandres. Sadly it has since been closed, so we would need to retrace our steps and descend a new road linking Mulgannon to Distillery Road.

Walking down here a little over a century ago Bishopswater Distillery would have enveloped the view. The distillery was founded in 1827 and had a bonded warehouse cut into solid rock. It produced fine Wexford whiskey. The company had its own cooperage and cart-making shops. In 1912 the lands for auction on 14 February comprised of a boiler house, an engine room, a brewer's office, an elevator room, spirit store, waterwheel, still room, corn loft and nine distiller's warehouses. There was also a grain house, gauging house, excise office, forge, grain shed, distiller's house and garden, a dwelling house, managers' and clerks' offices, stables, coach house and harness room, all within half a mile of the town centre. The complex stretched over 12 acres, giving some idea of the importance of the business in its heyday. Pierce's purchased part of the complex and they used it to build houses for their staff and used some of the land to dispose of factory waste.

At the base of the hill and to our left is Casa Rio. This is one of the few Wexford sites named in Portuguese – probably because it was the language of Rio de Janeiro, where Pierce's had offices. The translation is 'house on the river' and it is fitting. The houses here are quite unique if you examine them. The Bishopswater or Horse River as it is called locally flows in front of them. The houses at the east end are all entered by hallways built as bridges over the river and four on the western end have short bridges leading to their doors.

As we move up Casa Rio heading west we find another Pierce edifice in a sad state. It is known locally as 'the spout'. This lovely brick structure on the left, with the legend 'aqua pura', was once the source of fine spring water for the locals when summer droughts caused the mains water to dwindle.

The housing estate of Bishops Park is built on the area once known as the Knock. Used as a dumping ground for Pierce's Foundry, it was a natural adventure playground. The large trees now visible behind Bishops Park were planted by schoolchildren on Arbour Day 1952 as part of a National Trees for Ireland Project.

The houses on our left are Bishopswater, an estate built in 1950. The neat bungalows on the right are another of the Pierce projects. This time the name is Alvina Brook. The houses have wonderful pillars and porches as entrances. After Alvina Brook is Casement Terrace, a relative newcomer built in the 1960s on a patch of land that previously had two or three thatched, white-washed cottages.

At Browne's Pub we turn right. We now walk through an area of Wexford that was primarily green fields a little over fifty years ago. To the right we can see the remnants of the Knock. The estate on our left is Kennedy Park, named after the American President. At the top of this hill we have St Aidan's Crescent and descending towards the town we pass Whiterock View and Whitemill Road. Wolfe Tone Villas were built in 1932, Devereux Villas in 1941, St Aidan's Crescent in 1950, Whiterock View in 1938, Corish Park dates from 1955, Kennedy Park from 1970 and Liam Mellows Park from 1971.

At Jack Bailey's pub we can look down Green Street. The street is named after John Green, who was elected mayor seven times and championed the idea of piped water. Into the 1950s Green Street retained its old character with lovely whitewashed houses. The lower end was called Black Cow and is now Thomas Street. A section called Black Cow had houses in a lane in 1880. St Michael's Club opened on 1 December 1963.

We turn left on to Talbot Green. This was Talbot Street in the 1900s with houses out to the footpaths. It was also called Bannister Terrace. Mrs Lacey had a little shop here frequented by the children going to a number of schools. Further along, Pierce Roche had another small shop, which later became Bridge's shop. After that shop on the left was a field with sheds and then a row of two-storey houses with walled gardens.

At the crossroads of Summerhill we continue straight ahead with the houses of Davitt Road on our left and Corry's Villas on our right. The houses of Davitt Road are built on former swampy ground where there were legends of people having seen fairies and not just after a visit by stage hypnotists.

Corry's Villas are built on land donated by businessman and athlete Jim Corry. Corry's Terrace was there originally. Residents requested a name change to Waterloo Road West in 1953. Following the line of Corry's Villas the lane to the right is called Paradise Row. No trace remains of the former houses.

Thomas D'Arcy Magee's family once lived here. D'Arcy Magee was a politician, poet and author of a history of Ireland. Magee left Wexford and was one of the founders of modern Canada. His mother and sisters are buried in Selskar Abbey churchyard.

We are now on Waterloo Road. In 1812 this street was called Methodist Row. The house named St Aidan's, on our left, was the residence of Fr James Roche when he was parish priest of Wexford in the mid-1800s.

Going up the hill we have Rose Rock Terrace on our left and the convent opposite is that of the Presentation Nuns who came to Wexford in October 1818. Thomas Moore, poet and composer, visited the convent in August 1835 and, after planting a tree in the grounds, entertained the sisters with some of his songs.

Rounding the corner from the convent we are in Francis Street, called James Street in 1840. Here the first Wexford praesidium of the Legion of Mary began in 1934. The Friary church is to the right. The Franciscan Friars are believed to have come to Wexford around 1240. They preached a gospel of penance and poverty, by example, and won a permanent place in Wexford hearts. For years this church served unofficially as the parish church of Wexford. In the early 1800s crowds gathered each Sunday afternoon under a tree in the churchyard to listen to Fr Corrin speak. Thousands of Wexford people attended a meeting there on 10 April 1841 to hear Fr Mathew preach a temperance crusade. An interesting shrine within the church is the reliquary of St Adjutor with a lifelike figure of the youthful martyr, originally presented by Pope Pius IX to Mr Richard Devereux. The reliquary was transferred from the Devereux home to the Franciscan church in 1883 on the death of Mr Devereux.

Turning left onto John's Street, we are now just two streets from Main Street and travelling parallel to it. The church of the Immaculate Conception is on our right. Opposite this church is Thomas Clarke Place, on the site of Duke Street or Duke's Lane. It was a street of whitewashed houses well into the last century. Perhaps the best-known character of the old Duke's Lane was John 'Buller' Wilson, who had a coal yard there and made deliveries by horse and cart.

As we move north, St Aidan's Mews guesthouse is where Hanton's livery and undertaking business was located at the beginning of the 1900s.

At the corner of John's Gate Street and John Street is St John's graveyard. Hidden behind whitewashed walls, it is the last resting place of members of the Redmond family among others. The annual pattern was held each June on St John's Eve. The ancient church of St John was located outside the walled town. It was granted to the Knights Hospitaller of St John in 1172 and is said to have been the only medieval Wexford church to have a steeple. The Redmond Vault is visible from the gate.

At the crossroads we pass John's Road on our left and Upper George's Street on the right.

We continue up John's Street until it opens out at the junction of Wygram, Hill Street and the N25 heading west. The double-fronted house behind railings on the left was a lying-in or maternity hospital. Beside was the barn in which John Moore died in 1793 following the skirmish with troops under Major Charles Vallotin. It was on the road here that the fighting occurred and the Corporation erected the monument to Major Vallotin's memory on the traffic island shortly afterwards. The monument is believed to be the oldest in the town.

Our journey takes us right and seaward again in Hill Street. Hill Street was a street similar in character to the Faythe at the opposite end of the town 100 years ago. It consisted of small, snug cottages with well-cultivated gardens. It was called Cabbage Row at one point in its history.

In 1737 the lower end of Hill Street was the location of the Wexford County Infirmary, situated on the banks of a millstream. This is reported to have been the first such institution built in Ireland. It consisted of an infirmary and a surgeon's house. In 1837 it had thirty-five beds in ten wards and a dispensary. Almost forty years later, the number of beds had increased to seventy-two (forty-two male and thirty female). Admissions to the infirmary in 1875, except for accident cases, were on Monday, Wednesday and Friday only. Nurses in 1889 were offered £25 per annum with rations, room, gas and coal and an indoor uniform. Many of those nursing there were members of the St John of God Order. This order of nuns was appointed permanently to the infirmary in 1918. With the transfer of the infirmary to the former workhouse at Stoneybatter around 1923 the premises became Dr Furlong's private nursing home. The car park on the left was the location.

The old County Council offices dominate the right-hand side of lower Hill Street. It incorporates a Garden of Remembrance beside the last remaining cellblock of the old gaol. The entire edifice on this corner was built as the county gaol in 1812 to replace one at Stonebridge. The original walls were 16ft to 20ft high and enclosed fifty-eight cells and sixteen exercise yards. Male prisoners were employed at breaking stones or on a treadmill while females were engaged in spinning, washing and knitting. Public executions were frequently carried out here during the 1800s. Some accounts refer to the niche above the main gate at Westgate, where a statue of St Brigid once stood, as the execution spot. However, this sounds more like the stuff of legend. In the *Wexford Directory* of 1878 there is a story of John Redmond and Nicholas Jackman being executed for the murder of three people and it relates that they died on a wooden gallows erected on the gaol green in March 1833.

Public executions continued until 1860. The building ceased to be the county gaol in the early years of the twentieth century. The buildings then came under the management of the Sisters of St John of God as St Brigid's Home for Inebriates. But it became necessary to use the premises to house prisoners again at the time of the 1916 Rising and to accommodate victims of the great influenza epidemic in 1918. During the Civil War it was used as a jail by the National Army and on 13 March 1923, the first Wexford executions of that war took place here. Those who died were James Parle, Patrick Hogan and John Creane, who had been found guilty of possessing arms at Horetown, Taghmon, a few days before. Today the old gaol is the County Council headquarters as well as containing Wexford Courthouse.

Spawell Road is named after a spa or well with curative powers popular in the sixteenth and seventeenth centuries said to have been visited by Jonathan Swift, author of *Gulliver's Travels*. Glena Terrace is a beautiful row of redbrick houses built by a female building contractor named O'Connor on part of the land of Wellington Cottage, now renamed Ardara.

Rounding the County Council offices, we pass yet another new street. This is 1798 Street, opened only a few years ago. It is built on Fortview residence and grounds. The residence was so named because the fort at Rosslare was visible from here. The house was of note principally because documents and records were stored there during the Civil War to protect them from destruction by opposing forces.

Beside the old County Council buildings stands Wexford Vocational College. It retains the older building at the kerb. This was once a private residence owned by the Harvey family. Later the house was divided in two, with George Jacobs residing in one portion and the County Club occupying the other. It was known as Spawell House.

The West Gate Bar, opposite the West Gate Yard, was the site of McDonnell's Westgate Hotel in 1856. In the intervening years it has had various owners including Walpole, Ryan and McCabe. Beside these buildings, a restaurant is located in a former grain store. The steep hill beside the restaurant was Kaat's Lane and led to the shipyard of Anthony Van Kaat, who came to Wexford from the Netherlands and built ships for the Confederate Navy between

1641 and 1649. After Cromwell had taken the town, the local Catholics were transported, some to Barbados, from this quay. The strand across the Slaney from here is often called Kaat's Strand. With the reclamation work of last century, the water's edge has been far removed from the old Kaat's Quay.

Walking through the old gate under the tower, we can see the recesses where watchmen waited 700 years ago to close the gates at dusk. This is not Westgate – that was demolished in the 1800s. The gate here is more properly Selskar Gate as it gave access to Selskar Abbey lands.

We are now outside the old Norman town of Wexford. Turning left, we are on George's Street. We stroll down this street where the gentry lived. Directly in front of us, on Main Street, is a house whose rent was donated to Wexford Corporation by the writer George Bernard Shaw towards civic works. We cross Selskar Street and enter Trimmers Lane West to bring us back to the harbour.

BIBLIOGRAPHY

Books

Basset, *Wexford County Guide & Directory* (Dublin, 1885)

Centenary Record (1958)

Colfer, B., *Wexford, a Town and its Landscape* (Cork University Press, 2008)

Griffith, G., *Chronicles of County Wexford* (Enniscorthy, 1877)

Hore, P.H., *History of Town and County of Wexford* (1906, reprinted Professional Books 1979)

Lacy, T., *Sights and Scenes in Our Fatherland* (London, 1863)

Leach, Nicholas, *Lifeboats of Rosslare Harbour and Wexford* (Nonsuch, 2007)

Ranson, J., *Songs of the Wexford Coast* (Wexford 1975)

Roche, Rossiter and Hurley, Hayes, *Walk Wexford Ways* (1988)

Rossiter, Hurley and Roche, Hayes, *A Wexford Miscellany* (WHP, 1994)

Rossiter, N., *Wexford Port* (WCTU, 1989)

Rossiter, N., *My Wexford* (Nonsuch, 2006)

Rossiter, N., *Wexford: A History, a Tour, a Miscellany* (Nonsuch, 2005)

Newspapers

Wexford People

Wexford Echo

Wexford Independent

Wexford Herald

Personal Notes/Unpublished Research

Rossiter, Nicky, Encyclopaedia of Wexford, unpublished

Tyghe, Sean, Personal Recollections

Walsh Dermot, 'A Right Few', one-man show, 2008

Also from The History Press

Wexford

Triangular UFOs of the United Kingdom

By

Colin Saunders

Published by

FLYING DISK PRESS

4 St Michaels Avenue

Pontefract, West Yorkshire

England

WF8 4QX

1

Dedicated to my good friend

Omar Fowler

RIP

Acknowledgements

I would firstly like to acknowledge the extraordinary debt I owe to the well-respected Philip Mantle for his tremendous help in writing and publishing this book. Philip's knowledge of the subject matter, his enormous number of contacts and of course his publishing prowess are second to none. Without Philip this book would never have been published and I will be eternally grateful to him.

My heartfelt thanks go out to the Kinsella twins, Philip and Ronnie; they were not only instrumental in encouraging me to write this book, but also were kind enough to appear in the book itself. A big thank you Philip Kinsella for writing the Preface to this book and another big thank you to his twin brother Ronnie Kinsella for the report and artwork regarding his close encounter with a triangular-shaped UFO.

I will always be deeply indebted to my good friend John Mills for the excellent 3D printed models he has made for me along the way. John never wanted any reward for all his hard work and thoroughly enjoyed the challenge of the manufacturing process. John's superb efforts culminated in the large model shown in the book. This model has enabled me to accurately describe the craft at UFO presentations and make the whole experience more tangible for the audience.

I would also like to express my deepest appreciation to Abel Perez Delgado from Canada. Abel is an exceptional graphic designer who took on the challenge of reproducing our craft and rendering 3D images. Many hours of hard work produced the most vivid and accurate CGI images I have ever seen, which again I have used in many presentations.

A big thank you to Michael Schratt from America, Michael has drawn many UFO's from witness statements and has allowed us to use of one of his superb images in this book. I am also extremely grateful to Clas Svahn from Sweden, for access to his incredible UFO database and especially his collection of Omar Fowler's journals.

Words cannot express my gratitude to John Hanson for supplying a wealth of triangle sightings for use in the book.

John is another incredible researcher and has written many books on this subject and our friendship goes back many years. I am also indebted to Dr. David Clarke for allowing us to publish the results of his painstaking investigation into the Calvine UFO, allegedly the best photo ever of a UFO.

And finally, I would like to express my appreciation to everyone who appears in the book, to all of you who took the time to write to me with your own encounters with a triangular UFO. Without your statements, faith and courage this book would not have been written, bless you all.

****

PREFACE

Philip Kinsella

I was honored to have been asked to write the Preface to Colin Saunders' book, 'Triangular UFOs of the United Kingdom.' I have known of Colin's experience with triangular craft for some time, and only just recently, and after attending 'The Outer Limits Magazine' conference in May 2022, which had been held in Hull, met the great man himself. His lecture both fascinated and chilled me; in the sense that his encounter has been meticulously analyzed, and some conclusions were reached which cast new light onto the phenomenon at hand. As an engineer, Colin's exploration and technical details are vital to the continual research surrounding Ufology, and I, (like indeed many others) urged him to write a book to document his sighting.

There is much debate within 'Triangular UFO' research as to whether such objects belong to us, or a separate and secret alien faction altogether. Varied researchers are adamant that these enormous, silent objects which defy gravity and commonly known as the TR-3B, are part of the Aurora Program, funded and operationally commissioned by the National Reconnaissance Office, (NRO) the National Secret Agency, (NSA) along with the Central Intelligence Agency, (CIA). Yet, I find it inconceivable to assume that such clandestine projects are flaunted above huge, populated areas. Surely, if this so-called military hardware is so Top Secret, there would be no need to make the public at large aware of its presence.

That said, there is also the suggestion that certain Triangular objects are the result of technology back-engineered from alien hardware salvaged from crashed UFOs. I feel more inclined to accept this hypothesis, but by the same token, the military industrial complex will still find the need to conceal their base of operations away from prying eyes.

The Triangular UFO phenomenon is nothing new, as they have been reported for decades, and especially at the height of the Cold War. Arguments aside, the subject has fascinated both researchers and witnesses alike.

Colin's book also deals with Triangular UFO sightings local to his area, plus others throughout much of England and the rest of the UK. Although we are aware of the

Belgian wave of these objects that received headlines back in the 1990's, this book addresses the British viewpoint. The author brings elements of, not only UFOs, but also paranormal and other high strangeness events into the equation. Many readers will find Colin's encounter, along with his thoughts, a vital part in at least postulating what it is we may be dealing with. To my mind, his documentation is one of the most important within the annuals of UFO research.

I am delighted that Colin has detailed his findings, and I am certain that many within this field of study take a good, hard look at his evidence. The author does not have the answers, but I am convinced his work will create much interest, especially within the scientific fraternity.

Philip Kinsella, Bedfordshire, England, 2022

Philip Kinsella

CONTENTS

****

INTRODUCTION

11

The author with a model of the UFO he saw in 1999

I think it is important that you should know a bit about me. Firstly, until our UFO sighting in 1999 I had no interest in UFOs whatsoever. I work as a self-employed graphic designer; I was born in 1958 and grew up in the Midlands in the UK. I have spent my whole life as a Technical

Design Draughtsman and my skills earned me AutoCAD user of the year in 1992.

Today I am still draughting but in the embroidery industry, although I started out as an Electrical Draughtsman. I have worked in Sweden and Germany as an Avionics Designer on civilian aircraft, and my hobbies include fishing, a passion for old watches and classic motor cars.

My encounter along with my family of a triangular UFO in 1999 totally changed my view of the world we live in.

In 1999 my family and I was fortunate to have a remarkably close encounter with a triangular UFO that I believe is extra-terrestrial in origin, since then I have met so many people that have had similar encounters, so it seemed logical to write a book to include these sightings as well as my own. This book covers UK triangular UFO encounters and includes a wide variety of descriptions of these craft, missing time, and men in black. What I soon realized from my own encounter and other witness statements, is that there is a definite link between UFOs and the paranormal, I have included a whole section about this phenomenon in the book, which also touches on alien telepathy. As strange as it may seem, I believe this is just a science we just do not currently understand.

****

Chapter 1

The Engineering Background

It has taken a long time for me to get around to writing this book about our encounter, there are two driving forces behind this work, the first being that this was such an amazing, earth-shattering experience, that I feel I need to write down a detailed account for the world to see. Secondly, from my own experience it will be comforting to those who have had this type of experience and have no one to talk to, to know that there are others out there who have been through the same experience. Hopefully, this will be of comfort to you. To have had an earth-shattering experience like this that turns your life upside-down and know that no one will believe you! I have spoken and shared emails with many people who have had their own encounters and struggle to come to terms with what they have seen.

I know I have helped some of them with subtle counseling, without realizing I was doing it! Just to talk to someone who knows the truth takes some weight of your shoulders. I hope this book helps many people, but my heart goes out to those who have undergone an abduction experience, this is often too much for people to cope with and they have no one to talk to, no one with whom to share their fears and anxiety, but there is no that doubt abductions do take place. Those who are researching UFOs, and especially triangular UFO's, will hopefully be able to use this as a reference book for comparisons with other encounters that occur around the world.

Seeing a UFO close up is something no one ever expects to see, and I was certainly no exception to this rule, it's a life changing moment, a paradigm shift in one's way of thinking but before I leap into the encounter I feel I need to give you some background information about myself.

Why, you may well be asking yourself, do I feel the need to do this, well it's two-fold, firstly it pertains as to why I think I make such a good witness to the craft we encountered that night and secondly, why the encounter had such a great effect upon me emotionally and spiritually.

I was born in Coventry in 1958 and at the age of twelve moved with my father and two brothers to Hinckley in Leicestershire. At the age of sixteen I started my first job as an Electrical Design Draughtsman at Saunders Electronics in Hinckley, this was my uncle's firm at the time and both my father, and I worked there. We mainly manufactured machine tool control equipment and my job covered electrical panel and cubicle layouts, electrical wiring and loom drawings etc. I also started college studying for a City & Guilds Electrical Technicians Certificate.

After two years' service, both myself and my father were made redundant, back in the 1980's there was plenty of employment around and I soon landed my next job with a company called EME Designs located in Cosby as a printed circuit board designer. This was an interesting job where we designed the layout of multi-layer printed circuit boards and I was also able to continue my day release to Leicester Polytechnic for my City and Guilds certificate, unfortunately, due to MS my father never worked again.

16

It was at EME designs I met an older draughtsman called Basil Meeks, Basil had contracted overseas and told me of the many good times he had and money he had earned along the way. In common with all young men, I had developed a passion for both travel and money and decided that I wanted to emulate Basil's contracting life and together we wrote out my CV, changing it slightly to suit the job I was applying for, and started posting out to as many agencies as I could find and Bingo! It wasn't long before I landed my first contract in Hamburg, West Germany and I was just 21 years old!

The following 12 months I was employed as an Avionics Design Draughtsman working for Messerchmitt Bolkow Blohm Gmbh based in Finkenwerder on the outskirts of Hamburg. I worked on the Airbus A300 and A310 on exciting projects such as waste water lever indicators and ground point earthing distribution! The print room was separate from our office and was located in a hanger with a part-built space rocket stretching up to the roof that I used to look at in awe every time I had to go and collect prints. Although the work was not particularly challenging the pay was good and the lifestyle different and exciting, just what I had been looking for. I enjoyed my twelve months in Hamburg and although I could have stayed longer, I decided to move on to pastures new.

My next adventure was with my girlfriend of the time (who later became my wife); she had decided to go back to New Zealand for a second time.

She had spent several years there previously and felt the urge to return, and I decided to go with her this time. New Zealand is a wonderful country, the outdoor life is amazing and as a keen angler I found myself in paradise.

We lived and worked in Auckland for twelve months and I was head draughtsman at a company called Refrigeration Engineering based in Penrose, Auckland.

The author as a young man busy at work

The work entailed designs for cooling storage, industrial wine chillers and carcass freezers etc. After twelve months we bought a campervan and for the next six months we went off touring around the South Island. I worked for several months in Christchurch at a company called Centreline Draughting just off the main square, lunchtimes I would often listen to the famous "Wizard" preaching in that square. After eighteen months in New Zealand, it was time to move on and we returned to the UK. After spending some time with my father whose MS was getting worse, I started my next exciting contract, this time in Aberdeen, Scotland working for Chevron Petroleum whose head office was based at Altens on the outskirts of the city. Again, this was a twelve-month contract and although I was based on shore in the drawing office, I did make two trips out to our platforms.

The platform the author worked on

To get to the platforms, which are 240 miles from Aberdeen, we would fly on a De Havilland short take-off and landing aircraft to Unst in the Shetlands, from Unst we would then take a large Sikorsky helicopter out to the platform. On one occasion I had to do some work on the Northern platform and to get there I flew on a small 3-seater Bolkow helicopter in gale force winds between the two platforms. Once my work was complete, it was back to the drawing office in Aberdeen to draw and record the installations I had been working on. Observation and record keeping offshore had to be 100%, as if I had missed anything I could not simply hop onto the next flight out to the platform and therefore you check and check again and make records whilst still fresh in the mind. This "training" would become invaluable on the night of the UFO encounter. After a great twelve months in wonderful Aberdeen, it was time to move on again.

My next contract was the best job I had during my entire career, back to aircraft avionics drafting working for Saab Aerospace in Linkoping, Sweden, with a job title of Design Consultant. Saab was manufacturing a 34-seater civilian aircraft called the SF340. I spent two years at Saab, the first year was spent working in the cockpit producing drawings of modifications to overhead control panels, centre console, avionics rack etc. The second year I spent working on the wings, engines, horizontal and vertical stabilizers.

The SAAB aircraft the author worked on

Back in 1985 Saab primarily produced fighter aircraft, the Viggen, at the Linkoping manufacturing plant, my drawing board (CAD was still in its infancy) overlooked the runway which was used by the military and civilian aircraft alike and I loved watching them take off every day, right next to my window, especially the Viggen with the after burners full on. After two years it was time to return to the UK and the birth of my daughter. I came back from Sweden one week before the birth of my daughter; it wasn't long before I was offered a contract locally working at Courtaulds in Coventry in one of their subsidiary businesses called Amtico, manufacturers of luxury vinyl flooring. I spent 8 years working at Amtico as Design Office Manager designing floors for the rich and famous.

It was here that I became involved in Computer Aided Design and in 1992 became Autocad User of the year for a project automating design floor production using CAD/CAM. Unfortunately, after 8 years I caught chicken pox from my daughter, this turned into post-viral fatigue syndrome and I was diagnosed with ME (Myalgic Encephalomyelitis) at the time, often referred to back then as Yuppie disease. After twelve months trying to recover, Courtaulds and I parted ways; it was now time for me to go on my own, mainly because I was still in pain and pretty much unemployable.

During my time trying to recover from the Chicken Pox I started taking Victoria to her Ballet lessons, it was here I met another parent called John Mills, we popped into a local pub whilst waiting for the ballet lesson to finish and became good friends over the next few years, John will feature later on in this book with his incredible 3D printing skills. It was on one of our Wednesday night meetings that John asked if I knew anybody who did embroidery. Amazingly enough I did know someone, a chance question that set me off researching embroidery with people I knew in the industry. I could soon see there was a market for producing embroidery designs (digitizing) and as I had been involved in CAD/CAM at Courtaulds, I decided to make this my new self-employed business venture.

The business took off well and I was soon able to employ a school leaver as a designer to help me grow the business, we had purchased an embroidery machine for sampling designs and for figuring out the complexities of embroidery and realized we could start selling embroidered garments too. We employed a local girl for sampling and production of embroidered garments and as the design side was going well we employed another lady as a designer too, we now had three designers and one machinist, all working from my dining room at home. This turned out to be a godsend, as we were fast approaching the encounter with the UFO and after the event I wouldn't be able to concentrate on work and needed my staff running the business whilst I was in the shed making models!

What I have tried to show here is that I have spent my whole working career as a technical design draughtsman with, notably, several years spent in the aerospace industry, I have lots of aircraft experience from working in Germany and Sweden as well as flying gliders here in the UK and having experience days flying helicopters and acrobatic airplanes. My work offshore taught me to pay attention to detail and record everything needed to reproduce accurate drawings when back onshore. The final model John Mills made for me is an exact copy of an alien UFO triangle, using all of my career skills to recall and recreate as accurately as possible the craft you will see here in this book.

***

Chapter 2

The Family Encounter

The 31st of March 1999 started off like any other ordinary day, it was a Wednesday, I had spent the day working from home in my newly created embroidery business, the staff had left for the day, and I was looking forward to the evening's excursion with family and friends for a bar meal at a local pub. It was my mother-in-law's birthday, and she was seventy-two that day. My brother-in-law's partner was a French girl; her grandparents were over from France to visit, and the plan was for all of us to get together at The White Lion public house in Pailton later that evening for drinks and a meal.

Pailton is a very small village nestled in the Warwickshire countryside and very rural. We lived in Hinckley (Leicestershire) at the time, which was just a few miles away. My wife was driving our car that night and our first stop was to pick up her mother from Coventry Road in Hinckley. My brother-in-law lived in the house next door to his mother, but his car was already full, which is why we went to collect her ourselves. We duly collected my mother-in-law, Madge, who sat in the front passenger seat next to my wife with myself and our twelve-year-old daughter in the rear of the car.

We set off for Pailton and travelled down the A5 (Watling Street) to the junction with the Fosse Way, two Roman Roads that intersect at a point called High Cross, we turned right and continued down the Fosse Way eventually turning left to the village of Pailton and The White Lion public house.

The meal was pleasant enough but pretty uneventful, the old French couple didn't speak English and we didn't speak French, so there was not a lot of conversation between us.

We finished the meal and duly paid the bill; the time would have been around 9.30 pm as we left the pub to head home. We got into my wife's car, again my wife was driving, and my mother-in-law was in the front passenger seat with my daughter and I in the rear. We started to head off and I remember looking through the rear window of our car to see my brother-in-law helping the old French lady into his car, a Range Rover, the step into the car was quite high and the frail old lady was struggling to get in the vehicle, we drove off fully expecting them to catch us along the way.

We left Pailton and drove through the countryside until we approached the Fosse way where we would be turning right heading back to High Cross and then Hinckley. Strangely enough someone said, "Here's the Fosse Way coming up," and my daughter replied, "There's been talk of headless horseman down here" and we all laughed and said we would keep our eyes open for him. We came to the junction and turned right onto the Fosse and were amazed to see some very bright red lights with some white mingled in hovering by the side of the road. I have been to many firework displays in my time but have never seen anything as bright as those lights in my entire life! The lights were deep red, like a rose red with a bit of white mingled in.

We drove down parallel to the lights, which I now estimate as being only 100 feet away! We had slowed right down by this point. I stared at the four lights which were in a row, but not level with the ground, I would say they were tilted at approx. 25% to the horizon. I stared into the light on the far left; this light was the highest side of the tilt with the far-right light being the anchor point for the 25% angle. It was at this moment I also noticed a fifth, smaller, spurious light off to the left-hand side which looked like a Roman Candle firework (Pic.1).

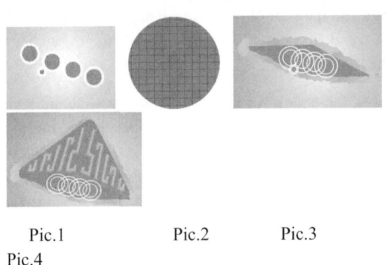

Pic.1   Pic.2   Pic.3
Pic.4

As I stared into the end light, I could see a crisscross of lines a bit like a traffic light lens (Pic.2), it seemed to pulse very rapidly in a digital fashion, i.e., on-off, not up-and-down. As I was looking at the lights I noticed a shape start to appear around them, the edges looked like the sky was rippling, but they and the body, I believe, were transparent at that time (Pic.3). I could see the shape of a diamond around the lights; you needed a keen eye to make out this shape as you could see the sky through it. As soon as I realized there was an object around the lights it materialized in front of our eyes, it fully "de-cloaked" and tilted slowly upwards in a most peculiar fashion, like a helium airship or submarine underwater, the object was now solid and had fully materialized into a triangular-shaped metal craft. The tilt was not from the centre of the craft but from the rear, i.e., the rear end stayed where it was, and the nose rose in the air (Pic.4).

It was so low that if it had pivoted from the centre of the craft, the rear would have struck the ground! It was so close I could have hit it with a cricket ball! I noticed the surface looked as if it was alive; it was like a lake of dark-grey liquid similar to Mercury. The liquid, although tilted quite steeply, looked as though it had waves running up and down the surface, like ripples on a lake in a breeze. On top of this "lake" were silver girders also running up and down the surface, they were like box sections raised off the surface which interlocked with each other like an old-fashioned maze (Pic.5 & 6).

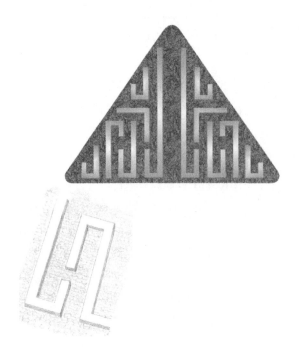

Pic.5

Pic.6

I could see how the craft's top and bottom surfaces joined to a lighter central core, like a sandwich.

No nuts and bolts, rivets, or welding seams visible. There were no apertures, no antennas, or protrusions of any kind. It was immediately obvious to me this was not an earthly object. As the craft's nose rose in the air I had three thoughts, the first one was *"my god aliens exist"* the second was that *"abductions must take place"* and the third one was *"this explains the unexplained in our history"* for some reason I had the feeling these guys had been around for centuries. I was shouting stop, stop, let me out, because

I wanted to get even closer, but my wife drove the car slightly forward to enable her to reverse into a gateway off the main road. The result of this was that a large hedge momentarily blocked our view of the craft. I thought to myself *"If it's going to clear off now would be a good time"* and sure enough it did!

We got out of the car, and it was gone. We could see a large craft in the distance with the same four red lights at the rear; it had a huge wingspan and seemed enormous. At the end of each wing was a steady, white light shining up along the top surface, you would only have seen the wing tip "lights" from above and not from below this craft. It was very, very quiet as we stood there, no smells of any fuel having been burnt. During the encounter we never heard a single noise from the craft which was hovering by the car and was the size of a large house. As we stood there it was so quiet, I believe it's called the "Oz Factor" a phrase coined by UK author and UFO researcher Jenny Randles, and then traffic started to come up and down the road again, as far as we were aware no one else was involved or saw the craft.

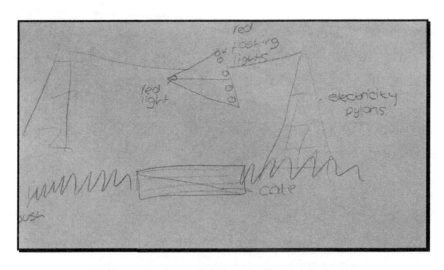

Victoria's drawing of the sighting

My wife checked her watch in case there had been any missing time, it was 9.50 pm, so we ruled that out as it seemed about right from the time we left the White Lion pub, however, we did not have an exact reference point. We got back in the car all excited and headed back to Hinckley talking about what each of us had just seen. It had been a surreal event and I think on reflection I must have been in some sort of shock, a "paradigm shift" in one's life, right there and then.

I say this because as we arrived back at my mother-in-law's house to drop her off her son, my brother-in-law, had already arrived home in the Range Rover before us, not only that but they, including the old French lady, were all inside the house and I did not feel the urge to get out of our car and tell them all about what had happened. I just sat in the back feeling mesmerized! Having dropped off my mother-in-law, we went home and drew pictures of what we had just seen whilst it was still fresh in our memories. My daughter and I drew the triangle with the watery surface and beams, my wife who had been driving did not have chance to see the craft as she was concentrating about our safety on the road. Her drawing was three red lights in a perfect triangle. This was odd because the rest of us had seen a mixture of lights, all mingled in like a Christmas tree laser light show, there was no way we could have seen three equilateral red lights amongst them.

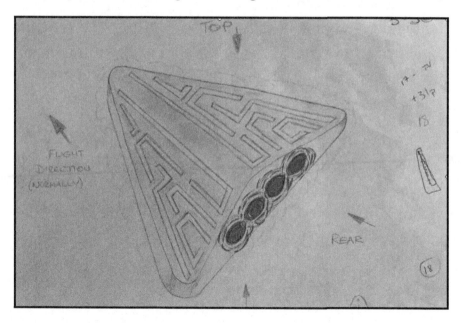

The author's drawing of the sighting

The next day was April Fools' Day, but this did not deter me from telling everyone I met about the UFO we had seen. I phoned the late Graham Birdsall at the UFO magazine who put me in touch with Omar Fowler, the respected Flying Triangle UFO investigator. Having spoken to Omar we wrote our witness reports and sent drawings of the craft to him before he sent us copies of his publication, "The Flying Triangle."

To my great surprise there was a report of a triangle from Stockis in Belgium from 1993, which clearly showed the same lines in relief on the bottom of the craft (Pic.7). Surely this was the same or a similar type of craft? The coincidence was too great for me, so I reproduced the bottom drawing of the craft (Pic.8) and used the Belgium sighting from Omar Fowler along with my own sighting of the rear and top to produce my first scale model of the craft.

My own research reveals that many people get to view the surface of these craft; they are normally viewed from below as one would expect. Ours was a very unusual sighting in this respect and I have tried to reproduce the surface as accurately as possible.

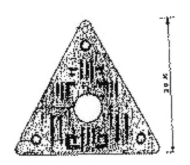

Pic.7

Pic.8

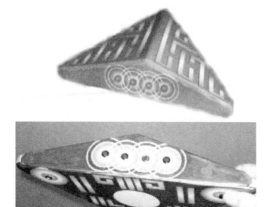

Pic 9   Pic 10

35

Wife and Daughter's Comments

Just for the record I thought it best to have my wife (now ex-wife) and my daughter go on the record. Sadly, my mother-in-law has passed away. Here are what my wife and daughter had to say today about that night. We begin with my daughter Victoria.

""Ok so I remember.

We'd been out for a meal and were on our way home down the fosse way, talking about the ghost of the headless horseman and saying we should keep an eye out for him. Someone in the car then spotted some unusual lights in the sky, to left hand side of the road. We decided to stop and reverse into a gateway where Dad got out of the car to look, but at that point I couldn't see much as I was sat in the back and the hedge way was obscuring my view. I remember feeling scared and asking everyone to get back in the car. The lights then disappeared as quickly as they'd appeared."

And from my ex-wife..

"My memories from that evening.

We had been out for mum's birthday (to Pailton). Colin and Victoria in the back of the car, me driving and mum in the passenger seat. As we turned into the Fosse Way, we joked about it being haunted by a headless horseman.

Immediately as we turned we could see three bright red lights in the sky to the left of the road - they looked like traffic lights in the sky, but in the shape of a triangle at the height of a large tree.

We commented on them being strange and not what you would expect to see there as there is nothing but fields around. I continued to drive towards them and was trying to peer to see them. We pulled up at the side of the road and I reversed into a field gateway, and we got out but there was nothing there. We looked all around but still could see nothing. I think it was Graham's car went past us but didn't see us parked there so then we pulled out & carried on home. That's about it!"

Omar Fowler became a great friend of mine over the years; I first met him when he came over to interview the four of us just after our initial encounter. He is sadly missed.

****

Chapter 3

38

The Models

I was like a man possessed; the model became a very important project for me. Having spent my entire working career as a draughtsman it was only natural for me to produce some CAD drawings of the craft. Using my training, I included as much detail as I could remember. I decided to use wooden doweling for the framework and printed my CorelDraw files to glue on top them. The end result was rather good; it was a bit on the flimsy side but still good enough to be able to show people what we saw.

Oddly, the van I was using at the time for work was broken into on our driveway at home. My car dealer friend who sold me the vehicle repaired the door lock for me; he told me that he thought that it had been professionally broken into! That was odd as only the old cassette player was stolen from the dashboard, it wasn't until a few days later I realized the model had been taken too! I know the last time I saw the model it was behind the passenger seat; it never did show up again. Was it just coincidence? We will never know, but whoever stole the cassette player also, I believe, stole that first model I made.

So, my next mission was the MK2 model version of the craft, this time I glued plywood around the doweling, which made the model much sturdier. I took a trip to Maplins in Leicester and bought myself some flashing LED lights and a battery holder. The new model looked fantastic, and the lights worked a treat, it would make me physically shake with excitement when I switched the lights on, and it instantly took me back to the night of the encounter.

I gained a wealth of information from this model, the first and most enlightening observation was that when you look at the rear of the craft and tip the nose down you end up with a silhouette of a diamond! (Pic.10) this would explain why I first thought it was a diamond-shaped craft around the lights.

The spurious small light that we saw was in fact the light underneath the nose at the front of the craft. I have referred to these as lights, but they were not lights as such, they did not emit light to the ground. The colour shown on the drawings is primary red, but from half a mile away they appeared deep rose-red in colour, I do not believe they changed colour, but more likely the colour changed depending on the distance. I believe the lights are a byproduct of their power source.

The crisscross lines on the surface of the four rear lights could have been generated from the light source itself, i.e., something along the lines of Newton's law of 'ring interference' rather than being etched material? I have seen a similar effect myself when using a laser pen. Also, whilst playing with the model I think I realized why the craft was tilted at an angle towards the earth. It wasn't some scientific technical reason as I first thought, but because I believe they wanted maximum impact from the "lights" and by tilting the craft towards us as we approached, we were given a view of all the "lights," albeit at an odd angle straight at us face on!

I started scouring the internet for reports of triangular UFO's and also started visiting UFO conferences, especially Graham Birdsall and Russell Callahan's amazing UFO conferences in Leeds. I even went to a UFO conference in Laughlin, Nevada (USA) which was a remarkably interesting experience. I also started doing presentations locally and the model was clearly an invaluable aid, a physical 3D model which enabled the audience to visualize more clearly what I was talking about. Eventually I was invited onto Central Weekend Live TV with Omar Fowler, I also took the model with me.

That was a night to remember, the other topics were tattooing and tribute bands. In the hospitality suite I found myself sitting next to a Robbie Williams look alike and a tattooed lady! I went on with my model and spoke to the presenters, Nicky Campbell was one, and I recalled the events of that night whilst showing the craft to the camera, apparently this was viewed by three million people live in the UK!

Good job I didn't know that was the expected audience that night before I started explaining what happened, I was nervous enough with the people in the studio!

After the death of Graham Birdsall, the UFO magazine eventually disappeared off the shelves and the conferences in Leeds also stopped. I found myself in limbo and had UFO doldrums until one day, out of the blue, a guy called Abel Perez Delgado contacted me via social media.

Abel is a graphic designer in Canada, and he said he wanted to model our craft in 3D computer graphics (CGI) and use them on his website. This was a brilliant and kind offer and also free of charge! We worked together on the design details, and he produced the most realistic images I've ever seen. These are the images he produced.

Pic.11

43

Pic.12

Pic.13

Pic.14

45

Abel made a fully accurate set of images from my information, Pic.11 shows the craft fully materialized with the four rear "lights" at an angle to the earth and the nose about to rise up into the air. Pic.12 shows the base of the Belgium sighting with the rear of our sighting. Pics.13 & 14 show the liquid surface similar to a lake of mercury with the interlocking silver beams on top of the lake. Abel has used these images and my description of that night on his website which is well worth a visit: http://ufo-explorer.com

The mark-two model I had made was a brilliant aid, however it was not exact; the girders on the top were raised off the surface as you can see on Abel's CGI images. The raised girders were something I hadn't yet achieved with my models but was hoping to find a way to do this one day. And then, out of the blue, my good friend John Mills came to visit me with some exciting news. John had bought a 3D printer, not only that, but he wanted to reproduce my model including the raised "girders" on the surface! Fantastic, I supplied John with as much information as possible and pointed him to Abel's website to see his images and he proceeded to make the prototype model. It was a bit of a learning curve for John, but eventually we ended up with a black triangle complete with working lights at the rear and underneath the craft in the centre, and of course the all-important raised girders on the surface.

The model, which was approximately A6 size, was brilliant however the colours were not, the surface needed to be a lighter liquid-grey and the beams on top were more of a silver colour, but I wasn't complaining. The cost of 3D printing is expensive, and John had spent a fair bit of his own cash getting this model into production, which gave me an idea. I suggested to John that now he had all the files needed to reproduce the craft relatively easily, that I should try selling some on a well-known internet auction site, and if successful he could build me a larger version with the liquid surface and silver beams as a reward.

John agreed and I duly started advertising. John was so impressed by Abel's website that he decided to 3D print both a saucer and a cigar shaped UFO. Much to my surprise the sales took off and eventually I sold enough for John to start on the next project, an A4 size model in full colour. This was quite a tricky project; we had several runoffs of the liquid effect paintwork on the surface before we eventually got it right. The next two images are as close as we are going to get to reproducing a genuine alien triangular UFO complete with "lights," silver beams and a central milky-white core that the top and bottom sections were sandwiched onto.

Pic.16

This is an absolutely fantastic model that John has made for me, and I will always be indebted to him for his efforts.

***

Chapter 4

Local Witnesses

Our local newspaper "The Hinckley Times" ran a small article on a UFO that had been spotted locally, I decided to write to the newspaper with my own experience and I ended up writing a two-page spread all about our encounter. At the end of the article, I invited readers to get in touch with me if they had witnessed a UFO themselves. Many people replied and interestingly enough UFOs that were reported were all triangular. Also, we have three separate occasions when these craft were seen over Transco (National Grid for Gas), and on one occasion a triangle was actually hovering over the large antennae array located at this site! Are the triangles interested in our gas distribution network, or simply recharging their batteries from the high frequency radio transmissions of the antennae? The sightings sent to me spanned forty years and these are listed below and in more detail on the following pages.

Michael Roberts 23rd Oct 1978 6.35pm, Triangular UFO seen over Transco, Hinckley, multiple witnesses.

Keith X 1978 11.00pm-1.00am Triangular UFO seen over Transco, Hinckley, missing time.

Michael Austen 1979 or 1980 evening, two Triangular UFO's fly over Barwell.

Alan Hydon, summer 1996, 03.30am, Triangular UFO over the area of Trinity Motors, Hinckley, plus two more Triangular UFO sightings over the next few days.

Kenneth Rush Aug 1996 late afternoon, Triangular UFO seen over Transco, Hinckley.

Debora Haines, month unknown, 1996 10pm Sunday evening on the A5 at Dowell's roundabout, Hinckley.

Rhys X summer 1998 10.20pm, Triangular UFO over Caterpillar Factory, Desford.

Mel Orton, 19th March 1999 02.30am, Triangular UFO, Sharnford (Mike's Granddad also had an encounter with a Triangle in 1997 at 8.00pm in Sharnford).

Colin Saunders, 31st March 1999 at 9.50pm multiple witnesses, Triangular UFO, Monks Kirby.

Frank (pseudonym), summer 2012, 2.00am, Triangular lights over back garden. Two beings seen inside glass dome underneath.

Stuart McKay, summer 2014, late evening, partially cloaked Triangular UFO, Earl Shilton.

Lou, 3rd February 2016 5:37pm, Triangular UFO, Clickers Way Elmesthorpe.

Nigel Bailey, 24/02/2019, 19:10 Triangular aircraft, Leicester.

I personally interviewed many of these people and I have no problem in believing the stories of their own encounters, after all, why would anyone want to make this sort of thing up to encourage ridicule? All of the sightings are in the witnesses' own words, as this gives a better idea of how they saw the encounter themselves rather than rewriting their encounters myself and inadvertently putting my own slant on things. The following information needs to be as accurate as possible and not embellished in any way. Here are the reports in more detail.

Keith X with missing time! Transco, Hinckley, Leicestershire

I was introduced to Keith X at my then local public house, The Prince of Wales, on Coventry Road, Hinckley. A genuine guy who had an extraordinary experience, I arranged to visit Keith at his home for an interview and took one of Omar Fowlers witness report forms as an *aid memoir*. Below is a detailed report on his incredible sighting.

"I was travelling from Nuneaton (Franklin Road) to Hinckley (Factory Road) on my motorcycle at around 10.45-11.00 pm when I saw what I thought to be a very bright star.

But the star caught my attention and made me feel a little uneasy, because it seemed way too low and too bright and also oversized in comparison to the other stars that night. It also seemed to stay in my rear-view mirror for around three quarters of my journey home. Upon reaching Coventry Road (Hinckley) I remember the star was positioned on my right-hand side and slightly behind me, e.g., over my right-hand shoulder. I slowed down to take a look and saw two much smaller lights, one red and one white, both in the same area as the bright star, but travelling away quite fast from it.

I turned back to look at the road and turned again in the direction of the star, but the two small lights had gone leaving the bright star on its own. I continued along Coventry Road, where upon reaching the site area of Hall & Sons (adjacent to the large Transco antenna.) I saw an exceptionally large dark triangle-shaped object appear flying from my left.

I pulled my bike up and stood astride my motorcycle to take a look at the object which came directly overhead, and then went away from me to my right travelling towards the direction of Hinckley Town centre and ending at a position which I believe to be around lower Bond Street e.g., Atkins building where I lost view of the object. The triangle-shaped object was massive; at least the size of 1.5 football pitches and it flew completely silently at a height of no more than 100 feet.

It was all black except for an illuminated area on the underside which looked to have some sort of framework around it, like a cockpit window. The object was flying at fifteen to twenty mph and remained in view for around one or two minutes. I continued my journey home and packed my bike up.

I noticed my bedroom clock was showing 1.00 am, which I thought must be wrong, so I recall waking my parents to tell them what I had seen and to confirm the time was correct, which it was."

I have met Keith a few times over the years and to this day he cannot remember anything about the missing time of approximately 1.5 hours. In these instances, most people would jump to the conclusion of an alien abduction experience, but could it be some sort of time dilatation due to the UFO?

Michael Austin, Barwell, Leicestershire

Hello Colin. I saw two of these triangular shaped UFOs over Barwell back in 1979 or 1980. I was in my car with two friends parked at the back of the houses in Chapel

Street, which would now be Willowdene Way. The driver's window was open, and I was looking at the sky when two of these objects came into my sight straight in front at high altitude over the houses of Chapel Street.

They were huge and travelling at high speed, one slightly behind and to one side of the other with no sound. I said to my friends, "Look at that," but they could not see clearly through the windows.

We all got out of the car, by which time they had travelled straight overhead and out of sight over the houses of Shilton Road, so they didn't get to see them. If you watch a jet plane do the same you can watch it for a while, these things did it in seconds!

I only say this now, because most other sightings are either bright lights or cigar-shaped objects.

It would be easy to jump to the conclusion that this is perhaps a secret military project such as the much-rumored American TR3B a.k.a the "Aurora", but there are many reasons that I do not believe this to be true. First and foremost are the statements from all those witnesses who have had a close encounter with a triangle, they all said that due to its flight characteristics and unconventional appearance, they did not believe it was from this world.

I do not personally believe that if we have this technology we would fly a secret craft over Hinckley town centre, hover over a Transco antennae array, or simply stop in the middle of the English countryside so individuals can get a good look at them! Then there is the question of how long these craft have been around, the earliest known reports of these unusual triangles can be traced to the Dutch East Indies in the late 1890s, around ten years prior to the Wright Brothers' first powered airplane flight in 1903. Triangular UFOs were also reported from Scotland and England in 1895.

Mr. Alan Haydon, Trinity Motors, Hinckley, Leicestershire

I used to be a security patrol officer; I was out in all weather's all year round with my dog. In 1996, when returning to my office on Coventry road's Trinity Motors site, I saw a large triangular 'something' flying slowly across the sky, almost as if it were following the Ashby canal. It was approximately 200 feet up and looked huge, there were red lights underneath it and as it slanted a bit towards my position, it seemed to have many decks, it made no noise that I could hear, but my dog started whining and all his fur stood up on end, I could almost feel a kind of low, soft vibration coming from it. The sighting lasted around nine seconds and the triangle was the size of a twenty-pack of cigarettes when held out at arm's length, possibly a touch larger, very dark grey in colour, it went from the northern perimeter road towards London.

In a further email he went on to say: 'Looking at your model I now see that I was looking at it tilting with the left hand 'wing' towards me making it look like a big cheese wedge, it was about 100 yards long if I remember rightly, (this is a sideways view). Also, if I remember rightly, it was about 03.30 in the morning, maybe just after, it was early daylight, and I was returning to my security office to finish my night's report.

A few days later a movement over towards the A5 made me look up and to my amazement the same kind of shape was just lowering behind a big black cloud. As it sank it seemed to shimmy and disappear, just before its total disappearance it left just the outline as it went see through, at first I wasn't certain of what I saw, but my job was to look out for anything unusual. A few days later I was taking a member of the forecourt staff home after her shift. When we reached the Northern perimeter road, from the end of Brodick road, I was about to turn right when we both saw a very large triangle like a shark's fin dropping down behind a big black cloud, it would have been over the A5 at the time. To be behind the cloud and look as large as it did, it must have been one hell of a size.

That is three triangle sightings in the space of about five weeks! About five to six weeks later as my dog and I were on one of our regular patrols, I again saw lights in the sky, this time two pale yellowish balls high in the sky, they came from different directions and came together as if following each other. After around ten seconds they seemed to catch up with what looked like a tube slowly going across the sky, until they joined it, (making a dumbbell shape) it was moving very slowly across the sky towards Hinckley town, but high up in a clear, dark, star-filled sky, the time would be around 02.30. Before the "dumbbell" went from sight, another yellowish ball of light came across the sky at a greater speed and seemed to slow down to follow just behind the others, they then carried on across the sky until out of sight.

Kenneth Rush, Transco, Hinckley, Leicestershire

Next to contact me, was Kenneth Rush (Pseudonym) with his incredible story of another town centre (Transco) sighting.

"It was back in the summer of 1996, not sure what month, but think it may have been August (I was nineteen back then). So, I left my then girlfriends' house on Brookside to go home, it wasn't quite sundown but not far off (also unsure of the time), as I turned onto Rugby Road from Brookside I spotted two largish bright lights close together, quite low in the sky.

As I went under the railway bridge and further along Rugby Road I could make out that there was something black above the white light (which now appeared to be singular).

When I got level with the Rugby road shops I could basically see it was a black triangle just stuck in the sky, possibly a couple of hundred feet up, then as I rounded the corner it was basically hovering near that Telemetry tower (or whatever it is at the back of the Leisure centre near British Gas).

Then, as I approached the leisure centre, I was directly under the triangular object looking up at it through my sunroof; it was black with a white circular light in the middle, and a red light in each corner. I can't remember as much detail as those in this week's paper, but I'd describe it as moving without moving if that makes sense. It was basically hanging there, but must have been drifting along, I could not hear any sound plus I was driving in my old Ford Fiesta, so there could have been some noise.

Anyhow, it was pretty much daylight and right in the town centre and my main goal was to rush home, grab a camera, and get a picture (which I didn't-sadly). With hindsight, people were walking around and didn't notice it while I was driving, and I can't for the life of me explain why I didn't stop or toot my horn at the pedestrians and point up. But when I got home, I could still see the twin bright lights from there, but couldn't find a camera, my family saw the lights too but basically thought it was a helicopter and I was mucking about (I was a pretty crazy teenager!!)."

Rhys X, Kirby Mallory, Leicestershire

In the summer of 1998, on a dark night, I was travelling by car with a friend between Barwell & Kirby Mallory along the Kirby Road route. As we approached a high point on the route, the Caterpillar industrial Plant came into view, about a mile away. Hanging in the air directly above the plant, was a huge triangular-shaped machine.

It was greater in size than the whole of the Caterpillar Plant. The craft shimmered, like the atmosphere around it was charged in some way. The Triangle had an unattached star-like object circulating at the back. I was fearful and quickly drove away. It was not an aircraft, it was not flying, and it hung in the air perfectly still. I'm sure it was not human technology.

Mel Orton, Sharnford, Leicestershire

Mel lived in the small Leicestershire village of Sharnford and had his triangular UFO encounter back in March of 1999. He recalls the exact date as he told me "My sighting was the 19th of March 1999; I remember the date as I went to Coventry speedway the same night"

60

Mel left home at 2.30am; he was alone as usual and driving to work where he would normally start at 3.00am driving a truck to London. Mel left the village of Sharnford heading in the direction of the A5, as he left the one-way system he could see some lights further along the road at an extremely low altitude. Mel wound his car window down to get a better look at the object as he drove towards it! The object was hovering at the junction to Bumblebee Lane. "I would say I was no more than one hundred yards away from the craft.

It just hovered above a tree (the tree now dead) that was near the road." Mel quickly parked his car by the post box outside Wayside Farm. Bravely he got out of the car and stood underneath a huge triangular UFO. He described the object as the size of a football pitch; the object was only 150 feet away and approximately one hundred feet off the ground.

The triangle was totally silent and just hung there in the sky not moving at all like a picture hung on a wall. It was crystal clear, no vibrations, no smells, no noise. The bottom of the craft was tilted towards him, and he could see the underneath quite clearly, a large, central red light with three additional white lights, one in each corner of the craft. Mel could also make out lines or "girders" on the underneath; they were raised off the surface. At this point he realized the object was not of this world and became frightened at the situation he found himself in, he quickly got back in his car and drove off, he could still see the object in his rear-view mirror as he sped away. With hindsight Mel now wished he had stayed and possibly got on board if invited. He went on to say "I know what I saw and, like you, I'm convinced it was not of this planet"

This is such an amazing coincidence, Mel's description of the craft was exactly the same as our craft, triangular with beams on the surface and "lights" in the three corners and middle, but what shocked me was the date of the encounter, 19th March 1999! That was just twelve days before our encounter and six miles away as the crow flies.

Strangely enough Mike's grandfather, (now deceased), also had an encounter with a silent triangular UFO, this took place in the village of Sharnford nearly a year later in early 1997.

His Granddad lived on Chapel Lane in Sharnford, and it was eight o'clock at night when he saw lights in the field which adjoined the bottom of his garden. The object was forty yards away and at first he thought it was a tractor, but the object then rose in the air to reveal a dark, triangular object with bright lights on the sides and a "shower of golden snowflakes or sparks" falling from the centre of the craft to the ground.

The object then started to move towards him and once the object was only ten yards from the bottom of the garden the lights went out and it simply vanished from sight.

The local vicar at the time, a Mr. Walter Evans, also witnessed a strange craft in Sharnford, probably the same one that Frederick saw that night.

Frank, Burbage, Leicestershire

"Hi Colin, I read your article on the Hinckley times page after a friend of mine suggested I should read it. I am amazed and excited to hear that other people have seen a UFO too, so I thought I'd tell you my story that happened in the summer of 2012.

I had just finished my shift at work at roughly 1.30 am and walked home to Burbage, which took me about half an hour or so.

It was a really clear night, not a cloud in the sky and was absolutely pitch-black. When I got home I decided to go out for a cigarette before I went to bed and decided to keep my earphones in and listen to my music whilst doing so.

As I stood in the garden with my back up against the house I could see three orange-red lights in the distance, as if it were coming up from the direction of town. I carried on smoking whilst watching the lights assuming it was an airplane just passing overhead, even though it seemed to be moving really slowly and at an extremely low altitude. The lights were perfectly in a straight line as it was approaching Burbage, still glowing orange-red, but then all of a sudden it stopped in the sky. I was a bit confused and thought it may have been a helicopter instead of a plane, so I took one off my earphones out to listen to the copter blades, but I heard nothing. So, I took my other earphone out and there was no sound anywhere.

I was frozen in shock watching the three lights in front of me (probably about 100 meters away and suspended fifty meters in the air), almost bouncing in the sky and I had completely forgotten about my cigarette.

Then, it slowly arched up to the right, (in a J shape) at least tripling its altitude and stopped and hovered as if it was bouncing again above the tree in my back garden, where it remained for a further minute or so. By this time, I was absolutely petrified, knowing that this was nothing I had ever seen before and didn't know what to think or do.

After hovering silently above the tree in my back garden, it slowly began to arch so the lights were directly above my house. I panicked so much that I ran inside and upstairs and into my sister's room: she was still awake. I blurted out everything that I had just seen. I looked out of her window, and I could see the lights in the distance, they were getting smaller.

So that's my story. Everyone I have told so far says that I was just seeing things, or just think I'm making it up and it's so frustrating! Also, I can't remember exactly seeing a shape behind the lights, but I know there was something there for certain, because it blocked out the stars above me. I was so fixated on the lights that I didn't pay much attention to what was behind them, and I was scared I was going to get abducted!

I remember the white light being the main thing I was concerned about. Because I believed the craft to be a police helicopter at first, I assumed this light was a searchlight. As the craft was slowly beginning to pass directly above me, fear got hold of me and I wanted to stay out of the white light beam, in fear of "being abducted". (Hence running inside)

I mentioned to you yesterday that my mind kept jumping from police helicopter to UFO, because the lights and the gliding and floating movements it made, plus the lack of sound, were unexplainable to me.

The account of the "figures" was relayed back to me by one of my friends and my older brother. I remember telling them what occurred and talking to them about it, but I don't remember seeing any the figures. The account I gave them was of a sort of dome-shaped cockpit just hanging down in front of the "search light", where there were two figures stood side-by-side. I could only see an outline/silhouette of them because the light was coming into the dome from behind them.

Kay, Sapcote Road, Hinckley/Burbage, Leicestershire

A big thank you to Dave Hodrien of BUFOG (Birmingham UFO Group) for this next report.

Late evening on the 13th of September 2007 Kay was driving home from work travelling towards Hinckley. It was around 10.17 pm and already fully dark. There were very few other cars around. She drove along Sapcote Road, passing a small shop on her left.

As she reached the turning onto Burbage Road she suddenly noticed a very unusual object in the sky. It was off to her left and appeared to be hovering just above the trees on the far side of the road. It was huge and at an angle. She could make out the left side, back end and tapering of the front end. It appeared to be the size of a large aircraft. The object was a strange shape. It appeared rounded at the front but had curved wings towards the back. There were no markings or windows as far as she could tell. It looked dark-grey metallic in colour, although this could have been partially due to the darkness. The object had a number of coloured lights along its underside. Kay cannot remember the exact shades of these lights; she just observed the entire object.

As soon as it came into view she pulled over at the side of the road. She was absolutely mesmerized by the object. There was another car a short distance ahead of her on the road. This carried on driving as if there was nothing there. It is likely that the driver did not look up into the sky. Kay had her phone on her, but as with many other sightings, did not think to take a photograph, she was too pre-occupied staring at the UFO. There did not appear to be any interference in the air. To her knowledge the object was completely silent, although she did have the windows up at the time.

Both astounded and puzzled by what she was looking at, Kay continued to watch the object hovering motionless over the trees. After what seemed like several minutes the object began to move. It passed across Hinckley Road to her left and then continued to veer off to the right over the houses. She watched it as far as she could, but it was not moving in a direction where she could easily follow it on the road, so she did not give chase. If it had carried on going in the same direction it was heading it would have passed over the M69 motorway to the Southeast, although Kay cannot confirm whether this did actually take place.

She continued her journey home, thinking about what she had just witnessed. She informed both of her sons about what she had seen. Her elder son was skeptical and laughed at her, but her younger son seemed more interested and started asking questions. She wrote down what she had seen so that she would not forget the details. Later on, she searched online to see if anyone else had reported seeing it, but nobody had posted anything. She added the sighting to a UFO website, but nobody commented further.

Stuart McKay, Earl Shilton, Leicestershire

The next sighting came from Stuart McKay of Earl Shilton, his sighting took place in 2014 in his back garden, this is what he had to say.

"I've just read the article in the Hinckley Times and was amazed that somebody else has seen this. I was out in the back garden having a cigarette (when I smoked) in the summer of 2014, it was late as it was dark, I don't remember exactly the time/date as I had put it to the back of my mind until now. Anyway, I usually look up to the stars during clear nights as it's a very nice sight, when I saw a (hard to describe) "fluid" looking triangular craft coming from the west over Earl Shilton (Park Road) I understand this sounds very weird hence I've not talked about it before. I don't think I would have noticed it if it had been at a different angle as it was "cloaked."

I could see stars as if I were looking straight through it, but I could clearly see the triangular shape of the craft and I still remember thinking to myself that it wasn't a particularly good cloaking device. It was moving very slowly and extremely low with no sound and no lights whatsoever, but it was huge, the size of a football pitch.

As it got closer visibility got worse, I'm guessing it's all about the angle of view, then I could no longer see it at all, I managed to see what I assume would be the front right side as it was approaching, then the underneath. It was all smooth or fluid with no sharp edges, very much like the picture in the Hinckley Times, but this craft had no markings that I could see. The first picture is spot-on regarding the edges, but the craft I saw had, like I said, a fluid, smoother edge to it.

Lou (Pseudonym) Barwell, Leicestershire

I have seen your article in today's Hinckley times and found it very interesting, I have also seen triangular objects (three white lights) moving silently across the sky extremely low.

Only a few weeks back it happened three nights in a row on my way back from work. On February 3rd, 2016, at 17:37, I was travelling from Stoney Stanton towards Earl Shilton, the lights seemed to be heading from Desford way, and following the Earl Shilton bypass across to Barwell. I wound down my window as it crossed overhead (I was at the bypass waiting to turn right onto Clickers Way).

The lights were very bright, I quite often stargaze, and these lights stood out immediately, there didn't appear to be any other lights on it, just the three white lights in a triangle shape, they did not flash, the lights were around the size of helicopter's search lights.

I would say the height of it when it passed overhead was around 300-400 meters high, I couldn't make out the size of the craft as the streetlights made it difficult, however with the distance between the two rear lights and the front light I would say it was the size of an articulated lorry and more of an isosceles triangle rather than equilateral. There was no sound as it passed over at approximately thirty mph.

Debora Haines, Hinckley, Leicestershire

This lady got in touch with me via social media, again another believable triangle sighting from a down-to-earth honest witness. As we chatted it became apparent that we lived in the same village, in fact just a few hundred yards away as the crow flies! Below is her sighting in her own words.

"Hello Colin., I sat and read your account of what you experienced. I cannot believe that I'm able to share my experience with someone who won't doubt or mock what I'm about to tell you. I used to work part-time at the Texaco Station by the Three Pots. I had just finished my shift at 10.00pm and was travelling home along the A5 towards the Dodwells roundabout as I live in Barwell.

As I approached the roundabout I noticed this massive black triangle that just appeared to my right-hand side. It was a perfect triangle with three red lights, one under each point.

I was probably only traveling at 45 mph and was slowing down to go around the traffic island and this object was moving so slowly it was almost hovering. I was neither frightened nor excited, but totally puzzled and confused as to how such an enormous aircraft/object could fly at such a low speed. As I took the second exit off the roundabout into the A47, my eyes were totally fixed on this object, and I slowed my speed right down to watch this incredible object go over my head. I turned my radio off and opened my window so I could hear the craft and was shocked to hear no sound or engine noise whatsoever.

I'm not particularly good at sizing objects by using 'meters or feet,' but this object must have been the size of a football pitch - if not bigger! And its approximate height was probably between 250-300ft above the ground. Again, I estimated the height against 'Big Ben' which I've seen numerous times when visiting London. It was most definitely no higher.

As I approached Tesco Distribution I'd reduced my speed to about 15mph just so I could observe this incredible object go overhead. As you've have described it, the underneath of this object was somehow molded with 'patterns.'

As it was just about to cross the flyover, there was a car coming towards me from the opposite direction. I was excited that somebody else was witnessing this with me and I was expecting them to either slow down or to stop like I had done, but they just passed by as though they were completely unaware of this magnificent 'thing' above our heads. It passed over and seemed to continue in a straight line of flight towards Mira. I couldn't wait to get home and tell my husband what I'd just seen.

Although he listened, I felt he didn't believe me when I told him how big it was, he said it couldn't have been that big. I told him another vehicle was passing at the time and other people must have seen it too and felt without doubt the following day it would be reported in the news on the TV or in the local newspaper the Leicester Mercury, and it would prove to him what I had just witnessed.

I rushed to get the Leicester Mercury the following day hoping to see an article reporting this sighting, but there was nothing. I've only told a few people of my experience, but after joining the UFO UK group a couple of months ago, I decided to share my story. Although I can't recall the exact year, it would have been about 1996 and it was a Sunday night because I only worked Saturday and Sundays. Also, I said I'd tell you about a flying object me and my father saw back in the 70's, I think it was 1978.

It was a winter's evening and we'd had heavy snowfall. We lived in a small village called Wymondham, the other side of Melton Mowbray. My father owned the village butchers and my mother the village shop. We lived on the Main Street directly opposite Station Road (now Butt Lane). It was a road leading out of the village, where the old railway station used to be, but that was closed in 1959. It was a great road for sledding down which we had done many times during my childhood years of living in this village. It was about 9.00 pm and I, my dad and our border collie had been out having fun. My dad would push me from the top and Bob my dog would chase after me to the bottom of the hill. I'd just reached the bottom and stood up to walk back up to my dad when I saw a mass of coloured lights in the sky behind my dad.

I shouted to my dad to turn around and look behind him as I was running back up the hill. It was quite low, possibly 150-200 ft, and cigar-shaped. There was also a very high-pitched sound coming from the distance and our dog became unsettled and starting whining and cowering down.

We both stood and watched it. I asked my dad what it was, and he said he didn't know.

We watched this object get lower until it disappeared behind the brow of the hill and behind the 'old station' which had been converted into a bungalow where an elderly couple Mr. and Mrs. Walker lived. Dad said it was time to go home and I couldn't wait to tell my mum what we'd just seen. I can remember sitting in front of the fire telling mum and she joked and asked if we'd been to the village pub instead of sledding. The following morning Mr. Walker came into my mum's shop and told them he'd been for a walk over the fields behind the 'Station' where he lived, and there was a huge area of completely melted snow in the shape of a circle. My dad then told him what we'd seen the night before! Mr. Walker contacted a local paper and I believe the authorities, and later that same day a group of people visited the site using what my dad said were Geiger counters!! There was a story published in the Leicester Mercury about this incident, but we never heard any more about it.

Nigel Bailey, Leicester

A huge triangular UFO with lights on each corner was witnessed slowly and silently gliding over Leicester, and three helicopters were flying above it! The UFO was seen by forty-seven-year-old commercial energy consultant Nigel Bailey. He wrote: "I've just seen a huge triangle-shaped aircraft flying slowly over Leicester. I caught up with it in the car, but lost it, however, I saw three helicopters flying around at a higher altitude than the police helicopter normally flies around at. The triangle was so low that I could make out the shape and the three lights at each corner and it had strobes flashing down the sides. It was silent!!"

He then said: "To be honest it looked like your typical TR-3B. Based on the flashing lights, it seemed to be a terrestrial aircraft, but it was quite low, lower than a commercial aircraft would fly, it made no noise at all and was flying very slowly. I could make out the general shape and it was definitely triangular. Nigel continued, "I had just come out of the front door around 7.15 pm to go to pick up my wife who works at Glenfield General Hospital. I looked up and saw some strange strobe lighting in the sky.

It wasn't the height of the normal commercial aircraft going over - nowhere near that height, more the height of helicopters as they're flying over."

He said that in the clear night sky he could easily make out a triangular shape with lights on each corner and there were red and green strobe lights splashing down the side. It was far too big to be a drone – it looked at least four times the size of helicopters that fly over.

According to the witness it looked around a foot wide at arm's length, probably no more than 5,000 feet up. It was travelling west towards the motorway. Nigel watched the craft moving across the sky for two minutes before it vanished behind a block of flats, so he moved into a car parking area near his home where he followed it again for three minutes before it also was obscured by houses. It was while in the car park that he spotted a helicopter flying towards the scene. He thought the sighting was over, so he drove off in his car for the five-minute journey to collect his wife from the hospital but spotted it again as he drove into the hospital car park, where he then counted three helicopters.

He watched the triangle for two minutes as it passed over the hospital before it again vanished behind buildings. He picked up his wife Emma and immediately told her: "I think I've just seen a UFO." And as we were coming out I pointed out one of the helicopters that was still flying around. He said that as a benchmark when they got home he and his wife saw a commercial aircraft fly over from the same direction at a much greater height.

"It was flying ten times as fast as the object I saw" he said, "The airliner had gone out of view in ten seconds" Nigel said that as a child he'd had a sighting of a UFO from his school playing field which was "an exceptionally large cigar shaped object." Then, a couple of years ago, while driving and waiting at traffic lights he saw, "what appeared to be an airliner flying over, but it had no wings" How did he feel when he saw the triangle? "Probably more excited than anything, and inquisitive. I didn't feel nervous or anything like that" he said.

He added: "I had my phone camera with me, but in my mind I was too busy taking in details and watching it rather than getting the camera on and knowing how dark it was. I was just gobsmacked as to what was flying over me" he said he thinks some UFOs may be military top-secret aircraft.

But he added "I don't think we can be the only life in the universe. I'm a strong believer that we are being visited. I think as a species we are in our infancy in the grand scheme of things. "About his triangle sighting he said "I don't know what to think, whether it was military or otherwise. But what I saw was completely unusual and something I've never seen before" I am grateful to Nigel for sending me the above report.

So many local reports and all triangles! Looking at the dates it's interesting to see three separate sightings in 1996, one at Trinity Motors on Coventry Road, which is a stone throws away from the A5 Dodwells roundabout and one at Transco, also on Coventry Road and about approximately one mile from Trinity Motors. Transco (National Grid for Gas) had three visits from triangles and Mel Orton's sighting was just twelve days before ours and approx six miles away.

Pic.17 Transco antennae array, Coventry Road, Hinckley

Witnesses share amazing UFO encounters

AFTER my last article in The Hinckley Times yet more local witnesses have come forward to tell me of their own amazing encounters with a triangular-shaped UFO.

It seems incredible that Hinckley and the surrounding area is quickly becoming a UFO hotspot for these craft rather than your traditional flying saucer.

The first witness to get in touch with me was Lou (not his real name) who with his sighting on three separate nights earlier this year.

He said: "I have also seen triangular objects (three white lights) moving silently across the sky very low. Only a few weeks back it happened three nights in a row on my way back from work. On February 3 2016 at 5.37pm I was travelling from Stoney Stanton towards Earl Shilton, the lights seemed to be heading from Desford Way, and following the Earl Shilton bypass across to Barwell. I would down my window as I crossed overhead (I was at the bypass waiting to turn right onto Clickers Way).

"The lights were very bright, I quite often stargaze and these lights stood out immediately then didn't appear to be any other lights on it, just the three white lights in a triangle shape, they did not flash.

"The lights were around the size of a helicopter at the height of it when it passed overhead was around 300m-400m high, I couldn't make out the size of the craft in the street lights made it difficult, however with the distance between the two rear lights and the front light I would say it was the size of an articulated lorry and more of an isosceles triangle rather than equilateral. There was no sound as it passed over at approximately 30mph."

I have in my files a report from a Rhys Dowdeswell of Barwell who observed a triangular UFO hovering over the Caterpillar factory in Desford back in the summer of 1996.

Next to get in touch with me was Alan Haydon with his sighting: "I used to be a security patrol officer, me and my dog were out in all weather's all year round. In 1996 when returning to my office on Coventry Road's Trinity Motors site, I saw a large triangular 'something' flying slowly across the sky, almost as if it was following the Ashby Canal.

"It was approximately 200ft up and looked huge, there were red lights underneath it and as it slanted a bit towards my position, it seemed to have many decks, it made no noise that I could hear but my dog started whining and all of his fur stood up on end.

"I could almost feel a kind of low soft vibration coming from it. The sighting lasted around nine seconds and the triangle was the size of a 20 pack of cigarettes when held out at arm's length, possibly a touch larger, very dark grey in colour, it went down towards the northern perimeter road towards London.

"Looking at your model I now see that I was looking at it sitting with the left hand 'wing' towards me making it look like a bug cheese wedge, if was about 100 yards long if I remember right, (this is a sideways view).

"Also, if I remember rightly, it was about 3.30am, maybe just after, it was early daylight and I was returning to my security office to finish my night's report.

"A few days later a movement over towards the A5 made me look up and to my amazement the same kind of shape was just lowering behind a big black cloud. As it sank it seemed to shimmer and disappear, just before total disappearance it left just the outline as it went see through, I wasn't certain of what I saw at first, but my job was to look out for the unusual.

"A few days later I was taking a member of the forecourt staff home after her shift. When we reached the northern perimeter road, from the east of Brodick Road, I was about to turn right and we both saw a very large triangle like a shark's fin dropping down behind a big black cloud.

"It would have been over the A5 at the time, to be behind the cloud and looking as large as it did it must have been one hell of a size.

"That is three triangle sightings in the space of about five weeks!

"About five to six weeks later as my dog and I were on one of our regular patrols I again saw lights in the sky, this time two pale yellowish balls high in the sky, they came from different directions and came together as if following each other. After around 10 seconds they seemed to catch up with what looked like a tube slowly going across the sky until they joined it, making a dumb-bell shape.

"It was moving very slowly across the sky towards Hinckley town, but high up in a clear, dark, star filled sky, the time would be around 2.30am.

"Before the dumbbell went from sight another yellowish ball of light came across the sky at greater speed and seemed to slow down to follow just behind the others, they then carried on across the sky until out of sight."

Next to contact me was Kenneth Rush (not his real name) with his incredible story of another town centre (Transco) sighting: "It was back in the summer of 1996, not sure what month but I think it may have been August (I was 19 back then).

"So, I left my then girlfriend's house on Brookside to go home, it wasn't quite sundown but not far off (also unsure of the time).

"Anyhow, it was pretty much daylight and right in the town centre and my main goal was to rush home and grab a camera and get a picture (which I didn't sadly).

"With hindsight, people were walking around while I was driving who didn't notice it, and I can't for the life of me explain why I didn't stop or toot my horn at the pedestrians and point up. But when I got home, I could still see the twin bright lights from them, but couldn't find a camera, my family saw the lights too but basically thought it was a helicopter and I was mocking about (I was a pretty crazy teenager)."

And finally a report from Michael Austin.

He said: "I saw two of these triangular shaped UFOs over Barwell back in 1879 or 1980. I was in my car with two friends parked at the back of the houses in Chapel Street which would now be Wilkinsons Way.

"The driver's window was open and I was looking at the sky when two of these objects came into my sight straight in front at high altitude over the houses of Chapel Street. They were huge and travelling at high speed, one slightly behind and to one side of the other with no makes sense? It was basically hanging there, but must have been shifting along, around was head plus I was driving in my old Fiesta so there could have been some noise.

"At about this time they had travelled straight overhead and out of sight, over the houses of Shilton Road so they didn't get to see them.

"If you watch a jet plane do the same you can watch it for a while, these things did it in seconds! I only say this now because most other sightings are either bright lights or cigar shaped objects"

It would be easy to jump to the conclusion that this is perhaps a secret military project such as the much rumoured American TR3B aka the Aurora but there are many reasons that I do not believe this to be true.

First and foremost are the statements from all those witnesses who have had a close encounter with a triangle, they all said that due to it's flight characteristics and unconventional appearance they did not believe it was from this world. I do not personally believe that if we have this technology we would fly a secret craft over Hinckley town centre, hover over Transco antennae array or simply stop in the middle of the English countryside so individuals can get a good look at them!

Then there is the question of how long these craft have been around, the earliest known reports of these unusual triangles can be traced to the Dutch East Indies in the late 1860s, around 30 years prior to the Wright brothers' first powered airplane flight in 1903.

UFOs were also reported from Scotland and England in 1895, interestingly enough all triangular UFOs, and also we have three separate occasions that these craft were seen over Transco, and on one occasion an FT was actually hovering over the antennae array.

Were these triangles interested in our gas distribution network or simply recharging their batteries from the high frequency radio transmissions?

Having seen one of these triangles close up I personally believe that these are not from this world, we have here multiple witnesses to these craft from 10 respectable and honest citizens in our local community who are of the same mind, this subject really does need to be taken seriously.

In my last article I wrote that the truth is out there, well actually that's not quite correct, the truth is already here, we just all need to open our eyes, look to the skies and start believing.

I'm indebted to all of the witnesses who have been brave enough to come forward and share their close encounters with me.

If you have your own encounter to share, contact Colin Saunders on Prck13@hotmail.co.uk

UFO ENCOUNTERS IN HINCKLEY...

As far Hinckley's own timeline here's a list of our own local encounters spanning the last 35 years in chronological order.

Michael Roberts, October 23 1978 8.45pm, triangular UFO seen over Transco, Hinckley, multiple witnesses.

Keith X, 1978 11pm to 1am triangular UFO seen over Transco, Hinckley, missing time.

Michael Austen, 1979 or 1980 evening, two triangular UFOs fly over Barwell.

Alan Hydon, summer 1996 3.30am, triangular UFO over the area of Trinity Motors, Hinckley plus two more triangle sightings over the next few days.

Kenneth Rush, August 1996 late afternoon, triangular UFO seen over Transco, Hinckley.

Rhys Dowdeswell, summer 1996 10.20pm, triangular UFO over Caterpillar factory, Desford.

Mike, March 19 1999 2.30am, triangular UFO, Shansford (Mike's grandad also had an encounter with a triangle in 1967 at 8pm in Shansford).

Colin Saunders, March 31 1999 9.30pm, multiple witnesses, triangular UFO, Monks Kirby.

Stuart McKay, summer 2014, late evening, partially cloaked triangular UFO, Earl Shilton.

Lou, February 3 2016 5.37pm, triangular UFO, Clickers Way, Elmesthorpe.

I was once asked if I thought Hinckley was a hotspot for UFOs and my answer to that would be no, the only reason we have so many reports is because of my own investigations and articles in local newspapers asking people to contact me. I believe if you put a Colin Saunders in every town from Lands End to John O Goats the results would be the same.

In other words, I believe these UFOs are visiting every town in every county of the United Kingdom with impunity, yet it is still scoffed at by the media.

The author in the news

A strange pyramid-shaped spacecraft has been spotted in the skies of the West Midlands. Not once, but scores of times over the past 10 years. Yet the sightings are dismissed by the authorities as the "crackpot" theories of overheated imaginations. Chief feature writer **PAUL DALE** asks: Is there anyone out there?

AS A FORMER aircraft designer, Colin Saunders reckoned he was pretty much an expert on the huge variety of flying craft to be found around the world.

But nothing could have prepared the 41-year-old draughtsman for the amazing sight that greeted him while travelling along the Fosse Way in March last year.

Returning from a family meal with his wife, daughter and mother-in-law, Colin was close to the village of Monks Kirby at about 10pm when he noticed several bright red lights across the road in the distance.

"It was odd because we had been along that road many times and there had never been lights in that place before," recalled Colin.

As their car approached it became clear to the Saunders family that a large pyramid-shaped flying machine was hovering 100 feet in the air.

"It had rounded corners and looked like a big blob of liquid mercury," remembered Colin. "There was a thickness to the edges which were definitely metallic but looked alive, shimmering as though they were covered in water.

"There were lines on the surface of the craft in the form of square box sections running through 90 degrees to give the impression of a garden maze."

Mr Saunders' wife, Karen, stopped the car and reversed a short distance to get a better view of the strange object.

OUT OF THIS WORLD EXPERIENCE: Aircraft designer Colin Saunders who made a model of the UFO he saw and (inset) how the public's perception of UFOs is portrayed

Scared

"We were not at all scared. With my interest in aircraft I wanted to get on board and have a look.

But before Mr Saunders and his family could get closer the craft tilted at an angle and shot off in a westerly direction towards Coventry.

At no time could he recall the machine making any noise. There was total silence.

"It moved towards Coventry, about 20 miles in a few seconds, still showing the red lights but it appeared to grow to an enormous width," he recalled.

The object had been in view for half a minute which was enough time for Colin to commit the detail to memory. When he arrived home in Hinckley he set about sketching the craft and then built a scale model of what he had seen.

He believes this is the first time anyone in this country has constructed an accurate model of a UFO.

Strange experiences for the Saunders family didn't end there. Over the course of the next few days they suffered numerous problems with electrical apparatus at home, including a clock that began to work of its own accord and faults with the television and a computer.

Similar inexplicable occurrences have been reported over the years by many others who have come into contact with UFOs.

UNEXPLAINED: TV shows like The X Files often investigate the UFO phenomena

Why Colin is saucer-eyed

"I am a down to earth sort of person and there's no way I would make up something like this. I know what aircraft look like and I knew it wasn't from this world"

Asked to make sense of what he had seen, Mr Saunders confesses he is mystified. He says a day hasn't passed since then when he hasn't thought about the experience and wondered whether he and his family really had stumbled over an alien spacecraft.

"I am a down to earth sort of person and there's no way I would make up something like this. I know what aircraft look like and I knew it wasn't from this world."

The case is just one of scores documented by former West Midlands police officer turned UFO hunter, John Hanson.

John, along with his partner Dawn Holloway, has interviewed witnesses all over the country who claim to have experienced extra-terrestrial happenings.

He is convinced there is something out there, but he has an open mind on whether aliens from other galaxies are involved.

He points to the fact that many sightings take place close to old Roman Roads, like the Fosse Way. He thinks certain people may be able to witness ancient energy sources.

"We firmly believe that these things are there all the time but they move in an invisible part of the spectrum. It's only occasionally that they can be seen."

What really angers John is the refusal of the authorities to take UFOs seriously.

The Ministry of Defence receives around 300 calls each year from people who are convinced they have spotted strange craft or unexplained bright lights in the sky.

But the men from the ministry are not amused.

Sightings

There have been numerous sightings across the West Midlands of a pyramid-shaped object with bright red and yellow lights hovering and then moving off at vast speeds. The MoD, however, has a stock answer. It doesn't believe the security of the country is at risk and therefore sees no point in investigating.

The British Astronomical Association takes an equally frosty view, having written to Mr Hanson describing UFO spotters as members of "crackpot" organisations. Bright lights in the sky and other unexplained objects are routinely dismissed by the BAA as fireballs or meteorites.

This isn't good enough for John and Dawn, whose research into the subject is meticulous. "Over the past few years we have attempted to get to the bottom of what all this is about. We weren't prepared to accept the sensationalised way in which the UFO subject is generally treated," said John.

"It would be impossible to calculate all UFO sightings over the past 50 years. They would fill a pile of books going up to the ceiling.

Reader tells us of his own close encounter

A model of a UFO and a graphic illustration of how it would look supplied by Colin Saunders

I knew instantly it was not of this earth

IT WAS with great interest that I read Michael Roberts account of his UFO sighting in The Hinckley Times and felt compelled to write and tell you of our experience along with some further information regarding Mr Roberts sighting.

I became interested in the subject of UFOs after my own "close encounter" back in 1999.

This occurred with my family and took place on the old Fosse Way close to the turning for Monks Kirby.

Our encounter has been described as one of the closest and most detailed ever in the UK.

We had been out for a family birthday meal at Pailton and were driving back towards Hinckley on the Fosse Way when we saw some very bright red lights hovering very low close to the side of the road.

We drove excitedly towards the lights which were now only approximately 100ft from our car, as we stared at the lights an object materialised around the lights, decloaking to reveal a triangular (delta) shaped metallic craft now hovering in front of us.

As an ex aerospace engineer I knew instantly that this was not an

Colin Saunders has contacted us having read Michael Roberts' article on a UFO sighting. He tells the story of his own close encounter with the unknown

earthly object.

The craft was so close I could have hit it with a cricket ball.

At this point the nose of the triangle rose in the air or rather "floated" up in the air to reveal a liquid like surface with white girder box sections sitting on top.

A model of a UFO and a graphic illustration of how it would look supplied by Colin Saunders

My wife, who was driving at the time, pulled the car off the road into a gateway so we could all four of us get out for a better look of the car the UFO had unfortunately disappeared.

Given the chance, two of us would have got on

board!

The experience really was earth shattering for me and totally "out of this world" but not at all frightening.

I decided to build a model of the craft we saw that night and armed with this I appeared on TV several times and made many presentations around the UK.

My own research into UFOs brought me into contact with a Hinckley man who we shall call Keith X.

I took a witness report from Keith in 2001, and his description of the UFO he encountered was identical to Mr Roberts.

Back in 1978, Keith was riding home from Nuneaton to Hinckley when his motorbike stopped working outside the old gas works (now Transco). This was approximately 11.30pm.

Keith looked up and to his amazement there was a huge black triangle, which he described as the size of one-and-a-half football pitches at an extremely low altitude (approximately 100ft), gliding silently overhead at 15 to 20mph towards the town centre.

Underneath the UFO he described a glass dome structure like a cockpit. After the triangle

was out of sight he managed to start his motorbike and continue his journey.

On arriving home he discovered the time was now after 1am, he woke his parents to confirm the time and realised he had lost approximately one-and-a-half hours.

I tried at the time to find other witnesses to this triangle but was unsuccessful until now.

It would seem logical that this has to be the same craft seen by Mr Roberts.

The only difference is the time slot, the latest report says the craft (with a glass cockpit) was seen by several witnesses over the old gas works at 6.35pm. Keith had his encounter outside the old gas works at 11.30pm.

I personally believe that this was a genuine UFO. What was it doing? Who knows?

Perhaps it was more interested in the goings on at Transco than the latest production showing at the Concordia Theatre that night.

More details of our encounter can be seen at ufo-explorer.com

Anyone wishing to contact me with their own sighting can do so by email to peckt3@hotmail.co.uk

More people say they have seen similar UFO in skies above town

UFO images created by Colin Saunders for his story about UFOs

More Hinckley Triangular UFO stories by Colin Saunders

IN MY recent Hinckley Times article printed a couple of weeks ago regarding local UFOs, I invited readers to contact me with their own encounters and I thought your readers may be interested in the follow up I have received.

Two local witnesses have been in touch with me after the article and I arranged a meeting with them so the three of us could get together and discuss the experience. What follows is an account of their own close encounters with the enigmatic flying triangle.

The first is from Mike (pseudonym) of Sharnford. Mike had his own Triangular UFO encounter back in March of 1996. Mike left home at 2.30am, he was alone as usual and driving to work where he would normally start at 3am trunk driving to London.

Mike left the village of Sharnford heading in the direction of the A5. As he left the one way system he could see some lights further along the road at a very low altitude.

Mike wound the window down to get a better look at the object as he drove towards it. The object was hovering at the junction to Bumblebee Lane. Mike quickly parked his car outside Wayside Farm by the post box.

Bravely he got out of the car and stood underneath a huge triangular UFO. He described the object as the size of a football pitch, the object was only 150 feet away and approx 100 feet off the ground. The triangle was totally silent

Stuart's drawing of his

and just hung there in the sky, crystal clear, no vibrations, no smells, no noise. The bottom of the craft was tilted towards Mike and he could see the underneath quite clearly, a large central red light with three additional white lights, one in each corner of the craft.

Mike could also make out lines or "girders" on the underneath, raised off the surface in relief.

At this point Mike realised the object was not of this world and became frightened at the situation he found himself in. He quickly got back in his car and drove off. He could still see the object in his rear view mirror as he sped away. On hindsight Mike now wished he had stayed and possibly got on board if invited.

Strangely enough Mike's granddad, (now deceased), also had an encounter with a silent triangular UFO. This took place in the village of Sharnford nearly a year later in early 1997. His granddad lived on Chapel Lane in Sharnford and it was 8pm when he saw lights in the field which adjoined the bottom of his garden.

The object was 40 yards away from his garden and at first he thought it was a tractor but the object then rose in the air to reveal a dark triangular object with bright lights on the sides and a "shower of golden snowflakes or sparks falling from the centre of the craft to the ground".

The object then started to move towards him and once the object was only 10 yards from the bottom of the garden the lights went out and it simply vanished from sight.

The local vicar at the time, a Mr Walter Evans, was also witness to a strange craft in Sharnford, probably the same one that Frederick saw at the bottom of his garden that night.

The second sighting came from Stuart McKay of Earl Shilton. His sighting took place in 2014 in his back garden.

He said: "I've just read the article in The Hinckley Times and was amazed that somebody else has seen this. I was out in the back garden having a cigarette (when I smoked) in the summer of 2014, it was late as it was dark, I don't

remember exactly the time or date as I had put it to the back of my mind until now. Anyway I usually look up to the stars during clear nights as it's a very nice sight, when I saw a (hard to describe) "fluid" looking triangular craft coming from the west over Earl Shilton Park Road.

"I understand this sounds very weird hence I've not talked about it before. I don't think I would have noticed it if it had been at a different angle as it was 'cloaked'.

"I could see stars as if I was looking straight through it, but I could clearly see the triangular shape of the craft and I still remember thinking to myself that it wasn't a very good cloaking device.

"It was moving very slowly and very low with no sound and no lights whatsoever...but it was huge, the size of a football pitch.

"As it got closer visibility got worse, I'm guessing its all about the angle of view... then I could no longer see it at all. I managed to see what I assume would be the front right side as it was approaching, then the underneath.

"It was all smooth or fluid with no sharp edges very much like the picture in the Hinckley Times but this craft had no markings that I could see. The first picture is spot on regarding the edges but the craft I saw had, like I said, a fluid, smoother edge to it."

I'm extremely grateful to Mike and Stuart for sparing the time to share their experience with myself and your readers. We are all of the opinion that these craft are not secret military vehicles and are definitely not of this world. Where they are from we can only speculate but I'm sure the truth is out there!

If you have a story for Colin please contact him at peck13@hotmail.co.uk

MORE TALES AND GHOSTLY GOINGS ON

Hinckley's
ufo!

We continue with Burbage historian Michael Roberts' ghost stories

STEVEN Spielberg's film Close Encounters of the Third Kind was released in 1977 upon a mainly unsuspecting public, although UFO sightings have been reported around the world for some years prior to 1977.

With the release of the film sightings increased dramatically - no doubt the film made us much more aware of the possibility of visitors from outer space and, thereafter, we were observing the night sky and also the daytime sky much more than we had in the past.

I must admit that the film fired my imagination. I hoped that one day I would see a UFO - but did not really believe that it would happen.

Well happed it did, and not on one of the occasions when I was searching the night sky - in fact, I was driving my car when the sensational event began.

It was the evening of October 23 1978. At the time I lived on Hinckley's Hollycroft estate.

On Monday evenings I drove my wife to Hinckley College to a class that she attended.

On this particular Monday I was driving up Hollycroft Hill at about 6.35pm when my wife said: "What is that strange

object in the sky?"

I glanced in the direction of the Gas Works in Coventry Road and saw it for myself.

The object appeared to be delta in shape and had lights dotted around it. On arriving at the junction of Upper and Lower Bond Street I observed that the object was high in the sky over the direction of The Borough.

I drove along Lower Bond Street into Council Road and then into Stockwell Head.

All the time my wife was saying the object was overhead. My curiosity overcame me and I pulled into the parking area near to the Concordia Theatre. I noticed that two or three other cars were doing the same thing.

We got out of the car - as did other people - and looked up. Immediately above us was the object.

It was now perfectly still. How high I could not say. There was no sound coming from it.

There appeared to be some kind of observation cabin below the main structure, which seemed to have numerous windows from which lights flashed on and off.

We all held our breath not knowing what was going to happen next, when all of a sudden there

> We got out of the car as did others and looked up. Immediately above us was the object.
>
> Michael Roberts

was a loud "whoosh" and then the object had vanished. My wife and I spoke with the other people.

None of us could say what it was we had really seen.

I believe it was a UFO in the true sense of the word. If our Government or any other earthly power was testing some new kind of flying machine, then they have certainly kept it quiet for these past years.

Some time later, I discussed the incident with someone far more learned

in astronomy than I am, and his belief is that it is impossible that it could have come from another planet.

Well, I can only say what I saw. It certainly was no hallucination as a number

of other people had also seen it.

So what did we see on the night of October 23 1978? Whatever it was, it was an unnerving and thrilling experience.

Jay walking ghost was 'knocked down' again

I JUST read

88

THE AUTHOR IN THE FLYING SAUCER REVIEW MAGAZINE

FLYING SAUCER
REVIEW

VOL 50/1
Spring 2005

http://www.fsr.org.uk

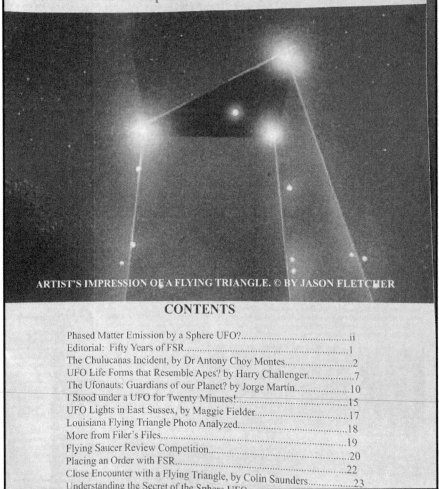

ARTIST'S IMPRESSION OF A FLYING TRIANGLE. © BY JASON FLETCHER

CONTENTS

CLOSE ENCOUNTER WITH A FLYING TRIANGLE.
© BY COLIN SAUNDERS.

As a recently new subscriber to your magazine I was very interested to read Tony Spurrier's article *When is a triangle not a triangle?* I recognised some of the drawings (Volume 49/4 page 5, figs. e & f) as originating from my own experience and decided to write to you with some of my own theories about FTs based on our own close encounter. This is how it all started.

31st March 1999, we had been out for a bar meal to a small village called Pailton in the Warwickshire countryside. There were four of us in the car that night. At approximately 9.30 pm we left the White Lion public house and headed home. We turned onto the Fosse Way near the village of Monks Kirby and immediately noticed some bright lights ahead of us. The lights were ½ mile away and just off the road to the left. The lights appeared as deep red, like a Rose red with a bit of white mingled in.

We drove down parallel to the lights, which I now estimated as being only 100 feet away! We had slowed right down by this point. I stared at the four lights which were in a row, but not level with the ground; I would say they were tilted at approx. 25% to the horizon. I stared into the light on the far left. This light was the highest side of the tilt, with the far right light being the anchor point for the 25% angle. It was at this moment I also noticed a fifth smaller spurious light off to the left hand side (Pic.1).

As I stared into the end light I could see a criss-cross of lines, a bit like a traffic light lens (Pic.2). It seemed to pulse very rapidly in a digital fashion, i.e. on off, not up and down. As I was looking at this light, and then the lights in general, I noticed a shape start to appear around them. The edges looked like the sky was rippling, but they and the body were, I believe, and were transparent at that time (Pic.3).

I could see the shape of a diamond around the lights; you needed a keen eye to make out this shape as you could see the sky through it. As soon as I had realised there was an object there it tilted slowly upwards in a most peculiar fashion, like an airship or submarine, and the object was now solid and fully materialised in a triangular shape. The tilt was not from the centre of the craft but from the rear, i.e. the rear end stayed where it was and the nose rose in the air (Pic.4).

It was so low that, if it had pivoted from the centre of the craft, the rear would have struck the ground! I noticed the surface looked to be alive, and it was like a lake of dark grey liquid similar to Mercury. The liquid, although tilted quite steeply, looked as though it had waves running up and down the surface, like ripples on a lake in a breeze. On top of this "lake" were silver lines running up and down the surface, and they were like box sections raised off the surface which interlocked like an old fashioned maze (Pic.5 & 6).

I could see how the craft's top and bottom surfaces joined to a lighter central core, like a sandwich. No nuts and bolts, rivets or welding seams visible. There were no apertures, no antennas or protrusions of any kind. It was immediately obvious to me this was not an earthly object.

I was shouting "Stop, stop, let me out!" (I wanted to get even closer!) but the driver pulled slightly forward to enable her to reverse into a gateway off the main road. The result of this was that a large hedge momentarily blocked our view of the craft. I thought to myself "If it's going to clear off, now would be a good time." and sure enough it did!

We got out of the car and it was gone. We could see a large craft in the distance with strange red lights at the rear. It seemed enormous to me with a huge wingspan; at the end of each wing was a steady white light shining up along the top surface. It was very, very quite as we stood there, no smells of any fuel having been burnt. During the incident we never heard a single noise from the craft, which was the size of a house, hovering by the car. As we stood there traffic started to come up and down the road for the first time. Noone else was involved. We checked our watches in case there had been any missing time; it was 9.50 pm, so that ruled out.

I have been a engineering draughtsman all of my life, and amongst other things I have worked for Airbus Industries in Germany on the Airbus A300 and A310, as well as Saab Aerospace in Sweden on civilian aircraft design. I have also worked for a major North Sea oil company and flown on many helicopters during my time there. I think I am well experienced to comment on whether this flying (hovering) triangle was man-made or not.

The next day was April fool's day, but this did not deter me from telling everyone I met about the UFO we had seen. I phoned the late Graham Birdsall at UFO Magazine, who put me in touch with Omar Fowler, the respected Flying Triangle investigator. Having spoken to Omar, we wrote our witness reports and sent drawings of the craft to him before he sent through copies of The Flying Triangle. To my great surprise there was a report of a Triangle from Stockis in Belgium from 1993, which clearly showed the same lines in relief on the bottom of the craft (Pic.7).

Surely this was the same or similar series of craft? The coincidence was too great for me, so I reproduced the bottom drawing of the craft (Pic.8) and used the Belgium sighting along with my own sighting of the rear and top to produce a scale model of the craft, complete with flashing lights. I could not understand the diamond shape that I had seen and instinctively built the model with a flat bottom (Pic.9).

I gained quite a lot of information from this model; the first and most enlightening observation was that, when you look at the rear of the craft and tip the nose down, you end up with a silhouette of a diamond! (Pic.10) This would explain picture No. 3 above, the spurious small light in fact being the light underneath the nose at the front of the craft. I have referred to lights but they were not lights per se, as they did not emit light to the ground. The colour shown on the drawings is primary red, but from ½ mile away they appeared deep rose-red.

I do not believe they changed colour, but more likely the colour varied with the focal point distance. The lines on the surface of the lights could have been generated from the light source itself, something along the lines of Newton's law of ring interference? I have seen a similar effect myself with a laser pen. Once the craft had disappeared there was no degradation left in the eyes, perfect vision.

The next obvious conclusion was why the triangle appears as different geometric shapes to different people. I believe our triangle was equilateral; however this depends on the aspect you are looking from at the time (Pic.11).

I have wondered about the lines in relief on the surface of the triangle and their possible purpose. They do not appear to be aerodynamic, but we are not dealing with a conventional craft behaving according to our known laws of physics. Although the craft's surface was "shimmering" like liquid mercury, the solid lines on top displayed no distortion at all. This would rule out the effect of heat or electromagnetic distortion. You can see that the pattern I have shown varies between my first drawing and the model; this is because I cannot recall the exact configuration. However, the quantity and layout appears in the correct ratio, as in Pic.5.

One theory that came to me was that these raised lines could be used for docking to a larger ship (I now believe the large craft we saw in the distance was a

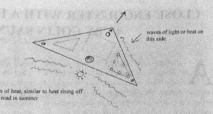

waves of light or heat on this side

waves of heat, similar to heat rising off a hot road in summer

Fig. 12

mother ship that the smaller craft returned to). This possible docking technique may be confirmed by an article I read in Omar Fowler's journal of March/April 2002.

A sighting was made near Titsey, Surrey by a Mr Herbert who stated he saw a large triangle about 200 yards wide, and underneath he could see smaller objects attached (Pic.12). The only problem I have with this theory is, what are the raised lines underneath the craft (Pic.7 & 8) used for? Maybe smaller triangles sometimes dock together?

The last six years have been very interesting for me. I have given several presentations to different groups, as well as appearing on television a couple of times with my model. The result of this is that many people have come forward to tell me of their own experiences, ordinary people who are not involved in the UFO world. I have also been encouraged by a 99.9% acceptance of our experience by everyone I have spoken to. Building the model helped me to understand and to come to terms with our close encounter. Others have been through the same experience and below are a few examples of other people's handywork.

And finally, in answer to Tony Spurrier's question "When is a triangle not a triangle?" - when it's a flying saucer! Yes, believe it or not, the last picture for your consideration is a front end shot of my triangular model (Pic.15).

Conclusion.

I have spent 30 years being a trained observer of electromechanical installations and transferring these images into legible technical drawings. I have been involved with many projects worldwide, and notably several years spent in the aircraft industry. I have received praise on the clarity and accuracy of my drawings on more than one occasion. I have absolutely no doubt in my mind that this craft was of extraterrestrial or inter-dimensional origin, but most likely both of these scenarios together. What you see here is an accurate scale model of a true alien spacecraft witnessed at first hand. ■

24

93

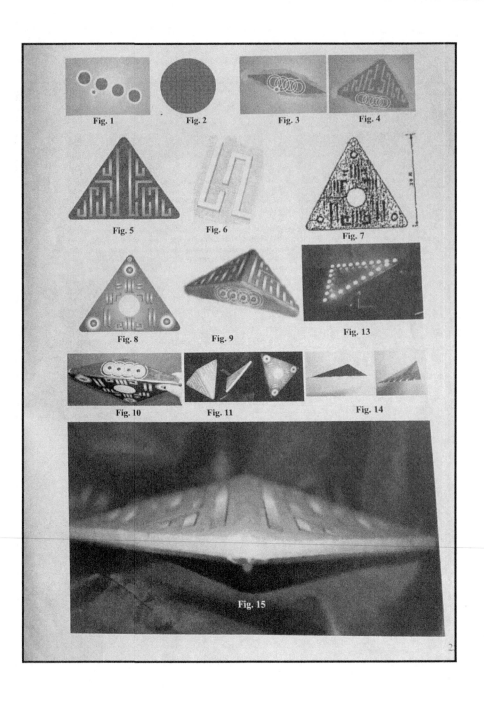

Fig. 1 Fig. 2 Fig. 3 Fig. 4

Fig. 5 Fig. 6 Fig. 7

Fig. 8 Fig. 9 Fig. 13

Fig. 10 Fig. 11 Fig. 14

Fig. 15

94

****

Chapter 5

Omar Fowler

Omar Fowler had been researching the mystery of Unidentified Flying Objects for over twenty-five years. He became interested in the possibility of alien craft visiting our planet while serving with the Fleet Air Arm in the 1950's. At the end of his Naval service, he moved to the Empire Test Pilots School at the Royal Aircraft Establishment at Farnborough for three years before returning to civilian employment in the early 1960's.

TRAINING ON SEAFIRE'S

He was founder member of the Surrey Investigation Group on Aerial Phenomena established in 1967 and served as chairman of that organization for over 10 years. During this period, the SIGAP group became well known and exchanged information with numerous UFO research organizations and scientists world-wide, including Dr J. Allen Hynek, Dr Jacques Vallee and Dr Joachim P. Kuettner (Chairman of the American Institute of Aeronautics and Astronautics).

Omar moved to Sinfin, Derbyshire in 1990 where he established the Phenomenon Research Association, we became great friends over the years, and I first met him when he came over to interview the four of us during the first few days after the encounter.

I joined Omar's Paranormal Research Association (PRA) in Derby and attended many meetings. It was at the Royal Legion Club in Derby that I did my first presentation to Omar's group using a scale model. I have to say I owed a lot to him; with his extremely calm nature he helped me keep my sanity over this encounter.

Over the years Omar introduced me to many famous people in the UFO world such as Stanton Freeman, Dr Roger Lear and Budd Hopkins. My brief conversation with Budd will appear later on in this book.

Omar Fowler, Chairman of SIGAP, discussing a point with Dr.Allen Hynek at the International UFO Congress.

97

Dr J. Allen Hynek (left) with Omar Fowler

Colin Saunders Shows Off His 'FT' Model

As a design engineer *(involved in the European Airbus & other aircraft)*, Colin knows his elevators from his flaps. His FT model must bear a close resemblance to the real thing.

An earlier FT model showing the red lights at the rear and the strange 'live' light pattern seen on the top surface.

The author's first presentation

Omar spent some time living in Spain with his wife and for a while he worked as a camera man. I wrote to Omar here in the UK back in 2003 and told him of some of the weird electrical problems we had after the close encounter, and this was his reply.

"I may or may not have told you about the experiences that my wife and I had when we lived in Spain. Briefly, we were about to complete the sale of our villa and were sitting in the lounge late at night when we heard a 'dragging' sound coming from the kitchen (all the floors are tiled). It sounded like someone slowly dragging a kitbag across the floor in a stop-go motion. My wife and I heard it and even the dog barked! I walked into the kitchen, but there was no sign of anything untoward.

From then on we started to have a series of strange experiences. That night the lights 'trip' jumped out nine times, I called an electrician the following day, but he could find nothing wrong. This was followed by a venetian blind falling down and light bulbs popping every time my wife touched the light switch. We completed our move back to England and had a short holiday in Malta. When booking in at the Gatwick Flight Desk their computer 'went down' The light blew over our Maltese hotel room doorway as we approached, then the large central room fan started to spin at a high speed (it was switched off as it was winter). This phenomenon stayed with us in England for some months afterwards. It included more light bulbs popping at home and while walking around the town.

More computers 'went down' when we were near them and a cheque printing machine in an M & S store refusing to work. Even when I phoned up to book a cross-channel ferry, the guy at the other end of the line said, "My computer's just gone down." So, it continued. I have no recollections of strange lights or UFO activity near our home in Spain, so why it happened it remains a mystery, but we seem to have been 'got at'! The observation that 'the more you learn about a subject, the less you understand' seems to be correct. I have said something similar in the past, the more we learn, the more questions we have to answer.

I will keep that observation in mind while looking for an answer, which I suspect is now venturing into the psychic realm.

Omar produced two booklets and many journals concerning the Flying Triangle mystery and it seemed only appropriate to include a selection of his UK witness sightings in this book. We start with an early sighting in 1956.

Robin Gibbard, Allestree, Derby 1956

One of the earliest reports that came to light, is that of Mr. Robin Gibbard, who witnessed an unusual event at I l am on April 9th, 1956. Mr. Gibbard and another joiner were working on a house roof in Allestree, Derby, when he heard the sound of an approaching aircraft.

At that time Mr. Gibbard was deeply involved in competition model aircraft flying and this, together with his hobby of aircraft recognition, made him familiar with all types of aircraft flying at that time.

Mr. Gibbard recounts the event- "The day was very clear, with very little cloud about. On hearing an aircraft approaching, I looked up to see a twin radial engine, propeller driven, Avro Anson (which even then was becoming a rarity).

The aircraft was approaching at an altitude of about 2,000 ft. or less. These aircraft were very slow flying and used mainly for reconnaissance." "I was amazed to see a delta-wing plane circling fairly close to the Avro Anson, actually circling around the plane at least twice, at a speed not much more than the plane's speed, but making no audible sound, the only sound came from the Anson." "After making two circuits, it (the delta) broke away and then increasing its speed to a phenomenal amount, disappeared upwards on a long curve in about 5-1 0 seconds." "My partner also saw this occurrence, but unfortunately he has since died and cannot corroborate this statement."

"It could not have· been a glider, because of its breakaway speed and any possible Delta aircraft of that period always made plenty of noise.

A 'Flying Triangle' Sighting 28-11-1977

By Ernie Sears

The date was the 28th of November 1977, and the time was about 8.00 pm with a beautiful clear sky. I'd gone out into the garden of my then Portswood, Southampton home, to let one of our cats out. There was a full moon visible over to the South. Being something of an amateur astronomer I gazed up at the sky, then, when I looked up over my head, I stood transfixed! Hovering, perhaps a thousand feet up or so, and totally silent, I saw a metallic looking triangular craft...complete with 'ribs' beneath it and what appeared to be 'rivets' of some kind. It also had weird, coloured lights around its edges.

Having seen a UFO being chased by two RAF Meteor jets in 1960, in daylight and having subsequently studied the subject deeply since then, I was not 'new' to such craft, but this (Flying Triangle) was big, awesomely silent and I got the strange impression 'it' was looking down on me. I turned my head and yelled out to my wife (who was indoors), to "come and look at this thing!" When I looked back up at the sky, just a few seconds later, it had gone! I gazed around from horizon to horizon, but there was nothing! Just the Moon over in the South, was I going nuts?

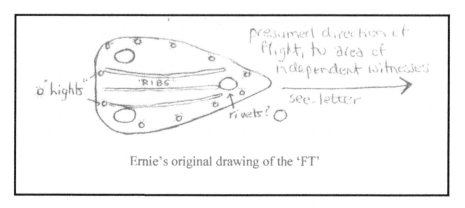

Ernie's original drawing of the 'FT'

I went to bed that Monday night, disturbed that I might be losing my marbles! However, the next morning I managed to phone my friend Monty and this time I spoke to him.

He went on to tell me that he had been in a car, driving along the M27 at Burlesdon, just five miles from my location, when he and four other people (all musicians) in the car spotted this "Huge Triangle" dashing about the clear blue sky in short bursts of terrific speed, seemingly leaving a short trail of 'light' as it did so! They stopped briefly on the hard shoulder to get out and watch this 'craft' performing these maneuvers, until they had to resume their journey to meet a radio program commitment. When I heard this, I was relieved. I wasn't going nuts after all!

A Flying Triangle Report From Northern Ireland August 1982

This encounter took place over a campsite in the Glen River Valley, Moume Mountains. Northern Ireland The witness, Mr. 'PS' describes the incident that took place on a Sunday in Mid-August 1982. Whilst camping at the above location in August 1982, a large, triangular object flew directly over the campsite, moving slowly and silently across the valley at an estimated height of 30ft. The object approached from an Easterly direction, moving through a ravine between Slieve Donard and Thomas Mountain.

It then banked to the 'Port' (left) side when cruising over the forest, which was due West of the campsite, before disappearing from view some 20 seconds later. In answer to the NIUFORP sighting report form, Mr. 'PS' stated that "The object moved between mountains and over the trees." It was viewed with normal eyesight (no visual aids). It was visible for approx. twenty seconds. There was no sound heard from the craft at the time.

The 'FT' was dark slate grey in colour. It appeared as a solid object. It flew over at 'rooftop level'. The speed was approximately fifty mph.

It flew within a quarter of a mile of the witness before passing overhead. The angle of the craft varied between forty-five and ninety degrees as it flew over. The craft had a large dim yellowish-white light under the centre. It was quite large; possibly 30-40 feet wide (equilateral triangle). The entire craft was very clear, and the domed light appeared transparent. There were a number of sheep grazing a short distance away, but I was not aware of any disturbance. No physical effects were felt as a result of the encounter.

Police Officers 'Flying Triangle' Sighting in 1984

We were recently contacted by a serving police officer regarding a 'Flying Triangle' incident that occurred in 1984. "I was searching the net for any information re the Flying Triangles and found your site. I am a serving Police Officer and had an encounter with one when I had just joined the service." "It was 1984 and I think something like October/November time. I was on night duty and posted on the Area Car (the fast response crime car) with my mate Bob, who had only just recently passed his advanced driving course. I was the radio operator. We were in a fully marked Rover SD1." "It was the very early hours of the morning about 3am and we were travelling slowly East along the Ruislip Road in Northolt. We were driving away from the White Harte roundabout towards Greenford and going slowly as someone had been setting fire to parked cars along this stretch of road during the week.

On our right was the estate where the cars had been burnt and on our left was a large, open grass area called Rectory Park. Beyond the park is the busy A40 and beyond that RAF Northolt a bit further West. As we drove with both driver and passenger windows all the way down (a must for night duty patrol), I noticed a large orange light in the sky. It looked extremely low and in the area of RAF Northolt. I remember saying to Bob "What the hell is that?" and him leaning forward and looking up at the light He had no idea." "The weird thing is that as soon as we acknowledged the light it started moving quickly towards us.

As it came over Rectory Park I could see that it was a huge, black triangular shape. The orange light being in the middle with a white light on each point and the rest of the craft being a dense black. I can't say how big it was, but it flew incredibly low (between 50-100 feet) over the football pitches in the park. It was far bigger than two of these pitches put together. The craft made absolutely no noise and flew directly at our car. It then positioned itself to the nearside and kept pace with us". "I remember being in awe of this thing, it was huge and silent. It seemed to block out the whole sky.

At this point I was leaning out of the window of the car and began waving up at it. I remember Bob saying: " What's it doing now?" We carried on towards Greenford and the park came to an end.

After that there were residential houses on our left. The craft shadowed us and was barely higher than the rooftops." "We crossed over the Lady Margaret roundabout and continued towards Greenford Broadway. The craft stayed right with us."

"Bob stopped the car in the middle of the Ruislip Road opposite Greenford Hall. The craft stopped and hovered directly above our car. It seemed really low, just above the rooftops. Again, it seemed huge and blocked out the sky. I remember feeling spooked at the size of the thing and that it made no noise at all. Bob turned off the car's engine and we both got out of the car leaving the doors open." "The craft just hovered directly above us. I was waving up at it and then put on the blue roof lights. There was no reaction from the craft." "After a while, the craft turned around and pointed back up along the Ruislip Road and then slowly moved off back the way we had come.

It then shot up into the sky at a speed which no plane or anything from Earth could have been capable of "We jumped back into the car and drove straight into Greenford Police Station which was just around the corner.

I called RAF Northolt from here and told them who I was and asked if they had any aircraft up over our area. I was told that there were no aircraft up and did I wish to report a UFO? I said 'Have you seen it as well then? "He said ' Officially, no'. I said, 'Have you got any idea what it is?" He said, "None whatsoever" I said '" Is it worth reporting?"

He said '" Not really mate" end of conversation". I know this all sounds a bit farfetched, but this is a true account of what happened that night. I cannot remember passing any other traffic during the incident. In those days traffic was virtually non-existent after lam. I cannot understand why neither of us tried to radio for help and get other units to join us. We told the Station Officer what had happened, and he offered to make an official report. We declined. It's a memory that sticks with me for obvious reasons.

Huge Triangular Craft Seen Near Banbury in 1988

A long journey lay ahead for Mr. Colin Harrison and his friend as they set out from Manchester in their van. The night was clear, cloudless and starry as they headed towards Banbury (Oxfordshire). It was about 2am on July 7th, 1988, and they were about three miles from Banbury, when both occupants of the van noticed a dark shape approaching them. It had first appeared low on the horizon, but there was something strange about it and they both sensed that it was something unusual. It was now only half-a-mile away and they could see that the object was not a plane, helicopter or any type of aircraft that they could recognize. By now Colin had stopped the van and switched off the lights.

As the object drew closer, they could see that the craft showed no lights and there was no sign of any wings or helicopter blades. It was soon within about 200yds of the van and at a height of 70ft above them, moving absolutely silently. "I knew this was a day that I wouldn't forget" remarked Colin. "By now I could see the front of the object, it was at least 60ft across, concave and had a matt-black body, there were also three lighter coloured 'circles' on the front of it." Colin was about to get out of the van for a better look, but his friend begged him to stay where he was.

Both witnesses sat quietly in the van as the huge craft passed silently overhead at an estimated height of 70ft. There were no markings visible on the craft, but they did notice five oblong 'hatches' underneath, lighter in colour than the main body. "By the time it had gone over, I realized that it must have been at least 300ft long," said Colin. "There was still no noise or any sign of lights." Colin then moved into the back of the van to watch the craft moving away. "It was about 600ft away and I was able to make out the shape of the object, it was tubular, tapering to a 'beaver' shaped tail." "The craft then did an 'impossible' maneuver on its own axis and shot off at great speed into the night sky", said Colin. "I was very excited, but my friend on the other hand was very nervous and scared, he just kept asking me to get going." Colin's final comment: "I have never forgotten that night!"

Triangular Craft in Nottingham, 1988 by Billy Booth

Strange events in Nottingham, England recalled. It happened quite a few years ago now. I was around eight or nine at the time and like most young boys, I had been sentenced to an evening of being grounded for something stupid I'd done. I had been in my room and playing on my games console, when my mum had passed my room and heard me. She advised me that being grounded isn't something you're supposed to enjoy, before taking the console away. I went to my bedroom window to watch my friends playing outside. My window looked out over our garden, which had an alleyway behind it, and then a row of buildings beyond that.

As I was looking out at my friends playing, I noticed movement above the roofs of the buildings at the alleyway. Assuming there was a spider or something on my window. I looked up to get it, but instead of a spider I witnessed a large, triangular craft passing above the buildings. Not directly above, but it appeared that way because of its position in the sky. It looked to be far away and was still visible and very clear ... and exceptionally large. I'd estimate it was approximately one mile away and was still as big as my finger is now. I observed the object for around ten seconds. It moved in a perfectly horizontal line and rotated to the right as it went at a speed of around one full rotation per three seconds.

It was a dark-coloured object, almost black. And the only way I know it wasn't totally black is because it had two thick, darker lines running across its width. There were also darker lines in between these lines but they weren't noticeably clear. They could have been markings, or they could have just been recesses in the surface. As I watched it I'd been totally frozen, until after about ten seconds I screamed and ran downstairs and wouldn't go back up no matter what, mother's wrath be damned! I have no idea what it was I saw; I've never seen anything like it since then. Oh, and a week or two after this we had some very strange occurrences in the house.

Firstly, my sister developed an imaginary friend that she never spoke to when we were around. This friend spent a while apparently just playing with her, but after a fortnight or so she began to wake up screaming in the night. She'd have marks on her and would literally stay up all night, so she didn't have to go to sleep on her own. It got so bad that she had to be moved first into my mum's room and then

112

into mine. For some reason, after moving into my room and having me tell her many times that if he comes back she should tell him to go away and to ignore him, it seems he did. My mum has always been a believer in 'other stuff' and was of the opinion that if you just ignore anything bad it will go away, which is a philosophy I have found extremely useful in life, believe me!

Huge Glowing Green Light Seen Near Bradford, West Yorkshire

6-8-1992

It was about 11pm on Sunday 6th of August 1992, as Russell Kennett drove back from visiting a friend at the famous 'Tunmy's' hospital in Leeds. Russell had set off from the hospital in his car at 10.30pm and as he approached the roundabout at the junction for Pudsey, his attention was attracted by a glowing green light in the sky. "I thought that it was a firework at first", commented Russell. "There was a Michael Jackson concert on in Roundhay Park and there were to be fireworks at the end of the concert." "Then as we were turning right onto the Leeds to Bradford road, I realized that it was a large, glowing green object moving in a cloud." "As it moved closer, I realized that it was a big 'Flying Triangle'. To my amazement, it moved overhead, very slowly and silently, heading from a NW to a SE direction, it seemed to glide." "I opened the car window to get a better view, but there were other cars behind me, and I moved on." "I looked again to see where it had gone to, but I could not see it, the 'Flying Triangle' had gone." The FT was described as glowing green, with no sound and exceptionally large. "It was so big, someone else must have seen it", commented Russell.

Bakewell, Derbyshire 26/09/1993

With a series of events that commenced at 7.45pm on the night of the 26th of September 1993, the town of Bakewell in Derbyshire was about to become another statistic in the series of world-wide sightings of the mysterious "Flying Triangle" While out walking near Alport, Bakewell, with her six-year-old daughter, Mrs. 'H' saw a brightly lit object in the sky, "It's shape was like three squares being placed on top of the other, with the largest square at the bottom and smaller squares on top and it just sat there quietly in the sky. It was about the size of a telephone box" commented Mrs. 'H.' It was then that her young daughter asked her mother what the object was, and she replied that it was an airplane. The six-year-old daughter looked at the object and then said, "I don't like that airplane mummy!" Mrs. 'H' felt uneasy and with her daughter turned and walked away from the area.

At 9pm on the 26th of September the activity around the Bakewell/Matlock area increased.

One witness reported an object in the sky "lit up like a huge fairground" Another witness out walking his dogs saw lights hovering in the direction of Bakewell. He noticed that the dogs became extremely excited. It was at 9.30pm that witnesses reported the shape of an illuminated triangle flying low and slowly across the town.

A Mrs. Hilda Hill drew a sketch of the triangle as it flew overhead "slow moving and silent" Mrs. Susan Shah, who lives on the hill overlooking Matlock Baths, noticed bright lights approaching her house. She opened the window to watch as the FT passed slowly and silently overhead. A Mrs. Pailing of Bakewell also saw the huge FT and noticed that it had red, green and brilliant white lights.

A key witness to the event was a Mr. Andrews who happened to be driving in the direction of Bakewell at the time of the incident. As he approached the town in his van, he saw a number of lights moving slowly and low down in the sky ahead.

As he proceeded through the town he noticed people lining the side of the road and looking up at what appeared to be a huge, black triangle flying low overhead. "It was lit up like a Christmas tree" said Mr. Andrews. "It had a bright white light on each corner, so bright that it illuminated the ground below. Suddenly he realised that he and the FT were travelling in the same direction, then driving at a steady 40mph he overtook it!

The FT then performed a series of slow, silent maneuvers over the town, including several U turns and right-angled turns. Finally returning to its original course and moving out of sight behind a line of trees.

Derby (Rolls-Royce Aero Engine Works) 29-6-1994

In the early hours of the 29th of June 1994, Mr. Alan Beardmore was driving his van on his way home from a snooker tournament. His journey took him past the engine testing facility of the Rolls-Royce Engine Co. On the side of the road there is a series of electrical pylons carrying lines to the test facility.

As Mr. Beardmore was driving along he noticed a series of lights hovering over a nearby field. He pulled up to a stop sign and peered out of the window, everywhere was deserted apart from a formation of three, bright white lights hovering over a nearby power line pylon.

The witness was able to make out what appeared to be a triangle of lights and close to the nose he noticed a bright red light, which was positioned next to the bright white light. Mr. Beardmore looked through the side window of his van and peered into the darkness. He was just able to make out the classic FT shape. Then as he watched, it slowly started to move away. He turned his van around to follow the FT, but it was now out of sight, suddenly his

116

headlights came on again! He surveyed the sky and had one last look for the FT, but it had gone.

May 1994 Encounter with Alien intelligence.

By PRA Member Richard Servante

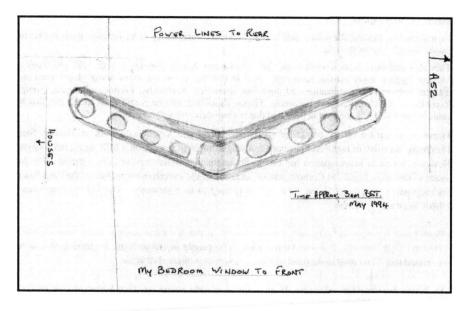

POWER LINES TO REAR

A52

SEVERN

TIME APPROX. 3am BST. MAY 1994

MY BEDROOM WINDOW TO FRONT

Richard's sketch of the object

I don't recall the exact date, but it was around May 1994. It was about three o'clock on a Monday morning when I was awakened by a sound. At first I couldn't make it out. I told myself it was 'just one of those things' and tried to get back to sleep as soon as it stopped- which was about five minutes later. About ten minutes after that it started again.

This time I really strained hard to listen. What I heard scared me, not the words themselves but the sinister, metallic tone of the voice. The closest I can describe it is that it sounded like a Dalek on a mission to scare the living daylights out of me! I don't mind admitting it was succeeding! The words, in a repeating phrase pattern were "Human being, human being" they were delivered like a call sign. I went to the window and drew back the curtain to see if there was any obvious reason for this intrusion, (although how there possibly could be at that hour, God knows!).

I looked across the field at the back of the house, and there,'hovering 'just in front of and just below the electricity pylon, was a boomerang shaped craft. The only detail that I can recall is that it was lit up along its entire body, but the light was not bright and dazzling: it was about the same illumination strength as what I call an old-fashioned car headlight. Having first heard the scary sound and then seen its apparent source, I wanted it to just go away and leave me in peace.

I went back to bed and, thankfully, the noise did not return. What happened next could well be described as my mind playing tricks. I saw an evil-looking face, like an eagle with reptile features. It told me that if I disclosed my experience 'they' would get me.

This next report Omar sent me was mentioned earlier on in the book. This was the inspiration for the bottom of the craft I was building. We never saw the underneath of our

118

triangle, but the lines in relief on the surface was very reminiscent of the Belgium sighting. It seemed logical to me to combine my own views with the Belgium view for a complete craft.

Belgium 3-11-1993

On the 3rd of November 1993, a young boy Nicolas, (aged twelve) observed a large 'Flying Triangle' over the town of Stockis.

The time was about 6pm when he saw "an enormous Flying Triangle" pass over his home, moving at a speed of only about 20km/hr. The FT had a small blue light at the nose, a red light, slightly inset from each corner and a large white light in the centre. The surface of the FT appeared to have some kind of relief pattern underneath

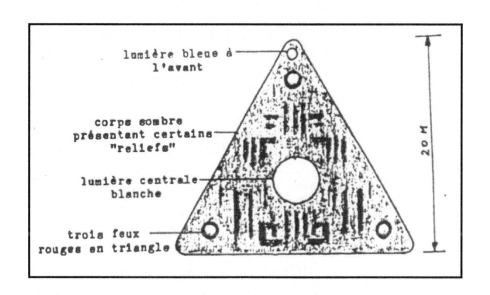

lumière bleue à l'avant

corps sombre présentant certains "reliefs"

lumière centrale blanche

trois feux rouges en triangle

20 M

120

The Author's Model

Long Eaton, Notts Sighting, 4-2-1997.

As Mr. Raymond Spybey walked down Oxford Street of his hometown, Long Eaton in Nottinghamshire, he noticed what appeared to be "lights in the distance." The time was 6.55pm on the night of February 4th, 1997. He took no notice of the lights at first, until he realized that they were stationary. "When I stopped walking, they came towards me, then, when I started walking again 'it' stopped."

"The next thing I knew was that the lights were above me and I could make out that the shape was triangular, with yellowish lights at each angle and one in the centre, there was a little red light on one of the sides." "Then I lost sight of it over some factories and although I made for a nearby bridge to get a better view, when I got there it had vanished." "I remember that I heard a faint humming sound as it was moving, but when it stopped it was silent." "I could clearly see that it was a black triangular craft, and it was about 400ft up." "It appeared from the North and disappeared heading in a NW direction."

Stoke on Trent 'Flying Triangle' 12-4-1996

Dear Mr. Fowler,

I saw you on the Controversial TV Channel in the past few days talking about the black triangle UFO phenomenon. I thought I would relate to you an encounter which my wife and daughters had back in 1996. My wife went out one cold Autumn night about 8.00pm to collect our youngest daughter from Brownies and to also collect her older sister from her friend's house on the way (the girls were eight and twelve respectively) Now, before I go any further I must say I normally went with her on this journey but curse the fact that on this occasion I did not. As she came back in about thirty minutes later, as soon as she came through the door she said "I think I've just seen a UFO" with a half-smile, I asked her what she was talking about.

She told me that as normal she picked up both girls and was only in the next street down, a matter of two minutes' drive, when she was aware of something in the sky above the car and low in the sky. She stopped the car and saw a large black shape above, so she got out to see better, she said it was a "huge black triangle shaped thing" in the sky just hovering in total silence. Now bear in mind the location of where she stopped was the edge of a newish housing estate, she said nobody was around and she told the girls to stay in the car whereby they dropped the windows and asked their mother "What is it?"

My wife said it started to move slowly back and forth and that she could hear a helicopter approaching, at this point she said she became really scared and thought it was watching her, so jumped in her car with a very strong thought, "Oh God, please start" which it did, and as she glanced up at it, in almost the blink of an eye she said it shot off upwards and at an angle. Now, as I said she was only in the next street and as she got to a junction at the end of the road she saw a police car parked up and two male officers out looking up at the sky. I went out myself into the garden, but of course I could see nothing but a clear starry night.

I remember my daughters excitedly getting their pens and paper out and drawing the triangle and one said to the other "was it isosceles or equilateral" to which the reply was "equilateral". What they described and drew is virtually identical to the triangle on your web page, dense black with white lights at each corner and a "duller" reddish light in the middle. I must say I have had a mild interest in the subject most of my adult life, but at the time this happened I had no idea that there were triangles being seen as well as the traditional saucer and cigar shaped UFO's. I made a point of keeping my eyes open in the local press, and a couple of weeks later saw a couple of reports about triangles, one being reported by an airline pilot as he was on approach to Manchester airport, and the other by a motorist who spotted a triangle near a motorway in the area. Of course, I thought to myself it must be something secret and military and largely pushed it to the back of my mind.

My wife has since said she is "Pleased the girls were with her that night otherwise she would have doubted her sanity!" It was not until quite some years later when we got on to the internet and read other people's encounters with identical craft I realized it was no military secret she has seen, rather something far more mysterious. Strange how they are so often at an extremely low altitude, my wife described it as "huge" and just a "few houses in height".

She never told anyone but me about it and in recent years I related the sighting in the local press just in case anyone in a nearby street witnessed it but there was no feedback to my printed letter. But then we know how some people prefer not to open themselves up to ridicule. I know you must get lots of email but being as this was not reported at the time I thought it may be of interest to you. I nearly forgot the location; we are in Stoke-on-Trent.

Scotland: Kennoway, Fife. 23-9-1996

What may be one of the most important UFO events ever, is alleged to have taken place on the night of Monday 23rd September 1996.

The 'close encounter' of two adults and two children with a landed 'Flying Triangle' and possibly a hundred-plus Aliens defies imagination. The story of the encounter has been investigated by Tony Dodd (Quest International), David Colman (SUPR) and Malcolm Robinson (SPI).

As yet none of the investigations have revealed the identity of the witnesses or the exact location, although it is believed to have taken place in a country area near Kennoway in Fife. Brief details of the alleged incident are as follows: 'Mary', 'Jane' and their two children 'Peter' and 'Susan' ·were travelling in a car en-route to and from a local village shop.

They first spotted brilliant lights low in the sky near a country farmhouse. They stopped the car and stepped out in order to get a better view. They were then able to make out the shape of a triangular craft in the sky. After a moment, it flew off into the distance and could be seen only as a point of light.

Later that night at 9.45pm, they were returning on the same road, when they saw what they described as a brilliant multicoloured 'pulsating star' on the ground. It then shot beams of laser-like light up into the sky and while the witnesses watched, they made out the shape of a figure moving across in front of the light. Although it was only visible in silhouette, it was by no means human!

It was long limbed, slender and with a head much larger in proportion to its body. As 'it' stood there, it was joined by four or five others who were similarly shaped, but much smaller.

They made out a black structural shape on the ground in the glow of the light and then they made out other 'beings' walking towards the black structure. The witnesses drove off but returned later with binoculars to study the UFO more clearly. They were able to see many small Aliens carrying boxes and cylindrical containers, picking them up and putting them down, seemingly under the direction of taller Aliens.

Shortly afterwards, the witnesses were confronted by the sight of 'hundreds' of aliens coming towards them, some appeared to be in 'cocoons'. With this, the witnesses jumped back -in the car and drove away at high speed.

Wales: Cardigan 21-11-1996

Mrs. Patricia James sat watching television in her home at Penparc, near Cardigan in Wales, the time was 8-45pm on Thursday the 21st of November 1996. Suddenly she heard a noise like the low rumble of distant thunder. It gradually grew louder, until it had developed into a very loud roar, "The sound felt as if it was penetrating my chest," said Mrs. James. "I asked my husband what it could be, then I decided to go outside and investigate." "At first I couldn't see anything, but the noise was so intense, I decided to stay outside."

"I looked up at the sky, over to the right of me and then I changed my position and looked over to the left." "It was then that I saw a huge triangular object travelling slowly, just above rooftop height." "It was clearly a triangular shape with curved tips and there were red and blue lights on the tips." "There was a silvery bright light surrounding the FT shape, which was clear against the night sky." "There was another object following it, with a single white flash." "The triangle travelled at the same speed until it was out of sight." Mrs. James reported that the FT was 'Grey, but not matt-grey.' The size estimate was approx. 8" wide at arm's length. The FT appeared from the NW and at a slow, steady speed, disappeared heading SE. UPDATE 21-1-97 "Tonight it was active again, at 6.30pm I heard the same noise as when I heard the FT on November 21st, 1996. I went outside to look and saw two red flashing balls of light flying through the sky, my husband also saw this." "What is going on?"

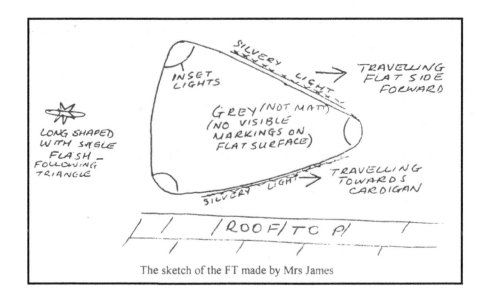

The sketch of the FT made by Mrs James

Littleover, Derby Sighting 2-3-1997

On the night of March 2nd, 1997, a Mr. B.M. of Littleover, Derby decided to go outside to his car and switch on his car alarm system, the time was 7.55pm. He continues with his story: "It was a clear night and I noticed how bright the stars were, I noticed the flashing lights of two aircraft in the distance, over towards Castle Donnington." (East Midlands Airport). "Then I looked around and as I looked straight above me, I saw a triangular shaped object come from above me and travel quickly towards the SE." "I looked at this triangle several times, to allow mind to register what I was seeing." "The FT seemed to be heading towards the aircraft, as if to go under and between them." "Then I lost sight of this object as it disappeared in the

128

night sky." "There was no noise whatsoever from the FT and it carried no lights." "It travelled in a straight line, with the point of the triangle going first."

M56 Triangle Sighting 1-6-1997

Peter and Wynn Seel, together with their two sons, were driving on the M56, returning from a holiday in North Wales. While travelling along they saw a brightly lit object in the distance. As they reached the High Lee area, a 'Flying Triangle' appeared and hovered above them. The family were stunned as it then 'zipped' across the motorway at a speed of approx. 100 mph and disappeared behind some nearby trees.

"It had red lights on each corner and a white light in the centre." "To be honest, we were very frightened, even now I find it hard to believe," commented Peter. 1999 was the year of our close encounter with a triangle and it seemed fitting to include encounters from the same year from Omar's files, this is a selection of those triangle sightings from 1999.

24-2-99

Mr. Adam Matthews was pottering in his back garden at his home in Brinsley, Nottingham. The time was 8.30pm, when he happened to notice a strange looking object flying in his direction (SSW). As it approached, it looked like a black square with white lamps on either side. It looked like a "flying wedge" as it passed directly overhead and Mr. Matthews noticed that it had a series of lights, like "an illuminated bar" along the side of the object. (see sketch). It flew over completely silently at a slow speed, estimated to be about 30 mph.

It could be clearly seen and was described by Mr. Matthews as being "triangular in shape." He observed for a period of 30 to 45 seconds as it passed over. "It was low, very silent and if it wasn't for the lights, I would probably not have seen it" commented Mr. Matthews.

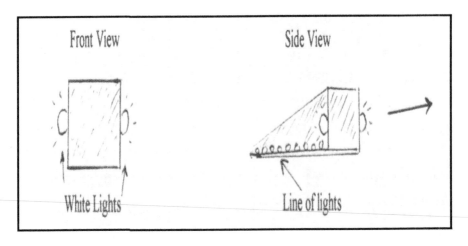

Mr. Matthews sketch of the wedge, note flight direction, flat end first!

3-3-1999

3rd March at 11.00pm, Helen Spencer-Smith was travelling by car along the A6, Northbound through Duffield Village, Derbyshire. She had experienced two previous FT sightings and was about to experience a third. The time was about 11pm, when she noticed a huge, bright light in the sky ahead of her. (The weather was cloudy, with drizzle.) The light "seemed to be stationary to the left of the road", observed Helen. "As I came through Duffield to the North side, I pulled over into a bus pull-in and wound down my window." As the light came closer Helen noticed "a blue flashing light to the rear of the craft." "There was no sound, so this discounted the thought that it might have been a helicopter, then as it flew over me, I saw very clearly, a flat, triangular, black shape with equal sides, flying point first."

Helen continued with her description of the event: "It had three lights; they were white and one at each point of the triangle." "As it sped off across towards Duffield Bank Hill (NW to SE), I saw huge, red pulsating lights, very bright and randomly flashing." According to Helen, she was able to observe the FT for two or three minutes, as it approached and flew directly over her.

"It was silent, large, brightly lit, like a spotlight and was a triangle shape." "It looked very thin and flat" commented Helen, who admitted that she felt exhilarated and excited at the time. When first observed, the FT appeared to be

131

stationary and flew over her car at about 50 mph. This is hardly the speed that a conventional aircraft would fly at, other than a helicopter or an aerial vehicle using high lift devices.

Even so, a conventional aircraft would have emitted some sound as the airflow caused turbulence in the air but are we talking about 'conventional' aircraft! I think not.

12-3-99

Miss Annette Doyle was travelling in her partner's car along the Nottingham Road, in Chaddesden, Derby. The car had just stopped at traffic lights, when the couple noticed a row of lights hovering over the road about 100 yards ahead.

At first they thought it was the new Police helicopter, but as they approached, it appeared to be a large black triangle with an orange light in the middle and three smaller red lights on the far side (see sketch). As they drove underneath it, they realized that it was hovering silently and completely still. Just after they had passed under the FT, they decided to turn the car around for a better look. It was then that the FT "took off" point first, silently and at great speed in a S.E. direction. It is believed that several other witnesses saw the FT. The total observation time was about two minutes. It was so low, that it "filled the sunroof as we passed underneath it!" "I have never seen anything like it" commented Annette.

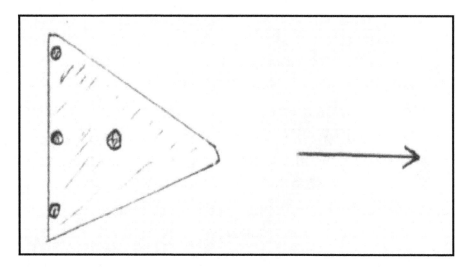

Annette's sketch

13-3-1999

A retired Rolls-Royce aeronautical development engineer Mr. S.H. is a man well-experienced in the field of aviation. He worked for the Rolls-Royce aero engine division for many years and was involved with the development of the turbo-prop 'Dart' engine, which has proved to be one of the most successful aircraft engines ever built. It was on the night of the 13th of March this year, when he saw something in the sky that left him dumbfounded. During his many years of involvement in the aviation industry he had never seen anything like it!

The time was about 8.30pm when Mr. S.H. made his way back to his bungalow home at Little Eaton, Derby. He had just parked his car in the nearby garage and walked up to his patio, where he stood for a moment and glanced up at the darkening sky. "The sky had broken cloud at about 1500ft, the sky appeared to be bluish behind the white clouds" stated Mr. SH. "Then I noticed a triangular shape that was black against the evening sky. It was stationary, quite sharply defined and was directly overhead. I could hear no sound and the object carried no lights of any kind. I must have stood there looking at it for about three or four minutes, when it started to rise up, increasing its altitude until it finally disappeared from sight." "Without going into details, I am fully conversant with all types of aircraft, and I believe that it was not an aircraft. Although it looked like a Stealth bomber, I do not believe that they can hover and make no noise." "When I came inside my house and told my wife what I had seen, I had the feeling that I had probably imagined the sighting, but I know I hadn't!"

2-4-1999

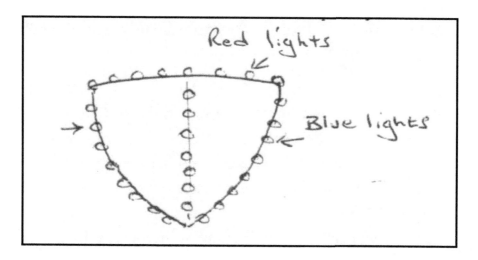

Mrs. Margaret Danaford told us "I don't sleep well, so when bright lights shone into my bedroom window, I got up to look." Mrs. Danaford lives in Wollaton, Nottingham and the time of her sighting was 1.30am on the 2nd of April 1999. Margaret continued, "What appeared to be an exceptionally large kite shape was just above the trees outside. It suddenly moved away, but made a circle and returned, where it stayed for about 30 minutes.

It was very large with a bar across the top, with bright red lights. There were also three rows of blue lights around it. It just sat there for a while and then went off quickly towards Derby."

7-4-1999

The 7th of April 1999 stood out as a prominent date in the midst of a UFO 'Flap'. A number of UFO incidents were reported from the East Midlands on this particular night, and they are given in sequence below:

10.10pm. Ms. Melanie Cunnigham saw a flashing formation of square lights "floating" in the sky, in front of her house in Belper, Derbyshire. The square formation had a white 'cone-shaped' light at each corner and a red light in the centre. As the lights approached, Melanie ran to the back of the house in time to see the block of lights pass overhead and out of sight behind some nearby trees at a speed she estimated of about 30 mph.

This was the beginning of a series of sightings made at Belper during the night from between 10.10pm to 11.30pm. Two triangles were later seen moving in a NW direction and three "balls" of moving light were also seen in the area. The FTs were seen to have "whitish" lights near each corner, together with a red light in the middle of the front line.

11.00pm. In the Strelley area of Nottingham, Mr. Kevin Radford was standing outside his house with his wife, when they both noticed what was described as a "strange craft", pass overhead.

The only view they had was underneath the craft, which they estimated passed over at a height of between 50-70ft. Kevin stated that "No way was it a plane, helicopter or any type of aircraft that I have ever seen before.

The base of the craft was oval and there were three lights across the centre (see sketch below). These were flashing alternately, the one on the right was red, the centre light was green and the light on the left was orange. There was no jet sound, no helicopter sound, not even a 'whoosh' of air, it was totally silent." The estimated speed of the craft was 30mph and it was heading in a Northerly direction in the clear night sky. Kevin confirmed that it was so low the oval shape could be clearly seen.

11.00pm. Again, another report from the Nottingham area, this time from Woodthorpe, where a witness reported seeing a large 'Triangular Craft' in the South. There were two ovoid lights seen upon two rear edges of a dark triangular structure. A single circular white light could be seen on what was described as the 'leading edge'. The FT was seen for a period of several minutes, at which time the craft appeared to be circling the area, as if in a 'holding pattern.' No noise was heard by the witness, who described the weather conditions as being clear, with moderate wind.

11.25pm. The final report came to us from Mr. Brian Payne of Lincoln, a retired Police Office and ex-Military Policeman, currently employed as a Security Officer on an industrial complex at Lincoln. It was a clear night, and the time was 11.25pm as Mr. Payne proceeded walking around on his night-time security patrol. He was about to enter one of the buildings on his rounds, this involved passing his electronic security card through a 'swipe' machine and he was just about to do this when he saw a light through the corner of his eye.

He paused and turned, to see what he described as an illuminated 'boomerang' or 'horseshoe passing slowly through the sky at a speed of only four to five mph. The boomerang shape had a leading edge full of lights and he had the impression that they were attached to a solid body/craft. The leading edge was lit up with a series of lights as though segmented. He was adamant that it was not a balloon, star or conventional aircraft. "I have seen bright stars before" commented Mr. Payne, "But never have I seen anything like this!" "I am no artist, but I have done my best to draw what I saw on that night."

Mr. Payne compared the brightness of the object to that of a streetlight, a sodium yellow-orange. When asked about the size, he said that a 10p piece would have covered it.

At the time, he was looking Southeast and the object moving from North to South at an awfully slow speed. The duration of his sighting was thought to be about three to four minutes. He looked at his watch to check the time and it was 11.25pm. Mr. Payne decided that he should continue on his security patrol and turned to 'swipe' his electronic card, as he did so, he glanced back to have another look at the flying boomerang: but it had gone! He then noticed that there were two, faint, fading pastel orange lights disappearing in the same Southeast direction. "I was not stressed about the sighting" commented Mr. Payne, "I just can't forget about it, it was very interesting." "I did not notice any time loss, but the speed, size, shape, lighting and sudden disappearance made me think the object was very unusual."

8-6-1999

Two maintenance engineers decided to take a short break from their work in the early hours of the 8th of June and watch the new Space Station passing in orbit of the over their works at Burton-on-Trent. But they were surprised when they spotted another unusual sight in the sky. At 0211 hrs Mr. Michael Akers and Mr. David Lakin were in position to view the passing International Space Station. "We had been on top of the water-cooling tower for about 5 minutes" said Mr. Akers. "Our eyes had become accustomed to the light, and I had watched the track of the I.S.S. for about 1 to 1/2 minutes, when Dave called out 'there's a plane', Dave was on my left."

"As I altered my gaze slightly towards him, while still looking upwards, I spotted the object." "At first I thought I was seeing a triangular shaped craft with a dull triangular window in each of the angles. However, after passing overhead I turned completely around, whilst watching it all the time, the trailing triangular light on my left veered away from the other two for a few seconds. It then immediately returned to the formation, before disappearing gradually into the night-sky maintaining the same altitude." "Dave and I questioned each other as to what we had just seen and making a note of the time and date, we independently sketched what we believed that we had just seen. When compared, the sketches matched exactly (see opposite)." Both witnesses stated that there was no sound and that the shapes were sharply defined in the night sky.

Mr. Akers described the objects as dull white, while Mr. Lakin described the object as black. Both agreed that there were bright lights at each corner of the object(s).

Michael Akers commented that "It may have been a man-made object, but I knew and felt I had never seen anything remotely like this before.

It was eerily noiseless and on a deliberate course, very puzzling somehow." Mr. David Lakin commented "I felt uneasy; it was not like an aircraft, not a sound and unusual lights."

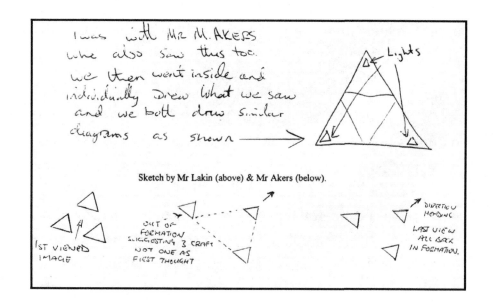

I was with MR M.AKERS who also saw this too. we then went inside and individually Drew what we saw and we both drew similar diagrams as shown ———>

Lights

Sketch by Mr Lakin (above) & Mr Akers (below).

1ST VIEWED IMAGE

OUT OF FORMATION SUGGESTING 3 CRAFT NOT ONE AS FIRST THOUGHT

DIRECTION HEADING

LAST VIEW ALL BACK IN FORMATION.

4-10-1999

We are grateful to Kevin Owen (PRA) and Sharon Larkin of Workington, Cumbria for the following report. "This sighting which I and a number of other people witnessed on October 4th (1999) was absolutely amazing! I have never seen a 'FT' before, but I can say that I have now, and I am glad that others were there to see it with me. Broughton Moor M.O.D. base is supposed to be disused and was previously believed to have housed Nuclear warheads, but the activity there continues. To see an 'FT' over the base shows that something must be going on!" said Sharon. The sighting of the FT (which took place about 7.30pm on the 4th of October) lasted for approximately three minutes, before the bright light faded and the craft vanished.

Twenty minutes later, we saw it again, only higher up, where it stayed motionless for hours! There was no sound with this craft and my friends managed to film it and I took photographs, so fingers crossed that they come out. During this time, the group noticed a white jeep driving behind the wire of the perimeter fence and they decided it was about time they 'disappeared'. Unknown to them, the jeep then came outside the fence and drew up behind the sky watchers, shining its lights on them and then two men in white overalls got out of the jeep and approached them. The sky watchers jumped into their cars and made of at high speed down the local tiny back roads with the jeep in pursuit while flashing its lights at the two cars ahead. By now the cars were approaching Camerton, and at this stage the white jeep was seen to turn away. Sharon continued: "When we got back to my place, I got a call on my mobile phone and a man said, 'We know what you have seen and you are not to contact the media', Sharon asked who the caller was, but the voice replied, saying that was no concern of hers and then rang off."

Apparently the film was developed, but only showed seven 'blank' negatives. The NW Cumbria UFO Group has since lost contact with the lad who took the video and although countless messages and letters have been left at his address, he has failed to contact Sharon. A sketch of the incident is shown below.

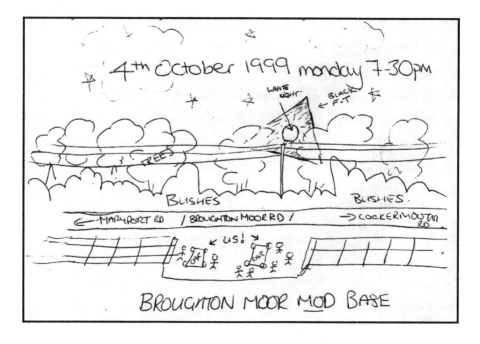

22-11-1999

A FT sighting was reported by a PRA associate, as he sped down the M1 on the night of 22nd November 1999. 'Paul' rang a PRA member on his mobile phone, to report that together with many other motorists, at 2005hrs. he had observed a huge Flying Triangle hovering close to the M1 Motorway, about a quarter of a mile north of the M1-M18 motorway junction (Jct.32). The witness saw a large, black, Flying Triangle hovering low down, just off the motorway. The FT was described as being huge, with an array of numerous lights and it appeared to be made up of a girder-like structure. The witness was unable to stop but noticed that many other drivers had pulled up on the 'hard shoulder' (emergency only lane), to look at the FT craft. We received a report from another driver, later the same evening. He stated that as he came off the M1, at about 2005hrs. heading towards the Sheffield area, he heard a roaring sound high in the sky. He said that he did not believe the sound came from an aircraft.

'Flying Triangle' Sighted Over The M1 17-11-2004

By Max Burns

If you live in the UK you will be familiar with the M1 motorway. The sighting occurred when we were heading southbound as we approached junction 37. The object was about two miles away slightly to my left, it was brightly lit, but at that distance I was unable to pick out too much detail. However, the object moved across the direct path of the M1 Motorway and was now slightly to the right of the motorway as we approached. We were heading down the valley south as the object was heading down the other side of the valley northbound approaching us from the opposite direction, as we got closer we were actually above the object for at least 45 seconds. It was remarkably close now.

We were just south of the Junction 37 marker of the Ml heading south. The object was illuminated on the top and the sides with white/red/blue/green/yellow/ orange strobing lights. the white strobes seemed to be more to the underside, but it was exceedingly difficult to make out any shape as at this point as we were still above the object but as we approached, and we were getting very close maybe 600 meters away the object gave the appearance of rising in altitude.

However, we were descending. It was also rising up now as it breached the base of the valley. We were travelling in a Mercedes Sprinter van towing as well; south bound at approximately 70 miles an hour. At this point the object was now above me and about 20 degrees to my right the object banked and started to come right across my path. The visibility was good because of the extremely low altitude we were at about 600 metres above sea level. An estimate, but I know the area. The object was just below the cloud cover I would have estimated that it was maybe 100/150 meters above the motorway. I estimated that the cloud cover from sea level was 700/750 meters (2200/2400 ft.) That is the reason I would suggest for there being no stars in the sky. The object had been approaching from behind us, but as I had my head protruding out from the window of the van, I could see that it was now directly above us.

It then passed through a wisp of cloud and at that point I saw that there were many white strobe lights. At least four all flashed together. The reflection from the strobes off the wisp of cloud reflected back on to the underside of the object and it was at that point that I shouted to the driver to stop the van. My exact quote was" stop the f***ing van it's a Flying Triangle!" I grabbed the company camera out of the case as we slowed to pull up on to the hard shoulder. We were towing two tons behind us, and it took a little time to stop. Then I jumped out of the van moved to the back zoomed in and managed to get one shot, I work on the motorways, and I carry out surveys on motorways throughout Britain. I am not colour blind and do not wear glasses. The driver of the van has confirmed the sighting and also added further details.

Huge Flying Triangle Dudley 28-11-2007

Readers have been calling in their droves to tell us they saw the huge "Dorito" UFO in the skies over the Black Country. The orange triangle with its three lights was seen over Wednesfield and Dudley by scores of people who phoned the newspaper after an appeal for information. A flurry of calls was made to the Stourbridge-based UFO Research Midlands, UFORM, from those claiming to have witnessed an unexplained aircraft in the sky. The flying object was spotted over Halesowen heading towards Stourbridge on Wednesday at around 7pm.Katherine

Hernmings, aged thirteen, of Beechwood Avenue, saw it at 4pm over Wednesfield High School in Lichfield Road.

She was walking home with friends Tasmin Jones and Chelsea Smith, when the three felt compelled to turn around. "It was weird because it wasn't making any noise, but for some reason we turned around", Katherine said. "We all saw this big thing with lights in the sky, We didn't tell anyone other than our families at first, because we thought everyone would laugh at us. Our families didn't know what to think until they saw it in the paper. I have never really believed something like that would be real.

I always just thought people who say they have seen a UFO are seeing airplanes or birds." Pat Scotford and her husband Mick saw the UFO when they were in their garden in Devon Road, Wollaston, at around 7.30pm. Mrs. Scotford, aged sixty-one, said she too saw three orange lights in the sky. "It looked like it was heading towards Kinver", she said. "At first I thought it was three planes flying information, but the lights were far too close together. I'm sure we're not alone in the universe."

Steve Poole, chairman of UFORM, said one man filmed over 30 seconds of footage of the craft. Driver Lisa Timmins, aged thirty-eight, saw the object while at her boyfriend's house in Whitgreave Avenue, Bushbury, sometime between 6.15pm and 6.40prn. She said: "I haven't got a clue what it was, but it was quite big."

147

Louth, Lincolnshire, 11-9-2009

Mr. Eric Goring

White Ball of light 140-150 degrees SE travelling extremely fast appeared from nowhere, a very bright white ball of light, it dives straight to the ground at terrific speed and is gone. I believe it is a Black Triangle (cloaked) coming in as a ball of white light and then 'decloaks' as a triangle again. I have seen this twice in the same area. Last seen around 2.00am. Friday 11th September.

During the 'Belgium Flying Triangle flap' 1979/80 there were reports of FT's shrinking to a ball of light and shooting off skywards, this is from a Belgian police report.

My night viewer is a great tool; I just wish it could be in full colour, not just green and black!

I would have liked to have had a heat-seeking (sensitive) camera with me, I believe that this would have shown the 'FT's when they are 'cloaked'.

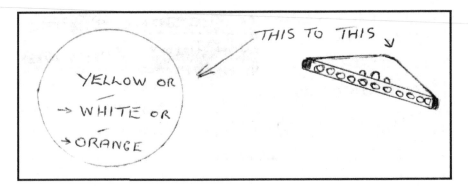

From the Leighton Buzzard Observer, 25-9-2011

After last week's report concerning a reader who saw a strange, triangular-shaped object flying over the skies of Leighton, a couple have written to the Leighton Buzzard Observer (LBO) telling of their strange, close encounter on the same evening. An email from a woman, who only identified herself as 'Christine', said: "After reading the Observer this week and finding out that someone has seen what they think to have been a UFO, I can confirm that both my husband and I also witnessed this on Friday, September 9th between 11.30pm and midnight as we walked along the Woburn Road in Heath and Reach heading towards the direction of Leighton Buzzard.

"A bright orange light larger than an aircraft's landing lights and travelling at a considerable speed passed over us heading in the direction of Milton Keynes. As it passed above us, we were aware that it was very quiet, almost silent, it looked like the shape of a triangle with rounded corners and a number of bright orange lights."

In another strange sighting, although more likely to some sort of military plane, reader Harvey Fryer said he saw an unusual sight over Leighton on Monday, September 19.

He said: "At around 3pm, I saw what looked like a very low-flying grey military plane (a Hercules-type). From my flat in Town Bridge Mill, I could see the plane about half a mile from the canal, in the direction of Soulbury. It then banked sharply, in the direction of Dunstable. It was so low that I thought it would crash.

Triangle Craft, Yorkshire from 'The Sun' 20-4-2012

The mysterious "Dudley Dorito" UFO has been spotted for the fourth time in five years flying through a cloudless sky over woodland in Yorkshire. The object, which looks like an extra-terrestrial tortilla chip, was captured by an amateur cameraman who posted the footage on YouTube. He can be heard saying "I don't know what that is" as the triangular aircraft glides silently across the frame above a forest in the north of England. The UFO was dubbed the Dudley Dorito after its first sighting over the Midlands in 2007, but it is unclear whether the YouTube footage is real or a hoax.

Eye-witnesses first saw the black triangle hovering over Halesowen and they reported the close encounter to UFORM, a local group of UFO-spotters. Then, in 2010, David Allan from Sutton Coldfield reported seeing a triangular object four or five times bigger than an airplane in the skies on Bonfire Night. A few weeks after that 21-year-old quality inspector Minuesh Mistry saw the Dudley Dorito hovering above his home in Tipton in the West Midlands. But the phenomenon of "black triangle" UFOs has been dismissed as similar to the effect ball lightening has on the atmosphere.

Peel Street, Derby, Sunday 12-8-2013

'Ken' telephones the PRA to report the sighting of three spinning 'pyramid' shaped objects, grey and silver in colour, at an approximate height of 400/500ft. They appeared similar to triangles in shape, there was no sound heard and they were travelling from West to East. 'Ken' had time to run inside his house and grab a pair of old army binoculars and watch the objects for a few minutes. The event took place on the 12th of August at 19.38 Hrs.

17-9-1980 Guildford, Surrey, two witnesses

Both witnesses were travelling in a car on their way home to Portsmouth and were driving on the A3 south of Cobham. The weather conditions were clear, and a few stars were visible. As they drove over the brow of a hill, they immediately noticed a brilliant light in the sky ahead of them and at a low elevation (approximately 15°).

The light was described as magnesium coloured and as being incredibly bright, with "spikes" of light being emitted by the object. As the car approached closer to the light, it became obvious that the light source was not one light, but two lights close together. Mr. Moore described the brilliance as "not a soft glow, but spikey". At this stage Mr. Moore pulled the car over to a lay-by, stopped and turned the engine off. He then jumped out of the car and ran along the hard shoulder. At this point it was possible to make out other lights associated with the object, there was a red on one side and green on the other, similar to an aircraft's light pattern. At first it appeared to be stationary, but then it moved across in front of the witnesses (Mr. Johnstone had now Joined Mr. Moore), it did not go up or down, but was travelling on a level plane.

It then passed over the witnesses, moving at a very slow speed and at a height of only a few hundred feet. Mr. Johnstone stated that he had always been skeptical about such things as UFO' s and had been sitting in the car up to the point where the object had started to move towards them, up to then he thought it may have been an airplane. However, as it approached, there was no sound and as it passed overhead, it was so large, commented Mr. Johnstone "it was absolutely massive." "You could almost feel the weight behind it, like watching a large liner moving slowly, you have that feeling of immense power". "I reckon it was at least two hundred feet long, judging the distance between the lights".

The object had no "glow" about it, but it was possible to judge the shape from the light pattern (two white 'headlamps' in front, red and green lights on either side, two amber lights on the tail section and a "rippling" series of amber, white and blue lights under the centre section).

The main impression made on the two witnesses was of the immense size of the object as it passed overhead. They did not feel any effects at the time, such as hair standing on end etc., indicating a source of electrical power.

Their car started immediately after the incident without any problem and there was no sign of any interference with any car instruments or their wrist watches (they checked). It was not possible to make out the shape of the object, it could only be judged by following the outline of the surrounding lights. The object was finally lost from sight as it passed over a nearby hill. Witnesses subsequently reported incident to Epsom Police Station.

A 1984 Triangle

A 64-year-old worker at the Little Eaton Water Works, in company with a colleague, noticed a "large set of red lights" over the A38 area at 2am (date not known). The lights were arranged in a triangular shape, with a bright red light at each corner and dull red lights along each side. No other details could be seen. The dart shaped object stayed in the same position for about an hour and then suddenly disappeared. The object had a sharply defined triangular shape and no noise was heard at the time. The witness is known and vouched for by the incident investigator.

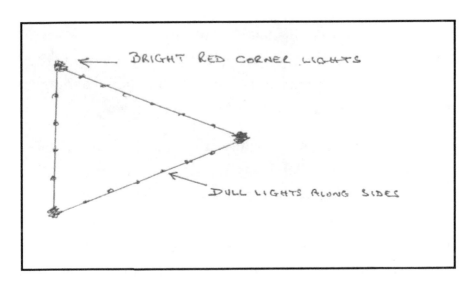

Witness sketch

Derby, 1985

Although this 1985 incident has only just come to light, the story has lost none of its impact and we thank Mr. David Bilton, a Derby resident, for giving us permission to disclose the details. By all accounts, the object was of gigantic proportions. The incident took place over Derby at 10.30pm during a night in November 1985. Mr. Bilton relates what happened. "I was driving along Warwick Avenue with Mr. Brough and I could see a dark object approaching. The car radio started to suffer some interference. We stopped the car, and we got out". "The object looked black and was silhouetted against a less dark sky.

154

It had three dull, red, steady lights set slightly in from the edges. It passed over at about 200ft high, with no sound". "I estimated it to be about 600ft long." "At one stage it bridged (extended) from the park, over the dual carriageway and over the houses ", (see sketch), "I have no idea of the depth of it, as it passed directly overhead. The air seemed very heavy or 'charged' as it passed over. It appeared to be one solid object".

Alan Hitchcock interviewed Mr. Bilton on the 8th of December 1992. In the investigation form notes, Mr. Bilton states:

(1) He observed the object for about one minute.

(2) The size of the craft, as viewed from his position, extended from fingertip to fingertip with both arms outstretched.

(3) It was travelling S.W. at an awfully slow speed of about 5mph.

(4) It made no sound as it passed overhead, and the atmosphere felt "heavy."

(5) The shape of the craft was triangular, and the outline was clearly defined.

(6) The object flew out of sight into the overcast, dark sky. Alan Hitchcock has pointed out that this craft appears to be similar in size to the object seen and photographed by

Garry Stapleton on 11th November 1992 near Breadsall, Derbyshire.

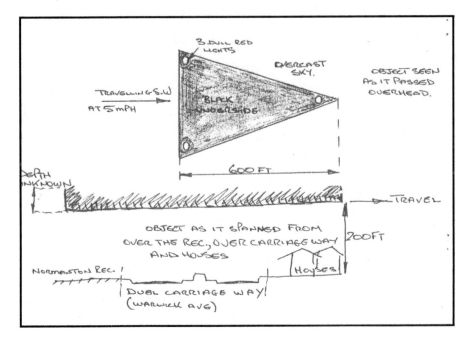

Mr. Bilton's sketch

Upper Pleasley, Derbyshire 3-11-1992

Mark Haywood, the investigations coordinator of the Mansfield based "Scientific UFO Research Association", had a nerve-racking experience, when driving down Newboundmill Lane, Upper Pleasley. He spotted what he described as a large, triangular shaped object through his car windscreen. Initially, the object appeared to carry three large very bright white lights.

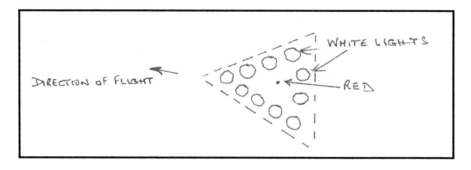

The object, which was heading towards the car, turned
slowly and it was then possible for Mark to observe lines
of four bright lights on each side of the object, with a small
red light in the centre of the triangle.

Although Mark had a camera with a telephoto lens on the
back seat of his car, he was so alarmed by the size of the
object that he accelerated away from the scene. However,
he did have time to notice the object disappear out of sight
over nearby rooftops. Mark commented that he heard no
sound and was certain that the object was not an aircraft.

Breadsall, Derbyshire, 11-11-1992

21.50, Garry Stapleton, his daughter Emma and her
boyfriend Shaun were driving along a country road near
Breadsall, when they noticed a single point of bright light
in the North-West. The light appeared to be approaching
them and the car was halted, and the windows wound
down. Fortunately, Garry had a pair of 8x50 binoculars
with him and was able to observe the approaching light. At
this stage, he was able to see a number of other lights

associated with the object (see sketch). All three occupants of the car got out and watched fascinated as the lights came closer. There was no discernible noise and the object appeared to be fairly low (estimated height 1,500ft) and moving at a steady pace, approx. 200mph. It was at this stage that Garry's daughter Emma became worried and wanted to get back into the car.

The lights continued their approach until they were nearly passing overhead. The object was by all accounts pretty large; Garry described it as "awesome". It was at this stage that Shaun took several colour photographs with a small Olympus 35mm camera. (The camera had no telephoto lens and had a coupled flash with each exposure.) As the huge object passed almost overhead, the group were able to make note of the lighting arrangements, no "strobe lights" were visible and it was not possible to see the shape. No noise other than possibly a faint jet (or airflow) noise could be heard. The object continued on its line of flight in the direction of Castle Donnington until it was out of sight.

The Investigation

Garry later telephoned the East Midlands Airport, who informed him that no aircraft should have been in that area at the time and certainly not flying that low! A Royal Air Force source has stated that the description of the object does not conform to standard aircraft identification lighting.

We have since had the Kodak film processed by the Mallard Laboratories at Kimberley, and special arrangements were made to increase the development to compensate for night photography (100ASA increased by two stops). The negatives revealed a number of lights in triangular formation, and this confirms the eye witness's description of the huge size of the object. Further means are being investigated to have the photographs enhanced; this should assist with further analysis and investigation of the object.

There has been some speculation that the object may have been an American Air Force "Stealth" aircraft. They are known to have gone to extraordinary lengths to maintain the secrecy surrounding this aircraft. The size of the craft could possibly have been compared to a B2 "Stealth Bomber" and the lighting arrangement could have been a modification of the "Yehudi" lighting used experimentally on earlier aircraft. In this instance, the lights could have been arranged to disguise the actual shape of the aircraft. If the line of the aircraft's flight is extended Southeast, it would bring it close to the American Air Force base at North Luffenham in Leicestershire.

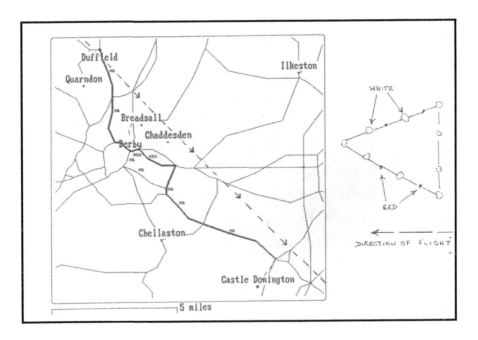

Garry Stapleton's sketch

The argument against the object being a Stealth aircraft is: (a) The extremely low altitude of the objects flight (b) The absence of flashing "strobe" lights (c) The quietness of the object at such a low altitude (d) The mounting of numerous lights along the wings, when the whole concept of the Stealth craft is to disguise its presence. For no other reason other than the aircraft is at present unidentified, it must be classified as an "unidentified flying object", a UFO!

Clacton-on-Sea, Essex, October 1993

Three witnesses walking their dogs along Clacton sea front, and one witness walking along Holland-on-Sea front, witnessed a large, black, triangular shaped object move in from the sea, pass over the coast in a westerly direction, having just come from the east. "It was at least the size of a football field, if not more. There was not a sound as this object passed just ahead of us. Height, I would not like to estimate, but it was not extremely high. We could see numerous red lights at the back of the object, no other lights were showing." "It moved over Clacton sea front into the residential part, where it disappeared from our view. The time was approximately 8.45·p.m. and the whole event only lasted for approximately two minutes.

I would estimate the speed of the object to be around 20-25 M.P.H. It seemed impossible for such a large object to be moving so slowly in the sky."

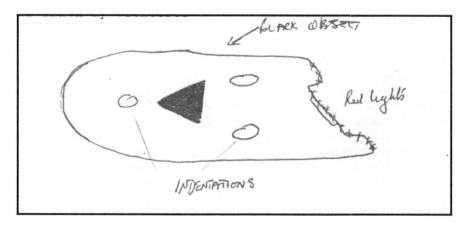

Holland-on-Sea, Essex, 5-11-1993

161

The 5th of November, Sunday, 7.30 p.m. looking out of our front room window which overlooks the sea (Holland-on-Sea). I saw a large triangular-shaped object moving along the sea front, approximately 2/300 yards out from the shore.

The object was massive, at least one to two times the size of a football field, it had one large white light at the front (that did not give out a beam) there were quite a few different coloured lights in the middle and there were either nine or thirteen red lights at the back. There was no noise, which was strange for a vehicle that size. I watched it until it disappeared towards the old Butlins site at approximately 40/50 mph.

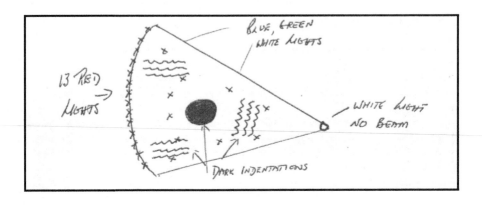

Cannock, Staffordshire 29-3-2015

A strange craft spotted moving slowly and loudly across the night sky has sparked off a UFO frenzy. Hundreds of Cannock (Staffordshire) householders took to social media after first hearing a loud drone, then spotting the massive object move slowly over their homes. Many believe that there is a very earthly explanation for a Close Encounter that has the community buzzing. Locals in the Staffordshire town believe they saw a secret military prototype, possibly from a US aircraft carrier currently stationed off Portsmouth. The British UFO Research Association (BUFORA) has not discounted claims that a drone might be responsible for the rash of reports. One thing is for sure, the people of Cannock saw something!

The area has been a UFO hotbed since the early 1980's, but last week's incident is the biggest in terms of the sheer volume of sightings. Shortly after the 'X Files' incident at around 9pm on Tuesday (24th March), Facebook sites were awash with details of the UFO alert. One individual posted: "My house was rumbling and I'm still shaking. It was slow and it was huge."

Another wrote: "Way too slow for fighter jets. It flew directly over our house, made a sharp left turn and carried on." The craft, sporting three red lights, was so low that many feared it was a plane in trouble. Paranormal investigator Lee Brickley witnessed the same phenomenon and began blogging as the drama unfolded.

He described the thunderous rumbling as like a WW2 bomber. "Before anything could be seen with the naked eye, there was a deep and very loud droning" he said. "After about three minutes, the craft came into sight. It seemed incredibly large and astonishingly low in the sky, with three red lights that were noticeable." "The UFO travelled very slowly, and many people thought it was about to crash." Lee claimed you could still hear the growl of the engines after the mystery machine disappeared." Cannock journalist Hannah Hiles, who has worked for the Sunday Mercury, was also alerted by the thunderous noise.

"It was ever-so-loud, and it went on for quite a while" she said. "It was much more prolonged than a military jet, It was very curious." Another resident described the sound of jets followed by a loud whirr, akin to propellers. The reports (and Lee is still collecting them), have spawned three theories: Members of the public did see something from another planet, or they witnessed a plane in distress, or they saw an experimental military craft, a so-called "black project", being tested over Staffordshire. Lee added: "I've checked on-line with flight tracking services and have concluded that it would be impossible for this to have been a plane in trouble. There simply weren't any flights in the area at that specific time." "I also contacted Birmingham Airport to make sure and they confirmed none of the flights leaving or arriving at the airport experienced issues that would have led then to fly so low."

A number of recent UFO alerts have turned out to be drones, BUFORA, which takes a skeptical view of alien claims, reveals that could well be an explanation for Tuesday night's sightings. A spokesperson said "I' m sure it is something that can be explained. Whether it will be explained is another matter." "There are so many drones around" She stressed that tests of secret military machines are fact, not fiction. "Development of new black projects - military hardware and vehicles can take between 20 and 30 years." "We are not going to know about the developments and tests that go on. There are so many reasons why people see things in the sky."

Triangular UFO Event in Cornwall, 28-4-2014

An unidentified flying object (UFO) was spotted by several people in the skies above Portreath last night. The mystery object, which has been described as "quite large" and "triangular", was spotted around 11pm by households in the Porthreath and Helston areas. Now founder of the Cornwall UFO Research Group (Cuforg), Dave Gillham, is appealing for witnesses to come forward to shed some light on the unexplained aircraft. Mr. Gillham said: "I like to log these things to find out what they are." Apparently there were quite a few people who saw the sighting last night. "It's nice to hear from people who have had sightings and most people do appreciate someone who is interested in it, as when they tell people who are not interested, they tend to get ridiculed, and they become reluctant to talk about sightings." Mr. Gillham said: "It had a lot of white lights at the front but none that I could see at the back." "It came from the Porthreath area and very slowly and quieter than a helicopter or plane [and] headed towards Helston." "It was definitely not a helicopter or plane." "It was quite clearly visible to the naked eye, but not on my camera phone."

One witness, who wishes to remain anonymous, had an eerie experience after attempting to capture the UFO on her camera phone. She said: "It was an odd shape, very bright and quieter than normal. It was not an airplane or helicopter "I videoed it, watched it [and] went inside and next morning it was gone from my phone. Just a mass of bright light." Mr. Gillham is keeping an open mind about the UFO and has admitted that it was seen on a flight path to the RNAS Culdrose naval base.

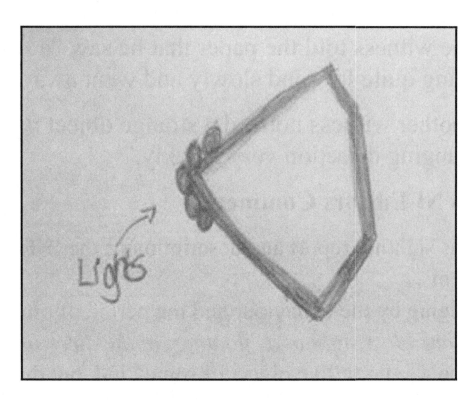

Witness Drawing

This chapter like the rest of the book isn't meant to be definite but I think it's fair to say that Omar contributed significantly into the research and investigation of the triangle-shaped UFOs and much more.

****

167

Chapter 6

More UK witnesses

There are literally thousands of UFO reports around the world of all manner of UFOs and strange lights in the sky, we have already looked at the local sightings I have collected in and around Hinckley, Leicestershire and now we shall look at other triangular UFO reports from around the country, again in chronological order.

Josephine Howard (pseudonym) November 1985, 7.30pm Darwen, Lancashire.

Full credit to Philip Mantle for this report.

On the night in question Mrs. Josephine Howard was walking to her car outside her home in Darwen, Lancashire. She just happened to look up and observed two round, red lights in the sky. The lights were about the size of car headlights. Her curiosity aroused; Mrs. Howard stopped to take a better look. There were no 'beams' coming from the lights and as they came overhead there was no noise. She described the scene: "I could not see the lights as it moved overhead, but I could see the underneath of the object. This object was exceptionally large and seemed to be very heavy-looking. I kept wondering how something so big and heavy-looking could move so slowly and not make a noise. I kept watching and took in as much detail as I could. The object was huge, and its underneath had what looked like round-headed studs. The object moved overhead, and I kept watching it until it was almost out of sight, at which point it seemed to tilt upwards and shoot off at a great speed and was gone."

Mrs. Howard reaffirmed to me and my fellow researcher, Rodney Howarth, that when passing over the object moved very slowly, but when moving off it was extremely fast indeed. The witness estimated that she had the object in sight for about eight minutes in total which is a long time for UFO sightings. It was a 'diamond' shape (Pic.18) with two lights at the front and it was totally noiseless at all times.

She estimated that to her it was 200-300 feet above her and that to the best of her knowledge no one else was around at the time to see this thing. The weather conditions at the time were reported as being overcast and cool with no wind.

Mrs. Howard lived in the town of Darwen with her husband and family and although she was interested in UFOs, she had never seen anything like this object before. A full interview was conducted by the investigators at the time and as a result the case was labeled as 'unidentified.'

Drawing of the diamond-shaped object done by witness Mrs. Josephine Howard.

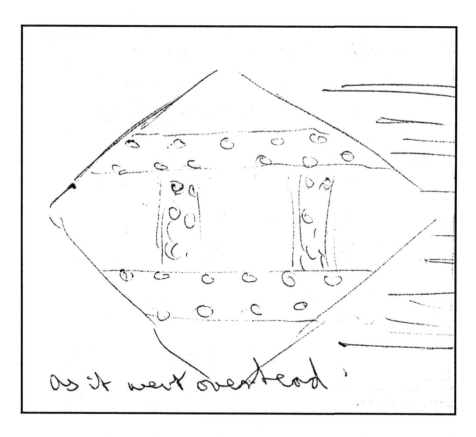

as it went overhead

Pic.18 Object seen by Mrs. Howard

John Stoddard, December 1986 7.22am, Bonsall Moor, Derbyshire.

Credit again to Philip Mantle for this report: Mr. John Stoddard, (real name) along with his wife and child, had been on holiday at a small cottage near Bonsall Moor. They had to get up early in order to vacate the cottage at 10.00 am on the 31st of December 1986. At around 7.22am Mr. Stoddard was standing outside of the cottage simply looking at the stars. It was a bright and noticeably clear morning when Mr. Stoddard noticed that one of the stars began to move.

It started to move in his direction from over the hills in the distance. At this point he shouted for his wife to join him and when she did, she too confirmed that the star was indeed moving in their direction.

By now the star was just above some trees at the bottom of a nearby field. It was still 'star-shaped' but had got bigger. The witness thought it had three 'fins' at the back of it but is not 100% sure.

The object came right by them and the back-end of it seemed to open up into a giant triangle with a lot of white lights all around it, but black in the middle. The object was moving very slowly, no more that 5-10 miles per hour, and all they could see was this giant 'thing' up in the sky above the trees and it made no sound at all. Both Mr. and Mrs. Stoddard were excited by this sighting but a little scared at the same time. The object moved slowly out of view over the moors.

Mr. Stoddard went on to inform us that his daughter had also viewed the object, she stood at the doorway of the cottage, but went back inside as she was a little scared of it.

The witness described the object as being the size of a double-decker bus and he has never seen anything like it before. Yet again, after an investigation by me and my colleague Dave Kelly, this sighting was labeled as 'unidentified.'

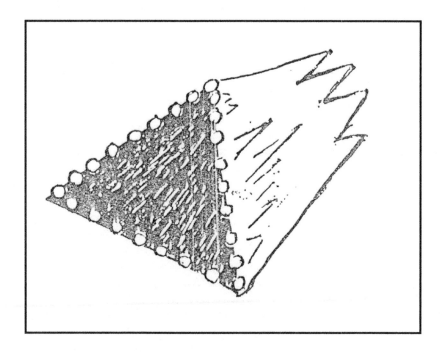

Pic. 19 Object witnessed by Mr. Stoddard

I would like to thank Philip Mantle for this interesting account:

My Mid-Atlantic Encounter

A few years ago, now a gentleman whom I will call 'Albert,' (real name on file), contacted me after listening to

173

me on a podcast and this is how he introduced himself. His message was 'my Atlantic encounter.'

"Hello Mr. Mantle, I am a Brit ex-pat now living in Florida. I fly for an airline and had an extended sighting of a 'classic' large, black triangle Mid-Atlantic some years ago, which has caused me to be interested in UFOs/UAPs ever since. I was just listening to you on the Paracast podcast from late last year. It is such a breath of fresh air to listen to someone like yourself, who is grounded, realistic and honest with a considerable depth of knowledge. Finding someone who is a genuine researcher rather than a person with extremist views is sadly uncommon in this field of study. I will take up no more of your time; I simply wanted to say Thank you."

As you can see Albert few details of a sighting he had 'some years ago.' Naturally, I was intrigued by this and sought further information. Thankfully, he was happy to oblige, but requested that I did not use his real name. Here are the details of his Atlantic Encounter.

"Hello Mr. Mantle,

Today I am a flying cargo specialist (known as a Loadmaster) with a major cargo airline, but in 1993 (Jan/Feb) I was a Senior Purser Flight Attendant with Northwest Airlines. I have been in the airline industry and flying professionally since 1984, - roughly 28,000 hours in the air. Not exactly a novice.

On that particular trip we were travelling from Boston in the USA to Glasgow, Scotland on a DC-10. After a breakfast meal service, I was fulfilling my role of basically being an 'ambassador' for the company, checking that all our passengers were happy, when I noticed the last half dozen rows on the left side of the plane were all staring intently out of the windows. I made some sort of a light-hearted remark about a pretty sunrise, and then asked, "What is so exciting, what are you all looking at?" - I remember that absolutely precisely - as I do the reply from a middle-aged Scottish gentleman, who said: "You tell us".

I had expected a cloud formation or nearby aircraft on a similar course (track) across the Atlantic, but actually saw a physical object which in my estimation was three times our size (450-500 ft) and about three or four thousand feet below us. It was moving gradually North-to-South in relation to our plane, and after about ten minutes it vanished below/behind our tail. It seemed to be moving slower than we were (200kts) and moving left to right diagonally. At the time our aircraft was flying at 32,000 – 34,000 feet.

The hull was like charcoal, virtually non-reflective, there were three faint white lights at each corner. I saw no features or windows. It exhibited no unusual flight characteristics and seemed to move consistently in the same direction, like it was oblivious or indifferent to us. I went up to the flight deck as fast as I could and asked the pilots what they thought it was. (The aft windows of the DC-10 are huge and have a very wide viewing angle).

All three pilots saw the object and the Captain said (quote); "That is very unusual, we should talk about that after the flight". At no time did it appear on our TCAS, (Traffic Collision Avoidance System).

DC 10 aircraft

Later (in the van to the hotel), the Captain told me he was not willing to say anything that would be recorded on the (CVR) Cockpit Voice Recorder - but he confirmed that he had seen precisely what I did, and he then also volunteered seeing a formation of three 'intensely reflective' disks the size of a house' when he was a Captain with the US Air Force flying F-18's back in the late 80's over a forest in Indonesia, the First Office also confirmed the sighting.

I have no evidence for my story; we all witnessed this a few years before the proliferation of mobile phones with cameras, but it is a moment forever stuck in my mind as it changed my universal view.

I have attached a picture from Google images that are simply the closest thing I can find on the internet to represent what I was looking at.

Best Regards, Albert"

As I have done on many previous occasions with witnesses, I went on to ask Albert a number of questions such as: 'Did you or your colleagues make an official report and what did you think was the nature and origin of the object you observed back in 1993 and looking back what do you make of it all now.'

Thankfully, Albert was prepared to answer my questions for which I thank him, and his answers are very thought provoking indeed.

"Hello Mr. Mantle,

I'm afraid not. The Captain was emphatic that he was not willing to report the incident. We actually had a few beers that evening and discussed the event. He felt that it was a 'career ender' for him. I felt that if I contacted BUFORA or MUFON I would be omitting a major part of the story if I didn't reveal that I had pointed it out to the crew on the Flight Deck but had to respect his choice not to get involved. I have thought on the subject many, many times and wish that I had made a bigger deal out of it, perhaps asking the passengers if I could get their contact information, to verify what we'd seen.

I'd guess probably a dozen people on the plane saw the object. I was just afraid that it'd become a circus and reports would get back to the company that I was being weird and bothering passengers. - Oh, for camera phones back then!!

So, in answer to your question, perhaps a mix of revelation and happiness at having seen this extraordinary thing, along with a sense of disappointment at myself for not making it as much of a 'big deal' of it as I should. Certainly today, a quarter century later, I would have been far more interested in getting this on the news or at least adding this story to the catalogue of mass encounters.

All the stories I had heard of before that, seemed to feature some version of a cigar-shaped object, a silver disc, or similar. I had never even heard of a black triangular craft.

When shortly afterwards I was doing some research, and for the first time saw images from the 'wave' over

Belgium, I was astounded and felt in some ways that my encounter was corroborated, for want of a better expression.

Back then, I was convinced that these things were physical 'nuts and bolts' interplanetary machines under the control of E.T's. Today I am less sure and feel that there is possibly a far stranger esoteric explanation. I have a hard time even putting my concepts into coherent words.

Time or Dimensional travelers perhaps? Something so peculiar that we have a hard time wrapping our minds around it, and this is how our brains express our experience? An as yet unquantified natural phenomenon seems to explain many of the mysterious lights to me.

The governments and military of the world are against us having any conclusive knowledge of what this is.

I'm sure a very mundane explanation such as military aircraft or disinformation campaigns account for a lot of reports, but certainly not all.

Sadly, I fear we never will know, but if any light is ever going to be shed on the subject, it'll be thanks to the hard work of people such as yourself.

Regards, Albert"

As Albert has outlined, he has no evidence to support his story but nonetheless it is an intriguing account. Over the years he has obviously pondered on what the object may or may not have been. Ultimately you will have to make up your mind whether he is telling the truth or not. It's as simple as that.

Michael James, Twickenham, London 1990's

"From 1990 onward I was living in Twickenham and working in central London as an Admin manager for a private Travel Agent. I lived in a house at the top of Clive Road a cul-de-sac which backed on to the open space playing fields and accommodation blocks of St Mary Teacher Training College. We had had two dogs, but one had died and every evening in 2001 we would give them a final walk usually around 10.30 or 11pm.

On this particular evening I took the dog out about 10.45, it was mid-November and most of the leaves had gone from the trees in the college grounds at the end of the road. As I reached the last but one house from the end I noticed two bright lights in the distance, like planes landing lights, shining directly towards me through the bare branches.

Now as we lived under the eastbound direction of the Heathrow flight path, I had a sudden panic as these lights were too low for a plane taking off, because they are usually in a steep climb...these lights were coming straight at me, and I froze. Was there a plane coming down it was much too low.

180

There was no moon that night and very few stars as we had old fashioned sodium lighting so you wouldn't see many anyway.

As the lights approached it became obvious that it was not a plane; there was no noise, the two bright forward lights vanished and were slowly replaced by a dull, almost florescent-like circular light emitting no illumination, at the height it was at the light would have been about 5 or 6ft in diameter. As the object moved overhead two more similar lights appeared at the rear forming a triangular shape and it was extremely large, dominating the sky above me. There was also a bright red pulsing light in the centre of the other three. I say pulsing, but it also spun slowly.

There was no one else around and the whole area was deathly quiet, and I was frozen to the spot engrossed and dumbstruck by what I was seeing. I should have gone back to the house to get witnesses, but I couldn't move, either not wishing to lose this spectacle or otherwise, even the dog sat and watched.

The object had approached from what I think was a north westerly direction as Heathrow is seven miles away to the west. It was about 200 ft in the air, working on the basis the average house is about 25/30 ft high, the trees were up to 80 ft high. As it moved overhead there was a very dull hum, there is an electrical transformer in the top left corner of the street, so it could have been that, but I have never heard it hum before.

It flew dead straight dead-level, there was no deviation in its path, I just watched in awe as it passed over the road and houses on towards the Thames and south London. It was only when it was directly overhead I realised the shape was triangular and formed by the 3 dull lights, but then I became aware of the darkness and depth of blackness. It definitely was not individual units.

As to its size when the first light passed over, the others were still over the college grounds so it must have been at least 400 ft long and 250ft? wide at the rear.

I am/was a travel agent; I have flown on everything from a Cessna to the Concord (luckily). As I said, we live under the Heathrow flight-path; I know the size of the planes taking off, the noise they make and the steep climb angles, this thing was no plane. I took six or so minutes from first sight to watching it pass over and vanish into the distance, it was slow, probably about 30/40 mph. I did not have a mobile phone and smart phones didn't exist then.

The other strange thing is that between 10.45 and 11.20 there were no planes taking off, there had been earlier, and this time of night is usually busy with long haul flights, mostly then Jumbo's, *there had been no planes for thirty*

30 minutes, but as I came back up the road after walking the dog, at last a Jumbo roared overhead in steep climb.

When I got back into the house I told of my experience to be greeted by not skepticism, but tolerant belief.

I sent a letter/report to a chap called Omar Fowler whom I had heard about through an article in a paper about the Belgian Incidents and through an address in a UFO magazine in the local newsagents. I did not speak to anyone else; I did not want to be the local nutter! The only computer I had was a works travel computer, this is twenty years ago, and a lot has changed since then.

I must state that from initial sighting to it vanishing in the distance I was rooted to the spot could not have moved even if I wanted."

Fiona Williamson, 1997, Fife, Scotland

I live in Fife in Scotland, and in 1997 my husband and I were living in a flat, which was next to the coast, with a beautiful view across the River Forth. On 11th September 1997, at 7.55pm, I looked up to the window and saw, literally no more than 50 meters away, a huge black triangle - flat triangular side facing me. It had lights in each corner. I screamed and jumped out my seat towards the window.

By the time my husband ran through (because I had screamed) it had moved slightly - rotating slowly - behind trees. My husband, although also witnessing it, didn't see it full on as I had. We opened the window, wondering if we would hear something like a jet engine, or something like that, but we could hear was a very low hum, similar to what you would hear walking past a small electricity substation.

We watched it as it went behind the trees, and it followed the perimeter of the neighboring park, which was also the beach. I reported it to BUFORA and a couple of weeks later they did get back to me, confirming there were no known aircraft in the area that night. They also asked me if I had any missing time, and if anyone had called asking me questions about it (apart from them obviously!). There had been nothing like that, although there was one strange anomaly that I don't go around telling everyone about, is that the day after the sighting, three small red spots, in the shape of a triangle, appeared on my forehead, just at my hairline.

At first I thought they were just that, spots, but they have never gone away. They have faded slightly over the last couple of years but are still slightly visible twenty-five years later. Not long after this, there was a TV show on one evening about UFO sightings, and it included an experience by some people in a car, not far away from where we are. What they described was exactly the same as I had seen. I think their experience is well-documented online, it happened around Falkland Hill and the villages of Falkland and Ladybank.

Nora Jones (pseudonym), South Wales, 1990

"I am from Southwest Wales and around the 1990's I saw a massive black triangular shadow, the longest side started to ripple like a wave and then it just disappeared. It did not shoot off. It was darker than the night sky. The black triangular shadow was remarkably close above me; it was about the size of a double decker bus.

My first encounter with a UFO was about forty years ago. I was driving with the children, and they said 'look at that' it was a vertical cigar shape with vapor trails from its points, it went behind a small cloud, and I said we will see it when it comes out again, but it did not reappear.

A short while later after arriving at my sister's, I noticed the vapor trails were visible by the same cloud. It dawned on me years later that the cloud should have changed shape or dissipated by then. Over the years this is what I have seen since - driving down on my own from a mountain in the dark there were clouds around and a light was moving silently around in a cloud close to me, there was no sound.

I have seen two bright stars next to each other and the right one sparkled like a diamond and shot off to the right, then the left one did the same and shot off to the left. Another time a bright star did the same, but I can't remember if it shot off. There was what I thought was satellite, it stopped and did a 90-degree turn.

Once, early in the morning, the sky was a pale blue and there was a bright, solitary star not moving, I watched it for about a minute and it moved slowly off. A few months ago, a large white orb was moving around the horizon, and it turned orange. I know seeing lights in sky doesn't prove anything, but to me, seeing the triangular shadow proves that aliens exist"

"Ps. the triangular shadow made no noise and did not have lights"

Arthur Wight (Pseudonym) Bristol, August 1991

"Hi Colin, have just seen your message on social media re Triangular UFO's and thought I'd recount my sighting. I was travelling home from work about 12.15am either August or September in 1991. I had just left the city of Bath, travelling on my motorcycle along the A4 towards Bristol, when I happened to notice a set of lights in the night sky off to my right. After travelling for around five minutes, I had reached the village of Saltford, and I was able see that this object was almost overhead.

In Saltford there is a fairly steep hill, and as I rode up it I was able to look up at this craft and saw that the outline

186

was made up of three white lights, with a really deep red (almost the colour of fresh blood) flashing light to their centre. The craft was travelling in a North-South direction crossing over the road and what appeared to be around walking pace. It was no more than a couple hundred meters above the top of the houses on the top of the hill. I vaguely remember that there was a car behind me, so I was unable to stop, but other than the noise of my motorcycle and the car behind, I do not recall hearing any other noise."

"After passing beneath the craft, I lost sight of it and never saw it again. I hope this sighting is of interest, thanks for taking the time to read this. Again, I asked the question, have you had any other experiences? His reply was: "Yes, I have had numerous other experiences, I have tended to work nights most of my career and being interested in the UFO subject, I do look at the skies as often as possible. My first experience of something unusual was when I was fifteen and have seen many things I don't understand or can truly explain."

"I am interested in most paranormal subjects and have experienced a few things that I still question and prefer to keep an open mind on. I have seen so many things and experienced unusual things I often question myself, I don't know if things happen because I am open minded and pay more attention than most people would. I just describe what I have experienced, but as with my triangle experience, I don't know if it was from this planet or not, only that I saw it."

Jason Gleaves 31ˢᵗ March 1993 RAF Cosford UFO Incident

There were many sightings across western Britain of triangular shaped UFOs moving across the sky at speed. Military personnel at both RAF Cosford and RAF Shawbury, including members of the public, reported seeing the triangular shaped UFOs. Coincidentally our sighting was also the 31ˢᵗ of March, but in 1999, obviously the next day was April fools' day, which made reporting just that little bit more difficult. Jason Gleaves was there on the night in Cosford, and I am grateful for this report he has sent to me.

"Over Twenty-nine years ago, on 31ˢᵗ March 1993 at around 1:15 am, there were several UFO sightings of a large, black, triangular shaped objects witnessed over the skies of England. One of the sightings happened at RAF Cosford Air Force Base over the airfield itself, I should know because I was present on the base that night and through work colleagues had firsthand account of the event.

"The craft was witnessed by base personnel including guard patrols, the guard commander and military police and was described to be the size of a battleship (huge in size), covering most of the runway because of its enormous size."

"Other sightings were witnessed across the entire U.K. that evening, including the West Midlands region, Cornwall and Devon, but what made the big news headlines at the time had been the important claim by Met Office staff and military personnel at both nearby RAF Shawbury and RAF Cosford, who reported the incident independently."

"Several UFO websites considered the UFO sightings as a major sign that Extraterrestrial life really exists, another plausible theory to consider is it could have possibly been a military covert project or part of the secret space fleet that Scottish computer hacker and systems administrator Gary McKinnon accidentally stumbled upon when hacking into the NASA administration computers back in 2002."

"The incident happened around the period, when throughout the 1980's-1990's, other sightings were seen of similar large black triangular-shaped craft all around the world. One memorable incident was over Belgium and involved F16 Belgian military jets is well documented".

LARGE BLACK TRIANGULAR SHAPED CRAFT INSERTED IN 2016 PHOTOGRAPH OF THE EXACT AIRFIELD GUARD POST LOCATION AT RAF COSFORD AIR FORCE BASE U.K. WHERE THE INCIDENT HAPPENED DURING MARCH 1993

Artist impression by Jason Gleaves

Retired British Ministry of Defense civil servant Nick Pope submitted a report to the MoD, saying that a UFO was able to operate in the UK Air Defense Region without being observed on radar. He added that this condition could be a threat to security and recommended further serious investigation."

"At the time of the incident in March 1993 a colleague of mine had been on duty as the Orderly Corporal in charge of the station main guardroom, also incorporated within the same building was the off-duty guard patrol personnel, where they would be during off duty periods awaiting their time to conduct their assigned guard duty or patrol."

"Everything was ticking over quietly as the late night rolled into the early morning, when suddenly, the handheld radio docking station located in the main guardroom burst into life, crackling out message after message of strange events unfolding over at the airfield guard post? The sender of the message was a young trainee airman 18 or 19 years old and he sounded quite distressed, so far as I'm aware the message contents had been a bit sketchy and at times inaudible, basically saying "it's huge, it's huge and over the airfield...get somebody out here, it's the size of a battleship" apparently upon hearing this all hell broke loose in the guardroom, things obviously quickly escalated and airmen and military police personnel got kitted up and ready to move under orders from the on-duty guard commander. They all got in their supplied standard Land Rover vehicles and Sherpa vans and proceeded to head out towards the airfield location which was only located approximately 800 yrs away from the main guardroom.

Upon arrival at the airfield gate the patrol and Air Force staff were confronted by the young trainee airmen, by this time was quite distressed by his encounter and the sight of the huge battleship-sized craft hanging there above the airfield quietly and motionless (no visible undercarriage). It was described as triangular in shape and jet matt-black in colour with few lights. I'm not too sure of the timescale, but it then silently accelerated away at high-velocity into

191

the distance, there was no sign of engine afterburners etc, towards its next location, RAF Shawbury, which was nearby.

Shawbury Air Force base at the time was an operational Helicopter base and had a twenty-four-hour operational air traffic control tower. It was the on-duty air traffic controller (Met Officer) who witnessed a triangular shaped craft of a similar description to that seen at nearby RAF Cosford approach the airfield runway at Shawbury.

It was flying in a very erratic manner, estimated at hundreds of miles-per-hour, and it appeared to be firing some kind of very thin light or laser from the craft to the ground. The opinion of the personnel who witnessed the event, thought, or got the impression, that the craft was looking for something or possibly surveying the area in general." "Other important and relevant information regarding the 'Cosford incident' is from a few years ago when the U.K. Ministry of Defense released important documents and reports of this encounter which back up what was witnessed and seen by the personnel in attendance at the military establishments."

Jason Gleaves, Ufonly, International author of UFO PHOTO, The Ufology Umbrella and UFO ENCOUNTERS up close and personal.

John Hanson and The Great British UFO Archive

Retired CID Detective John Hanson

There are many researchers in the UK producing books on all aspects of UFO's, but none is more prolific than John Hanson, a retired CID Detective from the West-Midlands. John has written a plethora of books on UK UFO sightings and encounters, and I would recommend that anybody researching the subject and looking for information would be well advised to get in touch with him via social media. John has been kind enough to allow me to reproduce some of his many triangle sightings in this book and here is a selection of his witness reports.

Glowing orange UFO seen over RAF Bentwaters/Woodbridge Air base Suffolk – January 1995.

Paul Pittock was driving from Woodbridge to Melton, Suffolk, one evening in January 1995, when he saw a bright light hovering in the sky above the now closed Royal Air force Woodbridge/Bentwaters airbase. Curious, he stopped the car by the side of the road and watched with surprise as the 'light' began to move from side to side in the sky.

Rushing home, he picked up his telescopic sight and, accompanied by neighbor - Richard Warnock, drove back to the Airbase, just in time to see whatever it was drop down towards the flight line and disappear. "As we stood by the entrance gate to the base wondering what was going on, over thirty military vehicles drove up. They included a military ambulance and a larger white vehicle, covered in aerials. After unlocking the gate, they then drove onto the Bentwaters Airbase, (closed some sixteen months ago). With tires screaming and lights flashing, the vehicles drove around the airbase, pointing searchlights into the sky, as if looking for something. There were even helicopters hovering overhead. We saw an orange/red glow emanating from the flight line - then a glowing triangular shape appeared. It had a distinct outline and could be seen clearing the slope. It stayed for a while and then left."

Civilian aircraft nearly collides with UFO! British Airway Pilots, 6th January 1995.

At 6.48 pm, 6th January 1995, British Airways Pilots - Captain Roger Wills, and First Officer, Mark Stewart - were preparing their final approach on-board a Boeing 737-200 Aircraft BA5061, with sixty passengers en-route from Milan to Manchester Airport, at 13,000 feet, over Saddleworth Moor, when something flashed silently past them, causing them to duck. The two men didn't discuss the matter fully, apart from radioing in to tell Air Traffic Control they had been 'buzzed by a 'V' shaped craft.' Mark said to the Captain, "Did you see that?" He replied, 'Yes, it was dark grey, and wedge shaped, with an even darker stripe down it, with no visible windows, not far from the starboard wing." According to the Air Traffic Control script, which was made public, some years ago, we learn of the following conversation: Wills: "We just had something go down the right-hand side, just above us, very fast."

Control Tower: "Well there's nothing seen on Radar. Was it, er, an aircraft?" Wills: "It had lights. It went down the starboard side very quick." Control Tower: "and above you?" Wills: "Er, just slightly above us, yeah" Control Tower: "Keep an eye out for something, er, I can't see anything at all so, er, must have been extremely fast or gone down very quickly, after it passed you I think. Wills: "Ok, well there you go." After landing, they independently sketched what they had seen. Both sketches were similar, although Mark suggested Captain Wills description of it

195

'resembling a Christmas tree, with a black stripe down its side' had been caused by reflection of the Boeing's landing lights, rather than the UFO being lit by an external source.

Another potential witness found to the above incident

Was there a connection with another UFO sighting (although the witness could not have known of the later incident, as details weren't released by the CAA until January 1996), involving Mark Lloyd, from Gatley, Manchester, who was driving along Style Road, adjacent to the Airport, at 3.30pm. (some two miles away), on the 6th of January 1995? "I was shocked to see a massive 'triangular craft' moving over the Airport, at a height of approximately 4,000 feet.

"I was so excited I had difficulty steering the car and had to pull up. I looked up and saw an Air Monarch aircraft, descending on its final approach onto the runway, and presumed they must have seen the UFO because it was so large."

"It moved from side to side in a sort of spiral movement in the air. I took a careful mental note. It was silver-grey in colour, glowing like the moon. Suddenly, its light came on.

All I could see was what looked like a black strip along its side. After it had gone I picked up my girlfriend and told

196

her what I had seen. She laughed at me. I was so annoyed I threatened to terminate our relationship."

"The next day, Mark telephoned Air Traffic Control, at Manchester Airport, and told them what had taken place.

They advised him to keep quiet, because two pilots had already filed a report regarding a near miss."

"Dissatisfied, Mark contacted the 'Sun' newspaper and spoke to one of the reporters, who promised to look into the matter, but nothing else was heard until the matter was brought to the public's attention, later, when he then contacted ITN News, who interviewed him and told his story, including an illustration compiled by Mark's colleague - Harold Withers. We placed an appeal in the newspaper, hoping to trace other witnesses present, according to Mark, but were unsuccessful."

"We weren't sure what to make of Mark; he appeared genuine enough, but seemed to be suffering from paranoia, with stories 'of a man in a dark trench suit, wearing a baseball hat, appearing at the end of his bed, who showed him a pump action shot gun.

He was apparently of American descent, although he never said a word during the encounter, and also of a Grey Alien who also appeared in the middle of the night."

None of these actions were witnessed by his girlfriend, who remained asleep. In addition to this, Mark complained of "being followed by sinister men, who were intimidating me"

■ FIRST Officer Mark Stewart. He and Captain Wills saw something which first made them duck, and then reach for the radio to call traffic control

First Officer Mark Stewart

Date/Time: 061848 Jan   **NIGHT**

Position: N5318 W0200 (8NM SE
                  Manchester Apt)

Airspace MTMA   *Class:* A

     Reporting Aircraft   *Reported Aircraft*

Type: B737   Untraced

Operator: CAT

Alt/FL: 4000 ft ↓
          (QNH 1027 mb)

Weather   VMC CLAC
Visibility: 10 km+

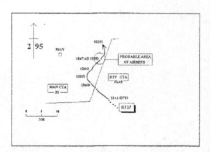

PART A: SUMMARY OF INFORMATION REPORTED TO JAS

THE B737 PILOT reports that he was over the Pennines, about 8 or 9 NM SE of Manchester Airport, at 4000 ft, while being radar vectored by Manchester radar on 119.4. He was flying at 180-210 kt on a N heading and squawking 5734 with Mode C selected. Although it was dark, visibility was over 10 km with a fairly strong NW wind (340/30). While flying just above the tops of some ragged Cu both he and the first officer saw a lighted (see JAS notes) object fly down the RH side of the ac at high speed from the opposite direction. He was able to track the object through the RH windscreen and side window, having it in sight for a total of about 2 seconds. There was no apparent sound or wake. The first officer instinctively 'ducked' as it went by.

The first officer reports that his attention, initially focused on the glare shield in front of him, was diverted to something in his peripheral vision. He looked up in time to see a dark object pass down the right hand side of the ac at high speed; it was wedge-shaped with what could have been a black stripe down the side. He estimated the object's size as somewhere between that of a light ac and a Jetstream, though he emphasises that this is pure speculation. It made no attempt to deviate from its course and no sound was heard or wake felt. He felt certain that what he saw was a solid object - not a bird, balloon or kite.

MANCHESTER ATC reports that the B737 was being radar vectored from Dayne to the ILS for RW 24 when the pilot reported a lighted object passing close by above and in the opposite direction. There was no known traffic in the vicinity at the time and no radar contacts were seen.

JAS Note (1): Telephone conversations subsequently took place with both the captain and the first officer. The captain remained convinced that the object was itself lit. Although he could not determine a definite pattern, he described it as having a number of small white lights, rather like a Christmas tree. He confirmed the high speed of the object, and though unable to estimate its distance, said he felt it was very close. Following the incident, the captain and first officer independently drew what they had seen, both agreeing about the shape but differing in their opinions about the lighting aspects. The first officer felt that the object was illuminated by their landing lights, which at that stage were switched on. He was unable to assess its distance, other than to say that he involuntarily 'ducked', so it must have appeared to him to have been very close. He was entirely convinced, as was the captain, that what they had seen was a solid object and not a Met phenomenon, balloon, or any other craft with which they were familiar, or a Stealth ac, which he had himself seen and which he feels he would have recognised.

JAS Note (2): Despite exhaustive investigations the reported object remains untraced. A replay of the Clee radar shows a number of secondary contacts, including the subject B737, being radar sequenced in the Manchester TMA and zone. The B737 tracks over two almost stationary primary contacts just N of Leek on a NW heading while descending through FL 70-60. On entering the Manchester TMA, passing FL 50, it is

Official 'Airmiss Report' no 2/95 part one.

vectored right onto about 040°, and continues to descend on a NE track along the E boundary of the Manchester TMA to within 0·75NM of the Daventry CTA, where the base of CAS is FL 45. At this point, passing 3600 Mode C, the ac is turned onto a L base for RW 24 as part of a busy sequence of inbound ac. At no time during this downwind leg is any other radar contact seen in the vicinity. An extract from the RT recording on 119.4, which shows that the B737 was given descent clearance to 4000 ft at 1845:30, follows:

From:

B737 (1848)-	"c/s we just had something go down the RHS just above us very fast."
Manchester -	"Well, there's nothing seen on radar. Was it er an ac?"
B737 -	"Well, it had lights, it went down the starboard side very quick."
Manchester -	"And above you?"
B737 -	"er, just slightly above us, yeah."
Manchester -	"Keep an eye out for something, er, I can't see anything at all at the moment so,er, must have, er, been very fast or gone down very quickly after it passed you I think."
B737 -	"OK. Well, there you go!"

The possibility that the object might have been a hang glider, paraglider or microlight was investigated, but all the operating authorities, without exception, agreed that this was an extremely unlikely explanation, for various reasons, but mainly because none of these activities takes place at night. In addition, there are the obvious hazards of flying in the dark, from high ground (the peaks in this area along the Pennine ridge range from 1600 to over 2000 ft), strong winds, and because these aircraft are unlit. JAS also explored the possibility of military activity, but could find no evidence in support of this from any official source. In any case, it seems most unlikely that such a flight would have been conducted in CAS and so close to a busy international airport. Because of the B737's proximity to uncontrolled airspace to the E of Manchester during the downwind leg, which covers the airmiss period, the possibility of unknown military or civil activity in the adjacent FIR cannot be completely discounted. However, the liklihood of such activity escaping detection is remote, as the area is well served by several radars and any movements at the levels in question would almost certainly have generated a radar response.

PART B: SUMMARY OF THE WORKING GROUP'S DISCUSSIONS

Information available to the Working Group included reports from the pilot of the B737, transcripts of the relevant RT frequencies, a video recording, and reports from the air traffic controllers involved.

The Group were anxious to emphasise that this report, submitted by two responsible airline pilots, was considered seriously and they wished to commend the pilots for their courage in submitting it, and their company, whose enlightened attitude made it possible. Reports such as these are often the object of derision, but the Group hopes that this example will encourage pilots who experience unusual sightings to report them without fear of ridicule. It was quickly realised by all members that, because of its unusual nature, they could only theorise on the possibilities once normal avenues of investigation had been explored. There is no doubt that the pilots both saw an object and that it was of sufficient significance to prompt an airmiss report. Unfortunately, the nature and identity of this object remains unknown. To speculate about extra-terrestrial activity, fascinating though it may be, is not within the Group's remit and must be left to those whose interest lies in that field. It is probably true to say, however, that almost all unusual sightings can be attributed to a wide range of well known natural phenomena. There are, of course, a few which defy explanation and thus fuel the imagination of those who are convinced that there is "something going on" out there. Usually activity of this kind is accompanied by a rash of ground sightings in the same geographic area; in this case, as far as is known, there were no other reports and therefore the incident has to be reviewed in isolation, with no other witnesses. The resources normally available when investigating airmisses are pilots' reports, corroborated by radar and RT recordings. Often these will provide all the clues necessary, but in this case there is no "reported pilot", and radar recordings do not show any unknown contacts. The lack of a radar contact is not necessarily

2

Official 'Airmiss' Report no 2/95 part two.

unusual if weather suppressors are in use on the radar, particularly if the object generates a poor radar response. In these conditions the radar can interpret a non-transponding (primary) contact as weather, and therefore disregards it. Enquiries into military activity did not reveal any ac in the area at the time, and it was considered inconceivable that such activity would take place so close to a busy airport without some sort of prior notification. Members put forward other suggestions, such as a large model aircraft or a commercially operated remotely controlled craft, such as those which are used for survey or photographic work. Considering the prevailing conditions - darkness, high ground, strong NW wind, and the proximity of a major international airport - the Group felt that this kind of activity, together with the hang glider/microlight theory, could not be regarded as a realistic possibility. As was pointed out by one member, however, the extreme actions of a foolhardy individual cannot be entirely ruled out and there remains, therefore, the possibility that someone, perhaps in a microlight ac (which most accurately fits the shape described), had defied the conditions and got airborne. Further talks with the microlight experts on this idea highlighted its extreme improbability; the strong wind, terrain and darkness would have rendered such a flight almost suicidal.

Having debated the various hypotheses at length the Group concluded that, in the absence of any firm evidence which could identify or explain this object, it was not possible to assess either the cause or the risk by any of the normal criteria applicable to airmiss reports. The incident therefore remains unresolved.

PART C: ASSESSMENT OF RISK AND CAUSE

Degree of Risk: Unassessable

Cause: Unassessable

Official 'Airmiss' Report 2/95 part three.

UFO kills fish in lake.? Ince Park, Manchester 23rd January 1995.

On 23rd January 1995, a number of people living near Ince Park, Manchester, contacted the Police, after sighting an orange-coloured object, approximately the size of a football, apparently having landed in the park, at 8.00 pm.

204

A search by Police Officers failed to reveal anything untoward. Coincidently, local UFO Investigator - Bill Eatock, sighted a triangular object crossing the sky over the main Wigan to Manchester road, during the same evening.

Bill told us on a visit to Ince Park: "I discovered a number of trees had been cut down, several holes were found in the grass, and a number of dead fish were discovered floating on the lake."

Further enquires made into the event, revealed part of the Park had been cordoned off by men wearing light-coloured overalls.

When the men were asked what they were doing, they showed MoD identification and ordered the residents to leave the area."

Schoolboy sees Triangle. Liverpool, March 11th, 1995.

March 11th, 1995, schoolboy - Steven Farrell, was at his home address, in Alvanley Road, Liverpool, when he saw "a triangular shaped object, with two red lights on the side, and a yellow one on top". Excitedly, he called his mother. She came running out and saw, "what looked like a large star, (except for the colours), showing red and yellow lights, making a buzzing noise." The sighting was corroborated by a local man, who was driving home, at the time, when he saw, "a bright light in the sky, flickering – like a strobe light, before dropping downwards behind a row of houses."

Light Aircraft Pilot sees huge black Triangle. Chorley Lancashire, 1ˢᵗ June 1995.

1ˢᵗ June 1995, Malcolm Smith - the Director of a printing company, based in Chorley, Lancashire, was piloting his light aircraft, five miles north-west of St. Helens, at a height of five hundred feet from the ground, when his co-pilot shouted out. "I looked downwards and saw 'a huge black, triangular shadow,' moving underneath us, over the landscape, at a speed I estimated to be no more than three hundred mph."

"I looked around but couldn't see any other aircraft, or object, which could have created this effect. Within twenty seconds the 'black, triangular shadow,' (rather than any structured craft), was out of view."

Black Triangular object over Somerset. Somerset, 15ᵗʰ June 1995.

At 1.30 am. 15ᵗʰ June 1995, Mr. Terrence McDonough, of Street, Somerset, was seated in his back garden, when he noticed a 'bright light' in the sky moving towards him. As it drew nearer, he was able to make out the shape of "a dark grey or black 'triangular craft,' showing a bright light

206

in each corner. It then halted in mid-air, a few hundred feet above him, overhead, making a strange sucking noise, like a giant vacuum cleaner, before moving away."

Sheffield UFO chased by two aircraft. Sheffield, South Yorkshire. July 29th, 1995.

At 12.15am 29th July 1995, Sheffield resident Wayne Brammer, and his brother sighted a triangular object showing a red light at each corner moving base first across the sky for about a minute until it disappeared out of sight towards the direction of Leeds. "About fifteen minutes later we noticed a bright amber ball of light appear in the sky from where the 'craft' had last been seen. This object travelled parallel along the horizon and then came to a stop, from out of this emerged a bright glowing red smaller object which headed upwards in a diagonal line. A few minutes later the amber ball reappeared in the sky this time being apparently chased by two aircraft which clearly were being outpaced by the object, seconds later they also disappeared from sight"

As a result of the matter being reported to BUFORA, it was ascertained that a similar object had been sighted around the Lincoln area by members of the Public and Police Officers twenty-five minutes earlier. In the same month, Mike Sutton, from Longbridge, Birmingham, well versed in aircraft identification, having worked in the

Aircraft industry for a number of years, was in his back garden, at 10.00 pm., accompanied by two friends, when they saw a black, triangular object, sixty degrees off the horizon, crossing the sky. "It had a bright orange light, set in the middle, surrounded by a dull red area. It reminded me of a gigantic piece of burnt paper, blown off a bonfire, without the flames but still glowing, I am sure it was a craft of some sort, rather than a natural phenomenon. We last saw it heading towards Northfield."

Gold Triangle spotted by police officers. Brislington, East Yorkshire, August 1995.

August 1995, Steven Turner from Bridlington was walking home along the sea front in the early hours of the morning when "I saw a dazzling gold coloured triangular object with a wavy spiral light underneath containing what appeared to be a rectangular box constantly rotating in different directions, there were at least two Police Officers who saw this UFO as well.

When we wrote to the Humberside Police asking for them to be put in touch with the Officers, they declined to do so, or offer any explanation as to why they wouldn't.

Triangle with force field? Powys, Wales, December 1995.

Mr. Emilio Petrosillo with a background in surveillance and systems crime prevention was driving through the army range in Bulith Wells, Powys, in December 1995 at 4pm, when he saw a metallic triangular object with a darker underside hovering silently in the sky to his right about a half a mile away a few thousand feet off the ground. "It seemed to be distorting the air around it as if generating some sort of force field; I estimate it was 60 feet long by 30 feet wide.

Triangular UFO over M6 Motorway with 'fridge' like pipe work. Birmingham, 22nd January 1996.

Midlands man Roger Smith was driving home along the M6 Motorway near Birmingham, just before midnight, the 22nd of January 1996 when he was astonished to see a triangular object hovering over the nearby electricity pylons, big enough to cover both lanes of the Motorway. "As I drove underneath it was able to obtain a clear view of its underside which showed a number of small red lights along its outer edges. In the middle was this huge white light. Radiating out from the centre were sections of what looked like the pipe work found at the back of domestic fridges, at each corner was a small white light, I wasn't the only one to see it others actually stopped on the hard shoulder to watch it'

Police sight Triangular UFO over Manchester. Broadheath, 7th February 1996.

Peter Wilson, a headmaster for a local Manchester school, was walking his dog on the evening of the 7th of February along a path by the side of the River Mersey in Broadheath when his friend shrieked and pointed directly above them "I looked and saw a large triangular shaped craft, showing three red apex lights and a large red light in the centre of the craft moving silently overhead." Alarmed, Peter reported the sighting to the local police station as soon as he reached home.

WPC Allen took the call at Altrincham Police Station and told Peter she would inform Officers who were in the area by the time they made their way to the scene the object had vanished.

Mrs. Spittle, an elderly woman from Stretford, was watching television in her flat on the top floor of a five-story block of flats in Urmston Road on the same evening, when a bright light flashed past her window. She walked over to the window and was amazed to see a "triangular craft flying at low level; it had three red lights at each corner and a large light in the centre of it. I watched the object darting backwards and forwards for about three minutes before going to get a neighbor. Mr. Thompson from next door who also saw the object before it shot off towards Manchester Town Centre."

Just after midnight on, February 8th, 1996, a Police Constable and two off-duty police officers reported seeing a low-level craft above the Lancashire County Cricket Club on the Stretford/Old Trafford border. It was described as "being triangular in shape with a 'girder' structure on its underside showing several lights, including three large, red, apex lights and four smaller white lights grouped together."

According to the officers, the object was massive, and made no sound whatsoever. After a short time, the object accelerated to an amazing speed and performed what appeared to be a display of aerobatics in the sky. The officers watched the object for several minutes before it sped off in a southerly direction. The following morning, one of the officers' contacted Manchester based UFO investigators and arranged to meet with them to discuss the sighting. During the afternoon of February 8th, the wife of one of the Officers received a visit by two men claiming they were from the Ministry of Defense at his home address asking for her husband.

"The two gentlemen were smartly dressed in dark suits and showed identification badges identifying themselves as Mr. Smith and Mr. Green and were invited in. They advised the Officer he should have reported the sighting to his Sergeant and should not have involved local UFO investigators.

They told him the object seen was a top-secret aircraft and the subject was considered extremely sensitive if he didn't co-operate he could lose his job.

The men left and said they would be in touch with him soon and not to say anything to anyone about what he had seen." As soon as they had gone the Officer telephoned the two other officers and was surprised to find out they had already received a visit from the 'two gentlemen' earlier that afternoon.

All agreed it was best not to talk about what they had seen. The next day, the officer telephoned the local UFO investigators and told them about the visit he and his associates had received and said he was no longer prepared to discuss the matter with them and no longer wanted to co-operate, as he feared he might lose his job or even worse. By February 11th, UFO investigators from the Manchester based group MAPIT, run by Steven Mera BSc, had received several calls from people who claimed to have seen the very same object; they included Michelle Booth and Gary Leigh who were travelling back from Michelle's mothers in Salford on February 8th.

As they drove down Barton Road Gary looked up and saw a 'huge triangular object' slowly cruising across the sky. The object met up with a smaller one and stopped over an industrial facility known as Courtaulds Chemicals. A woman walking her dog also saw the objects describing them as massive, mechanical type structures that hung in the sky without making a sound. she watched them for a few minutes before they slowly moved off towards Carrington. On February 14th, local UFO investigators visited Courtaulds Chemicals and talked to security officers Graham Mitchell and Roy Burgess who were in their guard house on the 8th of February. Roy told them he had heard a strange humming sound. He reached over and turned the radio down.

The humming seemed to be coming from outside. Graham grabbed a torch and went out to investigate. "About two hundred feet above us were two strange looking objects; triangular in shape with large white lights on them." Roy rushed back into the guard house and telephoned Chris Keaton the night manager. Two security officers, four truck drivers and at least sixteen members of the night staff watched as the objects silently turned and headed off towards Carrington Shell Refinery. The strange objects seen in Manchester did not reach Carrington Shell Refinery, nor did the local residents report seeing anything unusual that evening.

Some of the witnesses contacted Air Traffic Control at Manchester International Airport, who in turn alerted RAF West Drayton. The MoD later confirmed they had received reports from civilians which coincided with those of the Police Officers.

Whatever the objects were, the Civil Aviation Authority said they were not acknowledged on radar. We wrote to Chief Supt Hutchings B.A Hons MA at Talbot Road, Stretford Manchester asking him if he could put us in touch with the Police Officers involved in a UFO sighting over Old Trafford on the 8th of February 1996. We received a letter from Chief Constable David Wilmot Esq. QPM Dl BSc. on the 4th of April 2000. "Dear Mr. Hanson, I respond to your letter dated the 1st of April 2000, concerning your correspondence to Chief Supt Hutchings relative to alleged UFO sightings. I regret that I am unable to assist further as we do not appear to hold a report of such an event and have been unable to locate any officers who recall it"

Enquiries to the MoD revealed they had received three separate UFO reports between the 7th and 14th of February 1996, relating to a UFO sighted on the 8th of February 1996. A sighting at Sale (Bright green object lit up the sky) Stretford (A round red object moving erratically) Althrincham (single blue object moving north). Following another letter written to them they also sent to us a copy of a report containing the following information. A red-coloured object was seen moving up down, left and right, over Old Trafford Cricket Ground at 1am, whilst (witness details deleted) was travelling home along Kings Road Stretford. They claimed they knew nothing of Mr. Smith or Mr. Green. In fact, they stated 'no MoD Official would ever visit the homes of UFO witnesses' and as for the UFO's, they denied all knowledge of them, but did confirm a large number of reported sightings throughout the North West on that evening.

Pyramidal object seen hovering over Staffordshire field. Tamworth, Staffordshire, 7th March 1996.

At 12.30am 7th March 1996, Tamworth Staffordshire taxi driver Michael Sweet was driving back to the village of Sheepy Magna after dropping a fare off at 12.30am when he noticed a glowing light over a nearby field. "I thought a plane had crashed or was in trouble, so I stopped the car and got out to have a closer look, but was shocked to see a glowing mass of silver light resembling a pyramid made up of square blocks of silver light hovering a few feet off the ground, frightened, I drove away and had to take the rest of the week off to recover my composure"

Black Triangle follows the M5 motorway. Worcester, 7th March 1996.

At 9.30pm, 7th March 1996 the driver of a lorry parked overnight in the secure compound close to the M5/M50 Motorway services at Worcester was preparing to settle down for the night, when he saw, "a black triangular object showing a red light at each corner, one underneath and a green strobe light on top, hovering in the air a few hundred feet above me."

"I watched it slowly move away following the course of the M5 south before branching off towards the direction of Tewkesbury, imagine my surprise when a Hercules Aircraft appeared from the same direction and headed off along the path taken by the UFO. Being an ex-member of the Armed Forces I wrote to the MoD and explained what I had seen they wrote back saying it was of no defense significance"

Triangular formation of green lights. Lichfield, Staffordshire, 2nd April 1996.

Lichfield resident Lynda Bird was awoken at 1.45am, 2nd April 1996 by a quiet roaring noise and looked through the window to see a triangular formation made up of green lights moving point-first through the sky a couple of hundred feet in the air from her left to right over the treetops. "I leapt out of the bed with my heart thumping and managed to catch a brief glimpse of it before it went out of sight thirty seconds later; I found it an exciting experience and one that I hoped to see again"

Triangular UFO sighted over Eastbourne. Peckham, South London, 3rd April 1996.

At 4.20am 3rd April 1996, Olive Stookes of Peckham, who was staying overnight at a friend's house in Polegate, had trouble sleeping and got up to look out of the window when she saw what, " I thought was a satellite until I realized there were three different objects, silver red and green in colour each about the size of a small dinner plate in the sky heading from the direction of Hastings towards Lewes, as they passed overhead they appeared to change shape into triangles, within twenty seconds they were gone from sight" The Police who were contacted suggested she may have seen the Police Helicopter which was up during the same morning, which appears unlikely from the description given.

Black Triangular UFO panics boys out fishing! Milverton, Somerset, 4th May 1996.

At 8.30pm 4th May 1996, a 'large black triangular object with a white light in each corner and one near the centre making a low-pitched humming noise' was sighted flying overhead by James Rawle and Steven Wright while out fishing near Milverton, Somerset, panicking the boys who dropped their equipment and cycled away. Later that evening Jennifer Wilkins was driving home along the A44 towards Burton on Trent at 9.45pm, when near to the village of Overseal she noticed a light in the sky. "All of a sudden this massive blinding light swooped over the top my car; I flashed my lights on and off at it as it flew off northwards leaving me trembling with fear"

Did RAF jets attempt to intercept UFO? Chesterfield, Derbyshire, 7th May 1996.

From declassified Ministry of Defense (MoD) records released into the public domain during February 2010 we learn of a letter written by a woman from the Chesterfield area, who was looking out over Loch Linnhe at 10.5pm 7th May 1996 when she saw a red flashing object appear from the direction of Glen Tarben and cross the Loch heading in a southeast direction. "Five seconds after this we observed two military jets fly southwest down the loch and bank sharply SSE into Glencoeon what looked like an intercept course. We had not seen any military jets that day and this seemed too much of a coincidence."

"The flashing light was slower than the flashing light on a plane. The remarkable thing about this observation was the speed. When we got to the map we measured that we had observed the object over a distance of eleven miles.

It covered this distance in what I and my friend estimated to be six and seven seconds that puts it at a speed of

3600mph! What we observed could have been a 'Stealth aircraft,' 'Aurora' or similar, but why was it being pursued by a military jet? The object must have been picked up on radar. I would appreciate a sensible response to this letter not an excuse that nothing noticeable was brought to your attention on that particular night"

Five minutes later at 10.10pm David Parkes (aged 36) was with three friends enjoying the night air on Clacton on Sea beach, when they saw a black unlit triangular object in the sky a couple of miles away. A couple of minutes later it disappeared from view. Could there have been any connection with the previous, sightings, this is intriguing! Other witnesses included Stephen Johnson (aged 20) who was walking along the promenade with his girlfriend, when they saw four people on the beach who were excitedly pointing up into the sky, "We looked out and saw a black triangle hovering in the sky, a short time later it was out of view."

Triangular UFO sighted over Warwickshire with girders! Stratford-Upon-Avon, 5th August 1996.

On 5th August 1996, Carole Corden and Gillian Day, were travelling back from rehearsals held at Stratford-upon-Avon Theatre, Carole: "We were driving home along the A422, close to the Stag Public House, at Redhill, on the 5th of August 1996. We were a few miles out of Stratford-upon-Avon, when we noticed this massive bright light in the night sky to the North-west, but lost sight of it due to the trees lining the side of the road."

"As we approached Studley we were astonished to see the appearance of a triangular shaped object, showing an orange light at each tip, with what looked like girders, or lines, covering its outer surface. All of a sudden it was hovering over some tall trees on our left, opposite a caravan sales shop, before moving away for good."

Lancashire Triangular UFO chased by RAF. Wigan, Lancashire, 12th August 1996.

According to Wigan resident Bill Eatock, the local UFO Investigator, at 1.30pm., on the 12th of August 1996, a number of people living in the Wigan area of Lancashire heard the sound of a helicopter thrashing its blades overhead. "On going outside, they saw a Chinook twin rotor helicopter, flying extremely low, following a small matt black triangular object over the sky. Two minutes later, a Jaguar jet fighter passed low overhead with its undercarriage down and was seen to follow the course taken by the helicopter and UFO."

Bill happened to be in the area at the time and also witnessed the incredible sight of the UFO being followed by the helicopter, heading towards the direction of the Bury/Rochdale area, although he didn't see the Jaguar but heard it go over. In conversation with Bill, he told us the "Triangle was approximately 30 feet long, matt-black in colour and flying at a height of only 50 feet or so off the ground, in appearance it was very similar to the USAF Pilotless Drone." Even if it was the 'drone' we felt it was unlikely to be the answer for the many other sightings of what became labeled as the Flying Triangle which made their appearance in the early 1990's over the European skies.

Warwickshire Police notified after Golden Triangular UFO sighted in sky. Claverdon, Warwickshire, 26th August 1996.

The Warwickshire Police received a call from a member of the public reporting having sighted a "gleaming gold triangular shaped object in the sky about the size of a helicopter showing a number of lights along its side, at 10.30pm 26th August 1996, while driving near Claverdon. As it turned over it showed a number of black circles on the other side and was not any aircraft."

On this occasion we knew who the woman was as she had contacted us after having spoken to the local radio station after the event had taken place. Clearly from her description this was no aircraft.

I am not alone says UFO spotter. Henley, Warwickshire, 25th August 1996.

Gillian Hall a resident of Coventry, was driving home on a clear and dry night through Warwickshire at 8.15pm August 25th, 1996, along the B4095 just past Henley in Arden en-route to Warwick, when she noticed a brilliant light in the sky, "Far too bright to be an aircraft, I stopped the car and wound down the window, when I was astonished to see a triangular shaped object with a number of lights around it edges, and a red light at one end.

It was moving slowly over the landscape a few hundred feet off the ground. When I reached home I telephoned the local Radio Station, who informed me they had already been contacted by a local woman who I later spoke to about the matter, she asked me not to reveal her identity

Close Encounter Cornwall. Porthcurno, Cornwall, 9th September 1996.

At 3.45am 9th September 1996, a security guard (who asked for confidentiality) was carrying out a security check on foot at Porthcurno Lifeguard Station, Cornwall, which lies to the East of Lands' End. As he approached the station along a series of winding paths he noticed a pale-blue light illuminating the path approximately twenty-five yards away.

This was accompanied by the sounds of footsteps on the shingle. Curious he moved closer and shone his torch at the direction of the light emanating from behind a small group of trees, as he did so the light and 'footsteps' ceased. "My torch went out, in the dim light I just managed to make out the presence of two small figures moving away from me. I thought someone must be playing a practical joke, and after carrying out a security check of the Lifeguard Station made my way back to the car and drove home."

At 12.10am 9th September 1996, a grey-coloured triangular object 'the size of a duck in the sky' was seen at roof top level heading through the sky west to east at what was estimated to be 200mph over Shoeburyness.

The following morning the guard was once again on his way to the Lifeguard Station to complete his security check of the building halfway down the path, when he felt a band of hot, heavy air. Thinking it was residual warmth from nearby plant life he carried on walking. As the air cooled again, the man almost froze with fear at the sight of, 'Two strange glowing beings, four to five feet tall and milky white in colour. They were of slim build with large heads and almond-shaped eyes. There were two small holes, presumably noses, and a small slit for the mouth. They seemed to be examining plants in a small clearing; they had long arms and three fingered hands, they also had three toes on their feet.' Startled, the 'beings' halted whatever they were doing and turned to look at the guard.

One of them holding what looked like a torch projecting a blue light, pointed it at him – the next thing he remembered was running back to towards the parked patrol car, and driving back to work and arriving at 6.15am, an hour and a quarter later than his normal booking off time of 5am. The matter was fully investigated by Brighton UFO researchers Larry Dean and Patricia Begley, who journeyed to Cornwall to interview the witness whom they concluded to be an honest and sincere person who had experienced a remarkable close encounter.

Triangular UFOs seen over M42 Motorway.
Worcestershire, 22nd September 1996.

At 11.50 p.m. 22nd September 1996, residents in Alcester Road, Lickey End, Worcestershire - a quiet suburb, just off the M5/M42 Link Road - were disturbed by a loud buzzing noise coming from the top of the road. They suspected that the nearby Electricity Sub-Station was the cause but were amazed when a black, triangular unidentified flying object, showing a number of lights running along its length, was seen hovering fifty to sixty feet above the Motorway Junction. Mark, a student living a few doors away, was one of the first persons on the scene:

"I was amazed by what I saw. It had a soft white light on each wing tip, a red light at the front, and two white lights on its rear."

"The only thing you could hear was a high-pitched humming noise. Behind it appeared another identical object A few minutes later, the two of them headed off across the sky, side-by-side, and were gone within a minute or so."

Close Encounter in Fife, grey figures seen! Fife, Scotland, 23rd September 1996.

During the evening of 23rd September 1996, a car containing three occupants was being driven through a sparsely populated area of Fife, in Scotland, close to Newton of Falkland, when a huge 'white light' appeared in the sky, which suddenly split into two, crisscrossing the ground with beams of light. This was followed by the 'light' switching-off, revealing a black, triangular shaped unidentified object. It was round with curved 'tips.' One of the women in the car waved at the UFO and was staggered when it flashed back at her, three times. After making their way home and discussing what had happened with other family members, the three witnesses decided to return to the scene, where they noticed what looked like 'hundreds of stars sparkling in the night sky above a spinning blue/white 'light' on the ground.'

Underneath were seen a number of small grey 'figures', apparently in the process of picking-up what looked like boxes and cylinders on the ground, accompanied by a very tall 'being', tan/brown in colour. At this point, the people took fright and made their way to a friend's house, but, after further conversation about what had happened, plucked up their courage again to return to the scene. Upon their arrival, they saw the sky was still covered in bright stars, with a bright 'white light' flashing nearby in a sequence of three's. After sighting an object resembling a squashed ball, elongated from top to bottom with large, irregular indentations on it, the small 'figures' reappeared, accompanied by the tall brown 'being', eliciting the comment 'Oh My God, they are coming out of the woods. 'There is a mist coming towards us. There is a cocoon. There are hundreds of them. They are in these things'.

Huge Triangular UFO over roof tops in Farnborough. Aldershot, Hampshire, 22nd October 1996.

At 7.15pm 22nd October 1996, Farnborough based Hilary Porter of Beams (British Earth Mysteries Society) was driving along Blackwater Valley Road, towards Aldershot, Hampshire, when a bright flash of light lit up the sky towards the east. "After arriving home, I looked out of the window and saw four red lights in the sky followed by the amazing sight of a gigantic matt-black object crossing the M3 over the Prospect Estate, Farnborough, barely a mile away from where I was stood. It must have been a thousand feet across by 700feet in length and flying just above the houses at 30-40miles per house, I felt fear creep over me wondering how such a large object could have stayed in the air without crashing to the ground."

"It circled the sky and flew over the centre of DERA Airfield, now in darkness, halted in mid-air and then flew past the control tower and rose upwards over the BA Business park before landing on the runway showing its rear left fin lights. I was shaking with fright and telephoned friend to tell him what I had seen, he offered to go and have a look himself. When he called round later this is what he had to say, "Although the base was in darkness, there was a lot of activity taking place around one of the hangers with white-coated men moving equipment." About a week later, Hilary was contacted by a woman living on the Heathside Estate near the motorway over Camberley, who told of having sighted a huge object moving through the sky at 9pm 21st October 1996, "It had a drooped nose and fin lights of red and white, I couldn't understand how a thing that size stayed up in the air"

Another Triangular UFO over Farnborough. Hampshire, 16th December 1996.

Again, Farnborough resident Hilary Porter from British Earth Mysteries spotted another triangle. "I was about to get into her car at 7.50pm 16th December 1996, when I noticed a pulsing shaped object flying through the air, cross a local cornfield and schools before heading over a large housing estate scattering beams of white light over the rooftops".

"As I drove onto the A325 road I felt a sudden change in the atmosphere, as if things were slowing down. I made my way to the Frimley Interchange and onto the A331 where I was astounded to see the object no more than fifty feet above the road saturating the traffic with beams of light and slowly heading southwards. It then came to a halt, now hovering in the sky above the centre of a bridge spanning the road. To my amazement it changed to a gleaming white triangular craft approximately thirty feet long by fifteen feet wide still bathing the traffic below with beams of light emanating from its underside. In a split second it changed back into a pulsing object and flew over a water treatment plant nearby at speed before doubling back on itself."

Triangle shines beam down onto road. Wigan, Lancashire, 30th January 1997.

30th January 1997, Miss Sonner was driving from Shevington, near Wigan, to Gathurst at 7.45pm. As she passed under the motorway bridge she was startled by a bright light shining down on the car from above. "I stopped the car to have a look at what was going on and saw a black triangular object hovering silently above me in the sky, it was huge and had a spotlight shining down onto the road about a 100 feet away from me, suddenly it flew away towards Up Holland at a speed of only about ten miles an hour" Miss Sonner attempted to give chase in her car, but by the time she reached the traffic lights at Orrell it was out of sight, interestingly she noted that during the time the sighting was taking place no other vehicles passed by.

Triangle with bronze 'lights.' Burntwood, Staffordshire, 19th March 1997.

On 19th March 1997 Mrs. Susan Wells of Burntwood, Staffordshire, was stood in her garden looking for the Hale Bopp Comet at 9.15pm 19th March 1997, when "Two bronze lights appeared in the sky one above the other, giving an impression like aircraft banking as they flew silently overhead. I was able to see a triangular object showing three bronze-coloured lights set into its base. I continued to keep my eyes on the object till it disappeared from view five minutes later.

Blue Triangle over Birmingham and a case of angel hair? Birmingham, 20th March 1997.

20th March 1997. A man was awoken by barking dogs at 4 a.m. going to the window he saw a large, blue, triangular shaped object hovering over his garden in Birmingham, England. When he went outside, he says the object took off into the sky and disappeared, leaving behind a silky

229

white substance on the treetops. The man collected the substance and put into a jam jar as proof. What an intriguing report this was, did anyone from a UFO organization visit the witness, carry out an investigation and view for themselves what appears to be the recovery of a UFO by product, known as angel hair, (which usually disintegrates quickly) or is there a more mundane explanation? We shall probably never know.

Four days later on 24th March 1997, a very strange incident took place, this time over the Peak District of Sheffield involving many calls made to the Police from members of the public after the sighting of what was believed to be a low flying aircraft, which disappeared over the Peak District near Sheffield followed by a flash and loud explosion. It appears a major incident was initiated by the Police and RAF who disclosed that none of their aircraft was missing. Despite a thorough search covering an area of forty square miles, nothing was found to explain the incident. This has led to claims of a Government cover-up following the crash landing of a UFO following sightings of 'Flying Triangles' reported earlier in the evening.

Triangular UFO over Wigan motorways. Standish, Lancashire, 1st June 1997.

At 10.30a.m 1st of June 1997, Steve and Leanne were driving towards the M6 Motorway at Standish near Wigan.

As they approached the traffic island near the M6 Motorway, Leanne shouted out she had just seen what she thought was a plane crashing and urged Steve to stop the car which he did. The couple jumped out and looked into the sky and saw a mat-black triangular object hovering in the sky near to a lake in the vicinity of Wrightington Hospital half a mile away from them. Suddenly, it began to rise and headed in the direction of Parbold Hill at a speed of about 30mph, and then it accelerated away at an incredible speed, it was out of sight in seconds.

At 11.45pm that evening Peter and Wynn Seel, accompanied by their two sons, were driving home to Stockport, Cheshire, along the M56 Motorway heading east between Junction 11 and 12, when they noticed an unusual light low-down in the sky, which they presumed was a warning light on a tower. After crossing a bridge over the M6, they were astonished to see that the light was in fact a greyish coloured triangular shaped object showing red and blue lights at each corner. There was a large white light in the middle and it suddenly it shot off into the distance and disappeared. At 10.50pm on the 2nd of June 1997, strange lights forming a triangle in shape, with a bright light on top and a smaller light on either side, were seen over Bradwell, Staffordshire, by Claire Tideswell, a hospital worker driving home. The object drifted sideways and disappeared into a gap in the clouds'

Triangle drops oval object down to earth. Tamworth, Staffordshire, 8th January 1997.

Ronald Mathias from Glacote, Tamworth, was in his back garden at 12.10am on the 8th of June 1997, when he saw a very bright object moving across the sky at an estimated height of between 4-5000feet, some three miles away heading SSE. According to Ronald, "Suddenly something roughly oval shot out of the object leaving a thin trail behind it and dropped down to earth, I watched it for over a minute till I lost sight of it."

A Triangle visits Ayrshire. Galston, Scotland, 26th June 1997.

On the 26th of June 1997, a resident of Galston, Ayrshire, living near the local school contacted the authorities after sighting a "large black silent Triangle with a white light at each corner heading across the sky southwards at 11.pm".

At 11.35pm on the 27th of June 1997, members of the Ralston family living in Saltcoats, Ayrshire, arrived home and saw what looked like 'three layers of electric blue triangles inside an oval shape 'which hovered above nearby rooftops, tilting occasionally, before dropping slightly and then rising upwards once again'. Another witness to a strange event on the same evening was Philippa Knapp of Dundonald, who was with her husband, son and his friend, when they saw what looked like a cloud substance of a purple shade, it was made up of small circles rotating, forming a larger circle that headed over the rooftops of Castle View. "As it got closer it changed shape, swirled to its right the left and disappeared, but reappeared two or three minutes later when the same thing happened all over again. We watched it for about an hour, from 11.35pm onwards."

Triangular UFOs over Gloucestershire. Lyndney, Gloucestershire, 25th July 1997.

Finding it difficult to sleep a Lydney, Gloucestershire, resident Mark Adams, sat looking out of his bedroom window at 3.15am on the 25th of July 1997, when he was astonished to see over the next twenty-five minutes, a total of "eight triangular objects fly across the sky, making a rumbling noise, each one had a white light on the tail with red flashing lights along the sides. To make sure I wasn't dreaming or imagining it, I woke my wife who confirmed she could see them as well. At 7.30pm on the same day a 'silver cigar shaped object showing a red and green light on each sharp wing tip' was seen hovering in the sky over the Humber Bridge before heading away at speed. It was seen by at least nine people who contacted the Hull Daily Mail to report the incident

Police officers see Triangle at Chippenham. Chippenham, Wiltshire, 12th August 1997.

On the 12th of August 1997, two Wiltshire Constabulary Police Officers were travelling along the Corsham to Laycock Road Chippenham and had just reached a point near the railway bridge, when a 'triangular object showing two red lights on its rear about fifteen feet apart with a white light on the front, flew past them in the same direction at a height of thirty feet just above tree top level.

It then headed northeast towards Chippenham and met up with a second object, which appeared to be following it.

Their speed increased and they were soon out of sight. Later that afternoon a 'triangular shaped object with black wings and what looked like a 'sausage' in the middle for a body' was seen flying through the sky at 5.30pm by a resident of the Cwmbran area. At 9pm an object like a jellyfish flew through the air and was sighted over the Stourbridge area of Worcestershire. At 10.16pm on the same evening a 999 call was made to the Police reporting a yellow ball of light seen passing over houses at Leighton Buzzard heading towards Milton Keynes.

Huge Triangular UFO over Hull flying blunt end first! Sandtoft, Lincolnshire, 7th October 1997.

On the 7th of October 1997, a bright orange ball was seen moving slowly across the sky near RAF West Raynham by a man walking his dog. This was followed by a report of a 'Delta formation of over a dozen flashing red lights' seen moving across the sky heading Northwest over Sandtoft North Lincolnshire at 7.30pm by a couple who complained that its passage through the sky had interfered with the colour on their TV.

At 7.45pm, Mr. Pete McGowan, an engineer living in Hull, was adjusting the new security lights at the back of his house, when his wife drew his attention to a series of red streaks forming in the sky directly in line with the Humber Bridge, about a mile away.

"The centre one was straight, a second 'streak' of light appeared and curled over on the right, followed by a third which curved to the left of the original making five in all. Then I heard a buzzing noise, and the lights went out. I looked around and saw the lights again, they were flickering like a blacksmiths forge in the sky, and I wondered if they could have been helicopters but knew this could not be the explanation as the lights were about ten times the size of any helicopter.

Then I saw an orange glow appear and realized it was the city lights being reflected of the base of this huge triangular craft, which was moving blunt-side forward at about 30mph, you could see the lights curling around the edges of the triangle.

It then halted in mid-air and turned apparently moving to far forward as it corrected itself and stopped and did the same thing again. I looked up and was amazed to see right above our heads something resembling a rib cage and two giant circles underneath it with a 'tail' on the one end. I tried to memorize as much as I could there were over a thousand pale blue lights underneath it, it was high, but you could see everything quite clearly. I estimated you could have put three Jumbo 747 Jets wing to wing tip that's how big it was"

At 7.55pm a male passenger in a car being driven along Bricknell Avenue, Hull, noticed a triangular shaped object showing flashing lights in the sky above him. Another sighting made at more or less the same time involved the appearance of a semi-circle of red lights 60-70yards apart being seen in the sky over the Scunthorpe area.

Triangle over East London. Walthamstow, London, 8th December 1997.

On 8th December 1997, Brian Jessop was standing on the garden steps of his house in Walthamstow, East London, at 11.37am when he noticed what looked like a military jet passing through the sky. He brought the sighting to the attention of his mother, who pointed out a second black triangular object motionless in the sky. Brian ran into the house, grabbed hold of his camcorder and rushed outside, but by then there was nothing to be seen. Brian panned the sky looking for any sign of the black triangle, then a jet aircraft appeared, prompting a response from his Mother who shouted out pointing into the sky. "A black object came into view on the handy cam about the size of a penny coin held at arm's length, it shot across the sky and seemed to intercept the jet before diving into cloud cover.

I carried on recording for a few minutes longer hoping it would reappear, but it didn't." Brian contacted Roy Hale from the East London UFO network and explained what had occurred. Roy Hale then telephoned the MoD asking them if they had any military aircraft in the locality, they replied in the negative.

A letter was sent to the local newspaper, the Walthamstow Yellow Advertiser, asking for any members of the public who may have seen the object to come forward, a man contacted Brian and Roy, this is what he had to say, "I was in the sun lounge having just finished work in the garden, when I happened to look up into the sky and saw this peculiar object resembling a UFO from a science fiction magazine, heading east to west across a clear sky at about the same height of aircraft on their way to Heathrow. As it approached closer I could make out quite clearly a black and triangular shaped object. The front seemed so thin, with an absence of nose cone or fuselage. I was so excited that I ran in to tell my wife, but realized she was next door, so I rushed back into the garden to see it still heading on the same course. Suddenly it turned nose up tail down and began to spiral upwards like a falling leaf rather than downwards, and it was soon lost from sight."

Three Triangular objects over Powys. Llanidloes, Wales, 3rd June 1998.

Welshpool resident Paul Best was travelling along the road between Newtown and Llanidloes at 10.30pm 3rd of June 1998, when he saw "Three triangular shaped planes just below cloud cover, they were perfect triangles with a round shape underneath, and completely stationary in the air, then they moved away slowly to begin with before increasing speed like no aircraft I had ever seen. RAF Community relations officer, Brian Sidebotham, confirmed there was no unusual flying or exercises taking place at the time given, and suggested "Sometimes the lights on any aircraft can cause unusual effects and I do know that laser light shows have been known to cause people to see something that they have never seen before"

UFOs over the West Midlands. Erdington, Birmingham, 9th January 1998.

On 9th of January 1998, three men were driving to the Dunlop factory in Erdington near Birmingham at 6.20am, when they saw a man standing on the street corner looking upwards into the sky. Following his gaze, they saw a "single red flashing light with the hint of what appeared to be something triangular behind it. Margaret, a traffic warden based at Birmingham International Airport, was driving north along the M6 Motorway between Junction 3 and 4 at 5.23am 10th of January 1998, when she saw 'an oblong shaped object stationary in the sky, it was highly unusual and like nothing I had ever seen at the Airport, after about 30 seconds it moved away and out of view. Margaret rejected the explanation that she had seen the Goodyear Blimp, which was in the area later in the day passing over the Wolverhampton Football Ground.

Merseyside Multicoloured Triangle lights. Thurcroft, South Yorkshire, 21st February 1998.

At 8pm 21st of February 1998, a "Triangular shaped object surrounded with brilliant blue green, red and orange lights was seen 'darting bizarrely around in the sky'" according to Susan and Steven Butler who, along with their two children, were driving home between Thurcroft and Whiston along the Rotherham Road when the object appeared. The object followed them for some distance. Enquiries with the Police Manchester Airport and RAF Linton Upon Ouse failed to identity what the family had seen.

Triangular UFO over Exeter drops ball of light. Exeter, 9th March 1998.

A motorist and his two passengers were driving along the M5 Motorway at 7.45pm on the 9th of March 1998 heading south approximately 40 miles away from Exeter, when they noticed a light in the sky high up at approximately 30,000 feet.

As they continued on their journey the 'light' descended to about 3000 feet displaying an array of bright, white lights with a red one in the centre or tail part.

It then descended even further, now showing a triangular shape with the light now far more discernible as three white lights with a large, reddish pulsing light in the centre. As it climbed upwards, a small yellow and orange ball of light dropped away from the reddish part of the 'craft.'

This ball of light shot off towards the south, immediately followed by the larger object. According to the occupants of the car, a number of other drivers on the Motorway witnessed the fly-past of the object.

Dartford tunnel Triangle. Dartford Tunnel, Summer 1998.

Summer 1998, Kent housewife Irene Brennan witnessed unexplained aerial activity during the summer of 1998."I was driving to Maidstone in Kent from Suffolk one evening and somewhere on the road after the Dartford tunnel, I noticed a bright light in the sky that seemed to be staying in the same place all the time. It stayed in the same position for quite a long while as I continued on my journey down the motorway. As I drove underneath whatever it was, I saw it was triangular shaped with lights at each corner, with an underside divided into sections. I wondered if it could have been a Harrier or the "invisible" Stealth bomber or something, but I didn't see any wheels hanging down, just the lights at the corner of the triangle".

Triangular UFO over Hastings. Hastings, East Sussex, 9th August 1998.

Seen at 9pm, 19th of August 1998, by Gordon Griffin from Hastings, who wrote to us about what he and his wife Ruth had seen from their home address. Gordon said, "I went to the widow and saw this cigar-shaped object side view on, moving from right to left above Christchurch, it had green lights to the front with red to the rear. When it was over the sea it halted in mid-air as if observing the Carnival Celebration taking place below. It then moved slightly showing a blue light on the top, and moved inland, we ran downstairs and into the garden when we saw, instead of a cigar, it was now triangular in shape with a glowing white light at each corner. It stayed in the sky for about fifteen minutes then disappeared from view"

Triangle over Birmingham Airport. Sutton Coldfield, 6th November 1998.

On 6th of November 1998, an enormous, dark, triangular object showing three green/blue lights in each corner was seen stationary in the sky over Sutton Coldfield on the approach lane leading into Birmingham National Airport. According to the witness an aircraft descending to land actually flew underneath the object, which suddenly shot upwards into the sky and out of sight.

M1 Triangle. M1 motorway, 22nd November 1998.

A motorist travelling along the M1 Motorway a quarter of a mile north of the M18 Junction 22 at 8.5pm 22nd of November 1998, saw a large black triangular object hovering nose-down in the sky. The man concerned described the object as "huge and covered in numerous lights apparently made up a girder like structure. I was unable to stop but saw other drivers had pulled onto the hard shoulder."

White Triangular UFO with multitude of 'lights.' Glanarfon, Wales 7th January 1998.

At 6.30pm 7th January 1999 a white, flat, triangular object like a shield 'larger than a fighter jet, but smaller than an airliner showing a number of orange, white, green and purple lights around its body with a larger 'spotlight' underneath, was seen moving slowly through the air at a height of about 200feet off the ground over Glanarfon, Wales.

Triangular UFO over Cumbria, Broughton MoD base, Cumbria, 4th October 1998.

At 8pm on the 4th of October 1999, Sharon Larkin, head of Cumbria UFO Research, was taking part in a sky watch outside Broughton MoD base, when, without any warning, a black triangular object appeared over the top of the hedge a short distance away. "It had a large light in the centre with smaller lights on the three points (I took some photographs, but they never turned out). After about ten minutes it moved slowly towards us, at which stage, fearing what might happen, we decided to leave. When we plucked up the courage to go back and have a look, it was now stationary in the sky over the MoD base. After watching it for three hours still there in the sky a few thousand feet up we decided to leave for home'"

In conversation with Sharon, who had found the experience exhilarating, but puzzled as to whether there was any connection with the nearby MoD base. She told us of having received a threatening telephone call made to her mobile phone from an unidentified male who said, "I know what you have seen, and I know you took some photos, under no circumstances should you go to the press with them" Sharon asked the caller to identify himself, he replied, "there's no need to know that" The phone then went dead.

We learnt that at about the same time (excluding the likelihood there was more than one UFO moving across the sky over the UK that evening) an object described as a 'square shape' with a light at each corner, was seen by a motorist driving from Dinnington to Thurcroft. The object shot away at high speed, was this the same UFO seen by Sharon?

Curiously on the following evening (5.10.1999) Sharon saw what she believes to be the same if not similar triangular UFO hovering over Broughton Moor.

Another Triangular UFO flying blunt end first over Gloucestershire. Hucclecote, Gloucestershire, 7th December 1998.

Dave Cosnette from Hucclecote, a small village four miles from Gloucester, was taking his dog for a walk at 6.30pm on the 7th of December1999, when he noticed a large white light in the sky with many different colours shimmering inside it, "Creating an oil-on-water effect as big as an open daily newspaper at arm's length with pinkish, orange-coloured lights forming a triangular shape flying with the 'point' to the back. It was moving through the air about a mile up. I noticed another man who had been walking towards me had stopped and was gazing upwards at the UFO.

I ran home and got my brother out of bed, and we made our way to a motorway bridge close to the house. We saw the same man watching the object now moving over a hill around four or five miles away. The next day I heard that people had phoned in to the local radio station and newspaper reporting having seen it go over"

Mark Haden, August 1997, RAF Shawbury

Hi Colin, this is a report that I gave to a Midlands UFO network earlier this year. Place - old, disused railway lines adjacent to Hortonwood industrial estate coming from the approximate direction of RAF Shawbury. Date - middle of August 1997. (Unsure of precise date, but by looking at sunrise times on Google they tally with days around the 15th) Time - somewhere between 05.30 and 05.50a.m. While walking to work from the Donnington area of Telford, to my right I noticed two bright, horizontal lights in the distance moving towards me in an SSE direction. I would estimate a couple of miles away at least, and about 10° off the horizon, (although I was walking on elevated ground). The sun was just coming up, but they were still extremely bright. As I continued walking the lights came closer and I could then see the object was flat and black. The closer it got I could see there were three lights, one in each corner. At the point on the railway lines there was an old siding.

This had a few hundred army trucks and vehicles painted Khaki that were UN peacekeeper vehicles ready for the Middle East. (MoD Donnington, at the time the largest

Army ordinance depot in Europe, was to my left rear. Further on down the line is GKN Sankey, who make the vehicles.) At this point the triangle came directly above my head at a few hundred feet if that. It was approximately 40 ft across. Dull black with no sign of protrusion or propulsion engines. Just completely smooth. It made a slight low hum. Its movement was so smooth and easy. As it got just past me it started to turn in a smooth arc without banking.

It looked the same on all sides. It more or less went back towards the way it had come. I would estimate that it didn't get above 30mph. I didn't feel threatened and got the impression it was surveying the area. The Google Earth image has the approximate grid coordinates of where it went over my head. Somewhere around 52°42'53" N 2°27'31 W.

Chris Rolf, March 1997 Burmarsh, Kent FT & the Home Secretary!

I am indebted to Chris Rolf for his permission to reproduce this next report that he has supplied me with. "During the early hours of 8th March 1997, a flying triangle was observed at Burmarsh, Kent, by local journalist Sarah Hall. "It was early morning" explained Sarah, "I think it was about 3am and I was driving back from dropping some friends off and as I was coming down the road I felt weird and a bit scared. I saw something in front of me and thought "Oh my God what the hell is that?" I slowed down because I thought it was coming at me, but it stopped in a field in a field three to four hundred yards away.

It was a huge triangle thing, which was a lot bigger than an airplane. "It had lights all around the outside and this disc attached to the back and a big light on the front. I pulled up to stop and as I did so it shot off and stopped again approx 500 yards away from me, it did that four times, the object was moving westwards all the time and it was making this weird humming sound. It was really peculiar; I wouldn't say shiny, but looked more like tinfoil, sort of shimmery. It was shiny in places and not others. The lights were really bright, a very bright one at the front."

"When it shot off I saw a light in each corner, they were white in colour. The ones around the outside were a sort of yellow-white and there was also a circle of light in the middle. When stationary it looked like an object suspended in the sky and had no wobble or anything like that. When it moved off it was like s fluid movement, it was really odd. The object was like an equilateral triangle about the size of an airliner, maybe as big as a football pitch. It wasn't very thick but seemed thin along the edges. There was a humming sound like the sound you hear when you stand under power cables."

Shortly afterwards Sarah's story appeared in the Folkestone Herald newspaper as did the testimony of two additional witnesses to the unknown object, Ji Lang and Christopher Lee. Local UFO investigators Chris Rolfe and Jerry Anderson looked into the case and uncovered a stunning fact, the location of the triangle was practically on the doorstep of the residence of the former Home Secretary, Michael Howard MP! Recognizing the potential significance of this, Rolfe and Anderson began to dig deeper into the affair and inadvertently found themselves plunged headlong into a dark and disturbing world full of covert telephone tapping operations, political intrigue, official obfuscation and more.

Rolfe and Anderson also succeeded in locating new and important witnesses, including two firemen who had seen the UFO hovering directly over the roof of Michael Howards home.

Original Report by Chris Rolf

During the early hours of 8 March 1997, one of the most significant UFO events of modern times occurred, when an unidentified aerial object of the now-familiar *Flying Triangle* variety was seen at Burmarsh, Kent, by a local journalist - Sarah Hall of the *Folkestone Herald* newspaper. Little did she know it at the time but Sarah was to serve as the catalyst for a complex and curious chain of events that would tax even Mulder and Scully of *The X-Files*!

'It was very early in the morning,' explained Sarah, who, oddly, seemed to be aware that all was not as it should be even before the *Flying Triangle* loomed into view as she drove along Donkey Street, Burmarsh.

'I think it was about three o'clock. I was driving back from dropping some friends off and I was coming down the road and I felt, I said afterwards to other people since, that I felt really weird. I was really looking over my shoulder on the way home. I was a bit scared, a weird feeling anyway.

'And I saw something in front of me, and thought, "Oh my God; what the hell is it?" [I] sort of slowed down because I thought it was coming at me, and it stopped in a field in front of me. Probably three to four hundred yards away, and I slowed down looking at it. It was just this huge triangle thing, which was a lot bigger than an aeroplane, but there is no way that I could have mistaken it for an aeroplane or anything like that.

'It had lights all around the outside, and this disc attached to the back, and a big light on the front. I pulled up to stop, and as I did it shot off. Literally shot off. I thought "Oh God; what is this? This is really, really scary." And it stopped again, sort of another five hundred yards away from me and it did that four times. It just shot further and further away, but stopped four times, sort of moved for about five-to-six seconds, stopped for two secs., then moved again for another five-to-six seconds and so on. The object was moving westwards and all the time it was making this weird humming sound. There was no other noise, like an aircraft engine.

'It was really peculiar; it was, I wouldn't say shiny, but looked more sort of tin foil, sort of shimmery. It was shiny in places and not in others. I just don't know what it was; it was so weird. The lights were really bright - a very bright one at the front. And when it shot off, I saw a light in each corner, which were white in colour. The ones around the outside were a sort of yellow-white and there was also a circle of light in the middle of the same colour as the outside ones.

'When I first saw it, the point was facing me, but when it shot off it sort of...I don't know, it must have swivelled. But I don't remember it swivelling because I could see it side-on then and I could see underneath as it shot off and there was this circle of lights.

'I probably got a good look at it literally for a matter of seconds and then it flicked off. [It] then stopped for a few seconds, and then it flicked off again and so on. I would say no more than twenty-five seconds - if that. I saw it for quite a long time in the distance. It wasn't until I got closer that I thought "Bloody hell; what is that?" So maybe I saw it for a lot longer than I thought.

'It wasn't something like you see on television like the futuristic planes - you can always tell that they are planes. I was really frightened by it and I'm not stupid. I don't believe in anything like [UFOs]. This is not something I've ever seen before or like something we would have built. It was just too weird, too odd and the strange shimmer effect. It looked like an object suspended [and] had no wobble or anything like that. And when it moved off it was like a fluid movement; it was really odd.

'The object was like an equilateral triangle about the size of an airliner; maybe as big as a football field. It wasn't very thick but seemed thin along the edges [and] sort of mounding in the middle. As I said, there was this humming sound, like the sound you hear when you stand under overhead power cables. When I first heard the noise I

Rolfe and Anderson also succeeded in locating several new and important witnesses including two fireman who had seen the UFO not just in the general vicinity, but hovering directly over the roof of Michael Howard's home!

Also, according to Rolfe, a further source had seen shortly before the events of 8 March 1997, an equally curious phenomenon at Aldington Lympne - only two miles from Michael Howard's home.

As Rolfe reveals: 'A man out walking his two dogs late at night some three weeks earlier had seen a bright flash in the sky. He and the dogs immediately stood rooted to the spot as an object came directly over them.

'He recalled seeing some sort of tail, different coloured lights, and then after two-to-three seconds, there was a loud "whooshing noise" and the object shot off in a westerly direction towards Rye on the Kent/Sussex border.

'The man was very frightened by the experience, as were his dogs, who cowered at his feet. One refused to move for quite some time, but eventually he managed to bring them home. All the while both animals were very wary of all around them.

'The larger of the dogs has been very apprehensive ever since, and is very reluctant to go on walks that hitherto he would have relished.

'Interestingly, the man had previously observed "bright flashes" in the Aldington Lympne area during the previous two months which he couldn't explain. This is just two miles north of Michael Howard's residence.'

Realising that they were in the midst of one of the most important UFO cases to have ever caught their attention, Rolfe and Anderson pressed on. Kent County Constabulary, the Home Office and the Ministry of Defence were all contacted for comment. The response was, perhaps, predictable:

'MOD Air Defence staff have confirmed that there is no evidence to suggest an unauthorized incursion of the UK Air Defence Region on 8 March,' Rolfe was informed by Kerry Philpott of the MoD on 3 July 1997. 'The Home Office has confirmed that no security incident occurred in the home of the former Home Secretary on this date...'

Rolfe and Anderson continued to dig for further information; however, it was a full ten months after the incident occurred that matters took a new twist. Despite the fact that the story had been reported in the *Folkestone Herald* newspaper at the time that it took place, it was not until January 1998 that the national media finally sat up and took notice.

On 18 January, the *Sunday Times* ran a feature that added a new piece to the jigsaw. The former prime minister John Major and the Conservative Central Office were fully aware of what had occurred over the home of Michael Howard; however, with a general election on the horizon, it was decided that matters had to be kept under wraps, reported the *Times*.

Melody Foreman of the *Folkestone Herald* was quick to point out that: 'Miss Hall's story was NOT tampered with by any Tory heavies, and encompassing this country's ethics which dictate a policy of a free press, the *Herald* would NEVER entertain such a spineless attitude.'

Michael Howard, himself, was keen to avoid entering the debate: 'I am just astonished by all this really,' he told the *Folkestone Herald*. 'While I probably was at my home that night as I often am, I certainly didn't see anything. It is all ridiculous and getting out of hand.'

Michael Howard may not have personally seen anything unusual in the Kent skies;

thought it was the car engine playing up and put my foot on the accelerator for a second or two but the noise was still there; and it was then that I realised the sound was coming from the object.

'When the object finally disappeared, I kept looking around the sky thinking "Oh God; where has it gone?" Looking for lights, anything - even aircraft lights and it was then that I noticed there were no stars visible.

'All the time I had the feeling of the hairs standing up on the back of my neck and I was convinced I had someone in the car with me. I felt really scared as I drove home. I think I arrived home about twenty-past-three, maybe half-past-three; I don't remember. But I woke everyone up and told them what I had seen and had a drink to calm me down. I was really shaken by the whole thing.'

Thus ended Sarah Hall's remarkable encounter. Shortly afterwards, her story appeared in the *Folkestone Herald* newspaper - as did the testimony of two additional witnesses to the unknown object: Ji Lang and Christopher Lee.

'It was crazy,' said Lang. 'I was getting a drink in the kitchen when I saw these strange lights in the sky just over the field across the road from our house. I wasn't sure what they were as they weren't moving so I called Chris and we both watched this weird floating object. We could only just make it out as we were quite far away, but when we ran outside to get a better look it had shot into the distance.'

Christopher Lee concurred: 'If it was an aeroplane of some sort you would have expected there to have been loads of noise but this was silent. Also it was a lot longer than a plane and moved incredibly quickly. I have no idea what it was and we were both left speechless.'

At the time that the incident occurred, local UFO investigators Chris Rolfe and Jerry Anderson of *UFO Monitors East Kent* were alerted to the events by the *Folkestone Herald* and began their own investigation of Sarah Hall's remarkable experience. Immediately, they were to uncover a stunning fact: the location where the *Flying Triangle* was seen was practically on the doorstep of the residence of the former Home Secretary, Michael Howard, M.P.!

Recognising the potential significance of this, Rolfe and Anderson began to dig deep into the affair and inadvertently found themselves plunged headlong into a dark and disturbing world full of covert telephone-tapping operations, political intrigue, official obfuscation and more.

Having gained the trust of Sarah Hall, Rolfe noted a curious anomaly. Sarah had initially believed that she had returned home at 'about twenty-past-three, maybe half-past-three'; however, she would later inform Rolfe that dawn was breaking when she woke her friends to tell them what she had seen.

'A case of mistaken timekeeping - or missing time?' asks Rolfe.

Rolfe then determined to take the investigation to a whole new level: he telephoned Michael Baxter, the former home secretary's Conservative Party Agent. Was Michael Howard in residence at the time that the incident occurred?

'No comment,' was the response.

Rolfe pressed further: had anything unusual been seen in the vicinity of Michael Howard's home?

'You mean the UFO,' came the reply. Abruptly, Baxter terminated the conversation. For the record, when he was contacted by the *Folkestone Herald*, Michael Baxter disputed mentioning UFOs in the brief conversation he had with Chris Rolfe; however, Rolfe maintains that such a comment *was* made.

however, on 19 January 1998, an admission was made to the *Daily Mail* newspaper by the Tory Party that the story was not exactly unknown to them.

As the *Mail* stated: 'Yesterday, advisers who worked closely with Mr Howard during the election campaign confirmed that the UFO story was well known in Westminster but denied there had been a "Men in Black"-style cover-up. They did admit, however, that the party had been keen to play down the sighting because of the risk of embarrassing headlines.'

According to John Major's press secretary, Sheila Gunn: 'There were calls about it because the local paper had done something. But while we take calls seriously, there are some that we'd rather ignore.'

It could be argued that the actions of the Tory Party were perfectly understandable. With a crucial General Election looming, who within the Conservatives would want to give mileage to a story linking the Home Secretary with UFOs? No-one, I would suggest.

Nevertheless, there is evidence that other, darker forces were at work. For approximately seven months things were relatively quiet. On 17 August 1998, however, Chris Rolfe received in the mail a highly-unusual letter. Written on official Royal Air Force stationery and signed by a 'Wing Commander A.W. Ward', it informed Rolfe that he was 'no longer permitted to carry on investigations into the supposed triangular-shaped object that was seen over Burmarsh, Kent'. The UFO, Rolfe was advised, was in reality a 'rapid response military aircraft' and the disc-like attachment that Sarah Hall had reported was a 'distance radar'. 'Once again, this is a conditional warning,' Rolfe was ominously advised.

Rolfe immediately dismissed the matter as a hoax but felt duty-bound to inform the Ministry of Defence that someone had sent to him what amounted to a thinly-veiled threat. Curiously, the MoD displayed nothing more than casual indifference.

The Ministry's response was made all the more mysterious when Rolfe learned that there was a real 'Wing Commander A.W. Ward' based at RAF College Cranwell! To his credit, Chris Rolfe wasted no time in contacting the wing commander.

No, the wing commander informed Rolfe, he had not sent him the letter. However, he *did* concede that the signature attached to it was indeed a 'reasonable forgery' of his own signature. Significantly, Rolfe told me, Wing Commander Ward's work did not normally involve him liasing with the general public, which begs an important question. From where would an outsider obtain a specimen of Ward's handwriting? But even more bizarre and disturbing things were afoot - as Chris Rolfe explains:

'Ever since we became involved with the Burmarsh incident, Jerry [Anderson], who uses a B.T. answering service, found that someone was trying to gain unauthorised access to retrieve messages left by callers. Then in September [1997], very loud radio telecommunication noises came over my own telephone. It got so bad at times that I couldn't hear the person on the other end of the line and they couldn't hear me. Some callers couldn't get through at all, and if it wasn't the interference that put people off, others would hear a message saying that the line was out of order.'

Rolfe decided that enough was enough and took steps to have the matter resolved once and for all.

'In the end,' he explains, 'a B.T. engineer came round to tackle the problem and pronounced that the telephone equipment in my house was perfectly okay, but that there was definitely a fault on the line - somewhere between my residence and the B.T. exchange.'

According to Rolfe, the problem persisted and a second engineer was called out and

the matter was apparently resolved: all of the problems were due simply to moisture on an extension line in Rolfe's home. Or were they ...?

On 8 February 1999, Anderson received in the mail a manila envelope that contained an audio-cassette tape-recording of a telephone conversation between Rolfe and himself that had taken place twelve months previously! Interestingly, the subject matter of that conversation was an important witness who had surfaced at the time with vital new evidence and who had approached Anderson during a lecture given by Timothy Good at Waterstone's bookshop in Canterbury, Kent.

Chris Rolfe takes up the story again: 'This witness claimed that he and his wife, whose house overlooks Michael Howard's country residence, had been woken from their sleep in the early hours of 8 March 1997 by a bright searchlight. They went to the bedroom window and saw the light sweeping across surrounding fields, into the night sky and Michael Howard's property: it came from a helicopter.

'On the ground, teams of security men carrying torches darted about the property as if looking for something; and the following morning, the couple watched possibly the same helicopter hovering over the area.

'The witness told us that on more than one occasion, Howard's security team came to their front door late at night to ask several bizarre questions. Such was the case around midnight on 4 January 1998, when the couple had just finished watching a late film called *Red Rock* on Channel 4 when there was a loud knock at the door.

'It was two members of Howard's security team, who wanted to know if they had seen any unusual lights in the area that evening. They replied that they hadn't, and asked why, but were told that it wasn't important and the two officers left. This story is essentially what was on the cassette tape that Jerry had been sent in the post. It had arrived in a plain brown envelope, which bore the Canterbury post-mark, with Jerry's name and address stencilled in red ink.' And more was to come.

On 9 February 1999, Joe Showler, an engineer from British Telecom's Communications Investigations Bureau, visited Anderson but maintained that there were no problems with his telephone. Showler also examined Rolfe's telephone and could find no fault.

Showler did note, however, that the cover that protected the electrical components on Rolfe's telephone connection point had been changed from the old green design to a new, white cover. Rolfe explained to Showler that he had received two visits from B.T.engineers; however, to the best of his knowledge, none had installed a new cover.

Puzzled, Showler made additional checks and discovered something highly curious. British Telecom's own records showed that only one engineer had visited Rolfe's home. So, who was the - presumably bogus- engineer who maintained that all of Rolfe's problems were due to nothing more sinister than 'moisture' on the extension line? Then, to cap it all, forty-eight hours later both Rolfe and Sarah Hall received in the mail identical copies of the audio-tape recording sent to Jerry Anderson!

In the four years that have passed since Sarah Hall's extraordinary encounter with the unknown on that dark stretch of Kent road, of several things we can be certain. In the early hours of 8 March 1997, 'something' manifested itself in the direct vicinity of the home of one of Britain's most senior politicians. Furthermore, it was that 'something' that led the Tory Party to construct a wall of silence and caused some hidden hand to launch a covert surveillance of the principle investigators of the case.

But, inevitably, questions remain: who was responsible for the thinly-veiled threat made to Chris Rolfe? Why was he warned to keep his nose out of the events of 8

March 1997? Why was the MoD so unconcerned that the good name of a Royal Air Force Wing Commander was being exploited and blackened? Why were Chris Rolfe and Jerry Anderson subject to such intense surveillance? And most important of all: what was the origin of the object that was seen in alarmingly-close proximity to the home of the then Home Secretary, Michael Howard?

In conversation with Chris Rolfe in October 2000, he told me that he is inclined to believe that the object seen by Sarah Hall was a military device of some kind and points to the fact that situated nearby is the Army's test range at Lydd. It will be recalled that a vehicle similar to that seen by Sarah Hall in 1997 was also witnessed near a military firing range on the Cannock Chase, Staffordshire, in 1985. On the other hand, as we have seen, Nick Pope of the MoD is adamant that these are extra-terrestrial devices as opposed to anything man-made.

The final word I will leave to the lady who started it all, Sarah Hall: 'Yes it was odd and I am sure to many totally unbelievable, but I certainly do not proclaim it as anything "alien" as suggested in some newspaper reports! But it WAS…a UFO, an unidentified flying object, which until someone can come forward with a cast iron explanation, will remain a total mystery.'

Chris Rolf recalls "This witness claimed that he and his wife, whose house overlooks Michael Howard's country residence, had been woken from their sleep in the early hours of 8th March 1997 by a bright searchlight. They went to the bedroom window and saw the light sweeping across surrounding fields into the night sky and Michael Howard's property, it came from a helicopter. On the ground, teams of security men carrying torches darted about the property as if looking for something, and the following morning the couple watched possibly the same helicopter hovering over the area." The witness told us that on more than one occasion Howard's security team came to their front door late at night to ask several bizarre questions. They wanted to know if they had seen any unusual lights in the area that evening. They replied that they hadn't and asked why but were told that it wasn't important, and the two officers left."

A strange case indeed, which calls into question the security of our airspace, especially around high-ranking politician's home. The final word I will leave to the lady who started it all, Sarah Hall "Yes it was odd, and I am sure to many totally unbelievable, but I certainly do not proclaim it as anything alien as suggested in some newspaper reports!

But it was a UFO, an unidentified flying object, which until someone can come forward with a cast iron explanation will remain a total mystery."

Nick Mellors, October 7th, 1997

Another encounter with the triangle the size of a football pitch!

"Basically, we saw a huge, black, solid FT, with a light at each end, flying silently over West Hull. The craft was flying just above house and tree level, I'd estimate at 150 feet and no more. We jumped into car and followed it for about six miles as it silently and slowly headed in a northerly direction.

My ex-partner was driving; I was in the passenger seat with the window down, all the time the craft was on my left. We drove from Bricknell Avenue in Hull, into the village of Cottingham, through the other end, on into Skidby. As we left Skidby on the Little Weighton road it disappeared. True story"

Andy (pseudonym), October 2002, Stanley, County Durham

Andy got in touch with me after seeing my original article in the Hinckley times, this is his story:

"OK, so around October 2002 me and a friend were walking home in Stanley County, Durham, towards Craghead, a small mining village and from the town centre it's roughly two miles away. We were about halfway home, and I spotted a fire off in the distance to the west and said to my friend that it looked like one of the farms was on fire as it was all fields and pitch black, and the only thing over there were farms. As we continued to watch, this fireball got closer, then oddly ceased to be a fireball and a beam of light came out the front of it and started scanning the fields, which was odd. At this point I said to my friend that it was maybe a police helicopter's searchlight, shortly after which the searchlight disappeared, then whatever this thing was split into two orbs, one red and one white, and both silently went over the brow of the hill out of sight."

"To be honest I was blown away at this point. You have to remember that this wasn't so long after September the 11th and I honestly couldn't make sense of what I'd seen. I actually said to my friend I think we're under attack, thinking it was some kind of missile and asked him if he'd actually just seen this thing"

"At this point we excitedly carried on with our journey discussing the object and spotted another fireball to the south over the nearby golf course. This time the object got closer and again oddly ceased to be a fireball. but this time didn't split into orbs.

It was a large black triangle. We could only make out the solid triangle shape against the clouds as it was very dark. It had blue strobing lights going down each side from the front to the back, kind of like LED strips I guess, but the strangest thing was how it flew. If you can imagine drawing a staircase on a piece of paper, it was flying in 45-degree sharp angles with no observable inertia.

I don't know much about planes, but this thing wasn't obeying the laws of physics as far as we know them to work."

"As far as distance overhead is concerned. I honestly find it extremely hard to say, unfortunately it was very dark so could only see a very dark triangle with the lights against the dark clouds, so it was difficult to judge. I'd say maybe a couple of hundred feet tops.

It moved from the south to the north and flew directly overhead. Like I tried to articulate in my last message it was how it flew that was so odd.

Normal aircraft bank left to right when making a turn, but this thing had a weird flight path moving in short equally distanced bursts. I can only describe as if I drew a staircase. Inertia and gravity seemed to be out the window. At that point I was convinced it was either from 'somewhere else,' or our military was light years ahead of what we'd been told."

Marion Goode 2003 Birmingham

"I saw my first one in 2003, there was no noise just lights in a triangular pattern and a sense of pressure as it went over my car. My car suddenly died on me, then I saw the lights. I got the impression it was large due to the spacing of the lights.

I don't know how long it was there before it disappeared out of my sight; I must add that it happened at night on my way home on country lanes.

I also lost time which it shook me up and it took till I saw one like it again to tell anyone about it. Luckily, my sister was with me that time, again it was late at night driving home and the car cut out and it appeared.

Over the years I have tried to rationalize what it could have been, but we could never lock it down to anything specific. However, each time my car started up immediately after it had moved away."

"I've seen them over the years and just accept it now, it doesn't feel like it's threatening me, but it's still a shock to see them. Most of my encounters have been in the West Midlands near Birmingham and they were definitely not with normal aircraft."

Jan Edwards-Rigg (pseudonym), Monmouth in 2007/8

'I saw the same thing in Monmouth in 2007/8 ….it had a white light at each corner and a red one in the centre …..silent and flying slowly from east to south west ……also in 2015 saw I saw one in Cardiff, a large triangle flying slowly North to South towards the Bristol Channel, and it was dusk …and the strange thing was it was cloaking, I could see the outline of it very clearly and could also see the darker clouds through it, ….I call it my ghost triangle'

"There was some car traffic at that time so was not super quiet. This event was not more than thirteen seconds. This object literally touched the treetops and was remarkably close to the ground.

I had my phone with me, but I knew a recording from the phone at night wouldn't work as the phone video recording camera at night is terrible. Overall, this ship felt like out of this world.'

Ronald Kinsella – 9th-11th August 2010

Triangle witness Ronald Kinsella

At a recent UFO conference where I gave a presentation using my models as visual aids, I bumped into Ronald Kinsella and his twin brother Philip. These twin brothers are two of the kindest gentlemen I have met in the UFO world. Ronald had his own close encounter with a triangle, and I am indebted to him for this next report.

"I must make it perfectly clear, before I address the particulars of my encounter back of August 2010, that I have only ever seen the infamous 'Triangular Craft' once.

265

There are a few interesting points to also note concerning it which came to light much later."

"I had heard of the Triangular-shaped UFOs that appeared to frequent our skies back in the 90s, especially when a famous case was broadcast on 'Unsolved Mysteries' hosted by Robert Stack at the time. This was 'The Belgian UFO Wave.'

"The testimony back then was enough to convince me that we were being visited by an unfamiliar force, with the evidence supported by Law Enforcement Officers who witnessed the UFOs first-hand and were extremely credible. Indeed, I have personally seen enough of the phenomena myself to appreciate our world is being invaded by things that defy explanation."

"But that's the thing that helps to tie-up loose ends regarding this topic. If something cannot be explained or rationalized, alternative theories are proposed, which regularly sway towards the negative, debunking a sighting, or encounter and downsizing it to an explainable anomaly. It is true to say that certain variables must be taken into consideration, such as satellites, planets and stars, atmospheric irregularities, terrestrial aircraft and so forth.

Nonetheless, and if these are indeed refuted, we are then left with another and more annoying explanation which, to my mind, has been stirred up to dampen perhaps the true nature of these incredible vessels. That explanation concerns the military, which is possible in terms of their super-secret tech."

"I do not subscribe to this opinion, as my encounter with one of these remarkable UFOs left no doubt in my mind that the engineering involved was, quite simply put, a few hundred years ahead of anything we could possibly conceive of today. That's not just based on its ability, but also the sheer nature of its composition."

"I can say, with hand on heart that I experienced just such a backlash from a gentleman who purports to be an expert on the subject, simply by attending conferences where the speakers told him as much. My astonishment was equally heightened when he spent a whole day, on-and-off, batting my testimony back and forth and stating it was nothing short of military hardware. I continually opposed this, with him putting words in my mouth by stating 'I'm so glad you agree they're military,' when I stated nothing of the kind. This really annoyed me, as the tunnel-vision approach, coupled with sheer arrogance, marked this man as ignorant.

I saw this thing in broad daylight, so my confident antagonist must come to realize that I also had a good look at it, never once taking my eyes off the thing as it silently glided overhead. It was so close; I was afforded a remarkable glimpse into something which I have come to accept as not being part of our natural world."

"I cannot place the exact day this occurred, as I had no intention (back then) of reporting, documenting or even publishing such an encounter, since I was not part of any UFO group, and had no plans to discuss the encounter. I had sorely learnt, prior to this, the sheer mockery and heartache caused by the Press, and I had endured that with past sightings which were published to much amusement and mockery."

"But it was this, and ultimately this, that changed my perspective in terms of approach. Not straight away, mind. But that sighting spurred me to write a book based on the supernatural, which was eventually published by Capall Bann entitled, 'TWIN SOULS' of 2012. The book received virtually no recognition at the time of print, though I was extremely proud to have documented the case, amongst others, if only to nip at the heels of debunkers who appeared to have the entire scenario figured out. This topic can be a snake-pit, with smoke and mirrors lining your journey as you seek only truth and a yearning to understand just what exactly it is we're dealing with."

"Roughly, I'd gauge the sighting as having been between the 9th – 11th August 2010, and I recalled the time very well. It was around 7.15pm or thereabouts, with the evening pleasant and moderately sunny. We live in a small town on the outskirts of Bedfordshire, Kempton, which leads on to numerous other villages which spider out. I had entered the back garden for a cigarette, never smoking indoors, and distinctly recalled the distant sound of children playing in the park some way off. There was very little wind, and the sun was still up in a northern direction.

I had been watching a DVD on television and had just nipped out for a quick smoke with the DVD on pause."

"Something caught my attention after lighting up. Above me, and to my immediate left, I saw a shape moving across the sky. Curious, I turned to look up and was utterly astonished to realize that what I was observing was a huge (and I mean huge) triangular thing. There was no immediate first thought of it having either been 'this' or 'that,' as I discerned the peculiar nature of it. This gigantic black triangle just drifted above me, evidently having come from the east, heading west. It was around the size of a battleship and its surface reminded me of a jet-black tar. It was shiny. That's the first thought that came to me; raw and untainted tar. As I watched it closely in absolute amazement and was curious to note that it did not have sharp edges. They were rounded. Unmistakably so. This feature was prominent. Also, it was thickset, very thickset indeed.

269

Judging from my observation I wager you could get about fifteen decks on that thing. I had originally labeled it, 'The Fat Triangle,' though I felt that classification was too biased, especially in today's climate. I had a good look at the side of it, its underbelly and rear, because this was the angle it presented, searching for any tell-tell signs of machinery, components, or seams to perhaps deduce a kind-of mechanical feel to it. In other words, engineering of some kind or anything else that would offer an acceptable explanation in terms of an advanced terrestrial craft. There were none.

It was as though the thing had been molded in one piece, but the sheer scale of it caused me to wonder just how such a ship could be constructed. The lack of lights might well be attributed to it still being daylight, though I cannot be certain." "It made not a whisper as it travelled at about the speed of a conventional jet, slowly passing overhead and beyond. This is when I noticed the Sun, which was casting its rays from the north and illuminating the side of the craft."

"I observed on tar-like composition fine indentations, running along the entire panel as though machine-grooved – perhaps grills? Apart from that, the belly and rear of the thing were as smooth as glass. I wish to remind the reader that I have not coloured one ounce of this description, sticking only to what I observed. The rear was bland and flat, curved – as I stated- at the edges, with no engine, lights or any outward means of propulsion.

I remembered thinking to myself, "How the hell can it just hang there like that?" It was massive and looked weighty. Extremely weighty. It's hard to judge the exact height of it, considering its size and all, and since it was evidently unconventional, comparisons are hard to make. Suffice to the craft was utterly colossal."

"So, it was moving at the speed of a conventional aircraft, but I had no witnesses whatsoever. People ask me why I didn't race in to collect my mobile phone in order to film it, but this was the furthest thing from my mind. It's not a cheap copout, it is the honest truth.

I guess I was just so astonished I merely goggled at it. Besides, who would believe me?

To think I'd race in to fetch recording equipment to satisfy the whims of others (and perhaps to debunk it too), was not on the agenda as I observed the gargantuan thing that seemed to prove that some kind of anti-gravity mechanism is possible. Up there in the sky, it appeared as light as a feather. Nothing here on Earth, absolutely nothing, can perform the effortless feats that this craft demonstrated."

"We could perhaps reach the Moon using that thing, and also travel comfortably to Mars. We have nothing like that.

Absolutely nothing. And, considering this, even if it were some kind of exotic military hardware, why on Earth would they be flying it over civilian airspace? In terms of stealth, I think they're much smarter than that. They quite simply wouldn't. It just drifted off over the horizon never to be seen again."

"I will also add that something peculiar occurred as it flew overhead. The noise from the children's playing in the park some way off, was muted as the craft made its passage. On that note, another interesting point to observe for this report, is that we have many birds flitting about the region. But there was not one single bird in sight, while the craft made its passage. I felt no vibration, had no feelings, and lost no time during this encounter. I was merely awestruck at the apparent technology on display."

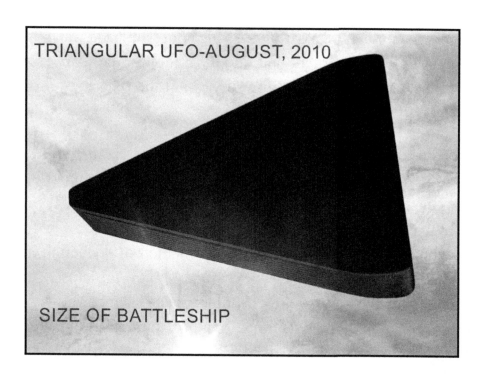

Pic. 20 – UFO witnessed by Ronald Kinsella

"As to why others never reported it I cannot say. I did wrestle with the fact that, having been so large, it surely must have been spotted by others. But, there again, and as in most cases concerning the paranormal, the strange case of the tar-like triangle disappeared that day, never to be spoken of by others other than myself.

I did not hallucinate it and do not drink. I do not take drugs and am of sound mind. But I will wager this, perhaps it will be of no surprise to those who investigate such things; we are being visited by something that even the military cannot control."

"Something is casually entering our airspace, and it appears unconcerned and aloof, bridging the gap (for some) announcing that humanity is not the only master of the Earth and Space."

"The rounded corners of the craft were interesting, as I do know – from 'The Belgian Wave' – that all were reported as being sharp. At the time I had no knowledge of them looking like this. This unique distinction caused me to apply a kind of 'Sherlock Holmes' method of deduction in terms of reports which now vary. I am no closer to understanding it, nor the phenomena as a whole, but have seen enough to convince me, being of rational mind, that there is more to our universe that we're currently led to believe."

A truly fascinating account of a huge triangle, Pic.20 shows Ronald's drawing of the battleship sized triangular craft.

Charles Bee (pseudonym) 28th October 2011, Darlington, County Durham.

This next report is one you would definitely call a close encounter, in fact so close that Charles was able to raise his hand and touch the underneath of the craft, an utterly amazing close encounter. Here's his report.

"There's a lot to tell but it's probably best to start in 2011 when I first saw the triangle. On 28th October 2011, my ex-partner and I, along with our two daughters, attended a large firework display in Darlington South Park. During the display we both saw a croissant shaped object lit up by the fireworks flying west to east. I actually thought it was one of the cartridges of the fireworks, so I dismissed it, although later it became clear it wasn't. My ex thought it was a UFO, but few weeks later seemed to have forgotten it."

"On 6th November 2011 in the evening, I was driving home after collecting my dog from my mother's house.

As I drove along Fulthorpe Avenue, Darlington, I was approaching a sharp left-hand turn when I noticed three lights in a triangular formation in the sky.

These swooped down and it was clear it was a large, black, triangular craft with the lights just inside each piece. I pulled over and dropped the window and tried to get a photograph of the object, but my hands were shaking too much. I lost sight of the object not long after. All sorts of weird things started to happen after that night. Both my daughter and I heard strange bleeping sounds in the night, almost like Morse code.

I also developed tinnitus and began to get the impression that someone or something was trying to communicate with me. It is difficult to explain, but I was being shown visions of things and felt a presence. Later, in November 2011, my then teenage daughter told me that she and two friends had seen a triangular craft over Salutation Road, Darlington, and had observed it from directly underneath.

It matched the description of what I'd seen. Her friends were positive about the sighting, but years later denied it."

"I no longer have dates as published accounts have disappeared off the internet, but in December 2011, I believe my daughter and I were walking our dog along the path between Crammond Close and Granton Close in the evening, when a white orb the size of a football descended to treetop level about thirty feet right in front of us and we were able to observe it for several minutes from a short distance. Over the next few weeks, I saw a light moving over the town on a number of nights. I also believe I saw the outline of several cloaked triangles during the day.

They were displaying a "false sky" and there was shimmering distortion around them. I was also getting the tinnitus and seeing visions of a planet with a dim, blue twilight sky, a large moon, and a large dim sun and a much smaller brighter one. The atmosphere was stuffy but breathable, causing me to constantly yawn and the gravity stronger than here, so I felt heavy and sluggish. I don't think I actually went there, but rather it was a vision sent for me to see?"

"I discussed these things with my daughter, and we decided to look for the light and try to get closer. We saw it one night moving over the Mowden area of the town. My ex-partner tried to say it was Venus, but Venus was also clearly visible, and the object was also clearly visible. My ex's daughter who was seven at the time, became hysterical and said it was aliens. We pursued the object, which was very bright, but as we followed slowly in the car into North Yorkshire, it seemed to be getting lower.

We both reasoned it was maybe a helicopter but there were no strobes and no noise. Somewhere between Cleasby and Manfield we lost sight of it as it got too low. We looked for the object but decided to give up and turn back home. As we drove back along the A67, I said 'let's look down by the river at Low Coniscliffe.' With hindsight I think 'they' told me it was there.

After driving down the track to the river, it was probably about 300 ft above ground level. It was huge, at least 1000 feet across, the lights at the apices were dim yellow/orange and there was a dimmer orange light in the body towards the back. I got out of the car and stood staring at the triangle. There was total silence; I could no longer even hear the traffic from the nearby A1-M motorway

The body was black, and it blocked out the stars, but I could see stars around it and also a nearby farmhouse on a hill south of the river. It also seemed to block out the breeze. I don't know whether I got closer to it or it to me, but I seemed right underneath it. I could see black channels etched into the underside of it, which you have now made me think are a docking mechanism. I can't explain how, and I've never told anyone until now, but it seemed to be just a few feet above me.

It seemed to be made of a slate or graphite material, very dark-grey and a smooth matt texture. I could feel the presence in my whole body and a dental implant was vibrating in my mouth. I could see the channels covered the underside of the craft: they are probably six feet across and of a similar depth. I raised my hand and touched part of the craft's body between the channels. I was terrified and even thought it could harm me but did it anyway. I brushed my fingers over it and then put my entire palm on it. It felt like a hard, kitchen worktop with a matt finish, but it was not cold. The next thing I remember is my daughter shouting to me to come back to the car. She hadn't wanted to get out."

Darren Cooper 12th January 2014

Again, I am indebted to Darren for this report of his remarkably close encounter.

"On the night of the January 12th, 2014, my friend Christian McGailey and I went to work as usual between 6-6.30pm, the same as any other day. We were working as industrial cleaners at the time where we travel between destinations during the day and this one is our last job of the day, but we could not enter the building before 6pm".

Darren Cooper (right) with Philip Mantle

"When we got into the building and the first thing we always did was grab a coffee, because there was a free-vend machine in the canteen. So, while we are drinking our coffee and I am showing Chris a new app I have from

279

Dr. Steven Greer called 'The ET Contact Tool.' I played a few tones from the app and then went onto the meditation part, and I believe we listened to this all the way through, while looking at the instruments part with my phone on the table!! The alarm on the magnetometer sounded and we both look at each other and said something like 'There is something here if it's going off.' I picked up my phone and took a screen shot before it stopped!"

So, after being a little freaked-out that the app was either working or just faulty, I didn't know what to think!! We both said at roughly the same time, 'Let's get out of here.' So, we made our way out to the fire exit for a cigarette before we started work."

"We were still talking about what had just happened when the alarm sounded, and this was about 8pm-8:10pm, when all of a sudden I believe it was the chilling silence that made us look up, and there was this 'V shaped' craft floating silently over our heads. I remember turning to Chris and saying something like, 'Are you seeing this, WTF is it"?

"I felt completely calm and mesmerized that the craft was so close, I could have jumped up and touched it! Now before the craft came so close to us there were birds singing and water running to our right, the sound of wind moving through the trees and various noises from the hotel to the left about 100 yards or so.

280

And then total silence, as if all sounds had just been muted or switched off. It felt like there was static from the craft and I felt like everything was going in slow-motion, because I specifically remember stepping forward to the front of the steps on the top of the stairwell and inspecting the craft as if it were standing still. I said out loud to Chris, 'It's too clean-cut and silent to be anything else apart from a UFO? It looked like it just came from a mould.'

There were no rivets, no seams, no engines, nothing similar to anything man made!! It had a surface like black glass or water, and from what I could see I believe we could see the stars straight through the craft. I have never in my life seen lights like those on this craft still today."

Artist impression of Darren Cooper's sighting

"Everything on the craft was too perfect, including the five white lights that I can only describe as the brightest white you can possibly imagine! When the craft was fully visible to us there was a bright red (orb) point of light in the centre of the V floating along with the craft and by this time my brain could not calculate what was going on, but I knew what I was seeing and feeling, because we could feel the heat from the lights and I called out again to Chris, 'Are you seeing this'? (I say, 'called out,' because it felt like I had to! Like we were in some sort of field of energy), and I said it looks like its flying backwards, because it's flying points first!! But the orb was not connected to the craft OMG!!"

"We are still talking about the craft while it glided silently away to our left, straight towards the back of the hotel about 150 yards away and then I turn again to Chris to my right and said,. 'I can't believe what we are seeing,' and I turned back to look at the craft again, and it had either disappeared/dematerialized, or accelerated to an unbelievable speed."

"We both turned round and went back into the building very confused regarding what had just happened, and only just realizing we hadn't even attempted to take a picture! It felt like we had been incapable of doing so!! We just walked towards the canteen again to start work, when Chris stopped me and said, 'Do you realize the time?'

I said, 'No, that's the last thing I care about mate, not after what we've just seen.' We then realized that more time had passed than we thought! It is now way past 10pm and I don't understand why? We didn't get out of there till gone 1am and the job only took roughly two hours?"

Darren JM, 2014 Beeston, Nottingham

Another report from social media, interestingly this triangle was brown in colour, here's his report, "2014 sitting in my back garden, I'd just finished work and looked up and noticed the outline. Shaped like a triangle or triangular boomerang with five circles underneath, no lights, no noise, gliding over me at about 300ft up. Dark brown maybe in colour, I stood up and watched it glide away at slow speed like something from an X Files movie. Didn't faze me in slightest as I've seen others (different) kinds of UFO before throughout my life."

"I saw a saucer-shaped disk in sky at five years old, but due to my age I now question myself on this, but the memory stuck... And through the years I've seen many silver orb sightings. Singular sightings and multiple sightings. The wife just laughs it off when I talk of these." I'm sure the reaction of his wife is quite common for those who have a sighting without their partner present."

Leigh Smith, April 2016 Marlborough

"I've seen about five UFOs in the last five years. I spend a lot of time looking up at the sky since my first encounter. The first sighting was unbelievable. I had just dropped of a Hi- Fi in Marlborough, Wiltshire, from an eBay sale and when I set the satnav for home, it sent me back in a completely different direction. I was travelling down a long, empty road about 10pm towards Upavon. To the right of the road about a mile ahead I could see what I thought was a combine harvester with a bar of five lights on the top in a straight line."

It was slowly heading towards the road. I thought why, would it be out at this time of night. As I got closer I then thought that this might be an extremely low-flying helicopter carrying a forward-facing bar of lights, as it seemed a little too high to be a vehicle on the ground.

As I got closer it changed course and headed toward me. At this point it was 200 meters away. I thought "This helicopter is too low and it's going to hit me. When it came within fifty meters of me I slammed my brakes on and got out of my car. The car has stop/start, so the engine cut out and I could hear everything perfectly.

This was definitely not a helicopter as it was silent. I froze as I could see the sheer size of this thing was huge. As big as a passenger jet; a matt-black perfect triangle 50ft directly above my head. As I went over my head I could see only three lights, one on each corner with one red light in the middle. The lights were not like bright LEDs, more like dull amber but were all aiming off skew. The red light was not for illumination, it had a clear lens, but what was inside can only be described as mechanical. This thing stayed at 50ft from me, so where the hill dropped to my left it went down the hill and disappeared out of sight. I went back to the same spot the next day to investigate, and I noticed that this was military land.

There was a huge warning sign right next to where I stopped the car. No trespassing or you will be detained. blah blah. I know this is a military drone using secret anti-gravity technology. Don't ask me why; I just know this isn't ET. I've been researching these things from the moment I got home on that night. From the information I have it's definitely a gov project. My other sightings point to something completely different.

I think we are being visited but the triangle is one of ours. I know so many people that have seen these and we all agree on this."

Luke Midgley, Elland, Halifax in 2021

"My friend and I were walking down the street at night; I looked off to the right and saw what I thought was a flock of white birds flying in the dark and I thought that it was odd. So, I stopped and quickly realized it was not birds. I told my friend about it, and initially thinking it was some kind of mist, I suddenly realized it was hundreds of sparkly lights in a V. Then we realized there was a huge, black triangle, not even high up - just low over the houses, cruising in complete, eerie silence. This huge thing had just sneaked up on us. It seemed to be light absorbing and you could only make out its shape from how it cut out the stars in a triangle.

The triangle flew point first in a V with the back end being more convex. We watched it float off into the darkness and through the valley. This happened in Elland, Halifax in 2021"

Robert Peter 25th February 2021 Christchurch, Dorset

Another report via social media which took place on 25th February 2021 in Christchurch, Dorset at 20.22 the sky was completely clear sky.

'Good day Colin, I'm happy to share what I seen if you interested, it's hard to talk about this with people, mainly because they don't believe me and they twist my words like I saw something else. I had just set up my camera to take some pictures of stars and satellites, when I saw a triangular flying object hovering in the sky extremely low, it was very close to the ground. I estimated the speed at less than 40mph and the speed was constant. The object was as large as a building and looked very solid, I couldn't hear any noise and it moved a bit sideways.

There were four lights shining like stars, one light in the middle and three lights equidistant from each other were light blue. The colour of the four lights were somewhere between x-ray and ultraviolet. I was literally underneath the object; it was so close it was awfully hard to see the edges and the object was the same colour as the sky.

I could feel a pressure which is hard to explain. I have been out watching stars and taking pictures of the night sky for a long time now but have never seen anything like this before.' I asked Robert a few questions and these were his answers.

'Yes they are all same light blue colour. The pressure was similar like when you are under water. Like I felt extremely low frequency pressure-sound, but I couldn't hear'

Mark Leeper, August 2021, Odiham, Hampshire

"Monday 30th August last year, bank holiday 11pm, I hear a Chinook thudding away in the distance, nothing unusual but could tell by the sound it was low and hovering or moving very slowly from the sound of it, not flying overhead as normal, we were very close to RAF Odiham, home of the Chinook. Anyway, being a helicopter nerd, I went outside in the back garden, it was a clear night, no wind or cloud, I looked toward the Chinook sound as it was getting closer to the point where I can feel it almost overhead but could see no navigation lights at all.

Then, all of a sudden, one green dot came into view, at first I thought it was the nose light on the Chinook, but no, then a second green light followed the first perfectly, low and slow as the first green dot passed where I was standing. I saw the whole craft, it was triangular in shape; all sides were the same size, green dot at front, purple burn of some kind from point to point on the back of both craft. This was all under the noise of a Chinook which I couldn't see but it was there, they headed straight to RAF Odiham, I think perhaps the Chinook was giving them radar cover"

"Points to add which I don't think I said are as follows, I would say the height was under 100ft as they went over the top of the next-door neighbors' bungalow, so it was easy to estimate the height and speed. It was very slow, no more than 30mph, as to the size of craft, I would say about the size of a small plane or fighter. Really close to each other, a couple of car lengths apart, can't say about noise of the craft because of the deafening sound and vibration of the Chinook. One way I can try to explain the configuration of the illuminated rear of the crafts is as follows.

Try to picture four or five really wide, flat, TV screens put in a row, with each screen lit up with a purple blue glow, it's the only way I can describe it.

Personally, because of the military connection I think that what I saw were reverse-engineered, man-made UFOs. I found out two days later that the previous weekend in the Basingstoke Gazette (online), someone had filmed and sent to them a video of spiraling acrobatic lights in the sky late night over Winklebury in Basingstoke, after watching the footage I determined that what I saw could well have been made by these craft, but that's just a theory. I contacted the gazette, but no-one got back to me, but after leaving messages and some colourful language, someone finally did get back to me. They said that they were interested until I started swearing, the video was later debunked as a father and son drone display team, load of rubbish in my opinion, I contracted Nick Pope, MUFON and Richard Hall of Rich Planet, I didn't see any point of reporting it to the police or ask the RAF at Odiham."

Steven Bate, 2016, Mansfield Nottingham

A short but interesting sighting I'm sure you will agree.

"I was watching the Persied's meteor shower about 2016 with my daughter, when what looked like two shooting stars went over slowly followed by an orange triangle in the middle of them, it looked like it was on the edge of the

289

atmosphere and the orange glow was heat friction. It shimmered in and out of view just for a second or two, the only thing I could find on the internet was a picture of the hypersonic glider [wave rider] that the main powers are developing"

****

Chapter 7

The Alleged TR-3B

There have been many rumors about the TR3B, an alleged secret US military triangle, possibly back-engineered from captured alien craft. Whilst there is no proof it even exists; the internet is buzzing with alleged information regarding this top-secret craft. I remember in the early days of my involvement in UFO's, that when a secret plane came out of Area 51 the authorities were happy to encourage the belief it was a UFO, somewhere along the line this has now changed. Every time someone mentions an ET triangle, anywhere in the world, everyone jumps on the bandwagon and shouts TR3B! So where has this all come from? Rumor has it that the TR3B legend was started by the late Edgar Fouche as a disinformation project. Edgar Fouche claimed to have worked at Groom Lake (Area 51). His TR-3B is most likely pure science fiction and there has never been any single, credible, photo of a TR-3B.

In the 1980's when the U.S. was testing prototypes of the new stealth aircraft, there were many reports of massive football pitch sized flying triangular craft over the East coast of England, which had nothing to do with prototypes being tested by the U.S. Air Force. And these had nothing to do with the alleged TR-3B disinformation promoted by the late Edgar Fouche.

I have no doubt we are manufacturing some sort of triangular shaped craft, after all the Vulcan Bomber had a triangular shape to it and I would guess it's a natural progression that we err towards triangular craft, such as experimental hypersonic wave riders.

The TR3B, even if it exists, would not count towards the worldwide sightings of triangles; let's look at the different models that exist. A quick look on the web shows hundreds of different configurations and construction of triangles around the world, this is not in keeping with any manufacturing process whether black budget or otherwise.

Look at the stealth fighter and bomber, remarkably similar construction with little variation in appearance due to constraints of manufacture and budget. The F117 stealth fighter had only fifty-nine production models and only twenty-one Stealth Bombers were built. That being the case, one would then assume the large quantities of triangles seen around the world are not from the US, otherwise they would need a production line similar to the 'Model T' Ford!

When a stealth fighter is downed retrieval teams pick up the pieces or bomb hell out of the downed craft to avoid parts falling into the wrong hands. Therefore, do you seriously think that a government would fly such experimental craft, including triangles, over densely populated areas sometimes at roof-top height, knowing that any problems would need immediate retrieval?

All manner of vehicles and cranes etc. would need to be deployed, not to mention a heavy presence of armed military along with the extremely high possibility of civilian casualties and media exposure. If you believe all these triangles are the alleged US-built TR3B, then you have been brainwashed by Edgar Fouche, and by the way, do you think any government would patent secret technology for their competitors to copy? Examples of this can be seen doing the rounds on the net.

So, what are these enigmatic triangles? I have already stated earlier on in the book that I think these are dimensional craft, rather than extra terrestrial, coming here from a parallel universe running alongside our own. These craft are using technology we have yet to discover, but I have a few ideas that I shall explore with you as to their manufacture. I was sent a link to a YouTube video by a friend of mine, the video was from a guy called Boaz Almog on 'quantum levitation.' Boaz took a piece of metal and cooled it down to zero degrees Kelvin by immersing in liquid nitrogen.

The effect of this was the metal became a superconductor and when introduced to a magnetic field quantum levitation was achieved. The metal just hung in the air without any movement, just like Mel Orton's triangle at Sharnford which hung in the air like a picture on a wall. This is called quantum levitation.

The noticeable thing about the experiment was the amount of vapor or condensation that surrounded the object. This got me thinking as our craft had fluffy white clouds on the wingtips as it materialized (Pic.21). I have heard people say that because there is smoke surrounding some UFO pictures then they must be faked, like a Doctor Who set, but I believe it's not smoke but condensation for these reasons.

Pic.21

Pic.22 reproduced with kind permission by Michael Schratt

Let's suppose the liquid I saw on the surface of the craft was something like liquid nitrogen trapped underneath a transparent skin, the beams on the surface would then protrude through the skin into the liquid turning them all into super conductors.

This would then cause the craft to have quantum levitation and the effect of the cold craft in our atmosphere would cause vaporization to occur. Like a heat sink on a printed circuit board where the heat goes to the point of least resistance, then the same thing would happen with the points of the triangular craft, the three corners would naturally dissipate the vapor. There are many worldwide reports of triangular craft covered in pipe work similar to the back of a refrigerator; you can see this in Pic.22 sent to me by Michael Schratt.

I surmise that these pipes are carrying liquid nitrogen (or something similar) so again we have superconductivity and hence quantum levitation. You may have noticed throughout the book that many witnesses when talking about the craft's movement, say things like "it glided" or "floated" and I assume this is down to the antigravity operation of the craft, certainly our craft floated it's nose up like a submarine under water.

The best description I heard about their movement is the effect you get when two people put a clean sheet onto a bed, the trapped air in the middle slowly lets the sheet descend and that's a good analogy of the way they have been seen to move. If antigravity is being used keep these craft afloat, would this work in outer space where there is no gravity? It may be another pointer to these craft, along with their occupants, being dimensional.

So, what about the "lights"? You can see from the book they vary and can include all the colours of the rainbow; one common factor is the brightness of these lights, and I can vouch for that myself. I have never seen anything quite as bright as the lights that night. I even persuaded John to make me a 3D model out of transparent material to show how bright the lights looked when we approached the invisible craft just before it de-cloaked.

Our craft had red lights in the corners and white in the middle, Mel Orton's huge craft at Sharnford had the reverse, white lights in the corners and red in the middle.

Again, we can only guess what these may be, my guess is that the corner lights may be used to change the vibrations (frequency) of the craft to enable it to travel through dimensions. From my years of research, I surmise that the middle, larger light may be some kind of tractor beam or searching device.

Another observation of mine from our close encounter was just how perfect the craft was, it looked like it had just come out of the showroom, no burn marks, no wear and tear. This also applies to the way it had been manufactured, no nuts and bolts, no welding seams, no rivets; I like to use the phrase "sympathetically assembled," just a beautiful, immaculate piece of engineering.

Throughout the book we can see lots of similarities between these craft, generally three lights in the corners underneath, and a central, larger light, although colours can vary between red and white. All the colours of the rainbow pop up at some point or other. The craft are normally black or grey, but silver and orange and brown have been spotted too. In most cases there is no noise, but when noise is detected it's described as a 'low hum or droning sound.' And then there's the cloaking effect often referred to as 'rippling' which we saw as our craft materialized in front of us, and of course the movement, always described as floating, like the craft is under water, which may be due to anti-gravity technology being employed.

I have no doubt in my mind that these craft are not of this world, and I believe they are dimensional rather than extra terrestrial. The next part of this book will look at the relationship between close encounters with a UFO and the paranormal world.

****

Chapter 8

UFO's and the Paranormal

(A science we do not understand)

There is a connection between UFO's and the paranormal which is not often talked about or recognized. Those having had a close encounter find it difficult to talk about these "other" events to the general public and often keep it to themselves. I am indebted to those people who have written to me about these connections, and they will appear in this section of the book. Having spent my whole working life as a design draughtsman involved in many technical projects worldwide, including the aircraft industry, the close encounter was, as previously stated, a paradigm shift in my way of thinking, but what was to come next changed my perception of life here on earth for good. What we are about to explore many will find incredible, especially some of my friends and family who will think I'm completely mad, but for those of you who have had close encounters of your own, I'm sure you will be able to empathize with me. Let's go back to that night of the 31/03/1999 at 9.50 pm, this is what happened.

As the craft floated it's nose up into the air I was looking at the surface and could see box sections interlocking quite clearly, I was then looking at the nose when I thought to myself "This nose is very round and also very big" in fact I had realized it was out of proportion to the rest of the craft. It was like someone had put a pair of binoculars in front of my eyes. I then realized it seemed I was so close to the nose (maybe six feet?) I couldn't see the rest of the craft's surface or any of the box sections, just a big, round, grey nose stuck in front of me.

Next I had a side view of the nose; I could see how the craft's top and bottom surfaces joined to a lighter central core, like a sandwich. No nuts and bolts, rivets or welding seams.

I do not remember seeing anything between the front and the side view; it was like I had flipped from the front to the side instantaneously. I don't remember seeing the craft roll to show me both views. And same again, I'm back in the car and I don't recall seeing the craft between the last close-up of the side view of the nose and being back in the car itself. I say that, but there is a final, hazy recollection of being away from the craft in the darkness and the most peaceful feeling enveloping me, but I can't bring it fully to mind.

The next I can recall is shouting 'stop, stop, stop,' and my wife driving forward to enable her to reverse into a gateway of the main Fosse Way. The result of her driving forward was that a large hedge blocked our view of the craft and I thought to myself "If it's going to clear off, now would be a good time" and sure enough it did. We jumped out of the car, and it had vanished, but we watched a huge triangular craft flying away from us, the biggest flying craft I have ever seen. I now believe this was a mother ship.

300

Now I'm not sure what took place there, it seems to me a possible out-of-body experience, however I spoke to the late Budd Hopkins at the Leeds conference here in the UK and he thought maybe images were placed in my mind by the aliens. Unfortunately, he did not have time to elaborate on this as we were rudely interrupted by a crazy woman brandishing a crystal she had found in the forest!

At this point in time, I believed I had had an out of body experience (OBE) but decided to keep an open mind on this for the time being as the whole experience was surreal. I did read books on OBE's and tried a few times, but never managed to achieve it again.

The first week after the encounter we had many electrical problems, TV switching channels on its own, video recorder recording on its own, electric clock started working after many years of being broken and I lost a hard drive on one of my PCs. It turned out the receiver on the TV had blown and the video recorded had programmed itself to record every two weeks. The TV repair man who came said it was very unusual, the sort of thing that only happens after a lightning strike. It was put to me from someone I met along the way that maybe 'they' followed us back that night and scanned the house to see our reaction and thus the electrical interference? Sounds reasonable and the best explanation I have heard so far.

I had started to watch the sky more and started to see unusual things and I also started having other weird things happen to me, so I started to keep a record with dates. I must admit I was finding all of this fascinating from a scientific point of view and like I say, this is all a science we do not yet understand.

June 7th, 2000, standing on the back patio two spheres of bright, white light the size of a five pence coin held at arm's length came overhead. Around midnight, the first one came directly over our house; it was approximately 5,000 feet in the air heading from South to North. A bright Omni directional white light with no trail, the same colour coming towards me then going away at a tremendous speed (two or three thousand mph?). Within thirty seconds a second sphere came over, more to the left of me from my position, lower down this time at a height of approximately 2,000 and at the same speed. It was glowing white, which included a view of its side this time. Both spheres were travelling horizontal to the Earth, i.e., they were not meteorites coming down to Earth, but intelligently controlled objects. The approximate height is based on own my glider flying experience of being towed to 2,000 feet and released.

Around 24th June 2000, I was captain for the Black Horse darts team in Hinckley and we are playing the Anchor in Burbage that night. It had been a lovely day so when we arrived we decided to sit in a pub garden for a beer before the match. As I was sitting there I distinctly felt a "splat" on the crown of my head. I exclaimed a bird had just 'pooed' on me, but when I felt my head there was nothing, no poo, no water! The sky was clear blue, no clouds or rain drops and left me wondering if I had had some sort of muscle spasm on the top of my scalp.

On its own this would have meant nothing, but the following Saturday 26th June, it happened twice more, this time in my back garden in St Georges Avenue, the same feeling of bird poo hitting me on the head, but twice this time. The first one happened when I was walking from my shed to get a coffee from the house and then twenty minutes later, same again on the way back down to the shed – splat, right on top of my head!

I was obsessed with building the model in the shed at the time of the second splats and I felt like some sort of message had been sent down from above, maybe to spur me on with making the model. It's been twenty-two years since then and whatever it was, it's never happened again.

Unknown date in 2000, sometime around midnight. I had been watching the stars, when one started to move quite slowly. It became more interesting as it turned through 90 degrees and disappeared behind a cloud. It didn't return so I went to bed, as usual I looked out at the sky from my window and I couldn't believe what I saw, a large bright light moving slowly over Hinckley Town centre. Definitely not a helicopter, the light again was shining all around the object. I woke my wife up to come and have a look, but by the time she got to the window it had completely disappeared. She said it must have been just for me so next time not to bother waking her up! This experience had me investing in a new digital camcorder so I could record future events!

Autumn 2000. You would have thought being next to a UFO was frightening experience, but for me it was the opposite, like meeting God. It was in fact a beautiful moment, but this next experience was by far the most disturbing and frightening so far. I have always loved fishing, especially river fishing and I was a member of the Greenhill Angling Club in Leicester. The club had a stretch of the river Soar near Rothley in Leicestershire, and this was quite remote at the rear of Rowena Garden Centre. I was taking part in a small club competition, probably no more than ten anglers.

I ended up being pegged in a field on my own opposite an island where it's possible to wade into the water to fish. I had to go down a steep bank at the peg so I could then stand in the water and happily fish away. The fishing was going well, and I was in my element, a perfect Sunday morning when suddenly I heard the sound of what I thought were footsteps coming towards me. It sounded like two people, i.e., four footsteps and the noise was getting louder as they approached my peg. Being a polite sort of gentleman, I climbed up to bank to move my fishing tackle out of the way of the towpath, but much to my surprise there was no one there, more surprising the footsteps continued to get louder and were coming towards me!

My first thoughts were that it was a big cat (big African cats have been illegally released into the wild in the UK), probably hungry and wanting me for its dinner! My mind was racing as to what to do, I could swim to the island, but I know cats cat swim too, especially if hungry, so I then decided to take a pointed spike out of my rod holdall that I use for my fishing umbrella and use that for defense. I figured if it were a cat I'd go back down the riverbank and force the cat to jump on me from above and using its own body weight to impale it on my umbrella spike. It's amazing how quickly you can formulate a plan in your head when you are in a life-threatening situation, I was bricking it!

Whatever it was it came towards me and passed from my left-hand side to my right-hand side at approx. six feet in front of me, I could see nothing moving, no animal, no grass or branches moving, nothing at all. I was petrified and now thought my best form of defense was attack, so I took the spike and started swinging it at the grass and shouting, I put the stick under my arm and started clapping and shouting but nothing became visible. The noise just faded away. I calmed down and thought 'cats would not make loud noises like that,' plus the grass and bracken were only six to eight inches high, so any animal that close would have been visible. I decided it had to be a paranormal incident, some sort of 'space time continuum' and that whatever it was wasn't actually here, but somewhere else.

I knew this had come from the UFO encounter as I can't remember having had any other experiences before the triangle, only afterwards. This was the moment I decided that our visitors were not extraterrestrial at all, they were in fact inter-dimensional! Having deduced this was the case and not a big cat at all, I calmed down and felt extremely relieved, rather an inter-dimensional being than a big, hungry cat. I felt calm enough to carry on fishing and actually won the match!

2000, date unknown. I was driving my wife's recently purchased car with my daughter and two of her girlfriends sitting in the back; I was taking them all to Bosworth Hall to go swimming.

As we pulled off from some traffic lights there was a very large cracking noise in the car, it was like a whip-crack or a large electrical discharge. I stopped the car to have a look at what it could have been.

The car was a recent purchase, and my first thought was it was two cars welded together and it had snapped in two as the noise was so loud. We got out to examine the car, but there was no visible sign of anything untoward.

I drove on gingerly but nothing else happened, the car was fine. On its own this could be nothing and soon forgotten, but a couple of weeks later it happened again. I was on my own this time in my works van. I was on my way back from Bosworth when the same happened again, a loud whip-crack, I slowed down but didn't stop this time. On my return home I checked the van for a bullet hole or lighting strike, nothing could be found. There were no plastic pop bottles in the car and the cracking noise would have been far louder than a bottle could make when expanding. I once read a report of ghost hunters who heard a loud crack near them, like someone had stood on a branch and snapped it. I did wonder if it was some sort of electrical discharge from an entity that was going back to where it came from. Me, an engineer starting to have these strange thoughts, these things were impossible but there were happening.

Spring 2001. I was on the back patio watching the stars at night again. I swear they were all stationary and then one started to move slowly across the sky. I initially thought it was a satellite, but when it turned through 90 degrees I got excited. This time my camera was at my side and ready to go, but by the time I lifted it to the sky the object had disappeared completely. I stood there and for a brief moment and thought I was going insane. But I wasn't going insane; I know what I saw but failed to record it in time.

Date unknown, year 2000. Channel 5 came round to make a short video for the internet; this was to coincide with a SCI-FI weekend on the TV.

The cameraman, who was French, had been up and down the country talking to and filming different experiencers. He told me he was convinced that aliens were real, so many people saying the same things and he thought he would meet one himself soon! I took the opportunity to ask many questions and he said he had interviewed someone who had had many abductions and out of body experiences. He said every time he was taken he was left with a cigarette type burn mark on his arm. I showed him one on my arm that I had also had for some time. He was so amazed he called over his colleague to have a look. He reckoned it was exactly the same. I had already been to the doctors and had used different creams to no effect. It eventually cleared of its own accord.

This next one is a bit on the strange side and may well have an Earthly explanation. Spring 2000. I had a dreadful pain in my stomach making me double up, it passed fairly quickly. The next day after visiting the toilet and flushing the chain there was a shiny object left behind.

The object was bigger than a £1.00 coin but smaller than a two pence piece. The object looked like a 'big smarty;' the surface seemed to shine in the water.

I retrieved and dried the object which was brown in colour with almost a metallic looking surface which I took to be chemical deposits, possibly magnesium which I take for cramp. I accidentally dropped the object which broke into several large pieces.

The inside was honeycombed like a crunchy bar, but white in colour. I took this to my doctor who was amazed! He had never seen anything like it before and sent it off for analysis. After several weeks, the surgery phoned to say the object had mysteriously disappeared and could not be traced at the hospital. A couple of months later I received a letter from my surgery with a lab report.

Somehow, after several months, the sample had reappeared, unfortunately it doesn't throw any light on what the object was, the report said "The outer brown layer consists of fibrous fragments containing traces of carbonate and phosphate, this appears to be fecal material.

The inner layer consists of white crystals of a water-insoluble, aromatic organic compound or compounds. Cholesterol was not detected. The crystals may be ingested material." I still have the report today, it may well be nothing out of the ordinary, but the fact it went missing and then reappeared is a bit suspicious, but it may just be a simple NHS mistake.

Date unknown. A short while after the encounter I went and spent an afternoon with ex-police officer John Hanson and partner, they told me many interesting things, but some were very frightening. John took some excellent pictures of my model onboard the narrow boat where he was living at the time.

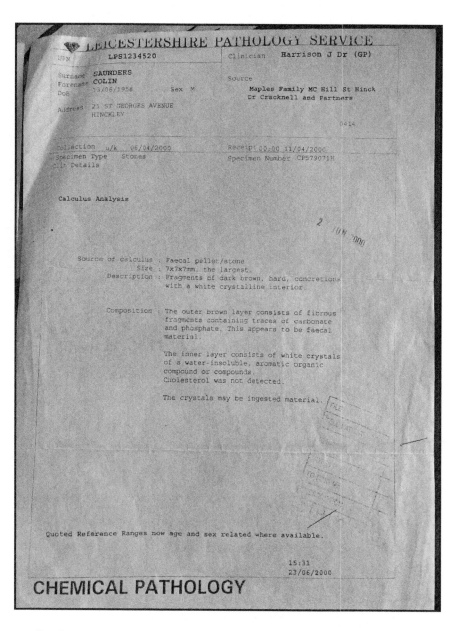

UPN LPS1234520   Clinician   Harrison J Dr (GP)

Surname SAUNDERS
Forename COLIN   Source
DoB   23/06/1958   Sex M   Maples Family MC Hill St Hinck
Address 21 ST GEORGES AVENUE   Dr Cracknell and Partners
        HINCKLEY
                                                                    0414

Collection u/k 06/04/2000   Receipt 00:00 11/04/2000
Specimen Type   Stones   Specimen Number CP579071H
Clin Details

Calculus Analysis

Source of calculus : Faecal pellet/stone
              Size : 7x7x7mm. the largest.
       Description : Fragments of dark brown, hard, concretions
                     with a white crystalline interior.

       Composition : The outer brown layer consists of fibrous
                     fragments containing traces of carbonate
                     and phosphate. This appears to be faecal
                     material.

                     The inner layer consists of white crystals
                     of a water-insoluble, aromatic organic
                     compound or compounds.
                     Cholesterol was not detected.

                     The crystals may be ingested material.

Quoted Reference Ranges now age and sex related where available.

                                           15:31
                                           23/06/2000

CHEMICAL PATHOLOGY

Lab report from Leicestershire Pathology Service

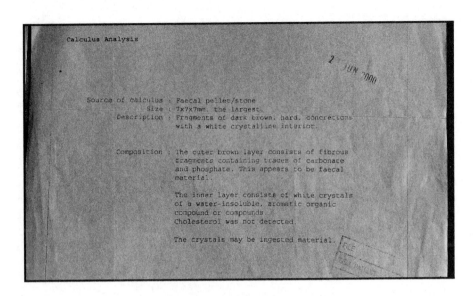

Details in the lab report

On my return home the house was empty, and I went upstairs and looked out of the bedroom window across the estate. Thinking about what John had been saying I said aloud, "Come on boys give us a sign" and this object came down in front of my eyes over the estate, it was like a meteorite or shooting star. You could not see the object itself as it was travelling so fast, but there was a trail left behind with all the colours of the rainbow flashing away. It was a bit like a firework but much bigger, no sound, and it just burnt itself out before hitting the ground, for a brief moment it looked like a rainbow had filled the sky, it was daylight too, a marvelous coincidence perhaps?

November 2001. It was the Sunday night and I had just returned from Graham Birdsall and Russel Callaghan's

UFO conference in Leeds. I was the last one to bed as usual and I normally look out of my bedroom window to the south and scan the skies. This particular night as I reached the landing, a light caught my eye looking north over the park which we lived next to. It would be about half a mile maximum, maybe closer, and inside a cloud, orange and spherical. The cloud base was extremely low and heavy that night and you could not see the sky through the clouds. The object in the cloud was quite big (five pence at arm's length) and was glowing orange, there was a beam of light the same diameter and colour as the object shining through the cloud like a torch beam. However, this beam was not omnidirectional but dead straight, more like a laser beam.

I watched this for a minute or more in amazement before making the usual fatal mistake – I went to get my camera from the bedroom. As I picked it up I thought it's going to be gone when I get back, and sure enough it had disappeared. Amber light is not associated with aircraft, and it was not Mars as it was the wrong time of year, and we normally see Mars looking South.

Date unknown. I had been looking at Sirius through my small telescope when I noticed what look like a small planet drifting along in Earth's atmosphere, This object glowed white, green then red, the object kept cycling through these colours all the time that I watched it, probably half an hour or so, I was amazed there were no reports on this in the UFO community

I don't normally take notice of my dreams as they are so vivid and have been intense all my life. I tend to dismiss them as the brain sorting itself out, but I feel I must put this one in writing. Approximately one year after the encounter I had a dream that a UFO was hovering over our house.

I dreamt I heard the noise of an alien scuttling down the roof tiles to my bedroom window, I also dreamt I was sitting on my bed and that my wife walked into my room (we were sleeping in separate rooms at the time, but still amicable and our twelve-year-old daughter had the third bedroom) and sat on the bed next to me. A dark, shadowy figure came through the window towards us with a silver glowing rod in his left hand, I started screaming and I awoke to find I was screaming in real life! I'm surprised I didn't wake my wife or daughter up as I screamed so loudly. I collected my wits and went back to sleep.

In the morning when I came downstairs, my wife was in the kitchen and before I said anything at all she said, "I had a dream last night that a UFO was over the house, and I was walking from room-to-room looking for Victoria (our daughter)." Well, this is from a woman who rarely remembered a dream in the thirty years we were together.

I've never heard of a synchronized dream before, people tell me it was probably a real occurrence. I have to say this one still haunts me.

03/10/2019

This is the most recent sighting I've had. It was 6pm and I was walking my dog over the fields next to Barwell Lane, Leicestershire where I now live. There was a clear blue sky that night and I noticed an object in the sky flashing away, initially I thought it was a plane covered by a vapor trail from another plane catching the sun intermittently, however there was a plane above and also below the object. The two planes were flying in opposite directions, but both catching the sun and reflecting yellow light from the rays (one hour to sunset). I watched the object leave the vapor trail but continue flashing a very bright white light, when the light was not flashing you could just make out a sphere, possibly greyish metal. It was definitely not a Chinese lantern and not a gas burner suspended below a hot air balloon.

When the object flashed the light was crescent shaped, but only on the left-hand side, covering about a quarter of the object, like half a moon. I assumed the light must have been emitting from one side only, i.e., the rear and I was looking at a side-view and hence the crescent shape. The whole object was not flashing, just on the left side at the rear as it floated away to the right. The object moved smoothly and slowly and flashed intermittently, like dot dash, dot dash, dot dot, dash, dash dot dot dash etc, it gave the impression it was malfunctioning. The object was between two and five thousand feet high but was possibly coming down slightly as it drifted away. I ran round the field and got a better view, but now it must have been a mile or more away and as we are quite high up here I could now see green countryside behind the object, so it was definitely down here in Earth's atmosphere and was definitely not the space station.

It was weird to see it heading towards a motorway still flashing away. Its path was mainly across open countryside, I took lots of photos and video, but it was too distant to show anything significant. Interestingly enough, the video I took is all distorted and I have never seen this before on my phone. On another video I took you can see an orb-type image flying in front of the camera whilst I was trying to video the object.

That's the majority of the strange things that have happened to me so far, there are many others that have occurred along the way, but less exciting, so I'll just keep them on record for myself.

Some of the above could be natural occurrences like the meteorite in No.10, and the cigarette burn mark was probably a small viral infection. I keep an open mind on all of this, but I believe that some of the above are definitely paranormal. I list them in order of magnitude with the most significant first: the UFO encounter, invisible creature at the river, two fast spheres directly overhead, orange light in the cloud over the park, whip-cracks in car, bird splats on the head and the sphere over Barwell fields. I'm sure there are more to come!

Over the years I have read of many other people having strange experiences before and after seeing a UFO. Many people go on to have further UFO sightings throughout their lives, many have experiences before seeing a UFO and often we find these things run in families.

For the purpose of this book, we shall only be looking at triangular UFO's and the paranormal, but this type of activity exists with all types of UFO close encounters. We shall explore some of these examples in the next few pages in chronological order.

Lynn Lodge (nee Lynn Brown) Narborough, Leicester, 1970's

This close encounter includes a visit from the infamous men in black!

"Ok, I remember, reading about the Hinckley case, just down the road. I know I just had no recollection of the object I first saw which appeared to be hovering just above a high hedge lining the turn into Desford lane, approaching from Kirby Muxloe. I was on my motorcycle having finished nursing shift at 9pm in Narborough.

As I made a right turn the object appeared as a long cigar-shape, it was red, glowing red in colour. At the right-side end, it appeared to look white hot. I pulled my bike up off the road, walked onto the wide, grassed verge. My brain was suggesting a Harrier jet fighter! But why the hell so low, why here?

I lifted my visor up, then continued to remove my helmet for a quick few seconds, but I was shocked as the object was no longer on the hedge-line but above me, which did not seem possible. It had risen so quickly; I was aware of a droning noise and almost as soon as my head was tilted back the craft, which I could clearly see from underneath, was triangular in shape.

A lower rectangular shape ran the entire length of the fuselage with a central circular shape. There were lights emitting from each corner, very white and it was at breakneck speed heading away across Ratby. There was a slight raised area as if it were a cockpit?

I stood and watched it move into the distance, excited I got back onto my bike and raced down the hill into Main Street, turning up to the Plough Inn. I used the booth to call the operator asking for the Air Control, she gave connected me to the MoD (Ministry of Defense). I was told that there were no flying aircraft at that time in that area. It had been below radar tracking level. They thanked me and I never stopped talking about it to my boyfriend who I had been meeting and other friends in the pub. I was working a morning shift on the ward, when a phone call came through for me to report to my room as I lived in as a student nurse, I had visitors who wanted to talk to me.

My room looked out over reception and the driveway sweeping round an island, indeed two men in black suits wearing bowler hats got out of a car and more surprising was when there was a knock on my door, it was the same two men. They had been shown to my room and they introduced themselves as being from the MoD. They asked me to recollect my account, including drawing as many detailed sketches as I could. They said I should not discuss this with anyone and that there had been other witnesses over Leicester. I was shocked but felt a little worried as I had put an account in the Hinckley Times newspaper. I didn't tell them though. I seem to have a natural ability to look up and there is always an object there, often a plane, but I have captured other such phenomenon, which I sent to MUFON where my original account can be found."

In a second email Lynn said: "Thank you Colin, I am pleased to hear it's not just my experience that these objects can avoid being captured on film, not even registering on your lens. It has happened so many times, you account is magnificent in presentation and like you, I just know they are here frequenting our skies. My late husband Brian Lodge lived at 25 St. George's Ave Hinckley. I would love to keep in touch if you wouldn't mind. The two men that visited seemed regular enough, obviously working for Government."

The last email was quite amazing as I used to live at 21 St Georges Avenue, just two doors away from her late husband who I remember well as he was a respected doctor at the time. What a coincidence!

The Flying Triangle Seen by Serena Bradbury

I was walking to my friend's house about 4.30-ish in daylight on a Sunday, November 27th, 2016, in my hometown. I got to the traffic lights on a junction, and something caught my eye. I looked up and it looked like a small fireball coming down fast. I thought 'oh well I'm going to die.' By the time I crossed this road I looked up again, and there it was, this black metal, seamless hovering triangle very low down, I need to learn trigonometry to know how close.

Well, I laughed (because I always wanted to see one). I live in Caldicot, Wales. I saw a red car pass by me; I did think about walking out into the road to stop it.

I was filming, but MUFON said good job I didn't, because they might not have been able to see it and by then it wasn't as spectacular, just being the glowing, moving ball of light. No noise, silent but warm, I could feel the heat from it. It had four beams of light, a red one in the middle, three yellowish/whitish ones by the corners, but not fully in the corners. I then thought 'oh no, I'm going to be abducted,' then I thought, I'm going to be a billionaire if I take a photo, so I got out my phone, unlocked it, put it on camera, looked up and it was gone.

So, I looked around, and there, above a nearby tree, was this fireball, well, a yellowish light, hovering, moving. So, I took two rubbish pictures, and decided to film it. I only filmed for less than a minute, I stopped, because (now I don't feel so foolish, to admit this) I thought it was coming back to get me.

I managed to film it flying, moving, fast, it looked small compared to what was above my head. But when I slowed the video down very slow, you could see the side lights (orange) like flashing and kind of cloaking it. I saw that too when I were filming but slowed down you can see it was actually bigger than that small beam of light. Lately I haven't been thinking about it every day, but I do think about it a lot.

Photo by Serena Bradbury

It was not that big a UFO, but it was surreal and out of this world, I always believed in ET's and at first I thought maybe it might have been the supposedly TR-3B, but no it couldn't have been. It was seamless, and magnificent, and the way it was a solid object, and then turned into just a flying light. I am trying to get someone to draw what I saw. It's like what's on the front cover of the book you recommended but not exactly. Luckily, I have connected with a few people now who have also witnessed a triangular craft, but as yet I have found no one who I could chat too who saw one so close.

Honestly, the craft were so close; I was totally shocked by what I saw. I think I could have climbed a ladder to get into it, when it was directly above my head, being a solid metal, magnificent, triangular hovering craft! I feel privileged to of seen it so closely, at the time I was depressed, but it seemed to have helped me.

I don't mind my name being used, the more people who do not mind being ridiculed when they see such craft the better.

 I often get drawn to the spot where I saw it, and sometimes it's just so overwhelming, but now I am 100% certain we are not alone.

Philip Shepherdson, Easingwold, near York February 1979

Credit to Philip Mantle for this report.

It was a crisp, 1979 February morning and my newly-built scooter ran smoothly along the twisting country lanes near Easingwold (near York, North Yorkshire, England). As I turned left towards Huby, my personal world seemed to abruptly switch off into a hushed silence. I looked to my left and my heart flipped at what I saw.

Hovering in a corner of a small field was a black, triangular shaped object. I stopped to get a better look not believing what I was seeing. The object was smooth with no control surfaces and no sharp edges and at the top was a cockpit with a figure inside it.

All I could see was a black helmet and a black overall of some kind. By the side of the craft, I now realized there were two more slim-looking figures who also wore black overalls, and they were trying to push the vehicle into the next field, perhaps to conceal it amongst the standing crops. They abruptly stopped to look in my direction; the cockpit figure too, turned to gaze at me. I felt transfixed with fear.

I was shaking. The silence was stifling as we gazed at each other and I felt some form of contact taking place, but I just don't know what that was. Time appeared to stop.

Suddenly my mind couldn't take any more and I got on my bike and took off to work. I don't remember getting there, in fact everything after that seemed surreal. I appeared to forget the experience as if told that this was something I shouldn't have witnessed. What struck me at the time was this was nuts and bolts technology, no fuzzy lights with a smudgy image. I freaked at the fact that an aircraft floating like a silent kite with not a blade of grass out of place and without jets, it was way beyond our technology!

My nightmares didn't start right then, but I was under the impression that WW3 was remarkably close at hand and, "For my own safety," I was to join a military establishment. Frankly, I have hated anything official– but the Royal Observer Corp was looking for recruits. At York, which was a major Control Centre, they had sections consisting of Crew One, Two and Crew Three and the latter, Crew Three, suited my requirements precisely: they worked hard and played hard.

Only military personnel can appreciate what that means: you make firm, lifelong friends and I gained many. And let's face it – this was the height of the Cold War and if an imminent WW3 developed, you would need them. The York area suddenly became a UFO hotspot, with puzzling crop circles suddenly appearing as well, it looked as if something were about to happen. I appeared on Arthur C. Clark's Mysterious World program regarding York's crop circle as a scientist investigator. At the time of my sighting many more were witnessed.

A UFO was spotted (Jenny Randles UFO Retrievals) in the Rossendale Valley near Todmorden around 2am and was then tracked to Blackpool, where a guard at Blackpool Pier claimed it could have gone in and then came out of the sea when chased by military jets. At 3.30 am, a man driving to Easingwold (near Huby) claimed a black, triangular shaped object flew alongside his car. "It had an orange light in the centre and there were lights all around it. Then it shot off at great speed into the sky." Then, at approximately 8am, my own experience took place. I had to find out more. Going back to my field near Huby I walked across the small field to where the UFO had landed.

What I found strange was that there was a bald, triangular shaped patch where nothing had grown, and for many years afterwards that continued to be so.

Then misfortune struck me when I had a motorcycle accident which left me concussed. However, it seemed to have triggered deep unconscious memories which now began to trickle into my dreams: nice to start but then with horrific nightmares. My first was being held in a dentist-like chair with a masked face bearing down on me. Black eyes appeared to sooth my senses and then I witnessed a laser swan-like instrument being used upon my upper face and body.

The next nightmare consisted of being in a dark cavern-like room; the only illumination came from an oval-shaped window above my head.

I appeared to be on a soft-to-touch leatherette slab. Also, about this time my life appeared out of synch with the time of our world. A classic case was where a girlfriend of mine ditched me for being an hour late, yet I had arrived on time by my watch. The fact that I had gone to a previous meeting in perfect time added to this mystery, a displaced missing hour out-of-time mystery.

I was lucky enough to obtain brief counseling with none other than Dr John Mack, Professor of Psychiatry at Harvard Medical School, who became an expert on alien abduction, and he appeared very impressed with my case and included it in one of his England lectures. Trying to get rid of my demons and have closure, I spent some years writing my novel 'Earth Zoo.' This is purely science fiction, but fact and fiction can become extremely blurred!

My nightmares became relentless until I knew I needed help, but from where? With the help of a spiritual healer who gave me regressive therapy, more disturbing memories surfaced, but were now controlled due to my guiding friend. Further from my dentist chair experience, I now appeared to be walking – or more aptly hopping (due to a feeling of weak gravity) along winding corridors which held gothic like archways. Abruptly I reached a cave-like small room, which held a weird, triangular table.

It had uneven odd-shaped legs and should have fallen over but it was held in perfect balance by an unseen force. There was a box, which had a lens on top, upon the table.

At my approach it flickered into life and through the lens I saw what I assumed was our sun – but it had a luminescence-like ring around its inner core, which behaved like a skipping rope. I gained the impression this was paramount for our solar welfare, yet totally unknown to our science at this time.

Suddenly the view changed, and I gazed at close quarters upon our home galaxy festooned with bright tiny multicoloured dots – all suns in their own right.

My line of sight was along our galactic arm, but at (by rule of thirds) thirty-five thousand light-years there appeared behind our galactic centre (and therefore invisible to us) a smaller 'Z' shaped bar-like galaxy. I awoke in a cold fearful sweat. Luckily, my spiritual friend first gave me a brandy to ease my shredded nerves and then some valued words of advice:

"We reside in many altered states of consciousness and treat your experiences as such. Whether these are mere dreams or past interwoven memories, allow them to be as guides of enlightenment towards truth; there is nothing to be afraid of anymore." His words gave me extreme peace even to this day.

However more trapped memories surfaced whilst writing this article. My last sessions with my healer were very enigmatic indeed. So much so that, fearing ridicule if I attempted to scientifically clarify what I am about to reveal, I have left this to the last. It also unnerves me due to its importance.

Philip Shepherdson at the scene of his encounter

I was regressed back inside my UFO craft where a solid wall became transparent, revealing a solid mass of multicoloured stars. I was not alone this time. By my side there was a humanoid figure about the same height as myself, but my focus was outside. Abruptly, but without any sense of feeling the motion of speed, we were chasing a small, red disc at tremendous velocity.

It plunged deep into our Earth's atmosphere and suddenly we were flying at tree-height through a forest type jungle. I gained the impression that this was subtropical – perhaps Australian bush land. Suddenly we stopped and close by in front of us was a strange pineapple-shaped tree. I gained the impression that this was extremely important to them, and they came here to collect samples. Apparently this was the first tree type/plant type that evolved here on our planet. I cannot comment here because I am scientifically completely ignorant regarding what I witnessed.

I was now completely exhausted both physically and mentally and my healer allowed me to rest. It was our last session together; I informed him that I had had enough!

I can give no logical explanation to my story, but hopefully catalogue this strange narrative for reference amongst the many other UFO experiencers. We all give witness to this enigma of the UFO that appear to be examining our world; let's hope with benign intentions.

Pic.23, Artists impression of the object seen by Philip Shepherdson

Lindsey Turner (pseudonym) Cotgrave, Nottingham 1983

Lindsey got in touch with me via social media, with one of the most intriguing witnesses reports I have come across. She phoned me and it was obvious to me she was telling the truth, she was so enthusiastic even after all these years, her encounter was in 1983 at Cotgrave, Nottinghamshire and this is what she told me.

'Cotgrave is a small mining town in Nottinghamshire I think the year was 1983 and it was the height of the miners' strike, it would be August/October time and I was eighteen years old.

My friend was three years older than me, and we were unemployed at the time. We decided to go and visit Dad's property, a ten to fifteen minutes' walk away, and we arrived at 8-9pm. The house had a football pitch just beyond the back garden, with wild space surrounding it, the weather had been, dry all day. When we came to leave late that night, we glanced over to the football pitch, via an entrance. We both spotted the mist and the pyramid, so we both decided to go and investigate. The pyramid object was the size of a council house and not quite on the ground but hovering just above the ground by about a foot or two in height. The pyramid looked to be made of glass and was transparent and I could see swirls of coloured gas inside, yellow, blue, green, in fact like a rainbow.

As they approached the pyramid it backed away from them, but when they backed away the pyramid returned to its original position. The craft then became solid, in fact Lindsey described it as metallic with Egyptian hieroglyphs on all sides, one of these hieroglyphs was a man with a bird head carrying a long spear.

Lindsey and her friend became nervous and decided to go home, where they believe they lost between half to three quarters of an hour in time. Lindsey's friend plucked up courage and went back to the football pitch, but the pyramid and the mist had now gone. I asked Lindsey if she had had any other experiences and she replied. 'I've seen an odd few lights throughout my life and as a very young child had an experience whilst playing with her toys.' Lindsey said she looked up, and there was an old lady milking a cow and a bale of straw in the room with her!

The lady wore an old-fashioned milkmaid clothing, (perhaps from the 1800's era) with the long dress, white apron with white hat and she kept speaking to Lindsey and commenting on how nice her hair was, she was referencing her interest, she was touching my hair at the same time, then she started to simply fading away.

Nigel Ross, Georgeham North Devon, March 30th, 1993, 22.15hrs

Nigel has been kind enough to allow me to use one of his sightings in this book. Nigel has had five sightings in total and has appeared in several books already.

Nigel went on to form NUFORS the National UFO Reporting Service www.facebook.com/nufors. For the purpose of this book, we shall just concentrate on the Triangle encounter that Nigel had that night. This is his amazing story.

"Weather dry cloudy, windy but not blustery, and I lived with my then girlfriend at Davids Hill, Georgeham, North Devon, UK. We both worked at a factory in Braunton, North Devon. We normally worked opposite shifts, alternating from 6am-2pm and 2pm-10pm. So, when one of us was in bed the other would be working. This is why I can be certain down to the exact minute of the sighting."

"I'm writing this in an attempt to still understand what we saw that night and to maybe gain some answers, and to also add another piece to that Cosford jigsaw. The following conversation between me and my girlfriend will be seared into my mind as if it were just last week."

Time 10:15pm, 30th March 1993.

"I was bed at this time when she bust into the house and shouted, "Come and look at this". I jumped out of bed thinking that there was an injured animal or something like that around the front of the house, she pointed across the valley over Georgeham as we live on a hill overlooking most of the village and to another hill opposite the village. Our house was situated approximately thirty feet above the village below. The view between our house and the neighbors' house where we can see the village is around forty-five degrees, including the other hill facing west. Within seconds this craft slowly comes into view, from my understanding she had seen and tracked this craft over the

334

hill from Braunton to Georgeham after finishing her shift at 10pm allowing five minutes to change at the factory and was always a ten-minute car journey "over the tops" to the village. We were presented with a craft that was approximately 150 feet in length and approximately seventy-five feet in width at its widest point. I would like to say it was triangular in appearance, but as we were almost level with the craft and that as the craft moved slowly north up the village it blocked out streetlights and they would appear again after it past, so getting an exact shape was exceedingly difficult.

I now liken it to a rough shape of a stealth-bomber aircraft, lots of different angles, wedge shape with one very defining feature of the craft being a (viewing gallery) a cockpit of thirteen portholes approximately twenty feet back from the front, elevated. As it was level with me, I desperately looked into the five portholes that faced me to "see if I could see any humanoid figures", but to no avail.

The cockpit was lit up with a soft, lilac light that enabled me to see in, and to see through to the opposite side of the cockpit, there were five similar portholes on the other side. The cockpit size was approximately twenty feet in length and twelve feet wide, with three portholes at the front of the cockpit. As I watched this craft, I remember saying to myself that I must take as many details and feelings from this moment as possible because it was the chance in a lifetime. I listened for any engine noise coming from the craft, which was only fifty feet away from us. It was just slightly below us and there was absolutely no sound whatsoever. This was strikingly apparent at that moment; all I could hear was the gentle breeze. I remembered saying to myself to wait for the engine noise, wait for it, wait for it, but nothing! The craft moved up the village just above the roof tops, trees and telegraph poles approximately twenty feet above the village at approximately ten mph, very slowly!!

It was as if it was looking for something, or recording/surveying something. The craft had a few lights on it apart from the cockpit, but they were in various colours and had no set configuration. As we were level with it, we couldn't see the underneath of the craft, so we couldn't see the form, or if any lights were on the underside. There were no "searchlights". The craft passed our viewing point after about five seconds, and we were unable to see it any more as the end of our house stopped us. I do remember thinking that if it stayed on that course and altitude it would hit the village church, which had a spire of seventy-five feet and was approximately three quarters up the village to the north. Within two seconds I heard what seemed to be an engine noise, like a thruster noise, for two seconds, again I remember saying to myself "It's over the church".

My girlfriend then turned to me and said, "Go on then, explain that one away"! I said nothing, I was at a loss. We talked about it the next few days, but this just threw up more questions than answers, it was like we had just watched a film with us not in it, but this was so real, we had seen this. One of her brothers who lived at Velator by the estuary at the back of Braunton, half a mile from RAF Chivnor, had seen an object a couple of days prior to our sighting "zig zagging" around the estuary doing "incredible maneuvers" at "incredible speeds".

All of us had lived in the area around the estuary and sea for many years, so were used to seeing Air Sea rescue helicopters and jets etc. but we had never seen anything like this. My father, who lives at Croyde, North Devon, a village just one mile south of Georgeham saw, "Strange lights" that same evening further to the north of Georgeham around midnight.

He wouldn't have mentioned this unless I told him what we had seen the night before. As I have read a little about the Cosford Incident over the years, I didn't realize two things, one being that after reading "Open Skies, Closed Minds" by Nick Pope, this incident was one of the largest witnessed incidents across Southern England in recent years, approximately 300/400 witnesses saw this craft including military personnel at RAF Cosford, and some serving police officers including Devon and Cornwall police officers.

They said that space debris was the reason of these sighting, but this was between 1am and 1.15 am on the 31st of March burning up in the atmosphere. I say that 1% might be of the sighting, but my girlfriend and I weren't looking up at the skies, we were looking across the village to the hill opposite. Our sighting was three hours before the satellite burnt up in our atmosphere."

"This threw even more questions, which came to mind years later, why a craft of this size and huge weight was allowed to fly just above a village population in the dark. Had it crashed it would have wiped out half the village, this would never be allowed by local or national air traffic control. My girlfriend's brother who saw this object at Velator called RAF Chivnor and they said that "Nothing of theirs was flying around here on that evening". What was a craft like this doing over a tiny village at the back of North Devon anyway? There are no power stations, technology or anything else, yet here it was.

There were I believe more sightings of a strange craft in Braunton and Ilfracombe around the similar time as the National Archives stated, and that a small radar station near Winkleigh Aerodrome had seen something on radar flying around North Devon at low altitude and at low speeds on that evening again from the National Archive. One of the strangest things of all was that this craft could have sailed past my bedroom window on a very quiet evening, and I would never have known. Thanks to my then girlfriend I now see and think about technology totally differently, I have never been afraid of talking about it.

I know what we witnessed that evening and it wasn't anything we could have built, in addition there doesn't seem to be any lost time, but that's always hard to quantify after such an experience. The frustrating part about this is that what do I do about that strange craft on that evening? It haunts me to this day, so many unanswered questions. The colour of the "viewing gallery/cockpit" was a soft lilac colour, which, after twenty-five years of reading up on UFO's, I discovered that alien creatures only like a soft lilac colour because any other colour hurts their eyes."

"We were most likely the only people to see the top of the craft and the viewing gallery that night due to the location of our house." I asked Nigel if he had had any other paranormal experiences, and this is his reply. "Apart from very strange lights twice, I've recently seen a cryptid, a very strange headless bird flying over me, but strangely it didn't flap its wings, jet-black and very dinosaur(ish).... I'm also known for my premonitions which Mr. Kinsella can back up! I often have contact from "craft" lights that flash at me many times with witnesses around, almost to order."

Barbara Chapman, Triangle craft, June 1996

I am indebted to Barbra for this detailed report of her triangle experience and other subsequent 'paranormal experiences.' It takes a brave person to talk candidly about these things, as if seeing a UFO is unbelievable enough, the events that can follow often seem even more unbelievable to the uninitiated.

"After a sighting in 1995, I went back to the same place on holiday in Cornwall but told a few friends and family who came with me. Now this may sound strange, but I knew we were going to see something, so on the first night we waited till about 11.30 and walked up to the cliffs where about eight of us sat down and waited. To be honest I felt that we might see more of the ball-type things. We all had cameras and we had been waiting for about an hour, when my nephew, Gary, asked me when would we see something? I replied that it would not be long. Almost immediately to the east we saw a light, it was getting closer, and we all prepared to takes photos. I was dead calm, but the lads were getting more excited as it got closer."

"As it came towards us we could see more lights on the craft, it reached us and was about 100 yards away, it wasn't big, about the size of a bus in length and a triangular shape. It then stopped and floated there, the lights were located around the edge of the craft, they were multicoloured and flashing in sequence."

"We could all see the underneath which was an electric blue colour. I must admit that we were dumbfounded, a couple of the boys ran off to get others to come and see it, but the rest of us stood there in awe. There was a humming sound, extremely low-pitched according to someone there, but I was fully in awe of this thing. I think it stayed there for about a minute or so, we took photos and then it started to glide onwards and gently upwards. As it glided away, we watched till it disappeared very high up. Our initial response to all of this was a mixture of fear from some and amazement from the rest.

"This was a dark night, but you could clearly see the triangle. The thing is that subsequently I had regressive hypnotherapy and claimed that I saw a pilot on the craft, not alien but humanoid with a white crash helmet with red symbols on the side on its head. I don't know what to make of that, but it's a flash of memory that stays in my brain, I can actually see the face in my mind's eye.

He was smiling, young, almost boyish, and had blue overalls on. He was placed in a half-bubble shape, which was on top of the craft but very streamlined, no obvious hatch or anything."

Another fantastic story from a credible witness, I asked Barbara if she had also had any paranormal experiences, and this was her answer. "So, I'm going to try and write down what happened to us back in September 1995, it was a Sunday night/ Monday morning about 1.30am. We were on holiday as a family and had been visiting the same place for a few years. It's Hayle in Cornwall, we stay on a Caravan site on Upton Towans and it's beautiful up there, quite remote, no amusements, just miles of sandy beaches overlooking Carbis Bay. Anyway, this night we had all been to the club, and at closing time we came back to the caravan and a few of us wanted to go for a walk. We often did this as the stars are so nice when you haven't got light pollution like in London, so four of us got ready and set off.

There was me, my daughter (Corinne) aged fifteen at the time, her friend Kirsty who was the same age, and another girl, Kim, who was eighteen. We made our way to the moors and climbed the gate; Kim had a silly toy torch from the club in her pocket and switched it on so we could find a place to sit and watch the stars. We sat there for about five minutes when I saw a light to the left of us quite high in the sky, I pointed it out to the girls, it was travelling slowly towards us, no sound, then it suddenly kind of swooped towards us and before we knew it, it was right above our heads. It was not big, about the size of an Edam Cheese.

We all screamed and ran back to the relative safety of the caravan site. Once back at the site I began to think that it must have been a helicopter or something, I thought that our light may have attracted it, so I asked the girls if they wanted to go along the cliff top to see if it had gone that way out to sea. They agreed and we went to the end of the site on the cliffs. By this point I was less shaken and had calmed down. Kim got her torch out again; she put it on and held it up. I asked her what she was doing.

She said she thought it was sensible as we were on a cliff path. Kim put her light on, almost immediately a huge, orange fiery ball of light appeared out at sea.

She turned the light off and the ball of light disappeared. She put the light back on, and the light came back on. The two younger girls by this time were very scared. Strangely, Kim and I were fascinated by this. The light seemed to be gently bouncing, but then shot straight up into the air and did a perfect 90 % right turn and vanished behind the headland.

We turned to go back, but as we looked out to sea the ball came back along with another one. Then the two balls seemed to combine into one. At that point we had to leave, because the girls were hysterical. Kim and I knew that we wanted to put the girls in the caravan and go back out, as we were approaching the caravan I got the key out and had it in my hand, as I put the key in the lock the girls started

343

screaming and pushing at me to get in quickly. I asked them to tell me what was wrong, and the three girls said that they had seen a figure by the palm tree; it looked a bit like a Michelin man. I told them to calm down and started to make tea. I thought it might help.

Then as I put the kettle on, a loud humming noise started, and the caravan began to vibrate. The girls got under the table, and they were crying and shouting at me to make it stop. After about thirty seconds of this, I just shouted 'F**k Off,' and it just stopped there and then. That night we all eventually fell asleep in the living room, too scared to go to bed.

The next morning at about 7.30 there was a banging on my door. It was the caravan security people, they asked me how it had happened and were pointing to the roof, I stepped out to look and saw that our caravan, just ours, was covered in a layer of seaweed. Our caravan was further inland then the others, no-one else had seaweed on their roofs. Later that day, Corinne and Kim became ill with a sore throat and nausea.

I was ill too, and we could not wait to get back home. I nearly left on the Monday, but I was persuaded to stay by those who had not had this experience. After this experience, but without being conscious of what I was doing or why, I stopped eating meat, I did not want alcohol anymore and generally felt enthused to find answers. For a period of time after, I became more likely to experience the unusual as well.

This state lasted for about four years. In 1997 I was approached by someone called Robert Lamont who asked if I would be willing to undergo hypnosis to get greater detail of my experiences. I readily agreed, because I was unable to come to terms with what I had seen. The hypnosis took place at his home with my companion present. The episodes were taped so Robert could go over them later. I was regressed and can truthfully say that I do not remember anything about the experience or what I said.

This in itself is unusual I believe. Under regression I was able to give more detail, and had apparently told those present, that after the incident and the humming noise part of my story, I had gone outside and had had communication with a 'light-source,' which told me that I was not ready (I don't know what for) and that those with me were safe. On waking and hearing this I was unconvinced of what I had said. I had also made reference to another incident of missing time in Wiltshire. I was invited to attend again for further sessions, which I did, more of an experiment for me, because I was not convinced. After all the sessions had finished (seven in total) I was particularly concerned to start receiving strange images of alien beings in flashback form. Being a lucid individual who had a times held responsible jobs (Prison Warder) where psychological testing was required, I could not fathom out what was happening to me. I had drawings of my flashbacks done by an artist to see if it could provide answers. It didn't. So, I detached myself from the process and tried to carry on as normal."

"The above is my story. The others with me at the time are still close and we regularly go over the events of that night. I later saw the Michelin man figure in the same area. I call him the 'bowler hat man,' such a horribly fascinating figure that is the stuff of nightmares."

"In 1995 the week we had the experience up on the cliffs me and my son, who was eight at the time, were walking towards our holiday home at about 8pm at night. It was half light, that kind of gloomy light that happens just before nightfall. The Lane was deserted, and on our right there was wasteland with houses in the distance. On our left were scattered houses with side alleys and pathways that go straight to the sea.

Halfway up the lane on one of the pathways we saw a shape, as we got closer the shape was that of a human, but nothing like I'd ever seen before. He was wearing a long black coat with what looked like a bowler hat on his head. It was pulled tightly down almost obliterating the forehead and where the eyebrows should be. The face was bulbous, all folds of skin, and cold-looking lips.

The figure was squat and rotund; I'd say about five feet three inches tall. I wish I could draw because I have the face in my mind. His skin colour appeared to be pale and greyish in that light. He didn't move, but his eyes looked straight at us, there was an intense look in them. I held Nick's hand very tightly and walked so fast away from there. I didn't want to alarm Nick, but I was terrified. We didn't see him again that year. But in the following years we have seen him. He's not human as such, there's never anyone around when he appears, but he has a habit of appearing in roughly the same place. I don't go there alone anymore.

Often Nick will go looking for him, he is always with a mate or family member, but if it's late in the evening or night they are always spooked. They have heard whistling, scuffles and nearly always say they are being watched. Last time we saw him was in 2017."

Matt Ring Ipswich, August 1996, Suffolk

Matt got in touch with me via social media, this is his story: "It was around 2:00 am, I was living at my mum's house at the time on the Whitton Estate, Ipswich. It was August 1996; I can't remember the date as I put all of this to the back of my mind and only ever told my mum about it. I always thought a UFO was saucer-shaped until that night. I was watching a movie on TV, I believe it was 'Escape from Alcatraz,' I had just finished a cigarette and it was a warm night, I pulled back my curtain to flick the cigarette out of the window. As I did so I looked up and saw this large, black, triangle.

The sky was dark, but this was darker, in each corner there was a yellowish light and in the middle an orange coloured light with a tiny red light on the edge of the orange light, the red light spun around the large orange light, like it started at the 12 o'clock position and spun clockwise back to the 12 o'clock position, back and forth, back and forth, it made no sound at all, slowly moving but as it did so it spun slowly on it axis, there were no other lights on it. It was very low in the sky, and I would say about half a mile away, I kept thinking, should I go and wake up everyone, or should I stay and watch, it lasted for only a minute or maybe a little more before it slowly disappeared out of sight. It was very low in the sky, and I've never seen anything like it before, I've only just started to talk about it as I know what I saw that night was real now, I'm not saying it was 'little green men,' but something big is out there, I never felt scared or threatened, but it changed me in many ways."

I then asked Matt if he had had any paranormal experiences, and this was his answer. "Hi, so many things have happened at my mother's house. All of us have had experiences. I grew up with three brothers and three sisters in a three-bedroom house, it was the small bedroom that no one ever used or even went in. We would run past it and not even look, the first experience that really scared me was after my older brother and three sisters had left home, I decided I would move into the small room so I could finally have some space. The room always felt like someone was standing near the door, I never ever stood with my back to the door. I was fifteen-years-old at the time, nothing really happened for a few months, just that feeling of someone standing at the door and the hairs would stand up on my arms. Then one night I felt something pulling my bed covers down, I sat up and no one was there. This went on for a few years and then something started to touch my feet and legs.

Then one day I was going to sleep, and it started to touch my feet again, I thought to myself 'f**k this' and changed ends of the bed, I was falling back to sleep, and something started to grab my face and made the most evil laugh I have ever heard. It sounded a bit like Crusty the Clown from the Simpsons. As I opened my eyes there was a tall, black shadow but it had like points either side of its head, one was larger than the other, I actually screamed like a woman, and it was gone. My mom and younger brother came running upstairs to see what had happened. I've had many more things happen, including the black shadow that both my mom and I saw at the same time. I also had a glass cabinet that faces would appear in. I have a few pics and it's strange what you said about the paranormal and UFO connection. One pic has a demon face, but if you zoom in there is also a little face that looks alien."

"My four-year-old niece came one day with my sister; she went to play in the back garden, a few minutes later she started to scream. I mean a scream that says 'help.' We all ran out and she was deathly white and sweating, she could hardly breathe. After giving her water and calming her down she told us of a man who looked over the back fence and growled like a lion at her. She said he was all in black and had no hair, he was wearing glasses, then she said he looked like corned beef. We didn't understand what she meant; then her mom called and told us she meant his skin was all burnt." "I forgot to add the fence my niece saw the man behind was not from another garden, it was part of an abandoned school for special needs children and before that I believe it was a TB hospital, the school was called Thomas Walsey in Ipswich, Suffolk."

David Murphy-Bonner 2015, Tamworth with CE5

CE5 is a relatively new concept, which is short for 'Close Encounters of the Fifth Kind', whether by technological means or meditation induced telepathy, here's David Murphey-Bonner's CE5 Contact with the Yayhel/Assasani, (an extraterrestrial race).

350

"For a few weeks, I spent the odd evening sitting out under the stars in my back garden, trying to meditate (something I had never done before) and inviting any beings that could "hear" my call to come and show themselves to me. This was done rather skeptically, and I did not really expect much to happen, although I was hopeful, and excited at the prospect of being proven wrong."

"A couple of weeks went by with nothing happening. Then one night, sitting under the stars, I finally "got it" - I felt a deep understanding that I was part of one great, cosmic mind, and that consciousness was non-local, and present everywhere and in everything."

"That same night, a large, white orb appeared in the trees outside my house while I was asking for contact, hovered there for a few seconds, and then collapsed into nothing. I was stunned. And it was in that moment that I realized that I had made contact - with *something*."

"For the sake of brevity, I will fast forward here, but suffice to say contact became an especially important part of my life and lead me down a rabbit hole of discovery about the nature of reality. I started to "wake up", as the saying goes. In 2015, after mainly doing contact work alone for two years (with a fair amount of success), and a handful of groups that I attended (also with great success), I decided to start my own local group."

"There were four regulars who attended every week for a period of about six months. One of these folks has subsequently become one of my closest friends and actually introduced me to Rachel, who is now my wife (and also an experiencer and CE5 practitioner). It was actually our shared interest in the subject that led to us meeting, but that's another story for another day. During that six-month period, the four of us, and others who drifted in and out of the group at times, had utterly incredible experiences, which I am happy to recount at another time. It was a truly magical period in my life."

"Around that time, I had started watching a lot of Darryl Anka - who channels an ET known as Bashar. I had previously been dismissive of his material as nonsense, but with all the high strange activity we were having, and my spiritual journey well underway, I went back to it with fresh eyes.

"We had decided as a group that we wanted to deepen our contact experiences by reaching out to specific star races and had been discussing the Assasani (or Yayhel) in some depth. We were familiar with their alleged interest in humanity, their agenda and appearance, and the alleged shape of their craft. The weekend of our experience with the triangular craft (which I am personally convinced was Assasani) was one I will never forget."

"On the Friday night I had got back from work in London and gone to bed. On the Saturday morning, I had a fraught voicemail from one of the group (who I shall not name without his consent) stating that the previous night he and his brother had been out in the garden having a cigarette (they were both members of my group but were not trying to initiate contact at the time)."

"They looked up to see a massive triangular shape hovering directly over the roof of their house. Stunned, they watched as it suddenly shot up vertically and out of sight.

That night, my friend had a telepathic communication whilst lying in bed, where he found himself unable to move, and heard a voice in his head ask, "do we frighten you?"

"Needless to say, on the Saturday night the group got together (without my friend who had the telepathic contact, but his brother, and our other member came). We asked specifically during our meditation for the same craft to come and visit us, and we asked from the understanding that the craft was probably Assasani."

"Later in the evening, as we stood in my back garden watching the sky, I noticed a bright, stationary light in the distance, over some fields opposite my house. We quickly discounted it as an airplane, as they often appear that way

353

when flying directly towards the observer, and we were familiar with flight paths over the house after several months of standing out watching the sky from that location."

"About ten or fifteen minutes later, we noticed as a group that it was still there and hadn't moved - at all. Excited, we started asking for the craft to come closer, to come and make contact. To our surprise and delight, it began to move in our direction. As we watched, dumbstruck, it flew straight overhead, silently, and slowly, no more than 200 ft up."

"What we saw was a triangular dark shape that blotted out the night sky. There were white lights on each corner of the triangle that pulsed on and off irregularly.

There was also a central green light (it must have been on the bottom of the craft) which also pulsed slowly. I distinctly remember seeing a triangular, red symbol on the front of the craft as it came overhead, which looked distinctly like the symbol that the Assasani are alleged to use."

"There was no acknowledgement to our signaling (with our laser), nor our excited shouts for the craft to stop/land/take us onboard etc. It simply passed over the house, and drifted away across Tamworth and Fazeley, before banking slightly to the right and disappearing into the clouds.

We were stunned, and none of us had thought to grab our phones or record the experience, something we kicked ourselves for after."

"I feel it is too much of a synchronicity that we had been researching and discussing the Assasani and their craft in the weeks leading up to the sighting, for it to be coincidence. And it turned up on two consecutive nights, in two different locations, both of which were where members of our CE5 group lived - and the second time, on request. Of all of the encounters I have had over the past decade (and there have been a few) this one stands out as one of the most profound, and significant."

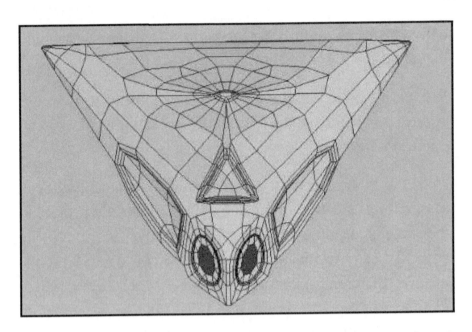

Pic.24 This is the amazing image produced by David of his triangular craft showing the red triangle on the front. There is also a second witness to the triangle sighting, a Mr. Nic Treadwell, which confirms what David saw that night.

Nic Treadwell, 2015, Tamworth with CE5

"In 2015, after a particularly active summer of CE5 sky watching with my then new acquaintance Dave Bonner, we had a spectacular sighting of a triangular craft above Dave's house in Tamworth. Dave, his friend Dan and I had assembled for the evening to observe any unusual phenomena.

We had watched many commercial flights coming across the sky and were familiar with their flight and light pattern, so when we saw what appeared to be another one off in the distance, we didn't pay too much attention.

As the lights got nearer though, we noticed they were distinctly different from those of a normal plane. They blinked much slower and had a different configuration.

We also noticed that as it approached there was no engine sound at all. At that point it must have been around 10pm as it was already dark. We could, however, make out the frame of this craft. As it came over us it was clear it wasn't a normal plane, this thing was triangular in shape, lights on the corners and in the middle as I recall. It was almost as if this thing had no weight as it seemed to just glide over the house and off into the distance without any effort. It was completely silent. No distinctive markings I could see, just a uniform grey/black in colour. All three of us were so shocked by what we had observed; we just stood there staring at it as it retreated into the distance. We didn't even think to take a photo. What it was I have no idea. Possibly some unknown military craft or perhaps something from much further afield."

Deborah Haines, Barwell, Leicestershire

Deborah appeared earlier on it the book under 'more local witnesses,' I asked her if she had seen any other UFO's or paranormal experiences, and this was her answer.

"I said I'd tell you about a flying object my father and I saw back in the 70's ...I think it was 1978. It was a winters evening...and we'd had heavy snowfall. We lived in a small village called Wymondham, on the other side of Melton Mowbray. My father owned the village butchers and my mother the village shop. We lived on the Main Street, directly opposite Station Rd. (now Butt Lane). It was a road that led out of the village, where the old railway station was, it closed in 1959. It was a great road for sledding down, which we had done many times during my childhood years of living in this village. It was about 9pm, me and my dad and our border collie had been out having fun.

My dad would push me from the top and Bob, my dog, would chase after me to the bottom of the hill. I'd just reached the bottom and stood up to walk back up to my dad, when I saw a mass of coloured lights in the sky behind him. I shouted to my dad to turn around and look behind him as I was running back up the hill. It was quite low, possibly 150-200 ft. and cigar shaped.

There was also a very high-pitched sound coming from the distance and our dog became unsettled and starting whining and cowering down. We both stood and watched it. I asked my dad what it was, and he said he didn't know. We watched this object get lower until it disappeared behind the brow of the hill and behind the 'old station' which had been converted into a bungalow where an elderly couple called Mr. & Mrs. Walker lived.

Dad said it was time to go home and I couldn't wait to tell my mum what we'd just seen. I can remember sitting in front of the fire telling mum what we'd just seen. Mum joked and asked if we'd been to the village pub instead of sledding.

The following morning Mr. Walker came into my mum's shop and told them he'd been for a walk over the fields behind the 'Station' where he lived, and there was a huge area of completely melted snow in the shape of a circle. My dad then told him what we'd seen the night before!

Mr. Walker contacted a local paper and I believe the authorities, and later that same day a group of people visited the site with some sort of 'testing' devices! My dad said they were Geiger counters!! There was a story published in the Leicester Mercury about this incident, but we never heard any more about it!"

"The other weird thing I've had ongoing is my 21-year-old daughter who is very sensible girl and not the typical teenager, claims to have seen a UFO right outside her bedroom window! It was shining a white light into her bedroom. I asked her why she didn't call me, and she said she couldn't because she couldn't move! It's played on her mind quite badly since it happened last year. I've tried to convince her it was just a dream, but she won't accept that.

"She's convinced she saw this huge, white orb. The following day after seeing this she had a terrible, terrible, nosebleed. It was quite alarming what came out of her nose. I actually took a photo of it, and she's convinced it was from seeing this orb! Have you ever heard anything like this before? "She said the orb was about 10ft in width, because she compared it to the trampoline we have in the garden, and it was the same height as her bedroom window!

She'd woken up and saw light coming through her curtains, she thought somebody was in our back garden shining a torch up at her window, so she got out of bed and opened her curtains, and it was just suspended in the air?"

"I was very concerned at the time about her mental health after seeing this, because she was frightening to go to bed at night in case it came back!! I've just reassured her the past few months it was just a bad nightmare. She became very paranoid, especially when her nose started to bleed the following day and these huge clots kept coming out of her nose, she even thought 'they'd' done something to her!"

"To be honest I haven't done a great deal of research. I have always been an open-minded person and it's a big universe. I think anybody would be foolish to think other planets with civilizations don't exist! But I must say after seeing the black triangle, I know that craft was not from this world! After speaking to you and knowing other people have had sightings I will most definitely be doing some research! I think, like you said, we've been very privileged to have seen it!"

Again, this is an intriguing twist to the subject where experiences run in families and paranormal activity is not far away. Amazingly enough I have often walked my dog in the fields that back onto Deborah's garden and must have passed the trampoline at some point recently.

And finally, an interview by Omar Fowler on 13-9-1998

The incident took place on the 3rd of July 1996 in a village called Bilton near Harrogate, North Yorkshire. Miss M.F. (32) had finished an early shift at her place of work and as it was a nice sunny day, she decided to take a walk into the nearby countryside.

As she walked along she came across a pleasant looking field and finding a comfortable spot, sat down to read a book, the time was 9.45am.

It was sunny and warm as Miss M.F. sat quietly reading, then quite suddenly, she was aware a large shadow was moving over her. She looked up and was astonished to see a large, black triangular craft overhead. It was twice the size of an aircraft and had a white light at each corner and hovered over her.

"I was amazed at the size of it and also the fact that there was no noise. In the quiet of the countryside there should have been a noise from it, but there was nothing and that unnerved me. There were three lights on the triangle but there were also other lights near it which kept on flashing away" commented Miss M.F.

Then suddenly a beam of blue light shot down from the triangle and covered her. "The next thing I felt that I was going upwards, very, very fast and I felt really sick. My nose was hurting, and I'm scared of heights, I couldn't see anything, I was going up so fast and just seemed to black out."

Omar Fowler with a model triangular UFO

"The next moment I was in a strange building, everything was a very bright white, so bright I couldn't see anything and there was a funny smell too to it. I couldn't see much because it was so white. I felt that I was laid on something, but I don't know what it was."

Miss M.F. then went on reluctantly to describe what happened next. There were strange 'beings' around her and they were doing something down near her legs, but she couldn't see or feel anything. She went on to say, "I know that people see these drawings of aliens on T-shirts and things, but these weren't like that."

"They had black eyes, there were no whites to their eyes, they had no eyebrows, no eyelashes, no cheekbones, no ears, no mouth or facial hair or anything similar to our kin. It was just one skin tone, a translucent white. I couldn't see any pores, any hair or any bone or anything."

"There was a taller alien, he seemed to be in charge of the others and looked the same as the others, but he was about six feet tall. I say 'he,' 'it,' I don't know what it was. He stood over me and then stared into my eyes and then I got this feeling of euphoria and happiness, which is odd. I thought that we could communicate, because I'm sure he could see what I was seeing and I had a feeling that I should be at peace, which is not a normal reaction, I should have been terrified."

"That was the last thing I remember. The next thing was I woke up in a field (from where she had been abducted), but I was in a different spot from where I had originally, and I found my book in a hedge. My watch had stopped, although I didn't notice this at the time, and I had a rash on my arm."

****

Chapter 9

Alien Telepathy

It was through Dave Hodrien that I was invited to give a talk to his group in Birmingham. I gave the presentation using my newly 3D printed model of the triangle. The presentation went well, and people were saying it was great to see the model to help visualize exactly what we saw that night. During the presentation I talked about the close viewing I had and a possible out of body experience. Dave said he had a report of a guy who was watching aliens across a field who had exited a UFO. The witness said all of a sudden there was an alien face in front of his face telling him (in no uncertain words) to go away, to leave this place. He said it was like the alien had telepathically come to him. Not quite the same as I had experienced, but along the same lines.

Then, two weeks later out of the blue, I receive an email from America, the email started off by saying, "I saw your presentation on the net and, just like you, I had three images placed in my head by telepathy during an encounter with a triangle." Well, that was a eureka moment for me, I'd heard of telepathy, but always thought it would be words in your head, like a conversation, but having listened to a lot of Dr David Jacob's work I now realized images were also used in telepathy between ET and humans.

So, Budd Hopkins was right all along, the images were placed in my mind by those onboard the craft, alien telepathy! It makes sense, as a picture paints a thousand words and I have spent my whole working life producing technical images. This would explain why I was the only one having other experiences as the other three occupants of the car that night were not. ET had opened my mind up somehow by placing the images in my mind, but why, to build the model, to write this book? I'll probably never find out. Here's the account emailed to me from America, the witness wants to remain anonymous so we shall just call him Sam.

Sam, Connecticut, 2014

"On January 3, 2014, I was driving home from work at 1130 pm. I live in a small rural town in northern

Connecticut. I was driving along the dark roads on the outskirts of town. I've driven on these rural back roads hundreds of times before. I often drive this route to avoid traffic in the centre of town.

The roads in that area are quiet farms roads and open fields. I'm a 58-year-old Army veteran, educated, business professional. I have no reason to make up crazy stories or tell lies. I've never been much of a storyteller and I'm certainly not going to start telling lies at my age. I remember most of the experience pretty vividly. However, I must admit that there are a couple of things that are a little cloudy in my memory."

The Sighting: "All was normal when I first started my drive home from the airport area. About five miles away from the airport is when I saw bright, white lights in the night sky. I thought nothing of it because there is a major International Airport so close and a small local airport nearby as well. I live in the town and was accustomed to seeing planes in the sky in that area. But these lights seemed different to me some way. The lights seemed to be flying extremely low and slow. I lost sight of them as I was driving through some hills that momentarily blocked my view. About five minutes later I see the lights again from about a mile away. I could see through the many trees that were bare due to the winter season. I thought it was a plane or helicopter in the sky. But then I felt these were very

367

bright white lights, some type of search lights or lights from a tower. I quickly dismissed the tower thought, because I knew these back roads and also remembered that there were no towers in that area of town."

"As I drove along the town's dark roads I was getting closer to the lights. There were no other cars at that time of night on that dark road that runs along the Farmington River. However, that's really not unusual for a very rural farm area of the town. Now as I drove closer I could see clearly that the lights were now just above the treetops and above an open farm field. There were three very bright, white lights spread out and I slowed down my car to a crawl to look out of the passenger side window to see what the object was.

At that point I could clearly see that it was some sort of black triangular craft hovering just above the treetops and the open field. The craft was less than 100 feet above the field, but a few hundred feet from my car".

The Encounter: "The lights were so bright that it took me a little time to figure out what they were attached to. A moment later, I could see the craft very clear. It was a big, gunmetal black hovering triangle. It was about an acre in size.

It had bright white lights and one pulsating red strobe light on the bottom of the craft in the centre towards the rear.

368

(Not in the centre of the craft but more toward the rear) There were rectangular white lights on the back end. Although I'm not sure if those were lights or windows. Some were lit and some were not, but all were stretched along the back end. The craft was gunmetal black, and it just floated in place. It was silent and looked sinister to me. The triangular craft was facing to the south in the same direction I was going. As I slowed my car down to a stop I watched the craft for a moment then it slowly turned on its axis a hundred and eighty degrees. It was now facing north."

"It was during the winter, and I had my windows rolled up, but the craft appeared to be silent. Somehow I felt that the craft knew I was there watching it. When I first came upon the object I fumbled for my mobile phone to take a photo, but I was too busy trying to drive and watch the object at the same time. I gave up on the idea of capturing the object in a photo. The night was so dark I would be wasting my time trying. The only thing I felt was that I had to remember the object the best I could to try to describe it later. I remember saying to myself that I needed to remember the craft very well. So, I took a hard look at it and tried to remember everything about it."

Phase 1: "At one point I remember thinking to myself that I needed to remember details of the object, because I would be better able to later describe what I was seeing. At that moment I remember that the object projected close up images in my mind of the craft.

There were three images that I can recall that that were projected in my mind. The first image was that I was seeing many round, white lights that surrounded the object. I seemed as if I was now ten feet in front of the craft.

This viewing of the lights was moving, as if I were taking a tour around the object. It appeared that I was moving slowly around the lights projected in front of me. While being shown the lights on the craft, I also saw some structure or girders between the craft holding it together. The second image view was a stationery image of the small red strobe light that was on the bottom of the craft positioned in the centre rear of the craft. It looked as if there was some type of protective cover over the pulsing red light.

The third image shown to me was a still image of a large industrial piping system on or in the object. It may have been some sort of cooling system with various pipes being shown to me on the bottom or inside the craft.

I don't know where this was on the craft. I believe whoever was inside it allowed me to see the three close-up projected images in my mind. There were no other markings or writings on the object that I could see. There were other lights that momentarily turned on the object as well. There were many small, circular white lights around the craft that I saw up close somehow but did not see them from the exterior of the craft."

Phase 2: "After the images were shown to me I was back in my car looking at the triangle from my car again a few hundred feet away. All I could see were the three white lights at the tips of the triangle and two large ones behind in the rear. The craft then made another maneuver and pointed straight up in the air. It hesitated in a vertical position for a brief moment. At that point I heard a deep humming sound from the craft, as if it were just put into gear and in a blink of an eye it moved at warp speed from my right front to just above the trees to my left front. As I was watching the craft on my left side, now it was dark without lights. As I sat in my car watching all this happen my car made a bucking forward and stop motion three times.

My car literally jumped forward and stopped three times. Then all of a sudden I saw a bright, glowing ball of light appear out my driver's window on the left side of my car. It was flying around the side of my car. Then it suddenly stopped directly beside my car, as if it were looking at me. It was about ten feet from the driver's window. It was as if the light was looking directly at me while I was sitting there looking at it.

It was bright white like a ball of plasma, with white rays a little larger than a basketball. It was just floating there next to my car window. It made a back a forth maneuver in a split second three times. It wanted me to know that it made my car buck and jolt three times. It was as if it were playing with me, or a better description would be toying with me. I didn't feel afraid though at that point.

But then all of a sudden the ball of light vanished with the craft. The area was dark and still again. But now I looked for the object and ball of light outside my car. It was not in my immediate vicinity anymore. I looked for it on the right side and all was dark and still. However, I looked up higher in the sky above the ridgeline now to my left side again, and I could see a large, completely dark, black object flying slowly north against the night sky. It was approximately 500 feet in the air at this point. The object was trying to camouflage itself and blend into the night sky.

This time there were no lights lit on it. But the shape of it changed to an almost baseball home plate diamond shape. At this point I don't know what compelled me, but I wanted to follow it. My car was facing to the south, so I had to pull into a street and turn around to follow the craft. I lost sight of it as I was now moving north on the dark road in the opposite direction to that in which I was originally driving. The craft was out of sight for a moment, when I decided to go to a clearing in an area I knew of, just a quarter of a mile up ahead on the right. I was thinking that I would see the craft again in the night sky in that area.

But the instant I got to the clearing, it must have known what I was thinking and as soon as I opened my moon roof shade to look above me, something cast a light inside my car. It scared the living hell out of me at that point.

I immediately hunched over in my driver's seat as I was really startled. A bright light was cast upon me, and it almost appeared that something was looking through my moon roof window at me. What was strange was that it knew what I was thinking all along. In that instant it knew that I was going to look up above the car through the roof window shade. But what felt like a second later, the light was gone, and I wasn't afraid anymore. I drove the remaining ten minutes home without any other high strangeness. When I arrived home I remember checking the clock, but it seemed to be just the time it should be, including the five minutes of the encounter. The next morning, I called the local police department to see if there were any reports of strange lights in the sky in that area. But the dispatcher on duty said that she was unaware of any reports made the night before."

"I try not to dwell on the experience. But at times it weighs heavy on my mind. I don't want thinking of it to consume my life. I realize that I will probably never figure it out. So, I don't want to waste my time trying. But I would like some answers or at least be free to talk about it. But I don't. I generally keep it to myself. I have only told a handful of people about the experience. I generally keep it to myself."

"When I was in my 20's, my friend and I saw a massive mother ship float over my apartment. It looked like something out of Star Wars. It wasn't triangle shaped it was more 'Enterprise shaped.' I saw it first and told my friend "look the mother ship." We watched it for 10 seconds and then ran into the apartment. It was the size of a city. It was in the 1980s. We both saw it, but never talked about it until I told him about the triangle."

"Last fall my wife and I were driving on the New Jersey Turnpike at night. I looked up and saw a strange flashing object in the sky off to my driver side. I thought it was a tower, until it stopped flashing, then started again and then disappeared.

Then five minutes further down the highway I saw the lights again. It was in the same spot (distance and height approx. 300 ft) as the first time I saw it.

Then I saw another one similar to the first off to my right. I knew that they were strange objects. I pointed them out to my wife. Then there was another one off to my right and it crossed over the highway and zoomed off into the sky flashing all the while. About a week later I decided to search NJ UFO sightings on the internet, and someone had contacted a local newspaper and captured UFOs in New Jersey on video on the same night and in the same area that I was driving while on the turnpike. Those were only lights, not close up and personal interaction with something from another planet or dimension."

I started looking for other "close viewing" encounters and managed to get this in-depth report from a Rob Fowler who now lives in New Zealand but had his encounter here in England. This is his story.

Rob Fowler, Bath, 1999

"Present at the same time as myself, (Rob Fowler), was Dave Reynolds, a long-term family friend. The Reynolds Family and I have known each other since I was eleven and he was nine, through regular cricket and subsequent socializing. We can be sure it was 1999 from where I was living at the time and where I was working. It was a (UK) winter's evening. I would be 26, Dave 24. Not quite Fosse Way, but within range of Bath, Cirencester etc.

Dave and I used to go to Chipping Sodbury Cricket Club to jam, using amps and drums. It was away from housing. Sometimes others used to join us, but that night it was just us two. We would have started 7.30pm (ish) and we

375

believe that the event would have occurred maybe an hour or so after that.

We can ascertain that it was February or March or early April. The night itself was unremarkable. A typical winter evening, not too cold, it was dry with a fairly clear sky.

We had both driven separately with instruments, from our homes in different parts of Chipping Sodbury. We may have drunk a beer each if that, but no more.

It was low key. I worked in the village, but Dave would have been worked away from home in the week, so an early start the next morning; Sundays were always low key for us both in the winter. After playing a bit of music I headed outside for some fresh air and a smoke. It was not a non-smoking club, but for some reason I went outside.

I saw above Wickwar Playing Fields, what almost looked like a gemstone in the sky, moving perceptively slowly northward. I very quickly ascertained that it was too unusual to be normal. It was too bright, too unnatural. In what seemed like seconds I knew I had to get Dave to see this, (to be in on it) and I went inside and said to Dave, 'come and have a look at this.'. We both recall me saying this very calmly, very matter-of-factly.

Dave now says, "I remember you saying it in a way that was pretty calm - not as if you had just seen anything particularly strange." "I remember thinking "Brilliant, I'll get Dave, someone is actually with me this time." It never entered my head that it would go, or that he might miss it. We went back outside. It was the same visually to me, but at this point we have a slightly different description to note."

Dave states: "I think there were around 8-15 lights in formation in the sky, the arrangement didn't really tell you much about its shape, not moving, just sitting there, above the rugby fields; maybe 500-800m away from us and it looked like 50m up. The lights looked to me like the sort of lights you'd get on a typical aircraft, but they didn't flash, they didn't beam cones of light towards the ground like you'd imagine from some sci-fi movie, and I can't remember whether they were all the same colour. What I could not sense was probably more interesting than what I could. Other than the lights nothing was there to suggest the presence of some sort of aircraft, no other shapes, no outlines, no surfaces reflecting the light and no noise, complete silence. They were in an oval arrangement. Longer in width than height."

"My memory is of the lights making up the faces of a gemstone, bunched together. To me they were morphing together rather than separate lights, they were changing almost into a disco ball of smoke, like a fireball but contained in the ellipsoid shape." We agree that it was

377

moving Northwards-ish from over the fields between Chipping Sodbury Golf Club and Wickwar Road. It was heading for Wickwar. We decided to try and get a closer look so locked the pavilion, jumped in Dave's car and headed up the Wickwar Road."

"Dave was driving and keeping an eye on it when he could; I was trying to track it as passenger. We don't think we ever got closer to it than a couple of hundred meters to our right, as the road wound its way. Dave was driving probably around the speed limit - 60mph, maybe a bit faster. We kept up with it as it travelled north, pretty much parallel to our route."

"We have both remarked that there was no sense of urgency to the whole thing. There was no chase; it was as if we were following it, even being led by it, in fact. Despite the seemingly perfect opportunity to photograph it, it never occurred."

"I seem to recall pointing a camera at this rugby ball of burning smoke, but it suddenly appearing on the other side of the road, but I have no other memory of there even being a camera there. It is feasible that there was one as I regularly had one if I was "into UFOs" that week, but when I try to remember I almost get a warning not to."

"Despite being two intelligent people, we cannot recall the route exactly either, but we think we drove through

378

Wickwar as if heading to the M5 and then carried on towards Charfield to get a bit closer - we got as far as a town/village which may have actually been Charfield before retracing our route to head back towards the M5 as it continued in that direction. We think we hung a right from the main road as we reached Tortworth, driving through the woods. We agree that it was Damery Lane which has a little lay-by near the bridge over the M5, immediately South of Michaelwood Services. We do not recall seeing that object again."

At this point the memories diverge.

Dave: 'We lost it as it travelled further over past the M5 towards Wales - it seemed to speed up at around this point, so we turned around, gave up the chase and headed back to the club. I recall nothing about the journey there or home or anything else that night.'

Rob: 'We stopped and got out at the bridge to study the sky, looking for the object. Parked up in the lay by, was a VW Camper-van, the sort with the concertina roof.'

'There was a light on inside and I wanted to go to see if they had seen the object. Dave did not want to. I walked down a very slight incline towards the cul-de-sac and turned to see Dave who was saying "No, don't" again and again, pleading with me not to go closer.'

"Don't do it, Rob!" I turned and the campervan was not there.

"There was a gun-metal colour wedge-shaped craft, very much like the side on view of an F-117 Nighthawk Stealth Fighter. It is the best description. It was angular, sharp, pointy, defined. It was more of a wedge, but the angles and surfaces reminded me. They were not smooth, they were flat."

"This image lasted one second and I was instantly on the other side of it facing what appeared to be its nose. It was remarkably close maybe a foot and it appeared to be alive, but artificial. This nose, whilst rounded and almost like a glove puppet shape and I had the sense of it sniffing me."

"Either side of it, the visible sloping away parts either side of the nose had the appearance of being like the cow-catcher on an old US Steam Train, but they had a pattern to them. It was like a maze, but with segments in it, like expensive chocolate, like a cattle branding-iron might appear, or embossed writing paper. I recall a red element to the "nose" but at this point I am unaware of any other surrounds at all. I am being sniffed by the nose of a hovering craft."

"The nose is gone and I'm in front of a panel with that embossed appearance, on the side of something that is now looking like the base of a pyramid. As I reach out my hand, I hear Dave saying "Rob, no!" My hand goes into the pattern, which now has a liquid texture, like immersing your hand in a bowl of paint. There is orange lightning and…There is a 'Fizzoom,' and like the turning off of an old TV I am back, on the bridge and with Dave. I say "Well, they were very nice."

"We look up and there are three white lights, like stars flying away from above us, North. We remark how perfect their formation s and note that it is a craft as the stars are disappearing behind it as it flies. "We do not speak again for weeks, long into the cricket season" Now this is quite an amazing story that Rob has sent me, not only did he have several different close views, which like mine could have been telepathy but actually immersed his hand into the liquid surface! Now that last bit I do not understand at all!"

Needless to say, Rob has had many paranormal experiences over the years, and we have become good friends, albeit over social media.

Betty Shine

I remember reading a book once by Betty Shine called, "The Infinite Mind," where Betty describes one night in Spain, where her husband, daughter and Betty saw a UFO in the distance whilst standing on the terrace of their villa. It was like a star in the distance, but then, all of a sudden, it

381

was on top of them, hovering over the villa. Betty and her daughter ran inside the villa and as they did the UFO disappeared. When they discussed the object later, it became clear that Betty had seen something much bigger than the others and even saw portholes in the side of the craft. "It was like my mind went out to meet it" said Betty.

I am convinced this is another case of telepathy whereby an individual is shown an enlarged detail of the craft. This last report on telepathy comes from America via a gentleman called Brian Hunter.

Brian Hunter

"Since you are one of the few I've ever come across who have had close contact with triangular craft that they know not to be TR3B, I'm going to detail out my whole experience (although it is a bit lengthy). On August 21st, 2007, there was going to be a solar eclipse. It was a full solar eclipse, and we were smack in the "path of totality."

I tiny bit of research led to my understanding that this would likely only occur once every 375-400 years in the general area I was in."

"In those days I didn't have any equipment yet, so I remember at the last moment going from place-to-place and everyone being out of those cheap paper glasses with the little, cheap solar filters. Finally, I got some from someone online about two hours before the eclipse and watched it with my best friend and his family. It was a good time for sure. After some of his family left, he and I went out in his back yard. He had a very large yard and behind it were trees, fields, trees, and more of the same (all kind of mountainous terrain as well) in North Georgia. We were both lying in the grass behind his house."

"As we lay there, I was thinking to myself "Please, if there really is anything out there more powerful than my own mind and consciousness, show me something big and let me know. Well, before I knew it I saw lights in the distance. They appeared white and I immediately told my buddy to look, and he was already looking at what we were seeing. They were travelling literally only a meter or two over the trees so we would see the lights and then they would dip below a tree line, etc until they got awfully close. Looking back on it, I wasn't nervous at all."

"The structure of the craft was also invisible to us until it got remarkably close. All we saw were what appeared to be three of the brightest, whitest lights I've seen from such a distance. When it got very close, I realized that it was a solid figure. I saw this misty substance that would float around, but there was not a lot of it. Because of its appearance and how it lingered and passed over the craft many times, I personally thought it was probably a form of cloaking that most likely wasn't in use at the time. The

383

craft was definitely black and solid, but at times it was seemingly translucent in places."

The three lights on the edges were absolutely incredible and seemingly had lives of their own. I don't even know how to describe them in words, other than to say that none of them were ever one single colour. It was like I was seeing, along with emotions and feelings, a colour scale I had never witnessed before. I believe this may have been when things started to get pretty telepathic with me.

The pull didn't really feel like a physical pull towards the craft, but more of a mental, visual, and more (as if there was absolutely no way I could have concentrated on anything else even if I had tried...not that the thought crossed my mind for a second).

One of the beings with connections to Lyra explained my lengthy history with the star system and then told me that I had previously been working on this craft when I died there, and that they had of course finished it. I received knowledge of numerous previous lives on earth and in other star systems. I have absolutely no doubt when we die that we will reincarnate elsewhere. I have no fear of death at all anymore. They led me to understand the process of life, death, and rebirth and how special that really is, explained the reasoning for the rise and fall of many civilizations and SO MUCH more. These specific beings included males and females and appeared to have a mixture of feline and human qualities. I would say more on the human side (except the height) but with distinctive feline features."

****

Chapter 10

The Calvine UFO Photo

The Best UFO Photo Ever?

The Calvine UFO photo - Credit Sheffield Hallam University & Craig Lindsay.

I think it is fair to say that photographs of UFOs in general are not great and the same applies to photos of the flying triangles. However, could one such photograph be the best UFO photo ever taken? Although not strictly a flying triangle the Calvine case has been the hottest UFO photo to be publicly revealed for quite some time.

The case, and the photo that have been made public, are still under investigation and it will be interesting to see where this all ends up. I will briefly cover this case and the photograph in question and leave you to draw your own conclusion. On August 4th, 1990, two hikers near Calvine in Scotland took a photograph of a mysterious, diamond-shaped flying object hovering in the middle of the sky.

For 32 years that image, dubbed the "Calvine photo," disappeared from the public eye, becoming the object of speculation, theories and myths. But now, the ground-breaking image has finally resurfaced thanks to the efforts of British journalist Dr. David Clarke. Dr. Clarke teaches journalism and media law at Sheffield Hallam University in the UK and has been involved in Ufology for decades and has written a number of books on the subject.

Craig Lindsay with the Calvine UFO photo. Credit Sheffield Hallam University and Craig Lindsay.

After thirteen years of research, Dr. Clark, who has worked as a curator for Britain's National Archives and is currently an associate professor at Sheffield Hallam University, found that former Royal Air Force (RAF) press officer Craig Lindsay, had held on to a copy of one of the original prints, waiting for someone to enquire about the mysterious image. In the photo, one of a series of six the hikers reportedly took, a diamond-shaped object can be seen flying in the sky, while a fighter jet can be spotted in the background not too far from it. It was 2022 that for the first time the public has had access to the elusive image, which has been described as the best UFO photo ever taken.

Back in 1990, the two hikers brought the photo to Scotland's Daily Record newspaper for publication. But instead, the newspaper handed the image over to the British Ministry of Defense, which kept it secret until now.

The Daily Record's picture editor at that time sent them to Craig Lindsay, who was the RAF press officer in Scotland. He passed the print to the Ministry of Defense in London; the Ministry of Defense in London then asked him to obtain the negatives.

So he went back to the Daily Record, asked the Daily Record to send the negatives to London, which they duly did, quite amazingly, and that's when they disappeared."

Dr. Clarke writes that the information linked to the photo, together with the image, should have normally been released by now, as 30 years have passed. But the identities of the two hikers who took the photo are still unknown and are not expected to be revealed before 2072, as the Ministry of Defense has cited "privacy concerns."

Oddly, despite all the publicity, the two chaps who took the photographs have never come forward and Dr. Clarke and his colleagues are still searching for them today.

The negatives have never been seen since they reached the Ministry of Defense. Now, the Ministry of Defense claim that they returned them to the Daily Record, but the Daily Record say they never received them, and they have no idea what happened to them. So, there are a lot of questions to be answered.

What Does The Photo Show?

While we do not know what happened to the men who took the photo, we do know what they described happened thirty-two years ago.

According to what Craig Lindsay told Dr. Clarke, the two men were working as chefs in a hotel in Pitlochry, in the Scottish Highlands, when, one summer evening, they decided to go for walk in the hills near Calvine. While out walking, the two spotted a huge, diamond-shaped flying object, moving silently in the sky.

They saw this thing in the sky, and it scared them. They ran into some woodland to sort of keep their heads down, and they heard this jet come down the valley and then, two minutes later, it returned and started circling around the object. And that's when they took the photographs. Whether what the two men saw on that summer evening in 1990 was actually a UFO, as the two men thought then, is still unclear.

Dr. Clarke had the photo analyzed by one of his colleagues, Senior Lecturer in Photography at Sheffield Hallam University Andrew Robinson, who said the image shows no sign of manipulation.

"It follows that this is either a genuine unidentified flying object in the sky," the report by Robinson reads, "or that any construction or manipulation used to create this effect occurred in front of the camera and not in the capturing of the scene on film, nor in the subsequent processing and printing of the image."

Craig Lindsay is also convinced that the image is not a hoax.

But while Dr. Clarke admits the photo is "by far the best UFO photograph" he has ever seen, the journalist says he does not believe the object in the image is actually an alien flying saucer.

"Sadly, I do not think that mysterious aircraft arrived from another galaxy," Dr. Clarke wrote in a piece he published in the Daily Mail. "I believe it was man-made somewhere in a secret hangar and whatever it was remains on the secret list and highly sensitive."

He thinks that the mysterious flying object could have been the "Aurora," a top-secret reconnaissance aircraft which the U.S. was rumored to be building in the 1980s, though there was never any evidence of such a project, and the U.S. government has consistently denied its existence.

"Although there has never been any substantial evidence that it was ever built or flown, there have been numerous unexplained sightings and incidents in both the U.S. and the U.K. over the years that have fuelled the Aurora myth Calvine included," wrote Dr. Clarke.

Dr. David Clarke and Craig Lindsay. Credit Sheffield Hallam University& Craig Lindsay.

Though Dr. Clarke is "100 percent sure that someone, somewhere in the military establishment in Britain or in the USA knows exactly what the photograph shows," the journalist also admits that it is possible the image could be anything, including a prank. "The other option is that the whole thing is a practical joke, a prank that got out of hand."

"The whole purpose of publishing this story is hopefully to get either the photographers themselves or someone who knows the photographers, or knows something about the circumstances, to come forward and solve the mystery."

Since the release of this information and the photograph in the UK's Daily Mail newspaper on August 12th, 2022, speculation has been rife with what it may or may not depict. There are those that like Dr. Clarke are of the opinion that it is indeed some form of secret American test aircraft. Others believe it is a photo of a rock in a pool of water and yet more think it is an outright hoax and it an item hung from the trees with a model aircraft also used. None of these possible explanations can prove what the photo depicts one way or the other.

The Calvine UFO photo under examination by Senior Lecturer in Photography at Sheffield Hallam University Andrew Robinson. Photo credit Dr David Clarke.

Dr. Clarke and his colleagues involved have done a great job in tracking down the photo and he has also had his Member of Parliament raise the issue for him all to no avail. Let us hope that the two men involved in this sighting step forward and/or the original negatives turn up and as a result we can learn more about this fascinating incident. If you know anything about this case or know someone that does please do not hesitate to contact Dr. Clarke.

****

Conclusion

I have tried to keep this book concentrating on triangle experiences due to my own triangular craft encounter, but there are literally thousands more sightings, not just around the UK, but worldwide of all types of craft, triangles, cigars and of course saucers. I have tried to explain why I think these craft are not of this world and that telepathy is used on many occasions by ET to communicate with humans, Dr. David Jacobs has written many books about the thousands of cases he has investigated, and telepathy frequently comes into the equation, and I very much admire his work.

I once heard that ET picks on certain people, and initially I was a bit skeptical of this, but as the years have gone by I believe there is some truth in this, because many contactees go on to have more than just one sighting. I did read once that ET picks on people who are telepathic which makes great sense, after all when we visit a foreign country it's always nice to find someone who speaks your own language.

One day everything in this book will become common knowledge, because it's a science, a science we do not yet understand but one day we will. I often wonder why we were chosen that night. Was it because they knew I would build the model or write this book? Am I part of a subtle disclosure project without even realizing it? Only time will tell. The truth is not out there, the truth is already here!

****

MORE BOOKS FROM FLYING DISK PRESS

http://flyingdiskpress.blogspot.com/

Flying
Disk
Press

399

Printed in Great Britain
by Amazon

41063244R00225